Insidious
Workplace
Behavior

SERIES IN APPLIED PSYCHOLOGY

Edwin A. Fleishman, George Mason University
Jeanette N. Cleveland, Pennsylvania State University
Series Editors

Gregory Bedny and David Meister
The Russian Theory of Activity: Current Applications to Design and Learning

Winston Bennett, David Woehr, and Charles Lance
Performance Measurement: Current Perspectives and Future Challenges

Michael T. Brannick, Eduardo Salas, and Carolyn Prince
Team Performance Assessment and Measurement: Theory, Research, and Applications

Jeanette N. Cleveland, Margaret Stockdale, and Kevin R. Murphy
Women and Men in Organizations: Sex and Gender Issues at Work

Aaron Cohen
Multiple Commitments in the Workplace: An Integrative Approach

Russell Cropanzano
Justice in the Workplace: Approaching Fairness in Human Resource Management, Volume 1

Russell Cropanzano
Justice in the Workplace: From Theory to Practice, Volume 2

David V. Day, Stephen Zaccaro, Stanley M. Halpin
Leader Development for Transforming Organizations: Growing Leaders for Tomorrow's Teams and Organizations.

James E. Driskell and Eduardo Salas
Stress and Human Performance

Sidney A. Fine and Steven F. Cronshaw
Functional Job Analysis: A Foundation for Human Resources Management

Sidney A. Fine and Maury Getkate
Benchmark Tasks for Job Analysis: A Guide for Functional Job Analysis (FJA) Scales

Insidious Workplace Behavior

Jerald Greenberg

RAND Corporation

Routledge
Taylor & Francis Group
New York   London

Also see www.workpsychologyarena.com

Routledge
Taylor & Francis Group
270 Madison Avenue
New York, NY 10016

Routledge
Taylor & Francis Group
27 Church Road
Hove, East Sussex BN3 2FA

© 2010 by Taylor and Francis Group, LLC
Routledge is an imprint of Taylor & Francis Group, an Informa business

Printed in the United States of America on acid-free paper
10 9 8 7 6 5 4 3 2 1

International Standard Book Number: 978-1-84872-858-5 (Hardback) 978-1-84872-859-2 (Paperback)

Library of Congress Cataloging-in-Publication Data

Insidious workplace behavior / editor, Jerald Greenberg.
   p. cm. -- (Series in applied psychology)
  Includes bibliographical references and index.
  ISBN 978-1-84872-858-5 (hbk. : alk. paper) -- ISBN 978-1-84872-859-2 (pbk. : alk. paper)
   1. Problem employees. 2. Employees--Psychology. 3. Work environment--Psychological aspects. 4. Industrial psychology. I. Greenberg, Jerald.

HF5549.5.E42I55 2010
658.3'045--dc22
                         2010017590

**Visit the Taylor & Francis Web site at
http://www.taylorandfrancis.com**

**and the Psychology Press Web site at
http://www.psypress.com**

To Carolyn, my best pal,

whose love has given me strength and comfort for over 30 years.

—JG

Contents

Series Foreword

There is a compelling need for innovative approaches to the solution of many pressing problems involving human relationship's in today's society. Such approaches are more likely to be successful when they are based on sound research and applications. This SERIES IN APPLIED PSYCHOLOGY offers publications that emphasize state-of-the-art research and its applications to important issues of human behavior in a variety of societal settings. The objective is to bridge both academic and applied interests.

In this fascinating new addition to the *Series in Applied Psychology*, editor Jerald Greenberg and his contributors take us on a tour of a form of behavior that is highly pervasive but about which little is known—*insidious workplace behavior (IWB)*. Although I leave it to Greenberg and his associates to define this concept formally, one can think of IWB as those seemingly minor harmful acts that by themselves appear to be innocuous but that cumulatively take a toll on its targets. As the contributors chronicle, IWB can take many forms, such as incivility, lying, sabotage, sexist humor, aggressive behavior (including bullying), and acts of revenge. Specifically, contributors describe the potentially insidious forms of these behaviors, including both antecedents and consequences, along with ways of discouraging their occurrence in the workplace. And to facilitate future advances in this field, additional chapters address the methodological challenges of measuring and researching IWB.

As a whole, this book blazes a new path in the fields of organizational behavior and industrial-organizational psychology. It promises to be of considerable interest to researchers and practitioners alike (be they students or current professionals) and we are proud to include it in our series.

Edwin A. Fleishman
Jeanette N. Cleveland
Series Editors

Preface

As a longtime Buckeye, the legend of Coach Woody Hayes is part of my heritage—mine and millions of other college football fans, especially in Ohio. With three national titles and 13 Big 10 championships to his credit during his 28-year reign as head football coach at The Ohio State University (OSU), there's little question about Hayes's proud legacy. But there's a dark side to it as well. Although basically kind-hearted and generous, Coach Hayes was a strict disciplinarian who was not reticent about using his volatile temper to express his disappointment with any player's poor performance. In the locker room he was a great teacher, albeit tyrannical. One day, the coach instructed one of his players to remove his helmet and then hit him in the head with it. Apparently, he demonstrated on a regular basis what today we call "tough love." As word got out about Coach Hayes's antics, most just brushed them off. After all, a football team is supposed to be tough and nobody was getting hurt—seriously, at least. Besides, Hayes's impressive record suggested that he knew what he was doing and no one wanted to argue with success.

Then one day—December 29, 1978, to be exact—Hayes went too far. In the Gator Bowl against Clemson, Coach Hayes's temper got the better of him. Late in the game, OSU's quarterback Art Schlichter was advancing the ball down the field hoping to erase a two-point deficit when Clemson's nose guard Charlie Bauman intercepted Schlichter's errant pass. As Bauman raced down the field along the OSU sideline, he came within inches of a frustrated Coach Hayes. Realizing that this meant his team's certain defeat, Hayes couldn't stand it. In a rage, he reached out and punched Bauman in the throat before also turning on one of his own players, Ken Fritz, who attempted to intervene. Outraged by this display of inappropriate behavior, Athletic Director Hugh Hindman relieved Coach Hayes of his duties the next morning.

As much as it makes me uncomfortable to recount the tarnishing of a widely admired coach's reputation, what it illustrates about the topic of this book, *insidious workplace behavior* (IWB), is just too perfect to ignore. For a long time, Hayes engaged in behavior that would have been considered completely inappropriate had it been more extreme in magnitude.

But, it wasn't. Yes, Hayes belittled his players. Yes, he screamed at them and he even hit them on occasion. These acts occurred repeatedly, characterizing his tough style, but no one thing was so egregious as to cross the line into blatantly inappropriate territory. In other words, Coach Hayes consistently flew under the radar. But his impunity ended abruptly when his aggressive behavior crossed the line separating acceptable from unacceptable behavior.

To the extent that we can characterize Woody Hayes's ongoing behavior before "the punch," as it is known in Columbus, as *intentionally harmful workplace behavior that is legal, subtle, and low level (rather than severe), repeated over time, and directed at individuals or organizations*, it is precisely what I mean by insidious workplace behavior. Dictionaries define *insidious* as "working harmfully in a subtle or stealthy manner." Indeed, this is what the coach did: The harm he brought to his players was delivered not in one big package but in many little ones delivered on a regular basis. My colleagues to whom I have described insidious workplace behavior have characterized it more colorfully as "death by a thousand paper cuts" and "being nibbled to death by guppies." These depictions, in keeping with the meaning of insidious, suggest that an actor is harming his or her victims. And we cannot say that Hayes's players did not feel his wrath in harmful ways. They simply accepted it given the small doses and the underlying belief that "it was good for me" and that "I deserved it."

Thus far, I have been talking about one individual, but as my accounts suggest insidious workplace behavior is inclined to occur all the time. Its stealthy nature, however, is unlikely to bring it to the forefront and uncertainties about its appropriateness (or lack thereof) may leave such acts unreported. As a result, we know little about this form of behavior. In fact, few are aware of its existence at all. This is potentially problematic to the extent that the adverse effects on a cumulative basis may be harmful to victims physically, emotionally, or both. Beyond individuals, insidious workplace behavior also may contribute to an organizational culture in which some forms of aggressive behavior are condoned, potentially interfering with cooperation required for organizations to function effectively.

The bottom line is clear: Some people on the job may be engaging in potentially harmful actions that go unrecognized. It is with the intent of shedding light on such behaviors that I have invited a cast of experts to chronicle the potential causes and consequences of various forms of insidious workplace behavior, along with suggestions about how to manage it now and how to research it in the future. This book reflects the fruits of their labor.

To begin, in Chapter 1, Marissa Edwards and I address a question that is fundamental to this book: What is insidious workplace behavior? To aid readers, we offer a detailed definition of IWB and then juxtapose IWB with other forms of inappropriate behavior that have been studied in the workplace.

Using this as a launching point, Chapter 2 begins our foray into various types of IWB with Joel Neuman and Loraleigh Keashly's analysis of workplace aggression. These authors contrast insidious acts of aggressive behavior with larger, more extreme forms that make headlines. As a heuristic for organizing their points, they introduce a framework in which various behaviors are differentiated in terms of means, motive, and opportunity. They then present the results of original research showing how these factors help explain insidious forms of aggression in the workplace.

In Chapter 3, Mark Seabright, Maureen Ambrose, and Marshall Schminke examine workplace sabotage as a form of IWB directed at organizations. These authors argue that in addition to the usual conceptualization of sabotage as being motivated toward harming organizations, it also can occur as a result of workers' desires to exercise control in the workplace. This latter form is usually insidious in nature, they claim, and as a result, has different antecedents and consequences. They explore these factors as part of their broader conceptualization of motives for workplace sabotage.

Revenge as a form of IWB is the focus of David Jones's contribution in Chapter 4. Specifically, he examines an important question: Why do some people refrain from striking back in response to IWB whereas others do not? In part, the answer he proposes rests on people's past experiences with being victims, which influences the likelihood of making the kind of hostile attributions about mistreatment that trigger revenge. Jones supports his notion by reporting new research findings, and he summarizes his conceptualization by proposing an organizing framework that specifies breaking points that trigger revenge.

Christine Pearson addresses the topic of incivility in Chapter 5. After describing its basic nature, she describes conceptual foundations for the study of incivility and reviews major research findings bearing on this concept. Pearson's emphasis is on the experiences of victims, such as their emotional and behavioral responses. With an eye toward mitigating these negative reactions, she discusses practical issues, such as ways for victims to cope. Finally, she offers suggestions for future research that promises to enhance our understanding of incivility.

Chapter 6 addresses an important issue that has received little attention by organizational scientists—sexist humor in the workplace. Christie Fitzgerald Boxer and Thomas Ford conceptualize this behavior as a subtle form of sexual harassment. In so doing, they examine why men engage in sexist humor and chronicle its consequences, both for individual targets and the broad culture of organizations. As an aid to practicing managers, Boxer and Ford conclude by offering specific suggestions for reducing sexist humor in their workplaces.

Lying may be insidious in nature, as Steven Grover chronicles in Chapter 7. We see this, he suggests, in white lies, lies made in difficult situations, lies used as negotiation tactics, and lies used to promote self-esteem. Grover examines the causes, consequences, and prevalence of these kinds of lies told to different audiences, such as subordinates, colleagues, and business customers. Arguing that lies are an inevitable fact of organizational life, Grover concludes by offering suggestions for coping with lies in the workplace.

Chapters 8 and 9 introduce methodological issues to our conversation. In Chapter 8, Steve Jex, Jennifer Geimer, Olga Clark, Ashley Guidroz, and Jennifer Yugo examine the challenges associated with measuring incivility. They focus on challenges from victims' perspectives (e.g., recall bias, recency effects) and from perpetrators' perspectives (e.g., causes of uncivil behavior). To help advance future research on incivility—and potentially all forms of IWB—they conclude by offering recommendations for improving the measurement of incivility.

Following up on this theme, Paul Spector and Ozgun Rodopman examine general methodological issues germane to studying IWB in Chapter 9. Their discussion focuses on ethical issues (e.g., identity protection), special considerations for institutional review boards, and considerations in accessing research participants (e.g., the special sampling techniques that should be used). They also offer suggestions for research techniques that are particularly useful in studying IWB (e.g., stress-incident records, designs, diaries, focus groups, and others). The authors conclude by discussing general research strategies to be used when studying IWB.

Finally, in Chapter 10, Marissa Edwards and I conclude this book with an integrative chapter. We discuss key issues that have arisen about IWB in this book and various challenges that confront future researchers.

Throughout, we offer some recommendations for scholars to take that will enable the study of IWB to advance beyond its infancy.

The contributions to this book make it ideal for use by professors and graduate-level management students as well as those from the parent disciplines from which the work is based—psychology (particularly, organizational psychology and social psychology), sociology, and communications. It promises to be excellent reading material in seminars and as a reference for professionals in these fields.

Given the relatively early stage of our understanding of insidious workplace behavior, the present work is of necessity scholarly in nature. However, practitioners also will find the topic fascinating—and all too real—and will pick up many good suggestions about how to recognize and manage insidious workplace behavior. Fortunately, contributors to this book have taken the first step toward making their work approachable to practitioners by discussing its implied implications. I thank them for reaching out in this way because it encourages the kind of rapprochement between academics and practitioners that will benefit both parties in their efforts to understand and contain insidious workplace behavior.

In closing, I wish to thank my editor, Anne Duffy, for her support and guidance—not to mention the patience of Job—over the years it took to bring this book to fruition. And, of course, I extend my heartfelt thanks to the various contributors to this book who have worked so diligently on their chapters as they drew upon what we already know to extrapolate into uncharted territory. All met the challenge brilliantly and rose to the occasion to create what I believe will be seminal contributions to a fledgling field of inquiry. I could not have asked for a more professional, talented, and kind group of scientists with whom to work. I am indebted to them for their contributions to this book. Finally, I thank my many students and colleagues on three continents with whom I have worked over the years and who have inspired me to undertake this project—not by any insidious acts on their part, but rather, by virtue of their rich intellectual support and stimulation.

Jerald Greenberg

About the Editor

Jerald Greenberg is senior psychologist at the RAND Corporation's Institute for Civil Justice and is retired as the Abramowitz Professor of Business Ethics at The Ohio State University's Fisher College of Business. He has served as associate editor of *Organizational Behavior and Human Decision Processes* and of the *Journal of Organizational Behavior*. In addition to 25 books, Greenberg has published over 150 articles and chapters, most in the field he helped develop, organizational justice. Recognizing a lifetime of research accomplishments, Greenberg has won the Distinguished Scientific Contributions to Management Award granted in 2007 by the Academy of Management, the Distinguished Scientific Achievement Award granted in 2006 by the Society for Industrial and Organizational Psychology (SIOP), and the Herbert Heneman Career Achievement Award granted by the Human Resources Division of the Academy of Management granted in 2005. Based on citation counts, Greenberg has been identified as the 37th most influential management scholar.

Contributors

Maureen L. Ambrose is professor of management in the College of Business at the University of Central Florida. She received her PhD from the University of Illinois at Urbana-Champaign. Her research interests include organizational justice, employee deviance, and ethics. Her work has appeared in the *Academy of Management Journal, Academy of Management Review, Administrative Sciences Quarterly, Journal of Applied Psychology, Journal of Management,* and *Organizational Behavior and Human Decision Processes.* She is an Academy of Management fellow, a Society for Industrial and Organizational Psychology fellow, and a member of the Society for Organizational Behavior. She served as associate editor for the *Academy of Management Journal* and was coeditor of a special issue on organizational justice called *Organizational Behavior and Human Decision Processes.* She has served on editorial boards for the *Academy of Management Journal, Journal of Applied Psychology, Journal of Management, Organizational Behavior and Human Decision Processes, Human Resource Management Review,* and *Journal of Managerial Issues.* She recently completed a five-year term in the division chair track for the Organizational Behavior Division, the largest division of the Academy of Management. She has also served on a variety of Academy of Management committees and as representative-at-large for the Organizational Behavior Division.

Olga Clark, PhD, is assistant professor of psychology at the University of Hartford in West Hartford, Connecticut. She earned her PhD in industrial/organizational psychology from Bowling Green State University. In addition to workplace incivility, Clark's research interests include employees' role definitions, welfare-to-work transition, and workplace safety.

Christie Fitzgerald Boxer earned her MA in sociology from Western Michigan University and is currently a PhD candidate at the University of Iowa. Her research interests include the intersection of social psychological and gender processes in the contexts of the family, home, and work.

Marissa S. Edwards is a PhD candidate at UQ Business School, University of Queensland. She holds a bachelor of psychological science with honors from the University of Queensland. Her research interests include emotions, decision making, employee silence, whistle-blowing, and workplace deviance. She coedited *Voice and Silence in Organizations* (with Jerald Greenberg) and has coauthored papers and chaired symposia at the annual meetings of the Academy of Management, the Society for Industrial and Organizational Psychology, and the Australian and New Zealand Academy of Management.

Thomas E. Ford is professor of psychology at Western Carolina University. He received his PhD in social psychology from University of Maryland in 1992. His research interests include disparaging humor and discrimination, humor and coping with stress, the relationship between religion and prejudice, and unintentional racism and stereotype threat in educational settings.

Jennifer L. Burnfield Geimer, PhD, is a senior staff scientist at the Human Resources Research Organization (HumRRO). She received her PhD in industrial/organizational psychology from Bowling Green State University in 2005, with a focus in occupational health psychology. During her graduate career she interned at the National Institute for Occupational Safety and Health (NIOSH), where she coauthored a book chapter on incivility and bullying. She was also a coprincipal investigator on a pilot grant awarded by the NIOSH-sponsored University of Cincinnati Education and Research Center to study incivility experienced by nurses and to develop a tailored measure of incivility in a hospital setting. Her dissertation focused on leadership behavior in subordinate stress and health. With over 10 years of applied experience, she currently manages large-scale projects in personnel selection and development, such as job analysis, the development and implementation of assessment centers, and test development.

Steven L. Grover is professor of management and deputy dean at the University of Otago School of Business in Dunedin, New Zealand (PhD, Columbia University). Previous appointments include Indiana University and Georgia State University. His research examines honesty and dishonesty in the workplace, with a special emphasis on leader integrity. His work has appeared in top journals, including the *Academy of Management*

Journal, Administrative Science Quarterly, Journal of Applied Psychology, Organizational Behavior and Human Decision Processes, and *Organization Studies.* He works with an international community of scholars on research in North America, Europe, and Australasia, and served on the board of the European Group on Organization Studies.

Ashley M. Guidroz, PhD, is a research consultant at Dennison Consulting in Ann Arbor, Michigan. She earned her PhD in industrial/organizational psychology from Bowling Green State University. During her graduate career she was coprincipal investigator on a pilot grant awarded by the National Institute for Occupational Safety and Health (NIOSH)-sponsored University of Cincinnati Education and Research Center to study incivility experienced by nurses and to develop a tailored measure of incivility in a hospital setting.

Steve M. Jex, PhD, is associate professor of psychology at Bowling Green State University and guest researcher at the National Institute for Occupational Safety and Health (NIOSH). Jex received his PhD in industrial/organizational psychology from the University of South Florida and has spent most of his postdoctoral career conducting research on occupational stress. His research has appeared in a number of scholarly journals including *Journal of Applied Psychology, Journal of Organizational Behavior, Journal of Occupational Health Psychology, Journal of Applied Social Psychology,* and *Work & Stress.* Jex is the author of two books, *Stress and Job Performance: Theory, Research, and Implications for Managerial Practice* and *Organizational Psychology: A Scientist-Practitioner Approach.*

David A. Jones obtained his PhD in industrial and organizational psychology in 2004 from the University of Calgary and is now associate professor in the School of Business Administration, University of Vermont. His primary research area is organizational justice, focusing on how justice perceptions form and how employees respond to fair and unfair treatment through organizational citizenship behavior, turnover, desires for revenge, and counterproductive work behavior. He also conducts research aimed at illuminating why job seekers and incumbent employees respond positively to socially responsible business practices. Reports of Jones's research have been published in journals including the *Journal of Applied Psychology,* the *Journal of Organizational Behavior,* and the *Journal of Management.*

Loraleigh Keashly is associate professor in the Department of Communication at Wayne State University, Detroit. Her research and consulting focuses on conflict and conflict resolution at the interpersonal, group, and intergroup levels. Her current research focus is the nature and personal and organizational effects of emotionally abusive and bullying behaviors in the workplace with a particular interest in the role of organizational structure and culture in the facilitation or prevention and management of these behaviors. Her work has appeared in *Work & Stress*, *Journal of Emotional Abuse*, *Violence and Victims*, *Employee Rights and Employment Policy Journal*, *Journal of Management and Organizations*, and *Journal of Healthcare Management*. Her book chapters have appeared in *Bullying and Emotional Abuse in the Workplace* (Taylor & Francis), *Counterproductive Work Behavior* (American Psychological Association), *Handbook of Workplace Violence* (Sage), and *The Destructive Side of Organizational Communication* (Routledge/LEA).

Joel H. Neuman is associate professor of management and organizational behavior and director of the Center for Applied Management in the School of Business at the State University of New York at New Paltz. His research and consulting activities focus on workplace aggression and violence, workplace bullying, and the use of collaborative inquiry within the action research process. His research in these areas has appeared in publications such as the *Journal of Applied Behavioral Science*, *Journal of Management*, *Journal of Vocational Behavior*, *Public Administration Quarterly*, *Employee Rights and Employment Policy Journal*, *Aggressive Behavior*, and the *Journal of Healthcare Management*. His book chapters, related to workplace aggression and bullying, have appeared in *Antisocial Behavior in Organizations* (Sage), *Bullying and Emotional Abuse in the Workplace: International Perspectives in Research and Practice* (Taylor & Francis), *The Dark Side of Organizational Behavior* (Jossey-Bass), *Counterproductive Work Behavior: Investigations of Actors and Targets* (American Psychological Association), and *The Destructive Side of Organizational Communication* (Routledge/LEA).

Christine Pearson, professor of management at Thunderbird School of Global Management, has focused her career on strategic preparation in heading off workplace crises. She has studied and developed causation theories as well as solutions with regard to problems that can escalate into disastrous individual and organizational losses, whether from faulty decision making, inattentiveness, or incivility and aggression in the workplace. With more than 20 years experience and faculty appointments in Asia, Europe, South America, and the United States, Pearson has helped numerous organizations plan for, avert, and contain crises from workplace homicide to executive kidnapping, from product tampering to product recalls, aircraft accidents, and consumer fraud. Her most recent book, *The Cost of Bad Behavior: How Incivility is Damaging Your Business and What to Do About It* (with Christine Porath, 2009) confirms the pressing need for leaders to address incivility or suffer the steep financial consequences.

Ozgun B. Rodopman is assistant professor in the Management Department at Boğaziçi University, Istanbul, Turkey. She received her doctorate in industrial and organizational psychology from the University of South Florida. She also has a master's degree in management from Harvard University. Her research interests include proactivity, mentoring, justice, citizenship, and counterproductive work behaviors.

Marshall Schminke is BB&T Professor of Business Ethics at the University of Central Florida. His research spans organizational ethics and justice, and focuses on the means by which organizational characteristics like structure and work climate influence individual ethics and justice outcomes. His work has appeared in the *Academy of Management Journal, Journal of Applied Psychology, Organizational Behavior and Human Decision Processes, Business Ethics Quarterly, Research in Organizational Behavior,* and *Research in Personnel and Human Resources Management.* He has edited two volumes on business ethics research and has served as associate editor at the *Academy of Management Journal* and as a visiting scholar at Oxford University. He is currently an associate editor at *Business Ethics Quarterly* and an academic fellow of the Ethics Resource Center in Washington, DC.

Mark A. Seabright is professor of management in the Division of Business and Economics at Western Oregon University. He received his PhD from Carnegie Mellon University. His research interests include moral reasoning, organizational justice, and workplace deviance. His work on these and other topics has appeared in the *Academy of Management Journal, Business Ethics Quarterly, Journal of Business Ethics, Journal of Management*

Inquiry, and *Organizational Behavior and Human Decision Processes.* He has served on the editorial boards of the *Academy of Management Journal* and the *Journal of Management.*

Paul E. Spector is distinguished university professor of industrial/organizational psychology and industrial/organizational doctoral program director at the University of South Florida. He is also director of the National Institute for Occupational Safety and Health (NIOSH)-funded Sunshine Education and Research Center's Occupational Health Psychology program. He is the associate editor of the Point/Counterpoint section of the *Journal of Organizational Behavior* and of *Work & Stress.* He is on the editorial boards of the *Journal of Applied Psychology, Organizational Research Methods,* and *Personnel Psychology.* His research interests include methodology, counterproductive work behavior, occupational stress, personality, and violence. In 1991 the Institute for Scientific Information listed him as one of the 50 highest impact contemporary researchers (out of over 102,000) in psychology worldwide.

Jennifer E. Yugo, PhD, is assistant professor of management at Oakland University. She received her PhD in industrial/organizational psychology in 2009 at Bowling Green State University. During her time at Bowling Green she was a principal investigator on two pilot grants awarded by the National Institute for Occupational Safety and Health (NIOSH)-sponsored University of Cincinnati Education and Research Center to study incivility and well-being related topics. Yugo's dissertation examined the role of work meaning in negotiating emotional labor demands. Her research interests include the meaning of work, emotional labor, employee well-being, and positive organizational scholarship. She has published research in several outlets including the *Journal of Applied Psychology.*

Section 1

Introduction

1

What Is Insidious Workplace Behavior?

Marissa S. Edwards and Jerald Greenberg

Headlines regularly chronicle audacious acts of criminal behavior that occur in the workplace. Whether it's a disgruntled ex-employee who fires a gun at his former coworkers (Leavitt, 1995), an investment broker who swindles billions of dollars from his clients (Efrati, Lauricella, & Searcey, 2008), or a governor of a U.S. state who auctions off a vacant Senate seat to the highest bidder (Keen, 2008), accounts of gross misdeeds are all too common. Despite what their prevalence in the news may suggest, such extreme acts are merely the tip of the iceberg of deviant workplace behavior.

Far beneath the surface, however, lays a broad base of deviant behaviors that fail to grab public attention because they are prosaic, sometimes covert, and seemingly benign in nature. Examples include an employee who makes one of her coworkers the target of her daily racial jokes, a coach who shoves one of his players each time he makes a mistake on the field, and an executive who badmouths his assistant whenever he walks away. Greenberg (2004) referred to such subtle but pervasive forms of deviance as *insidious workplace behavior* (IWB).

Given its under-the-radar qualities, it's not surprising that we only rarely hear about IWB, if ever. "Boss teases subordinate" is hardly newsworthy, leaving IWB to receive little attention by either the press or management scholars. Not only doesn't the behavior call attention to itself, but until now, social scientists didn't know to look for it. Yet, to the particular "boss" and "subordinate" involved, the incident may have value, especially when it's part of a repeated pattern. Indeed, as chronicled in this book, because the cumulative impact of IWB, furtive though it may be, is often considerable, taking a toll on victims, it is a potentially important area of study. For this potential to be realized, however, it is essential for IWB to be clearly defined and for its various forms to be identified. We perform these tasks in this chapter.

DEFINING CHARACTERISTICS

The word *insidious* has been defined variously as "spreading or developing or acting inconspicuously but with harmful effect" (*Oxford American Dictionary*, 1980, p. 342) and "stealthily treacherous or deceitful; operating or proceeding inconspicuously but with grave effect" (*Macquarie Concise Dictionary*, 1998, p. 584). Abstractions aside, the term's meaning becomes clearest in context. For example, the political scientist, Samuel P. Huntington (2004) contrasted the imparting of limited or incomplete information with lying, by noting that "partial truths or half-truths are often more insidious than total falsehoods" (p. 37). And in her groundbreaking memoir, *Prozac Nation*, Elizabeth Wurtzel (1994) explained that the challenge of living with clinical depression lies in the fact that its effects are "insidious and compound daily" (p. 191).

Our definition of IWB is in keeping with this general meaning, but narrowed to fit the context of workplace behavior. Specifically, we define insidious workplace behavior as *a form of intentionally harmful workplace behavior that is legal, subtle, and low level (rather than severe), repeated over time, and directed at individuals or organizations.* Importantly, IWB is not a unique behavior in its own right, but rather a particular form of several varieties of deviant behavior. The set of qualifying characteristics is as follows.

- *Intentionally harmful:* Acts that are performed in an effort to bring harm.
- *Legal:* Acts that do not break the law.
- *Low-level severity:* Acts that are subtle and incidental in nature, with minor (sometimes, seemingly unremarkable) effects that may go unnoticed when they occur on an isolated basis.
- *Repetitive:* Acts that are repeated over time (as opposed to single acts) with effects that are cumulative in nature.
- *Individually and organizationally targeted:* The intended victim of harm usually is another individual, although it also may be an organization with which the actor is associated.

This characterization of IWB paints a picture of subtle and stealthy behavior that cumulatively chips away at a worker's dignity—or, using morbid metaphors, "death by a thousand paper cuts," or "being nibbled to death by guppies." Although some authors have made passing mention to this type of behavior (e.g., Skarlicki & Folger, 1997), to our knowledge, it has not been examined fully to date. To shed further light on the nature of IWB, we now take a closer look at its defining characteristics.

Intentionally Harmful

In keeping with Robinson and Bennett's (1995) conceptualization of deviant behavior, we contend that the motive underlying IWB is to inflict harm (on either an individual or organization, as we will note later). This is important to note because several of the contributors to the present volume indicate that some acts that appear to be IWB actually may be driven by prosocial motives and can result in constructive outcomes. For example, Grover (Chapter 7, this volume) observes that employees sometimes tell white lies to protect colleagues' feelings; and Seabright, Ambrose, and Schminke (Chapter 3, this volume) suggest that sabotage is not always intended to be harmful. Appearances may be deceptive in these cases because the behaviors in question are not motivated by the desire to bring harm, and therefore, may not be considered insidious. With this in mind, we caution against labeling any acts as IWB in the absence of knowledge of the actor's negative intentions.

As Andersson and Pearson (1999) note in their review of incivility, the intention underlying many workplace behaviors is often difficult to detect. In the case of incivility, they suggest that perpetrators can deny all responsibility by arguing that the behavior was not intended to offend, suggesting that the target misinterpreted the behavior or is simply hypersensitive. In similar fashion, Einarsen, Hoel, Zapf, and Cooper (2003) state that it is extremely difficult to determine the presence of intent in episodes of workplace bullying and sexual harassment. Neuman and Baron (2005) observe that this is one reason why some researchers have elected to exclude harmful intentions from their conceptualizations of deviance. Although we acknowledge these points, we believe that it is essential to include negative intentions in our definition of IWB because without this criterion, IWB would be indistinguishable from accidental instances of low-level, pervasive negligence. For example, if an employee failed repeatedly to include a colleague in important group discussions via e-mail because he or she forgot that the individual's e-mail address had changed, this would not represent an example of IWB because the actor did not intend to harm that colleague.

By imposing this condition, we recognize that attributions of intentionality rest on the target's perceptions and interpretations of events, which are, of course, fallible and difficult to assess. We believe, however, that the inherent ambiguity of many subtle and frequently occurring forms of employee behavior underscores the importance of assessing employees' motives for performing the behavior before labeling them as IWB (Conte, 2009). Indeed, most acts we consider to be IWB probably should be referred to as "presumed IWB" or "apparent IWB."

Legal

Generally, discussions of workplace behavior focus on legal acts, but this is not always so. The literature on employee theft (e.g., Greenberg & Scott, 1996), for example, examines acts ranging from pilfering (generally not regarded to be illegal) to grand theft and embezzlement (highly illegal). Likewise, only most extreme acts of workplace violence are illegal (e.g., shooting or physically assaulting someone), although more benign, yet disruptive, forms of workplace aggression (e.g., a minor skirmish characterized by name-calling in raised voices) may be perfectly legal (Baron & Neuman, 1996).

For a behavior to be classified as IWB, it must be legal. This criterion is reasonable insofar as IWB, as will be noted later, involves repeated behavior. And assuming some modicum of law enforcement, it's unlikely that illegal behavior can be repeated too many times without being put to a stop.

Admittedly, the matter of legality is difficult to apply in the case of sexual harassment. In countries in which sexual harassment is illegal under state and national law (e.g., the United States and Australia), mild but pervasive instances of inappropriate touching and sexual comments in an organization may or may not constitute IWB. This ambiguity is based on the fact that laws are often framed using terms such as "unwanted" and "offensive," making the legality of any claims of harassment a matter to be assessed on a case-by-case basis. Thus, some but not all instances of sexual harassment may be considered IWB.

Low-Level Severity

Vardi and Weitz (2004) observe that the severity of misbehavior can be measured in behavioral and attitudinal forms. Behaviorally, severity may be evaluated according to its frequency, in addition to "the centrality of the violated norm or value ... [and] the degree of premeditation, preoccupation, or planning involved in the misbehavior" (p. 33). Attitudinally, the severity of misbehavior may be measured according to "the strength or intensity of the [individual's] intention, predisposition or propensity" (p. 33) to engage in the deviant behavior. Extending these foci, we contend that the consequences of the behavior are another critical component of severity. Specifically, in the case of IWB, we suggest that the outcomes of specific acts may not be especially harmful in the short term, although their cumulative detrimental effects over time can be considerable (Schneider, Swan, & Fitzgerald, 1997).

Using this consequence-based approach, acts of IWB, by definition, are low in severity. Each occurrence may be considered a deviant act of low severity, such as when a supervisor embarrasses an employee in front of others. The individual act may be so benign as to be unremarkable although the cumulative impact of many such acts repeated over time— the body of work in its entirety, so to speak—may be severe. As such, those rude and uncivil acts constitute IWB.

Several researchers have noted that deviant acts vary with respect to severity (e.g., Andersson & Pearson, 1999; Skarlicki & Folger, 2004). Bullying/mobbing, a phenomenon described in this book (Neuman & Keashly, Chapter 2), illustrates this variation. Some bullies, for example, terrorize victims through physical violence or verbal threats, whereas others engage in low-level personal campaigns designed to undermine victims' self-esteem and self-efficacy. Such efforts may take such forms as ostracism (i.e., exclusion and isolation; Lustenberger & Williams, 2009), setting unreasonably high work demands, or being unfairly critical of employees' performance (Simpson & Cohen, 2004). This same variation is addressed in the more general literature on aggressive behavior. For example, Baron and Neuman (1996) note that whereas some acts of aggression are extreme and overt (e.g., homicide), others are less visible and ambiguous with respect to their underlying aggressive motive (e.g., arriving late for a meeting, ignoring voice mail or e-mail messages). In all these cases of deviant behaviors, the low-severity acts may be considered IWB.

Finally, we note that severity was one of the dimensions used by Robinson and Bennett (1995) in their typology of deviant behavior. Among the most severe behaviors identified in their study were sabotaging equipment, stealing from the company, verbal abuse, and endangering coworkers. Less severe behaviors included blaming coworkers, gossiping about coworkers, and showing favoritism. Such acts may be considered IWB if they also meet our additional criteria (e.g., they are intentionally harmful and occur repeatedly over time). Robinson and Bennett noted that their "serious–not serious" dimension was related negatively to the covert or overt nature of the behavior in question: Serious acts tend to be overt in nature (because they are difficult to hide), whereas less serious ones tend to be covert (because they are easy to hide or are not even noticeable). This is in keeping with our depiction of IWB as being difficult to detect.

Repetitive

Our fourth defining characteristic of IWB is that it is repetitive. In other words, it occurs frequently and persistently over time. In contrast to a single act of aggression (e.g., a tantrum involving screaming at one's boss), employees who perpetrate IWB engage in repeated episodes (frequency: how often) over a series of days, weeks, months, or even years (duration: over how long a time).

Our definition may be juxtaposed with those of others who have elected to specify the frequency or duration of various deviant behaviors. Tepper's (2000) definition of abusive supervision—"subordinates' perceptions of the extent to which supervisors engage in the sustained display of hostile verbal and nonverbal behaviors, excluding physical contact" (p. 178)—is a good example of this because it acknowledges the persistent nature of the behavior in question. Also, we note that almost all definitions of workplace bullying specify that the behavior must occur on a repeated basis—typically at least weekly, over a duration of six months—in order to be classified as bullying (Einarsen et al., 2003). Additionally, Duffy, Ganster, and Pagon (2002) suggest that social undermining in the workplace involves ongoing attempts to hinder positive social interactions, explaining that such behaviors "are insidious, in that they weaken gradually or by degrees" (p. 332).

Keashly and Jagatic (2003) provide an excellent analysis of issues of frequency and duration in their discussion of workplace bullying in the United States. Commenting on the literature, they note that "even seemingly minor behaviors can have significant effects when they occur frequently and over extended time periods" (Keashly & Jagatic, 2003, p. 53). At the same time, they observe that a major limitation of the research thus far is that researchers have investigated discrete instances of bullying almost exclusively instead of examining the effects of persistent and repetitive behaviors over time. They note further that although some definitions of workplace bullying specify the duration of the behaviors, most researchers have failed to take duration into account when measuring deviance. In this connection, Keashly and Jagatic suggest that scientists would be well served to measure the frequency with which people are exposed to deviant behavior (e.g., in days, weeks, or months) and how they affect their experience and subsequent coping.

In summary, we argue that researchers should assess the number of exposures during each time period (i.e., frequency) when investigating deviant behavior. Greatest impact would be expected under conditions in which a high frequency of deviant acts occurs over long periods of time. In the case of IWB, low-level acts may have the most profound effects when the product of their Duration × Frequency is high. This multiplicative assumption is consistent with the notion that if either one of these values is 0, so too will be the effect. Additionally, lacking reason to do otherwise, we give equal weight to duration and frequency, although in practice, these may differ for various forms of behavior. Clearly, this is an issue in need of future research.

Individually and Organizationally Targeted

Some deviant behaviors are directed toward harming organizations (e.g., intentionally working slowly) and others are directed toward individuals (e.g., gossiping). Following the lead of scientists studying organizational citizenship (Organ & Ryan, 1995), who distinguish between acts aimed at organizations (OCB-O) and those aimed at individuals (OCB-I), we refer to these as *IWB-O* and *IWB-I*, respectively. If they otherwise meet the additional criteria, such acts, aimed at either target can be regarded as IWB.

This specification spans the distinction between individually targeted and organizationally targeted forms of deviance made by Robinson and Bennett (1995), and we are not the first to erect such a bridge. For example, Rayner, Hoel, and Cooper (2002) note that acts of bullying can be aimed at individuals, groups, or entire organizations. Their approach and ours are in keeping with Vardi and Wiener's (1996) claim that constructs of workplace deviance should be defined with sufficient breadth to allow for inclusion of several forms of behavior.

This is important because, as Berry, Ones, and Sackett (2007) observed, most instances of interpersonal deviance and organizational deviance are highly correlated. Yet, their meta-analyses revealed that these forms of behavior are also differentially correlated with other variables, suggesting that there are complex relationships between them. With this in mind, we encourage researchers to examine both interpersonally directed IWB and organizationally directed IWB to determine the degree to which differences exist with respect to their motives, antecedents, and outcomes.

More IWB-I Than IWB-O?

Casual observation leads us to suspect that more IWB is targeted toward individuals than organizations. However, in the absence of large-scale descriptive studies, this is merely speculation. Yet, assuming that such a skew exists, this possibility may be explained in several ways.

First, if we assume that employees are most likely to retaliate against those who have harmed them (Skarlicki & Folger, 1997), the prevalence of IWB-I may reflect a tendency for more harmful acts to be brought by other individuals than by organizations. Given that people usually work in proximity with others, they may be inclined to experience more harmful acts from them and also to suffer their impact sooner than they would experience harm stemming from the policies of an organization (whose effects have to trickle down to them). To the extent that this occurs, we would expect to observe more IWB-I than IWB-O.

Second, following from classic literature on displaced aggression (Dollard, Doob, Miller, Mowrer, & Sears, 1939), even when organizations are believed to be the source of harm, employees may be reluctant to strike back at them, fearing that they may get fired. This would lead employees to target "safer" others associated with the organization, such as individual managers or coworkers. This possibility also is in keeping with the relational model of workplace aggression (Hershcovis & Barling, 2007), according to which the relationship between aggressors and targets determines the aggressors' behavior. In particular, aggressors are expected to use less extreme forms of aggression when they have low amounts of legitimate power or when their relationships with targets are no longer ongoing.

A third possibility focuses on the nature of the responses rather than their quantity. Specifically, it's reasonable to assume that employees are harmed in different ways by individuals (e.g., interpersonal harm, such as a personal insult) than by organizations (e.g., financial harm, such as assignment to an undesirable sales territory), thereby leading them to strike back differently. And the ways they do this are more likely to take insidious forms when striking back at other individuals than at organizations. We base this on the notion that people desiring to harm targets may find it more gratifying to observe the suffering of others who they observe regularly than the organization—an abstract entity whose suffering they may only envision rather than observe directly. This thinking is in line with the socio-philosophical notion of *schadenfreude*, the tendency for people to delight in the suffering of others (Portmann, 2000)—a phenomenon that is now beginning to be examined by organizational scholars (Wiesenfeld, Blader, & Fortin, 2006).

FORMS: IWB IS A SUBSET OF …

Having defined IWB and discussed its key characteristics, we now turn our attention to a key question: What forms does IWB take? This question arises because, as we already noted, IWB is not a unique type of behavior itself but a set of characteristics that may manifest itself in various types of deviant behavior. As such, we now identify major types of deviant workplace behavior (Bennett & Robinson, 2003; Robinson & Greenberg, 1998), subsets of which may take insidious forms.

Noncompliant Behaviors

Puffer (1987) used the term *noncompliant behaviors* to describe "non-task behaviors that have negative organizational implications" (p. 615) and suggested that these typically involve "breaking rules and norms" (p. 616). She argued that employees may fail to comply with rules and regulations for many reasons, and that noncompliance is likely more "active, deliberate and premeditated" (p. 616) than simply following organizational policies and procedures (i.e., compliance).

Among the noncompliant behaviors she identified in her study of salespeople were (a) being late and taking excessive breaks, (b) complaining about the organization or fellow employees, (c) violating floor rules (e.g., taking sales from other workers), (d) making unrealistic promises to customers, and (e) failing to do one's fair share of noncommissioned sales promotions (e.g., phoning customers about upcoming sales).

Examining noncompliant behavior more broadly, Warren (2005) argued that it is crucial to distinguish between the various motives responsible for it. Specifically, these are as follows:

- *Ignorance about rules*: Employees violating organizational policies or procedures inadvertently because they are unaware that they exist.
- *Ignorance about rule application*: Employees know the rules but fail to understand how they apply to them in the situations they face.
- *Opportunistic noncompliance*: Employees are aware of organizational rules and expectations about appropriate behavior, but violate them for personal gain.
- *Principled noncompliance*: Employees intentionally break rules to protest rules they believe are wrong or morally corrupt.

All of Puffer's (1987) examples of noncompliant behavior are single acts of varying harmfulness, some of which are potentially severe. In practice, however, several of these acts may be minor in severity and it's possible—indeed, likely—for them to be repeated over time. This would allow them to be considered IWB so long as they are (a) not also focused on positive motives (e.g., principled noncompliance) and outside parties (e.g., making unrealistic promises to customers) and (b) take legal forms. In short, some but not all forms of noncompliant behavior may be considered IWB.

Workplace Deviance

Robinson and Bennett (1995) defined *workplace deviance* as "voluntary behavior that violates significant organizational norms and in doing so threatens the wellbeing of an organization, its members, or both" (p. 556). Using multidimensional scaling, they created a taxonomy consisting of four forms of deviant behavior:

- *Property deviance*: Serious forms of organizationally harmful behaviors
- *Production deviance*: Minor forms of organizationally harmful behaviors
- *Political deviance*: Minor forms of interpersonally harmful behaviors
- *Personal aggression*: Serious forms of interpersonally harmful behaviors

Like noncompliant behavior, some but not all acts of workplace deviance may manifest themselves as IWB. In particular, these would include only the minor forms of harmful behavior (production deviance and political deviance)—and among these, only those taking legal forms (thereby eliminating, for example, the destruction of equipment). Given the repetitive nature of IWB, an example would be repeatedly sabotaging the sales reports submitted by a coworker by inserting erroneous figures. And given the negative intent criterion, this would have to be motivated by the desire to make the targeted individual look bad (as is likely to be the case).

Employee Deviance

Warren (2003) defined *employee deviance* as "behavioral departures from the norms of a reference group" (p. 622). These can be either positive (e.g., whistle-blowing) or negative (e.g., lying and stealing) in nature. She distinguishes between behavior that conforms to or deviates from the norms of reference groups (i.e., local norms) and the more globally held norms of society (i.e., hypernorms). Specifically, Warren (2003) identified behavior falling outside both sets of norms (e.g., fraud) as *destructive deviance*, and behavior falling outside reference group norms but within hypernorms (e.g. whistle-blowing) as *constructive deviance*. Warren's approach highlights the importance of considering the consequences of behavior from organizational and societal perspectives, as well as the standards and norms from which behavior deviates.

Insidious forms of employee deviance would be those negative behaviors that occur repeatedly over time and only ones that are low in severity. Because not all employee deviance may be so described, IWB may be considered a particularly small subset of all employee deviance.

Organizational Misbehavior

Vardi and Wiener (1996) coined the term *organizational misbehavior* (OMB) to describe "any intentional action by member/s of organization/s which defies and violates (a) shared organizational norms and expectations, and/or (b) core societal values, mores, and standards of proper conduct" (p. 151). Additionally, these theorists classified OMB into three categories based on the intention of the person engaging in the misbehavior:

- *OMB Type S*: Misbehaviors intended to benefit the self (generally occurring inside the organization and target the company or its employees)
- *OMB Type O*: Misbehaviors that are intended to assist the employing organization and are usually directed toward outside targets
- *OMB Type D*: Misbehaviors that are designed to harm or damage the organization or its employees

In subsequent research, Vardi and his associates (2001; Vardi & Weitz, 2002, 2004) argued further that OMB can take the following forms:

- *Intrapersonal misbehavior* (e.g., substance abuse and workaholism)
- *Interpersonal misbehavior* (e.g., bullying and incivility)
- *Production misbehavior* (e.g., rule-breaking and absenteeism)
- *Property misbehavior* (e.g., sabotage and theft)
- *Political misbehavior* (e.g., misuse of power and favoritism)

The only forms of organizational misbehavior that may be regarded to be IWB are those in the category OMD Type D, but not all such behaviors qualify. Eliminated, in particular, would be those acts that are illegal and major in nature (e.g., bringing illegal drugs or weapons into the workplace). Also excluded would be any acts that are not repeated. Therefore, IWB may comprise only a small subset of all forms of organizational misbehavior.

Workplace Aggression

Neuman and Baron (1998) defined workplace aggression as "efforts by individuals to harm others with whom they work, or have worked, or the organizations in which they are presently, or were previously, employed" (p. 395). These authors argued that a distinction should be drawn between the term *workplace violence*, which is used frequently to describe direct instances of physical assault, and *workplace aggression*, which includes a wide range of harmful behaviors directed at individual or organizational targets. Subsequently, they (Baron, 2004; Neuman & Baron, 2005) drew on the classic social psychological work of Buss (1961) by crosscutting three dimensions of aggression in combination: physical or verbal, active or passive, and direct or indirect. The eight resulting forms of workplace aggression are as follows:

- *Physical, active, and direct* (e.g., homicide and assault)
- *Physical, active, and indirect forms of aggression* (e.g., theft)
- *Physical, passive, and direct* (e.g., exclusion and intentional work slowdown)
- *Physical, passive, and indirect* (e.g., denying promotions without good reason)
- *Verbal, active, and direct* (e.g., yelling and making racist remarks)
- *Verbal, active, and indirect* (e.g., spreading rumors and attempting to turn others against the target)
- *Verbal, passive, and direct* (e.g., intentionally failing to return phone calls and giving the silent treatment)
- *Verbal, passive, and indirect* (e.g., failing to refute false rumors about the target and failing to inform the target about important feedback)

Of these acts, those that are physical and active, regardless of whether direct or indirect, are not IWB because they are too serious and likely to be illegal (e.g., theft, homicide and assault). Instead, the passive and verbal forms of aggressive behavior may qualify as IWB so long as they also are repeated over time and intended to bring harm. Indeed, this is likely to be the case for some behaviors noted by Neuman and Baron (1998).

Organization-Motivated Aggression

O'Leary-Kelly, Griffin, and Glew (1996) used the term *organization-motivated aggression* to describe a particular type of aggression in the workplace, and like Neuman and Baron (1998), they distinguished between aggression and violence. Specifically, they defined organization-motivated aggression (OMA) as "attempted injurious or destructive behavior initiated by either an organizational insider or outsider that is instigated by some factor in the organizational context" (p. 229) and organization-motivated violence (OMV) as "significant negative effects on person or property that occur as a result of organization-motivated aggression" (p. 229). With respect to OMA, they make the following key observations:

- OMA does not always lead to OMV because individuals exhibiting aggressive behavior may be stopped before violence occurs.
- OMA may have negative effects even if it is not executed completely (e.g., threatening an employee with a knife or gun).

- OMA is injurious or destructive (i.e., harmful) in nature and is motivated by factors in the organizational setting.
- OMA can be perpetrated by people inside the organization (e.g., employees) or outside the organization (e.g., clients, customers or potential employees).
- OMA may be directed toward an individual or the organization itself.

By definition, the "major" nature of OMV precludes IWB. Furthermore, even many forms of OMA would not be considered IWB. Eliminated, for example, would be acts of violence (instead of aggression) and acts perpetrated by people outside the organization. Also eliminated would be those acts that are so severe as to be illegal (e.g., shooting a gun) and any that occur on only a single occasion. Therefore, IWB may comprise only a small subset of OMA.

Employee Vice

Moberg (1997) introduced the term *employee vice* to describe an act that betrays the trust of either individuals or the organizational community. He argued that different forms of betrayal exist in organizations, and categorized behaviors according to two dimensions: (1) the level of betrayal (high vs. low, measured according to the degree of organizational resources placed at risk as a result of the behavior); and (2) the beneficiary of the betrayal (the betrayer alone vs. the betrayer and other cobeneficiaries). Crosscutting these two dimensions results in the following forms of behavior:

- Behaviors involving a high level of betrayal that benefit only the betrayer (e.g., failing to disclose facts, lying about facts, self-dealing, insider trading, and embezzlement)
- Behaviors involving a high level of betrayal that benefit the betrayer and others (e.g., treason, espionage, corruption, whistle-blowing, and behaviors that are designed to cover up transgressions)
- Behaviors involving a low level of betrayal that benefit the betrayer only, such as withholding maximum effort while completing work (labeled *shirking*), rigidly complying with organizational policies and procedures to impede performance (labeled *bureaucratic opposition*), using organizational resources for personal expenditures (labeled *padded expense accounts and budget games*), and premature,

unexplained exit from the organization (labeled *untimely or symbolic exit*)

- Behaviors involving a low level of betrayal that benefit the betrayer and others, such as strikes, organized slowdowns (when all employees deliberately work slowly), sick-outs (when employees take sick days simultaneously), and unsanctioned partiality (when work units hoard resources that are supposed to be distributed to the entire organization)

The subset of employee vice that may include IWB is characterized by acts with low levels of betrayal. However, even this half of employee vice acts cannot be presumed to be IWB because whereas employee vice focuses on the benefits to the actor, IWB focuses on harm to another individual or organization, and a correlation between them cannot be assumed. In fact, one of the few "benefits" to be derived from IWB may come in the form of an actor's enjoyment from making the victim suffer (Portmann, 2000), and this would be difficult to assess (see our discussion of potentially beneficial side effects of IWB in Chapter 10, this volume). Considering this, in addition to overlaying the other criteria of IWB, it's possible but unlikely that much employee vice also can be considered IWB.

Organizational Retaliation Behavior

Skarlicki and Folger (1997) used the term *organizational retaliation behavior* (ORB) to describe "adverse reactions to perceived unfairness by disgruntled employees toward their employer" (p. 434). Consistent with our notion of IWB, they noted explicitly that, in contrast to more overt forms of deviance, they were interested in "the numerous subtle and covert forms of retaliation that are not as dramatic but still might have adverse consequences for an organization's effective functioning" (p. 435). Also consistent with IWB, Skarlicki and Folger (1997) note that ORB may be either direct or indirect and that it may be directed toward individuals or organizations.

Later, however, Skarlicki and Folger (2004) identified particular forms of ORB that in several ways disqualify from consideration as IWB. First, they argued that retaliation sometimes is a rational, measured response to wrongdoing, defying categorization as negative or positive (and only negative acts may be considered IWB). Second, they also contend that one of the reasons why people may retaliate against an organization is to educate it in ways that ultimately contribute to its survival. In his regard, ORB is similar to Puffer's (1987) notion of principled noncompliance, which also does not qualify as IWB. Third, these theorists also note that ORB can include acts that are unlawful (e.g., engaging in theft) and that they may be very severe acts. Such acts, of course, cannot be considered IWB. In short, as is the case with other forms of deviant behavior, ORB includes only some acts that would qualify as IWB.

Interpersonal Mistreatment

Cortina and Magley (2003) define *interpersonal mistreatment* as "a specific, antisocial variety of organizational deviance, involving a situation in which at least one organizational member takes counternormative negative actions—or terminates normative positive actions—against another member" (p. 247). As the authors observe, this form of deviance encompasses a wide range of behavior, ranging from minor insults to severe instances of harassment and violence. In this respect it shares some similarities with the overall construct of *interpersonal deviance* (Robinson & Bennett, 1995), which can range from minor (political deviance) to severe (personal aggression).

Here, we provide an overview of some of the most common types of interpersonal mistreatment, many of which are addressed in this book: (a) bullying and mobbing, (b) social undermining, (c) emotional abuse, and (d) incivility. We note further, and as emphasized by many other contributors to this volume, considerable overlap exists among these forms of behavior. Since sexual harassment, by definition, involves more specific behaviors, namely, unwelcome advances, requests, or verbal or physical conduct of a sexual nature (Cortina & Berdahl, 2008), we have not included it here. However, some instances of sexual harassment may be classified as interpersonal mistreatment that also may be considered IWB-I.

Bullying and Mobbing

The phenomenon of workplace bullying has attracted considerable attention from organizational researchers. As Einarsen et al. (2003) conceive of it, bullying in the workplace involves a range of negative behaviors, including "harassing, offending, socially excluding someone or negatively affecting someone's work tasks" (p. 6). They argue that to label the behaviors or process as bullying the behavior must occur on a regular basis and over a considerable period of time. Furthermore, they suggest that "bullying is an escalating process in the course of which the person confronted ends up in an inferior position and becomes the target of negative social acts. A conflict cannot be called bullying if the incident is an isolated event or if two parties of approximately equal strength are in conflict" (p. 6). Others agree that bullying involves a power imbalance between perpetrators and their target(s) and have incorporated this feature into their definitions. Salin (2003), for example, defines bullying as "repeated and persistent negative acts towards one or more individual(s), which involve a perceived power imbalance and create a hostile work environment" (p. 1215).

Extending the concept of bullying, Leymann (1996) introduced the term *mobbing* to describe "hostile and unethical communication, which is directed in a systematic way by one or a few individuals mainly towards one individual who, due to mobbing, is pushed into a hopeless and defenceless position, being held there by continuing mobbing activities" (p. 168). Leymann specified further that the behavior must occur at least once a week and for a minimum duration of 6 months to be classified as mobbing. In their review of the literature, Saunders, Huynh, and Goodman-Delahunty (2007) suggest that differences in terminology have emerged because the nature of bullying varies in different countries. Specifically, European researchers generally use the term "mobbing" because bullying in certain European countries (e.g., Germany) is often perpetrated by groups of people. In the United States and Australia, however, the term "bullying" is used in reference to the behavior of both individuals or groups.

The definitions reviewed here suggest that certain instances of bullying meet the criteria for IWB-I. First, researchers are in agreement that bullying and mobbing involve repeated instances of unwelcome behavior, a key element of IWB. And, as in IWB, some of these behaviors are minor in severity. Although some researchers (e.g., Randall, 1997) note that to constitute bullying the behavior must be deliberate and intended to cause harm, others (e.g., Einarsen et al., 2003; Zapf, 1999) have not included the intention of the perpetrator in their definitions of bullying and mobbing. The legality of workplace bullying has received attention in recent times (e.g., Namie & Namie, 2009), with legislation enacted in certain countries (e.g., Canada, Ireland) and in several Australian states designed to discourage such behavior by punishing perpetrators. Should the behavior in question be considered illegal, it would not be considered IWB. In summary, some forms of bullying and mobbing may be considered IWB.

Social Undermining

Duffy et al. (2002) defined *social undermining as* "behavior intended to hinder, over time, the ability to establish and maintain positive interpersonal relationships, work-related success, and favorable reputation" (p. 332). This definition incorporates three key features. First, for a behavior to be classified as undermining, targets must perceive that the behavior is intended to be damaging, thereby excluding accidentally harmful remarks or actions. Second, Duffy et al. emphasize that social undermining involves low-level, pervasive behaviors designed to harm an individual on a gradual basis. Like IWB, social undermining is destructive not because of any immediate and severe acts of deviance, but minor acts whose effects can accumulate to bring harm over time. Third, social undermining can take different forms, manifesting itself in terms of acts of commission (e.g., by making insulting personal comments) or acts of omission (e.g., by failing to share important information). Finally, as is the case for other forms of deviance (e.g., aggression), social undermining includes both verbal behavior (e.g., making hurtful comments) and physical behavior (e.g., deliberately misreporting information to colleagues).

It is apparent that social undermining shares several key characteristics with IWB-I, in that it involves intentionally harmful, low-level, and persistent behavior. Unlike social undermining, however, IWB also incorporates acts aimed at organizations (e.g., badmouthing the company to others)—that is, IWB-O. Furthermore, acts of social undermining may take illegal forms (e.g., theft), whereas such acts would not be considered IWB. In other words, people who engage in IWB may do so without getting into any formal trouble, and this enables them to maintain their ways.

Emotional Abuse

Keashly (1998) uses the term *emotional abuse* to describe "hostile verbal and nonverbal behaviors that are not explicitly tied to sexual or racial content yet are directed at gaining compliance from others" (p. 85). Extending this notion, Keashly and Harvey (2005) added that emotional abuse includes "repeated hostile verbal and nonverbal behaviors (excluding physical contact) directed at one or more individuals over a period of time such that the target's sense of self as a competent worker and person is negatively affected" (p. 205). Examples of behavior in keeping with this definition include humiliating or mocking an employee in front of others, giving someone the "silent treatment," name-calling, and deliberately withholding information (Keashly, 2001).

Keashly (1998) suggested emotional abuse incorporates the following defining behavioral features. Specifically, emotional abuse is

- Verbal and nonverbal (not including physical contact)
- Repetitive or part of a pattern of behavior
- Unwanted, unwelcomed, and unsolicited by the target
- A violation of standards of acceptable behavior toward others
- Harmful or causes physical or psychological damage to the target
- Intended to harm or under the control of the perpetrator
- Capable of exploiting the position power of the perpetrator over the target

Some forms of emotional abuse may be considered IWB-I (e.g., repeatedly chastising a coworker). However, emotional abuse may take forms that would not be considered IWB. Specifically, as Keashly and Harvey (2005) note, victims of emotional abuse may suffer lowered perceptions of themselves as competent employees. Indeed, victims' entire senses of self may be threatened. By contrast, it is not clear that IWB-I will lead to these consequences. Additionally, emotional abuse and IWB may be motivated by different factors. By definition, emotional abuse is motivated by the desire to gain compliance. However, acts of IWB are performed not with an eye toward getting others to behave certain ways, but rather to harm them. Finally, whereas emotional abuse precludes making physical contact with victims, minor forms of negative physical contact (e.g., pushing someone aside) may be labeled IWB.

Incivility

Andersson and Pearson (1999) introduced the term *incivility* to describe "low-intensity deviant (rude, discourteous) behavior with ambiguous intent to harm the target in violation of workplace norms for mutual respect," adding that "uncivil behaviors are characteristically rude and discourteous, displaying a lack of regard for others" (p. 457). The authors contrasted this behavior with workplace *civility*, which involves treating others with dignity and respect in line with normative standards of behavior in the organization in question. Further, they suggested that incivility is a particular form of workplace deviance.

Revisiting this concept more recently, Pearson and Porath (2004) observed that incivility differs from past conceptualizations of deviance in the following ways:

- Incivility (like IWB) involves minor, less extreme forms of deviance, such as making a sarcastic remark.
- Incivility (unlike IWB) does not include organizationally directed instances of behavior; it is only concerned with deviance directed at other individuals.
- Incivility (unlike IWB) is not always intentionally harmful and includes cases in which employees may unintentionally harm others through mistakes or oversights

Research (e.g., Cortina, Magley, Williams, & Langhout, 2001; Lim, Cortina, & Magley, 2008; Pearson, Andersson, & Porath, 2000) has demonstrated that incivility is a prevalent phenomenon that often has serious adverse psychological and occupational effects on employees.

When acts of incivility are intentional, minor, repeated, and intended to harm individuals or organizations—as some may be—they would be considered IWB. Clearly, many acts of IWB manifest themselves as incivility. However, because incivility excludes organizationally aimed behavior and includes acts that bring harm unintentionally, IWB is only a small subset of uncivil behavior.

Counterproductive Work Behavior

In the past few years, industrial psychologists have described counterproductive work behavior (CWB) broadly as "volitional acts that harm or are intended to harm organizations or people in organizations" (Spector & Fox, 2005, p. 151) and as "any intentional behavior on the part of an organization member viewed by the organization as contrary to its legitimate interests" (Gruys & Sackett, 2003, p. 30). Empirically, 11 distinct forms have been identified: (1) theft and related behavior, (2) destruction of property, (3) misuse of information, (4) misuse of time and resources, (5) unsafe behavior, (6) poor attendance, (7) poor quality work, (8) alcohol use, (9) drug use, (10) inappropriate verbal actions, and (11) inappropriate physical actions. These vary along the following two dimensions:

- *Interpersonal-organizational*: The extent to which the behavior in question targets individuals or organizations
- *Task relevance*: The extent to which the behavior in question includes tasks completed as part of one's job

CWB, like IWB, includes volitional acts aimed at individuals and organizations. However, IWB differs in that the acts are low in severity and occur repeatedly over time. CWB also includes potentially illegal behavior, such as theft and destruction of company property. Accordingly, IWB is only a subset of CWB.

CONCLUSION: CHALLENGES OF STUDYING IWB

We have depicted IWB as a particular form of various types of deviant behavior occurring in the workplace. IWB is not another one of these types but instead, a subset of behaviors within each type that conforms to our defining characteristics. Therefore, there may be insidious varieties of each of the types of behavior identified here. As such, IWB is unique relative to other manifestations of the particular type of behavior whose characteristics it takes on. This uniqueness poses two key challenges for studying IWB.

One of the greatest challenges in the study of IWB involves overcoming the fallacious assumption that small behaviors have small effects. Indeed, although individual acts of IWB may be subtle in nature, their cumulative effects can be anything but subtle, taking a toll on the lives of victims and the bottom lines of organizations. Indeed, people who are subjected to even seemingly minor acts of incivility (e.g., name-calling, the effects of which are trivialized in the children's rhyme about "sticks and stones") often show psychiatric morbidity (e.g., anxiety and posttraumatic stress disorder) when these acts occur repeatedly (Evans, 2002; Matthiesen & Einarsen, 2004). The pernicious effects of IWB also are found in organizations. We see this, for example, in statistics revealing the devastating financial impact of repeated employee pilferage on small organizations (for a review, see Greenberg & Scott, 1996).

Taken together, such evidence suggests that it would be worthwhile to assess the pervasiveness of IWB. However, the extent of the damage done by IWB is difficult to gauge for several reasons. First, its inherently stealthy nature makes IWB too far "below the radar" to be salient to people. Second, even if people are aware of being victimized by IWB, they are inclined to consider such behavior too low level to warrant taking any definitive response. And, absent a discernible response, measurement is difficult (on this, see Jex and his associates, Chapter 8, this volume).

The "smallness" of the behavior is not the only reason why people might not respond to IWB. Inherent in IWB resides some ambiguity about its inappropriateness that also may constrain responses. Thus, victims may wonder if the person who keeps chastising them, a superior, for example, is really doing anything wrong. "After all," they may wonder, "is my boss really so ill intentioned?" Also, they may rationalize by considering that "maybe I deserve it" or that "surely someone would do something about it if it were wrong." This ambiguity is compounded by the dynamic nature of the behavior. Any given act may be more severe one day and less the next. Additionally, it may not even occur in any patterned way (e.g., following a variable interval schedule). For such combinations of reasons, the inappropriateness of IWB may be open to questioning. And under such ambiguous conditions, victims may be reluctant to risk acting inappropriately by striking back (Solomon, Solomon, & Stone, 1978).

This issue of ambiguity is likely to influence responsiveness in another way as well. Specifically, even if someone is tempted to speak out about being a victim of IWB, he or she may fear counterreactions from the perpetrator, who may hide behind the excuse that his her insidious acts were, in reality, not worthy of response. In other words, fearing that the perpetrator may accuse the victim of "making something out of nothing," "being too sensitive," or "making a mountain out of a molehill," a victim may be motivated to overlook the offensive behavior despite being acutely aware of its uncomfortable effects. This may be especially so when status differences between the parties leave the lower status person feeling intimidated and wanting to avoid the potential conflict that questioning a supervisor's behavior may evoke (Moretti & Odgers, 2006), even if done politely and not in a challenging fashion.

Considering these points, both the incentives to manage such behavior and the opportunities to do so are likely to be limited. Together with the presumed assumption—although erroneous, as noted earlier—that IWB is too trivial to warrant attention, it's not surprising that only limited attention is being paid to IWB. We trust that the chapters that lay ahead in this book will go a long way toward turning this around.

REFERENCES

Andersson, L. M., & Pearson, C. M. (1999). Tit for tat? The spiraling effect of incivility in the workplace. *Academy of Management Review, 24*, 452–471.

Baron, R. A. (2004). Workplace aggression and violence: Insights from basic research. In R. W. Griffin & A. M. O'Leary-Kelly (Eds.), *The dark side of organizational behavior* (pp. 23–61). San Francisco, CA: Jossey-Bass.

Baron, R. A., & Neuman, J. H. (1996). Workplace violence and workplace aggression: Evidence on their relative frequency and potential causes. *Aggressive Behavior, 22*, 161–173.

Baron, R. A., & Neuman, J. H. (1998). Workplace aggression: The iceberg beneath the tip of workplace violence: Evidence on its forms, frequency, and targets. *Public Administration Quarterly, 21*, 446–464.

Bennett, R. J., & Robinson, S. L. (2003). The past, present and future of workplace deviance research. In J. Greenberg (Ed.), *Organizational behavior: The state of the science* (2nd ed., pp. 247–281). Mahwah, NJ: Erlbaum.

Berry, C. M., Ones, D. S., & Sackett, P. R. (2007). Interpersonal deviance, organizational deviance, and their common correlates: A review and meta-analysis. *Journal of Applied Psychology, 92*, 410–424.

Buss, A. H. (1961). *The psychology of aggression*. New York, NY: Wiley.

Conte, A. (2009). *Sexual harassment in the workplace: Law and practice* (3rd ed.). Alphen aan den Rijn, Netherlands: Wolwers Kluwer.

Cortina, L. M., & Berdahl, J. L. (2008). Sexual harassment in organizations: A decade of research in review. In C. Cooper & J. Barling (Eds.), *Handbook of organizational behavior: Micro perspectives* (pp. 469–497). Thousand Oaks, CA: Sage.

Cortina, L. M., & Magley, V. J. (2003). Raising voice, risking retaliation: Events following interpersonal mistreatment in the workplace. *Journal of Occupational Health Psychology, 8*, 247–265.

Cortina, L. M., Magley, V. J., Williams, J. H., & Langhout, R. D. (2001). Incivility in the workplace: Incidence and impact. *Journal of Occupational Health Psychology, 6*, 64–80.

Dollard, J., Doob, L., Miller, N., Mowrer, O., & Sears, R. (1939). *Frustration and aggression*. New Haven, CT: Yale University Press.

Duffy, M. K., Ganster, D. C., & Pagon, M. (2002). Social undermining in the workplace. *Academy of Management Journal, 45*, 331–351.

Efrati, A., Lauricella, T., & Searcey, D. (2008, December 12). Top broker accused of $50 billion fraud. *Wall Street Journal*, p. A1.

Einarsen, S., Hoel, H., Zapf, D., & Cooper, C. L. (2003). The concept of bullying at work: The European tradition. In S. Einarsen, H. Hoel, D. Zapf, & C. L. Cooper (Eds.), *Bullying and emotional abuse in the workplace: International perspectives in research and practice* (pp. 3–30). New York, NY: Taylor & Francis.

Evans, P. (2002). *Controlling people*. Avon, MA: Adams Media.

Greenberg, J. (2004, August). *Insidious workplace deviance: Causes and consequences*. Paper presented at the annual meeting of the Academy of Management, New Orleans, LA.

Greenberg, J., & Scott, K. S. (1996). Why do workers bite the hands that feed them? Employee theft as a social exchange process. In B. M. Staw & L. L. Cummings (Eds.), *Research in organizational behavior* (Vol. 18, pp. 111–155). Greenwich, CT: JAI.

Gruys, M. L., & Sackett, P. R. (2003). Investigating the dimensionality of counterproductive work behavior. *International Journal of Selection and Assessment, 11*, 30–42.

Hershcovis, M. S., & Barling, J. (2007). Towards a relational model of workplace aggression. In J. Langan-Fox, C. L. Cooper, & R. J. Klimoski (Eds.), *Research companion to the dysfunctional workplace* (pp. 268–284). Northampton, MA: Edward Elgar.

Huntington, S. P. (2004). *Who are we? The challenges to America's national identity*. New York, NY: Simon & Schuster.

Keashly, L. (1998). Emotional abuse in the workplace: Conceptual and empirical issues. *Journal of Emotional Abuse, 1*, 85–117.

Keashly, L. (2001). Interpersonal and systemic aspects of emotional abuse at work: The target's perspective. *Violence and Victims, 16*, 233–268.

Keashly, L., & Harvey, S. (2005). Emotional abuse in the workplace. In S. Fox & P. E. Spector (Eds.), *Counterproductive work behavior: Investigations of actors and targets* (pp. 201–236). Washington, DC: American Psychological Association.

Keashly, L., & Jagatic, K. (2003). By any other name: American perspectives on workplace bullying. In S. Einarsen, H. Hoel, D. Zapf, & C. L. Cooper (Eds.), *Bullying and emotional abuse in the workplace: International perspectives in research and practice* (pp. 31–61). New York, NY: Taylor & Francis.

Keen, J. (2008, December 10). Feds: Governor tried to sell Senate seat. *USA Today*, pp. A1–A2.

Leavitt, P. (1995, April 4). Ex-employee kills 5, self at Texas firm. *USA Today*, p. A3.

Leymann, H. (1996). The content and development of mobbing at work. *European Journal of Work and Organisational Psychology, 5*, 165–184.

Lim, S., Cortina, L. M., & Magley, V. J. (2008). Personal and workgroup incivility: Impact on work and health outcomes. *Journal of Applied Psychology, 93*, 95–107.

Lustenberger, D. E., & Williams, K. W. (2009). Ostracism in organizations. In J. Greenberg & M. S. Edwards (Eds.), *Voice and silence in organizations* (pp. 245–274). Bingley, England: Emerald.

Macquarie Concise Dictionary (3rd ed.). (1998). Sydney, Australia: Macquarie Dictionary Publishers.

Matthiesen, S. B., & Einarsen, S. (2004). Psychiatric distress and symptoms of PTSD among victims of bullying at work. *British Journal of Guidance and Counseling, 32*, 335–356.

Moberg, D. J. (1997). On employee vice. *Business Ethics Quarterly, 7*, 41–60.

Moretti, M. M., & Odgers, C. (2006). Preface: Sex differences in the functions and precursors of adolescent aggression. *Aggressive Behavior, 32*, 373–375.

Namie, G., & Namie, R. (2009). U.S. workplace bullying: Some basic considerations and consultation interventions. *Consulting Psychology Journal, 61*, 202–219.

Neuman, J. H., & Baron, R. A. (1998). Workplace violence and workplace aggression: Evidence concerning specific forms, potential causes, and preferred targets. *Journal of Management, 24,* 391–419.

Neuman, J. H., & Baron, R. A. (2005). Aggression in the workplace: A social-psychological perspective. In S. Fox & P. E. Spector (Eds.), *Counterproductive work behavior: Investigations of actors and targets* (pp. 13–40). Washington, DC: American Psychological Association.

O'Leary-Kelly, A. M., Griffin, R. W., & Glew, D. J. (1996). Organization-motivated aggression: A research framework. *Academy of Management Review, 21,* 225–253.

Organ, D. W., & Ryan, K. (1995). A meta-analytic review of attitudinal and dispositional predictors of organizational citizenship behavior. *Personnel Psychology, 48,* 775–802.

Oxford American Dictionary. (1980). New York, NY: Oxford University Press.

Pearson, C., Andersson, L., & Porath, C. (2000). Assessing and attacking workplace incivility. *Organizational Dynamics, 29,* 123–137.

Pearson, C., & Porath, C. (2004). On incivility, its impact and directions for future research. In R. Griffin & A. O'Leary-Kelly (Eds.), *The dark side of organizational behavior* (pp. 403–425). San Francisco, CA: Jossey-Bass.

Portmann. J. (2000). *When bad things happen to other people.* New York, NY: Routledge.

Puffer, S. M. (1987). Pro-social behavior, non-compliant behavior and work performance among commission salespeople. *Journal of Applied Psychology, 72,* 615–621.

Randall, P. (1997). *Adult bullying: Perpetrators and victims.* New York, NY: Routledge.

Rayner, C., Hoel, H., & Cooper, C. L. (2002). *Workplace bullying: What we know, who is to blame and what can we do?* New York, NY: Taylor & Francis.

Robinson, S. L., & Bennett, R. J. (1995). A typology of deviant workplace behaviors: A multidimensional scaling study. *Academy of Management Journal, 38,* 555–572.

Robinson, S. L., & Greenberg, J. (1998). Employees behaving badly: Dimensions, determinants and dilemmas in the study of workplace deviance. In C. L. Cooper & D. M. Rousseau (Eds.), *Trends in organizational behavior* (Vol. 5, pp. 1–30). New York: Wiley.

Salin, D. (2003). Ways of explaining workplace bullying: A review of enabling, motivating, and precipitating structures and processes in the work environment. *Human Relations, 56,* 1213–1232.

Saunders, P., Huynh, A., & Goodman-Delahunty, J. (2007). Defining workplace bullying behaviour: Professional and lay definitions of workplace bullying. *International Journal of Law and Psychiatry, 30,* 340–354.

Schneider, K. T., Swan, S., & Fitzgerald, L. F. (1997). Job-related and psychological effects of sexual harassment in the workplace: Empirical evidence from two organizations. *Journal of Applied Psychology, 82,* 401–415.

Simpson, R., & Cohen, C. (2004). Dangerous work: The gendered nature of bullying in the context of higher education. *Gender, Work & Organization, 11,* 163–185.

Skarlicki, D. P., & Folger, R. (1997). Retaliation in the workplace: The roles of distributive, procedural and interactional justice. *Journal of Applied Psychology, 82,* 434–443.

Skarlicki, D. P., & Folger, R. (2004). Deepening our understanding of organizational retaliatory behavior. In R. Griffin & A. O'Leary-Kelly (Eds.), *The dark side of organizational behavior* (pp. 373–403). San Francisco, CA: Jossey-Bass.

Solomon, L. Z., Solomon, H., & Stone, R. (1978). Helping as a function of number of bystanders and ambiguity of emergency. *Personality and Social Psychology Bulletin, 4,* 318–321.

Spector, P. E., & Fox, S. (2005). A model of counterproductive work behavior. In S. Fox & P. E. Spector (Eds.). *Counterproductive work behavior: Investigations of actors and targets* (pp. 151–174). Washington, DC: American Psychological Association.

Tepper, B. J. (2000). Consequences of abusive supervision. *Academy of Management Journal, 43*, 178–190.

Vardi, Y. (2001). The effects of organizational and ethical climates on misconduct at work. *Journal of Business Ethics, 29*, 325–337.

Vardi, Y., & Weitz, E. (2002). Antecedents of organizational misbehavior among caregivers. In M. Afzalur Rahim, R. T. Golembiewski, & K. D. Mackenzie (Eds.), *Current topics in management* (Vol. 7, pp. 99–116). Edison, NJ: Transaction Publishers.

Vardi, Y., & Weitz, E. (2004). *Misbehavior in organizations: Theory, research and management*. Mahwah, NJ: Erlbaum.

Vardi, Y., & Wiener, Y. (1996). Misbehavior in organizations: A motivational framework. *Organizational Science, 7*, 151–165.

Warren, D. E. (2003). Constructive and destructive deviance in organizations. *Academy of Management Review, 28*, 622–632.

Warren, D. E. (2005). Managing noncompliance in the workplace. In R. E. Kidwell & C. L. Martin (Eds.), *Managing organizational deviance* (pp. 131–150). Thousand Oaks, CA: Sage.

Wiesenfeld, B. M., Blader, S., & Fortin, M. (2006, August). *Empathy, schadenfreude and justice: Conflicts between what is right and what feels good*. Paper presented at the annual meeting of the Academy of Management, Atlanta, GA.

Wurtzel, E. (1994). *Prozac nation: Young and depressed in America*. New York: Houghton Mifflin.

Zapf, D. (1999). Organizational, work group related and personal causes of mobbing/bullying at work. *International Journal of Manpower, 20*, 70–84.

Section 2

Forms of Insidious Workplace Behavior

2

Means, Motive, Opportunity, and Aggressive Workplace Behavior

Joel H. Neuman and Loraleigh Keashly

In the world of police work (especially as portrayed on television), identifying individuals having means, motive, and opportunity often leads to the identification of potential suspects and, hopefully, the arrest of any and all guilty parties. As this suggests, means, motive, and opportunity (MM&O) are essential elements in the successful execution of a criminally motivated act and provide important clues for police engaged in criminal investigations. By extension, we believe that the consideration of these variables may prove useful in the study of isolated, occasional, and more persistent (insidious) acts of harm-doing in work settings. Furthermore, we believe that the utility of this framework may be manifest in both research and practice. In this chapter, we provide empirical and conceptual support for these assertions.

DEFINITIONAL AND CONCEPTUAL ISSUES

Since a broad array of actions may be subsumed under the heading of insidious workplace behavior, we begin by identifying the major focus of this chapter, defining the terminology we will be using, and providing a conceptual basis for our thesis. Following this, we will provide empirical evidence on the interactions among means, motive, and opportunity, and the utility of considering these variables in both theory and practice.

INSIDIOUS, AGGRESSIVE, AND ABUSIVE WORKPLACE BEHAVIOR

As relates to the behavior of human beings, dictionary definitions of the word *insidious* describe actions that "work or spread harmfully in a subtle or stealthy manner," inflicting gradual and cumulatively adverse outcomes on one or more targets (*Merriam-Webster's Collegiate Dictionary*, 2003). Furthermore, these behaviors are often described as "treacherous" and "intended to entrap" or "ambush." To the extent that we are talking about efforts by individuals to harm others in work settings, we consider these as instances of workplace aggression (Neuman & Baron, 2005).

While suggesting that such actions are, by definition, aggressive, we recognize them as a special class of aggression. Since insidious behaviors are often stealthy and enduring in nature, we would classify them as covert and persistent forms of aggression. As captured by the Buss (1961) typology, this might include passive, verbal, and indirect forms of harm doing. At the other extreme, aggression includes overt acts of physical violence—direct, physical, and active forms of harm doing. There is a range of behavior that falls between these two extremes, varying in degree of stealthiness (obviousness, ambiguity, and intensity), persistence (frequency of occurrence), and duration (overall length of occurrence). Finally, some forms of insidious behavior might include physical, active, and direct behavior (e.g., a male supervisor never missing an opportunity to "innocently" brush up against a female subordinate) just as serious confrontations (bordering on violence) may involve verbal aggression (i.e., death threats). While the MM&O framework can be applied to this full range of behavior, it may provide special utility in the exploration and management of insidious workplace behaviors, that is, recognizing their existence, identifying and addressing the underlying cause(s), and eliminating the opportunity for the behavior(s) to occur.

MEANS

As relates to means, we refer to an actor's wherewithal to commit an act of aggression as well as the method employed to deliver harm to the target(s). With respect to wherewithal, actors must possess the knowledge, skill, ability, capacity, and resources to engage in a particular act of aggression. For example, if you intend to shoot someone with a handgun, you must have access to the weapon and the bullets, know how to use (i.e., load, aim, and fire) the weapon, and possess the necessary psychological makeup to engage in such behavior. Similarly, engaging in computer sabotage requires knowledge of computer hardware and software; employing biting sarcasm involves certain verbal capacities; and insidious forms of political behavior require the ability to build constituencies, influence others, and engage in subtle, often covert, activities.

Along with wherewithal, means refers to the method used to deliver harm to one or more targets. As suggested earlier, aggressive behavior may involve overt, covert, physical, verbal, direct, indirect, active, or passive forms of behavior (Baron & Neuman, 1996; Buss, 1961). An enormous amount of work has been done in recent years focusing on the various means by which individuals may harm other individuals and organizations (Fox & Spector, 2005; Giacalone & Greenberg, 1997; Griffin & O'Leary-Kelly, 2004; Lutgen-Sandvik & Sypher, 2009). In addition to the aggression and violence literature, this includes (but is not limited to) social undermining (Duffy, Ganster, & Pagon, 2002; Duffy, Shaw, Scott, & Tepper, 2006), rude and disrespectful treatment (Andersson & Pearson, 1999; Cortina & Magley, 2009; Twale & De Luca, 2008), sexual and generalized work harassment and discrimination (Richman & Rospenda, 2005; Richman et al., 1999), lying (Grover, 1993, 1997, 2005), theft (Greenberg, 1993b, 1994; Kulas, McInnerney, DeMuth, & Jadwinski, 2007), bullying (Adams & Crawford, 1992; Keashly & Nowell, in press; Leymann, 1990, 1996), emotional abuse (Keashly, 1998; Penhaligon, Louis, & Restubog, 2009), and abusive supervision (Ashforth, 1994; Mitchell & Ambrose, 2007; Roscigno, Lopez, & Hodson, 2009; Tepper, 2000, 2007). In considering this list of diverse behaviors, it should be clear that method and wherewithal are inexorably connected, as actors are constrained to employ the methods under their control—consistent with their abilities, capacities, and resources.

MOTIVE

With respect to motive, we speak of the intent or purpose guiding an action and the motivating forces and factors evoking such intention. We ask the question, "Why did the actor do that to the target?" We are, in essence, asking "What prompted or caused the action, and what is its ultimate aim or objective?" As relates to insidious workplace behavior, there may be multiple motives, actions, and objectives. In many instances, aggression comes in reaction to some provocation—real or imagined (Bushman, Bonacci, Pedersen, Vasquez, & Miller, 2005; Geen, 1991; Harris, 1993). In this case, the objective may be to get even, exact justice, seek retribution, or simply retaliate (Bies & Tripp, 1996, 1998a, 2005; Bies, Tripp, & Kramer, 1997; Donnerstein & Hatfield, 1982; Greenberg & Alge, 1998; B. E. Lewis, 2004; J. McGregor, Hamm, & Kiley, 2007; McLean Parks, 1997; Tripp & Bies, 1997; Tripp, Bies, & Aquino, 2002, 2007). At other times, aggressive behavior serves some instrumental purpose and is not initiated in reaction to anything the target did (Buss, 1961; Feshbach, 1964; Geen, 1991; Hartup, 1974; Neuman & Baron, in press; Salin, 2005; Tedeschi & Felson, 1994). In such instances, actors engage in aggression to obtain some valued outcome or simply because it serves as a means to a particular end. Zillmann (1979) suggested that the terms reactive/hostile and instrumental/proactive be replaced by annoyance–motivated versus incentive–motivated aggression, respectively. Regardless of the terminology, different underlying motives are recognized as the impetus for aggressive behavior.

Other motives may involve fear or shame (Scheff, 1987; Tangney, Burggraf, & Wagner, 1995; Tangney, Wagner, & Gramzow, 1996). In the case of fear, people often become defensive and hypervigilant when anxious. This, in turn, may breed mistrust and the increased likelihood of making hostile and sinister attributions about the intentions of others (Kramer, 1994). With respect to shame, aggression is often employed to restore dignity, as captured in the notion of "humiliated fury" (H. B. Lewis, 1971). For example, Averill's (1982) examination of everyday episodes of anger among adults suggests that a common cause of anger is a loss of pride or a loss of self-esteem. The experience of shame among college students has been associated with a desire to punish others (Wicker, Payne, & Morgan, 1983) as well as anger arousal, suspiciousness, resentment, irritability, a tendency to blame others for negative events, and indirect expressions of hostility (Tangney, Wagner, Fletcher, & Gramzow, 1992). Among fifth-grade boys, shame proneness was positively correlated with both self-reports of anger and teacher reports of aggression (Tangney, Wagner, Burggraf, Gramzow, & Fletcher, 1991).

Clearly, the list of potential motives that might underlie aggressive/insidious behavior is endless but, in the case of intentional behavior, an objective must exist—as intentional behavior is, by definition, motivated.

OPPORTUNITY

With respect to opportunity, it is our position that an action must be possible (capable of happening) as well as practical and feasible (readily or easily employed in meeting one's objective). For example, insidious behaviors
often require the repeated application of low-level, low-intensity, subtle,
or stealthy "attacks" resulting in gradual (but cumulative) harm to one
or more targets—as captured in the saying "death by a thousand paper
cuts." Such a scenario requires the opportunity for these behaviors to play
out over time. This would require an ongoing relationship between the
actor(s) and target(s) or, at least, repeated access to the target by the actor.
In the absence of such a relationship, insidious actions are not possible.
In the case of more overt and severe forms of psychological abuse, workplace bullying (referred to as mobbing in some Scandinavian and German
countries) involves persistent acts of aggression occurring on a weekly or
daily basis over an extended period of time—typically 6 months or longer
in duration (Leymann, 1990). Again, actors and targets must come into
repeated contact with each other if bullying is to be possible.

Additionally, the nature of the relationship between actors and targets
impacts the feasibility and practicality of employing a particular behavior. In the case of abusive supervision or other abuses of power in organizational settings (Ashforth, 1994; Bies & Tripp, 1998b; Hornstein, 1997;
Tepper, 2000, 2007; Zellars, Tepper, & Duffy, 2002), practicality and feasibility results from power differences (either real or imagined) between the
actors and targets. Even in instances where there is no hierarchical difference in power, people may feel powerless to respond or feel that they are
unable to extricate themselves from the situation (due to economic considerations or limited geographic mobility). If this "opportunity" is lacking,
bullying cannot exist. By the same token, more active, physical, and direct
forms of aggression require only a single interaction. Consequently, verbal
hostility or physical assault is possible even within single encounters. As
we will demonstrate in a later section, in response to some real or imagined
provocation (i.e., motive), customers/clients/patients may resort to more
direct and overt forms of aggression as those are the only means available
to them, given their limited opportunity for interaction with their target.

Some forms of aggression require that the actor and target be in close
physical proximity to one another. If, for example, you wish to punch

someone in the nose (a desire that may surface during some faculty meetings), you must be within striking distance of your target. The opportunity for such physical aggression is lacking during a telephone call or e-mail exchange, assuming that some great distance separates the parties. Therefore, physical proximity will impact the choice of method as well as the practicality of using a particular tactic. On the other hand, computer sabotage requires no such physical proximity and knowledgeable actors can implement their attacks from great distances—often with anonymity (Gaudin, 2006; McEwen, 1990; Tahmincioglu, 2001).

In addition to time and physical proximity, contextual factors may either inhibit or facilitate the occurrence of aggression; that is, aggression may become more or less feasible given specific organizational policies and practices (related to interpersonal treatment, ethics, disciplinary practices, organizational culture, climate, etc.). For example, the presence of security cameras may reduce the likelihood of theft or vandalism, and electronic performance and computer monitoring may reduce the prevalence of other forms of aggression or counterproductive work behavior. Alternatively, organizational policies and practices may encourage overt aggression as well as more covert instances of insidious workplace behavior. This would include the existence of dog-eat-dog cultures in which tough and ruthless behavior is a sign of strength, and cooperation, collaboration, and sensitivity as signs of weakness. In these climates, compensation and recognition practices often encourage cutthroat behavior, and social undermining is viewed as a legitimate means for climbing up the corporate ladder.

MEANS, MOTIVE, OPPORTUNITY, AND RESEARCH ON "NEGATIVE" WORKPLACE BEHAVIOR

To the best of our knowledge, the MM&O framework has not been applied to the study of "dark side" behaviors in organizational settings (Griffin & O'Leary-Kelly, 2004). However, to varying degrees, means, motive, and opportunity have been integrated, explored, discussed, or implied in each of the constructs related to mistreatment at work. Later, we provide some examples of both implicit and explicit references to

MM&O in some of the key constructs in this field. For convenience, we have grouped certain constructs together. These groupings were not the result of any empirical procedure.

Workplace Aggression and Violence

The most explicit consideration of means, motive, and opportunity can be found in research related to workplace violence. This is evidenced in early workplace violence research done by the Division of Occupational Safety and Health for the State of California (*Cal/OSHA Guidelines for Workplace Security*, 1995). In these guidelines, Cal/OSHA classified incidence of violence based on the relationship of the perpetrator to the organization. In Type I violence (criminal intruder), the perpetrator has no legitimate nexus to the organization or workplace and usually enters the workplace to commit a robbery or other criminal act. In the case of Type II violence (client or customer violence), the perpetrator is either "the recipient or object of the service provided by the affected workplace or victim (e.g., the assailant is a current or former client, patient, customer, passenger, criminal suspect, inmate, or prisoner)." Finally, in Type III (internal employee) "the agent has some employment-related involvement with the affected workplace. Usually this involves an assault by a current or former employee, supervisor or manager; by a current/former spouse or lover; a relative or friend; or some other person who has a dispute with an employee of the affected workplace." A more recent formulation of this classification scheme (LeBlanc & Barling, 2005; University of Iowa Injury Prevention Research Center, 2001) adds a fourth category (Type IV violence) in which the perpetrator does not have a relationship with the workplace but does have a personal relationship with the intended victim.

In looking at this typology, and the definitions within each category, it seems clear that motive is an important consideration (robbery, revenge/retaliation, frustration, jealously, etc.). In addition, the violence literature focuses on the means by which harm is inflicted (physical vs. verbal assaults) and the consequences of the acts (fatal vs. nonfatal; Bureau of Labor Statistics, 2008, 2009). Opportunity is explicitly recognized in the workplace violence literature (especially Type I violence) as it relates to workplace security (Conte, 1993; Micco, 1998; Purdy, 1994). There also is an implicit recognition of opportunity as relates to the relationship of actors and targets (individuals and organizations).

Emotional Abuse

In the case of emotional abuse, this involves "hostile verbal and nonverbal behaviors (excluding physical contact) directed by one or more persons towards another that are aimed at undermining the other to ensure compliance" (Keashly, Trott, & MacLean, 1994, p. 342). This definition makes explicit reference to means and motive, in that the behaviors are designed (intended) to inflict psychological or emotional harm on the targets, pushing them into a helpless and defenseless position (Davenport, Schwartz, & Elliott, 1999; Leymann, 1990) and involve means (primarily nonphysical) to bring about this desired end (Koonin & Green, 2004; Penhaligon et al., 2009). As these types of behavior are truly insidious, they require time to play out and involve power differences (both real and imagined) between actor and target. Indeed, Keashly and Jagatic (2003) have argued that emotional abuse is about hostile relationships and not simply hostile events. Therefore, opportunity is implicit in the infliction of emotional abuse.

Workplace Bullying, Abusive Supervision, Petty Tyranny, and Social Undermining

Although not described as such in the literature, the notion of opportunity is clearly related to abusive supervision and petty tyranny. This is manifest in that mistreatment results from the abuses of power within an ongoing, formally established, hierarchical relationship. As relates to abusive supervision, superiors have the opportunity to "engage in the sustained display of hostile verbal and nonverbal behaviors" (Tepper, 2000, p. 178); or, simply put, lord their power over others (Einarsen, Aasland, & Skogstad, 2007; Harvey, Stoner, Hochwarter, & Kacmar, 2007).

Opportunity relates not only to the hierarchical relationship of targets and victims but also to the fact that they come into repeated and prolonged contact with each other in the course of their formally prescribed working relationships. This provides an opportunity for insidious (as well as more overt mistreatment) to play out over time. This may involve the use of social undermining, "behavior intended to hinder, over time, the ability to establish and maintain positive interpersonal relationships, work related success, and favorable reputation" (Duffy et al., 2002, p. 332). While social undermining is not restricted to superior–subordinate relationships, it would seem central to the demeaning and marginalizing behaviors heaped on defenseless subordinates.

In instances of workplace bullying, there may not be formal power differences in the relationship (i.e., the parties may be peers) but the targets may perceive that they are less powerful than the perpetrator or feel defenseless in the face of the mistreatment. As noted by Einarsen and Skogstad (1996), "bullying and harassment imply a difference in actual or perceived power and 'strength' between the persecutor and the victim" (p. 187). The importance of real or perceived power differences is a defining characteristic in most of the workplace bullying literature as is the importance of persistent and enduring mistreatment (Einarsen, Hoel, Zapf, & Cooper, in press; Einarsen & Skogstad, 1996; Hoel, Cooper, & Faragher, 2001; Hoel, Rayner, & Cooper, 1999; Lee, 2001; Quine, 1999; Rayner, Hoel, & Cooper, 2002; Zapf & Einarsen, 2003). It is our contention that even perceived (as opposed to real) power differences create the opportunity for bullying to occur.

As in the case with workplace aggression and emotional abuse research, scholars have generated lists of behaviors and explored the underlying dimensionality of workplace bullying (Rayner & Hoel, 1997), abusive supervision (Hornstein, 1997; Tepper, 2000), and petty tyranny (Ashforth, 1994). In fact, the bulk of the prevalence literature is devoted to empirical investigations of the methods (means) that people employ to mistreat others at work. A portion of this research has explored the motives, or motivating forces and factors, underlying these acts. In particular, this has focused on various dispositional characteristics that may precipitate bullying (Coyne, Seigne, & Randall, 2000; Matthiesen & Einarsen, 2007; Seigne, Coyne, Randall, & Parker, 2007; Zapf & Einarsen, 2003) and abusive supervision (Ashforth, 1994; Levinson, 1978). Some research has suggested specific motives associated with abusive supervision. For example, Keashly and colleagues (1994) define abusive behaviors in the workplace as those that are "directed by one or more persons towards another that are aimed at undermining the other to ensure compliance" (p. 342). Similarly, Ashforth (1994) identified intent to undermine subordinates' self-esteem through belittling, discouragement of initiative, and the withholding of consideration.

Revenge and Sabotage

As the terms *revenge* and *sabotage* clearly suggest, these are goal-directed behaviors in which the intent is to inflict harm, typically in response to some perceived provocation. According to Aquino, Tripp, and Bies (2001), revenge is "an action in response to some perceived harm or wrongdoing by another party that is intended to inflict damage, injury, discomfort, or punishment on the party judged responsible" (p. 53). In the case of sabotage, "the intention is to damage, disrupt or subvert the organization's operations for the personal purposes of the saboteur by creating unfavorable publicity, embarrassment, delays in production, damage to property, the destruction of working relationships, or the harming of employees or customers (Crino, 1994, p. 312). In terms of the destruction of working relationships, social undermining could certainly be a tactic (means).

Workplace Incivility

Research on workplace incivility has revealed many means by which people may be uncivil to one another (Cortina et al., 2002; Cortina, Magley, Williams, & Langhout, 2001; Lim & Cortina, 2005; Pearson, Andersson, & Wegner, 2001; Twale & De Luca, 2008). Since workplace incivility involves "low-intensity deviant behavior with ambiguous intent to harm the target, in violation of workplace norms for mutual respect" (Andersson & Pearson, 1999, p. 457), it seems clear that the list of incivilities is only limited by one's imagination. Everyday experience, and empirical research, demonstrates that this is the case.

Two important contributions made by Andersson and Pearson involve an explicit focus on motive and opportunity. As detailed in the definition of workplace incivility provided earlier, incivility may be an insidious behavior in which the intent of the actor (as perceived by the target) is ambiguous. This, of course, does not signify the absence of intent on the part of the actor but, rather, the difficulty in recognizing or establishing intent, especially as it relates to "low-intensity" behaviors. In the words of these authors, "One may behave uncivilly as a reflection of intent to harm the target, or one may behave uncivilly without intent (e.g., ignorance or oversight)" (Andersson & Pearson, 1999, p. 456). Clearly, the presence or absence of a motive is important in the commission, interpretation of, and reaction to the act. Effective strategies for responding to malice are likely to be different from tactics employed to address ignorance. In addition to recognizing the presence or absence of motive, the workplace incivility literature deals with the notion of opportunity—although not in those words. Specifically, Andersson and Pearson (1999) focus on incivility as an ongoing process in which there may be "spirals of incivility." This, of course, presupposes that there are opportunities for actors and targets to come into repeated contact with each other. Within these potentially escalatory spirals, attributions of intent (i.e., malice) may result because repeated acts of incivility are no longer "unambiguous" or are simply judged (rightly or wrongly) to be hostile in nature. We will have more to say about the utility of the MM&O framework where workplace incivility is concerned in a later section.

THE INTERACTION OF MEANS, MOTIVE, AND OPPORTUNITY: SOME EMPIRICAL DATA

The data provided in this section were derived from the Workplace Stress and Aggression Project, a 5-year action research initiative within the United States Department of Veterans Affairs (VA). Data were collected from 8,596 respondents using the Workplace Aggression Research Questionnaire (WAR-Q; Neuman & Keashly, 2004).

In completing the WAR-Q, respondents indicated the extent to which they experienced 60 different forms of negative workplace behavior (samples of these behaviors are provided later). In addition, respondents were required to indicate the actor most responsible for each of these behaviors (superior, coworkers, subordinate, customer/client, other). Using these, and other data from the instrument, we explore the relationships among means, motive, and opportunity. It is important to note that the VA data were not collected with the express purpose of exploring the MM&O framework. Rather, the data were collected as part of an action research project exploring issues related to workplace stress and aggression, and the development and implementation of various workplace interventions. During the analyses of these data, the utility of the MM&O perspective emerged. For this reason, we are not in a position to explore every aspect of our framework, and we view our initial data, and the concepts discussed in this chapter, as an incubator for guiding future theoretical and empirical research.

THE INTERPLAY OF MEANS AND OPPORTUNITY

For the following analyses, we derived the data as follows. Since each respondent indicated the frequency with which she or he experienced each of 60 different "negative" behaviors and the relationship of the perpetrator (superior, coworker, subordinate, customer, other), we were able to identify the "primary source of aggression" for each respondent. For example, if one particular source (e.g., coworker) was associated with 75% or more of the behaviors experienced by that respondent, we identified coworker as the primary source of aggression for that particular respondent. Using this 75% threshold as a criterion (a rather conservative number), 47% of the perpetrators (i.e., actors) were identified as coworkers, 40% as superiors, 9% as customers/clients, and 4% as subordinates.

Next, we sorted the behaviors from most to least frequently occurring for each primary source of aggression. Table 2.1 shows the top 10 behaviors (in terms of their frequency of occurrence) for each of four sources of aggression.

Consistent with findings from the workplace incivility literature, and our own research on workplace aggression, Table 2.1 reveals that being treated in a rude and disrespectful manner was among the top 10 behaviors initiated by coworkers, subordinates, and customers/clients in our sample. This was true of "being glared at in a hostile manner," too. More to the point, there are a number of behaviors that are uniquely associated with specific actor–target relationships. Again, referring to Table 2.1, the behaviors highlighted in bold italics are associated with one particular actor. For example, 8 of the top 10 behaviors reported for superiors (e.g., not being given praise to which you felt entitled, being given little or no feedback, being put down in front of others, or unfairly being denied a raise or promotion) are unique to superior–subordinate relationships. Looking at these eight behaviors, it seems evident that supervisors and other superiors have a greater "opportunity" to engage in (or control) these particular "means/methods" of aggression, as compared with coworkers, subordinates, or customers.

Similarly, four behaviors were unique to coworkers, three were related to subordinates, and eight were associated with customers only. In examining these unique behaviors, it would seem that the nature of the relationship

TABLE 2.1

Top 10 Aggressive Behaviors by Source of Aggression

Superior

Not given praise for which you felt entitled

Given little or no feedback

Had others delay action on important matters

Given unreasonable workloads or deadlines, more than others

Had your contribution ignored by others

Been lied to

Others fail to give you needed information

Put down in front of others

Been blamed for other people's mistakes

Unfairly denied raise or promotion

Coworker

Been given the "silent treatment"

Treated in a rude or disrespectful manner

Been prevented from expressing yourself

Had someone interfere with your work activities

Others fail to give you needed information

Been glared at in a hostile manner

Been the target of rumors or gossip

Had others take credit for your work

Had coworkers fail to defend your plans or ideas to others

Had others refuse your requests for assistance

Subordinate

Been given the "silent treatment"

Treated in a rude or disrespectful manner

Been glared at in a hostile manner

Had others consistently arrive late for meetings you called

Been lied to

Been subjected to temper tantrums

Had other people turned against you

Others fail to give you info you really needed

Been the target of rumors or gossip

Had someone interfere with your work activities

(continued)

TABLE 2.1 (CONTINUED)

Top 10 Aggressive Behaviors by Source of Aggression

Customer/Client/Patient
Been sworn at in a hostile manner
Yelled or shouted at
Treated in a rude or disrespectful manner
Been glared at in a hostile manner
Been subjected to obscene or hostile gestures
Threaten with physical harm
Negative comments about your competence
Been kicked, bitten, or spat on
Been subjected to sexist remarks
Subjected to suggestive and/or offensive stories

Note: Items in bold italics are unique to that actor, among the "top 10 behaviors."

between the actors and targets provides a context within which certain behaviors are more or less likely. This is particularly true in the case of customers, clients, or patients. Since such organizational outsiders typically do not have ongoing relationships with organizational insiders, aggression is more likely to be direct and active in nature, such as, yelling, swearing, or other hostile and inappropriate verbal expressions as well as threats or actual instances of physical aggression. We must point out that a large portion of our sample consisted of professionals involved in the delivery of healthcare services (nurses, medical technicians, case workers, etc.), a context known for high incidents of physical violence (Claravall, 1996; Forrester, 2002; Mayhew & Chappell, 2002; Simonowitz, 1995; Tahmincioglu, 2004; Whittington, Shuttleworth, & Hill, 1996; Winstanley & Whittington, 2004). While recognizing the special nature of a portion of our population, the fact that context plays a role in means, motive, and opportunity is consistent with our central thesis.

To complete the discussion related to Table 2.1, much of the aggression exhibited by coworkers might best be described as obstructional, covert, and passive in nature (Baron, Neuman, & Geddes, 1999)—certainly when compared with the behaviors exhibited by customers. This would involve behaviors that are designed to obstruct or impede the target's performance by withholding assistance or material resources. As suggested earlier, within the context of an ongoing relationship, coworkers have an opportunity to engage in subtler, but nevertheless damaging, behaviors. As shown in Table 2.1, this included taking credit for the target's work or failing to defend the target's plans to others. Some passive and obstructional behaviors seem to be related to both coworkers and subordinates, as in the case of being given the silent treatment or being the target of rumors or gossip. As discussed elsewhere (Baron & Neuman, 1996; Neuman & Baron, in press), aggressors often select strategies (forms of aggression) that inflict harm on the target while exposing the actor to a minimal (acceptable) amount of risk (i.e., retaliation by the target or others). This would be especially important in continuing relationships among peers or in which less powerful actors (subordinates) aggress against more powerful targets (superiors). With the exception of subordinates throwing "temper tantrums" (which sounds more childish than aggressive), many of the peer- and subordinate-related behaviors seem to fit into the "covert" (possibly insidious) category.

Figure 2.1 presents all 30 behaviors listed in Table 2.1 in a side-by-side comparison by actor (i.e., source of aggression). Each bar in this figure captures the percentage of respondents reporting a particular actor as the source for each of the 30 behaviors. For example, the first (uppermost) bar shows that 87.1% of the respondents reporting that they had "not received praise for which they felt entitled" indicated that a superior was the source of that behavior. Also, for this item, only 10.4% reported coworkers, 1.3% subordinates, and 1.2% customers as the source. Similarly, when receiving "little or no feedback," 94% reported a superior as the source, 5% coworkers, and less than 1% reported either subordinates or customers.

Even a casual review of this graphic reveals strikingly different patterns of behavior across actor–target relationships. Put in the context of the MM&O framework, the figure presents a visual representation of the interaction between means and opportunity. A closer examination of the actual behaviors reveals the rather obvious nature of this interaction. Specifically, the relationship of actor and target, and the context within which the parties interact provide (or fail to provide) the opportunity for particular kinds of behavior. It is no surprise that superiors control, and are in a better position to provide (or withhold), praise, feedback, information, raises, promotions, and work assignments. Nor would it come as a surprise to learn that nurses or other healthcare professionals working in psychiatric facilities, emergency rooms, or trauma centers are more likely to be kicked, bitten, pushed, shoved, and sworn at than hospital administrators or middle-level managers who may be less likely to come in contact with patients in traumatic situations.

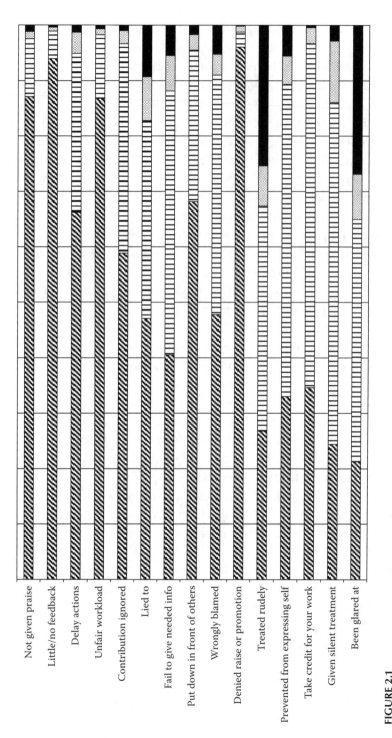

FIGURE 2.1

Side-by-side comparison of most frequently occurring forms of aggression initiated by superiors, coworkers, subordinates, and customers/clients, respectively.

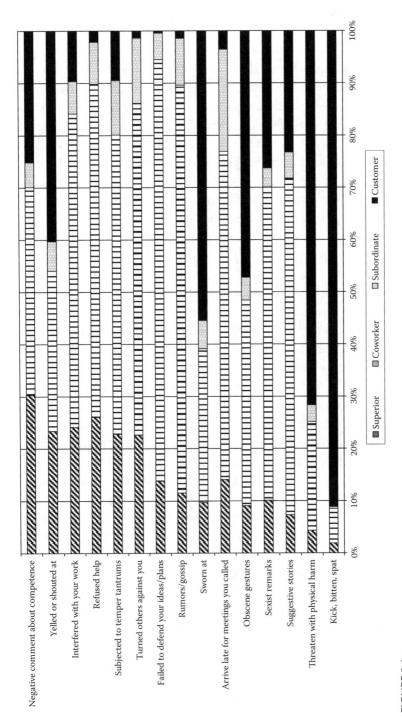

FIGURE 2.1
(Continued).

MOTIVE

Although our data do not provide self-reports from "aggressors" on their actual motives, we did collect data on the perceived causes for the behaviors that people experienced. Respondents were presented with 14 potential causes for negative workplace behavior. Table 2.2 shows the percent of those responding yes as to whether they believed that each of these 14 causes was associated with the aggression that they experienced.

Before presenting the results of our analyses, a few reminders about our sample and explanations about our process are needed. Because our sample is disproportionate across actors, side-by-side comparisons of yes responses, even when statistically significant, might be somewhat difficult to interpret. Nevertheless, we have included the chi-square and significance (p) values to show that statistically significant differences exist for 12 of the 14 perceived causes of aggression, across the four different categories of actors. In addition, we used a Statistical Package for the Social Sciences (SPSS) adjusted residual procedure to test for observed cell counts that differ significantly from expected (predicted) results. Adjusted residuals falling well below –2 or above +2 indicate cells that depart markedly from the model of independence. In Table 2.2, a superscript plus sign (+) indicates that significantly more yes responses were received for that category than could be expected by chance. Conversely, a superscript minus sign (-) indicates that significantly fewer yes responses were received than expected.

As can be seen, statistically higher than expected counts were found for age, office politics, and union affiliation when the primary source of aggression was a superior. Conversely, significantly lower than expected counts were associated with the target's sexual orientation, own behavior, personality traits of others, or work-related stress, when the actor was a superior. Rather than interpret these results (or the other results displayed in Table 2.2), we simply highlight the fact that perceptions of the causes of aggression seem related to the source of that behavior. Also, germane to the MM&O framework, people differ in the extent to which they perceive each of these causes to be operative. In essence, this means that motives are perceived, in part, based on personal attributes, job level, status, and union affiliation. Many of these variables are defined within the context of an interpersonal (business) relationship—an important element in our framework.

TABLE 2.2

Perceived Motivation as a Function of the Source of Aggression

Perceived Cause	SUP	COW	SUB	CUS	N	N-Yes	PCT-Yes	$\chi^2(df=3)$	p
Gender	39.75	47.55	3.09	9.62	2258	551	24	1.62	0.66
Race	43.06	47.69	2.78	6.48	2256	216	10	3.23	0.36
Ethnicity	44.91	49.70	1.80	3.59⁻	2245	167	7	9.40	0.02
Age	44.91⁺	46.74	2.87	5.48⁻	2258	383	17	11.34	0.01
Religion	32.39	60.56⁺	4.23	2.82⁻	2247	142	6	13.35	0.00
Political beliefs	31.58	64.66⁺	1.50	2.26⁻	2240	133	6	19.59	0.00
Health, illness, disability	44.50	51.38	2.29	1.83⁻	2244	218	10	17.64	0.00
Sexual orientation	22.06⁻	64.71⁺	4.41	8.82	2239	68	3	9.50	0.02
Job level	39.61	48.38	6.82⁺	5.19⁻	2258	924	41	57.70	0.00
Own behavior	29.24⁻	63.45⁺	3.66	3.66⁻	2232	383	17	48.89	0.00
Personality traits	36.87⁻	52.95⁺	3.74	6.43⁻	2274	1337	59	41.35	0.00
Office politics	47.22⁺	49.57	2.46⁻	0.75⁻	2259	934	41	154.75	0.00
Union affiliation	59.64⁺	38.57⁻	1.35⁻	0.45⁻	2238	223	10	54.83	0.00
Work-related stress	36.39⁻	56.49⁺	4.71	2.41⁻	2162	871	40	89.90	0.00

⁺ Significantly more yes responses than would be expected by chance.

⁻ Significantly fewer yes responses than would be expected by chance.

Notes: Sources of aggression—SUP = Superior, COW = Coworkers, SUB = Subordinate, CUS = Customer (i.e., U.S. military veteran). N = Total responses to each item. N-Yes = Number of "Yes" responses, PCT-Yes = Overall "Yes" responses for that item across actors (i.e., sources), p = significance level associated with χ^2 across sources.

DEGREE OF BOTHER

Our framework suggests an interaction among means, motive, and opportunity and, indirectly, differential outcomes and consequences for targets. For example, disparities in status and differences in the persistence and duration of aggressive behavior (all related to opportunity) have been linked to the perceived severity of impact on the target (Escartín, Rodríguez-Carballeira, Zapf, Porrúa, & Martín-Peña, 2009; Keashly & Neuman, 2002; Leymann, 1990; Rayner et al., 2002). In terms of superior–subordinate relationships, supervisors control important resources as well as opportunities for promotions, raises, work/office assignments, opportunities for training, and, of course, continued employment. The nature of the relationship between employee and supervisor is ongoing and consequential. Furthermore, the ability of subordinates to exercise control within an abusive relationship is minimal. Aside from being obvious on its face, the assertion that employees are most bothered by the abuse they receive from supervisors (as opposed to other actors) is supported in the workplace bullying literature (Einarsen & Skogstad, 1996; Rayner et al., 2002; Roland & Idsøe, 2001) and is consistent with theoretical models of stress and frustration—in which frustration of important goals, coupled with low levels of control perceptions, lead to higher levels of stress and frustration (e.g., Spector, 1997). Based on this research, we explored the differential impact of aggression on the subjective experience of targets in two ways.

First, we investigated whether the source of aggression had a differential impact across targets. After completing all 60 WAR-Q items, respondents were asked, "Overall, how much have the behaviors listed above bothered you?" Participants responded to this question using a 4-point scale (1 = not at all, 2 = a little, 3 = moderately, and 4 = quite a bit). Analyses of variance revealed a statistically significant effect for degree of bother across actors, $F(3, 2199) = 43.5$, $p < .001$. As predicted, respondents (targets) were "most bothered" when the aggression was initiated by a superior ($M = 2.49$[a], $SD =$ 1.17), followed by coworker ($M = 2.26$[b], $SD = 1.01$), subordinates ($M = 1.82$[c], $SD = .95$), and customers ($M = 1.64$[c], $SD = .77$). Here and subsequently, means *not* sharing common superscripts differ significantly, $p < .05$ using Tukey's test for our posthoc analyses.

Next, we looked at the relationship between persistence and degree of bother. Other research has demonstrated that persistence (regardless of actor) is related to degree of bother (Keashly & Neuman, 2002; Leymann, 1990; Rayner et al., 2002). However, since our current data suggest that mistreatment by superiors is the most bothersome, we explored whether persistence added any unique variance—while restricting our analyses to aggression by superiors. Again, as predicted, there was a statistically reliable effect on targets' subjective experience as a function of persistence $F(2, 6482) = 788.87$, $p < .001$. In this analysis, degree of bother was assessed for respondents experiencing aggression on an occasional basis (less than a weekly or daily), one to five events weekly/daily, or six or more events weekly/daily. Respondents reporting six or more events weekly/daily were most bothered ($M = 3.35^a$, $SD = .87$), followed by those experiencing one to five events ($M = 2.62^b$, $SD = .95$), and respondents reporting less than weekly/daily occurrences ($M = 1.93^c$, $SD = .87$). As in the previous analysis, means with different superscript letters differ significantly, $p < .05$.

To complete our discussion on the impact of supervisory behavior, we explored "intention to quit" as a function of aggression from a superior. Turnover intentions have long been recognized as an important variable in organizational behavior and management research. The results are dramatic, if not surprising. When the primary source of aggression was a superior, 65% of our respondents strongly agreed with the statement "I am considering leaving this organization," compared to 33% of those respondents subjected to aggression from a coworker, 1.5% from customers, and .5% for subordinates. These differences are statistically significant for academics and should be of practical significance for practitioners.

RESPONSES TO AGGRESSION

As demonstrated earlier, the ultimate response to insidious behavior may be withdrawal from a specific situation or the entire organization. Alternatively, there may be organizational procedures for addressing these issues or actors may choose to confront their tormentors. Table 2.3 presents data showing whether targets reported such incidents to a supervisor or union official, filed a formal complaint or grievance, or confronted the perpetrator. Similar to the analysis presented in Table 2.2, we assessed the

TABLE 2.3

Responses to Aggression by Primary Source of Aggression

Responses to Aggression	SUP	COW	SUB	CUST	N	N-Yes	PCT-Yes	$\chi^2 (df = 3)$	p
Reported experiences to a superior/union official	40	49	4	7⁻	2405	902	38	8.29	0.04
Confronted the person(s) involved	35⁻	50⁺	5⁺	9	2405	1195	50	24.19	0.00
Filed a formal complaint or grievance	53⁺	40⁻	2⁻	5⁻	2399	238	10	22.94	0.00

+ Significantly more yes responses than would be expected by chance.

- Significantly fewer yes responses than would be expected by chance.

Notes: Sources of aggression—SUP = Superior, SUP = Supervisors, COW = Coworkers, SUB = Subordinate, CUS = Customer (i.e., U.S. military veteran). N = Total responses to each item. N-Yes = Number of "Yes" responses, PCT-Yes = Overall "Yes" responses for that item across actors (i.e., sources), p = significance level associated with χ^2 across sources.

degree to which cell counts were higher or lower than expected by chance, as reflected in the adjusted residuals. As can be seen, cell counts were significantly higher than expected for filing a formal complaint or grievance when the source of the aggression was a superior; conversely, the counts were significantly lower than expected for filing a formal complaint when the primary source was a coworker, subordinate, or customer. With respect to confrontation as a strategy, cell counts were higher than expected for coworkers and subordinates, and lower than expected for superiors. It appears that targets understood that responding to mistreatment by a powerful actor requires the recruitment of allies (the need for strength in numbers). The strategy of choice in equal power relationships is to handle it on one's own, whereas dealing with powerful others requires increasing one's own power base. These results are consistent with our thesis that the context within which aggression occurs (i.e., the relationship between actor and target) affects the method and opportunity of the target to respond.

THE DIMENSIONALITY OF WORKPLACE AGGRESSION AS A FUNCTION OF MM&O

Several organizational scholars engaged in research related to aggressive workplace behaviors and related constructs (e.g., bullying/mobbing, petty tyranny, deviant workplace behavior, and counterproductive work behavior) have noted (in personal communications) the difficulty in establishing stable underlying latent structures/dimensions, and we have experienced the same problem. Factor loadings seem to vary across studies as well as populations within single studies. We believe that this may be due, in part, to the fact that different means are associated with different motives and opportunities. To explore this possibility within the present study, we extracted data from three groups of targets for which we had sufficient data. This included 574 first-line supervisors, 1,073 team leaders, and 6,139 respondents indicating that they had "no supervisory responsibility." Then, we conducted exploratory factor analyses (using varimax rotations) with these three populations and focused our attention on the primary factors to emerge for each of the three populations.

Table 2.4 shows the results that we obtained in our three factor analyses and the factor loadings associated with each item. Behaviors

TABLE 2.4

Primary Factor Loadings for Respondents Having No Supervisory Responsibility, Team Leaders, and First-Line Supervisors

No Sup Responsibility (n = 6,139)		Team Leader (n = 1,073)		First-Line Supervisor (n = 574)	
Contributions ignored	0.75	Excessively harsh criticism re work	0.64	Turn others against you	0.73
Delay actions	0.69	Accused of deliberately making error	0.64	Rumors or gossip	0.72
Not given praise	0.68	Rumors or gossip	0.58	Fail to deny false rumors	0.65
Fail to give info needed	0.67	Turn others against you	0.56	Silent treatment	0.63
Little or no feedback	0.62	Put down in front of others	0.54	Flaunt status	0.58
Take credit for your work or ideas	0.60	Fail to deny false rumors	0.50	Excessively harsh criticism re work	0.52
Unreasonable workload	0.60	Fail to defend plans or ideas	0.50	Storm out of room when you enter	0.51
Lied to	0.58	Little empathy or sympathy	0.48	Glared at in hostile manner	0.47
Prevented from expressing self	0.58	Blamed for other	0.47	Lied to	0.47
Flaunt status	0.57	Flaunt status	0.46	Neg. comments re competence	0.45
Fail to defend plans or ideas	0.57	Threats due to blowing the whistle	0.43	Fail to defend plans or ideas	0.45
Little empathy or sympathy	0.56	Take credit for your work or ideas	0.42	Treated rudely	0.44
Interfere with work	0.56			Embarrassing signs or notes	0.42
Blamed for other	0.55			Blamed for other	0.42
Refuse help	0.51				
Excessively harsh criticism re work	0.49				
Treated rudely	0.47				

Put down in front of others	0.46
Fail to respond to calls or e-mail	0.46
Denied raise or promotion	0.45
Silent treatment	0.42
Turn others against you	0.42
Temper tantrums	0.42
Negative comments regarding competence	0.41

Note: Items in bold italics are unique to that factor.

highlighted in bold italics are unique to the factor in which they are listed. For example, having one's contributions ignored, having others delay action on important matters, and not being given praise to which you felt entitled were (among other items) unique among people reporting no supervisory responsibility. Similarly, being accused of deliberately making an error and being threatened for "blowing the whistle" were behaviors reported by team leaders in our sample. Finally, first-line supervisors reported having others "storm out of a room" when they entered or being "glared at" in a hostile manner. The point of this exercise is not to uncover specific behaviors associated with certain actor-target relationships; rather, it is to demonstrate that the nature of these relationships—and the context within which behaviors occur—impacts the way such behaviors cluster with each other. Finally, although not explicit in this dataset, it is reasonable to assume that there are different motives underlying the behaviors reported by each respondent for each actor and category of actor.

CONCLUDING COMMENTS

Over the past 10 to 15 years, scholars and practitioners have paid increased attention to the nature, prevalence, prevention, and management of aggressive and abusive behaviors in work settings. We believe that examining means, motive, and opportunity, and, most important, the interaction of these variables in permitting, encouraging, and producing harm-doing behavior, may provide fruitful lines for future inquiry. Employing the MM&O framework may help integrate material currently fragmented across a number of different research streams, reconcile differences in empirical findings, and generate useful applications. Furthermore, the MM&O framework may shift some of the attention currently focused on reactive (hot, hostile) aggression to instrumental (cold, calculating) forms of aggression—an area that has received less attention by organizational scholars. When you consider the extent to which aggression is used (often successfully) to obtain valued outcomes in the workplace, it is surprising that little systematic research has been conducted in this area.

THE USE OF MM&O IN EXPLORING INSIDIOUS AND OTHER NEGATIVE WORKPLACE BEHAVIORS

Various typologies and taxonomies have been applied to the study of aggression, violence, and related constructs. For example, according to the Buss (1961), aggression can be captured within three dichotomies: (1) verbal versus physical, (2) active versus passive, and (3) direct versus indirect. This framework has been useful in exploring the nature and prevalence of aggression and violence in work settings (Baron & Neuman, 1996, 1998; Baron et al., 1999; Coombs & Holladay, 2004; Geddes, 1994; Geddes & Baron, 1997) and in guiding scholars in the construction of workplace aggression questionnaires (Baron & Neuman, 1996; Neuman & Keashly, 2004).

In the workplace violence domain, McPhail (1996) proposed a framework employing two dimensions: perpetrators and behaviors/outcomes. Perpetrators are characterized as employees, known outsiders, and unknown outsiders. In terms of behaviors/outcomes, this includes organizational delinquency, passive aggression, active aggression, verbal assault, destruction of property, and physical assault. Similarly, Mullen (1997) proposed three types of violence: intraorganizational conflict, occupational violence, and violence from the general public. This research preceded the workplace violence classification scheme (criminal intent, customer/client, worker-on-worker, and personal relationship) discussed earlier (Merchant & Lundell, 2001; Peek-Asa, Runyan, & Zwerling, 2001; University of Iowa Injury Prevention Research Center, 2001).

In the deviant workplace behavior domain, Robinson and Bennett (1995) proposed that deviance is either interpersonal or organizational in nature, and varies in its degree of severity (minor vs. serious). Examples of minor organizational deviance (which they label production deviance) include leaving work earlier or wasting resources, whereas serious organizational deviance (property deviance) might include acts of sabotage and theft. Finally, minor interpersonal deviance (political deviance) includes such acts as showing favoritism and gossip while serious interpersonal deviance (personal aggression) includes sexual harassment and verbal abuse.

Similar classification schemes have been proposed for many, if not all, "negative" workplace behaviors. These frameworks typically identify and classify specific behaviors, propose underlying dimensions, identify perpetrators and targets, define the boundary conditions for specific constructs, and even describe conditions under which the actions (such as theft) might be prosocial (as opposed to antisocial) in nature (Greenberg, 1997).

As noted throughout this chapter, we suggest that future research focus, more explicitly, on means, motive, and opportunity for at least two reasons. First, the presence, degree, or absence of any one of these variables may assist scholars in defining their constructs, establishing boundary conditions, and considering (or empirically validating) underlying latent constructs. For example, in framing the domain of workplace incivility, and distinguishing it from other forms of "mistreatment in organizations," Andersson and Pearson (1999) consider the intensity of a behavior, the ambiguity of intent to harm, the nature of the act (verbal vs. physical), and the degree to which it violates norms and harms individuals or organizations. It seems to us that this approach is useful in defining the domain and advancing research in the area. However, if we apply an MM&O perspective to this discussion, and introduce the consideration of real (as opposed to perceived) intent, the domain of incivility may come into sharper focus. Without considering circumstances under which the perpetrator might be motivated by some subconscious or unconscious drive (the subject for another paper), there is a clear difference (conceptually and practically) between intentional and unintentional acts of incivility. We would be inclined to call the former aggression and the latter insensitivity or callous disregard. These distinctions have important consequences for research and even more obvious consequences for practice, to which we now turn our attention.

THE MANAGEMENT AND PREVENTION OF AGGRESSION: APPLYING THE MM&O FRAMEWORK

As an example of the potential utility of the MM&O framework, consider the fire triangle shown in upper half of Figure 2.2. As demonstrated in this figure, three things need to be present to produce fire: heat, fuel, and oxygen. Remove any of those elements and you will not have fire, or the fire will be extinguished. In a similar fashion, we suggest that the MM&O triangle (depicted in bottom half of Figure 2.2) may prove useful in preventing an "ignition" (a sparking event) that leads to abusive/aggressive behavior; or, in the case of a "raging" fire (i.e., an episode of aggression), removing one or more of the elements might prove useful in extinguishing the "blaze."

The Fire Triangle

The MM&O Triangle

FIGURE 2.2
The fire and MM&O triangles.

Means

Since it is our contention that means refers to an actor's wherewithal to commit an act of aggression, as well as the method employed to deliver harm to the target(s), several strategies come to mind for the prevention of disruptive, threatening, or violent behavior.

First, preemployment background investigations may provide a useful tool for uncovering patterns of aggressive and abusive behavior, such as, convictions for crimes of violence, spousal and child abuse, threatening coworkers or supervisors, and workplace assaults violence ("How to predict and prevent workplace violence," 2005; Slora, Joy, Jones, & Terris, 1991; Slora, Joy, & Terris, 1991). Many organizations contract with firms that specialize in this type of investigation (Anfuso, 1994). Although these techniques may be somewhat effective in revealing a propensity for verbal and physical assault, they are less likely to be effective in determining whether a predisposition exists for more insidious (covert) behavior. However, preemployment testing can be used to screen for other counterproductive proclivities that have been linked to a wide range of negative workplace behaviors. For example, some preemployment questionnaires have been used to screen for unreliability, disciplinary problems, hostility to rules, absenteeism, substance abuse, dishonesty, and even "computer abuse" (Hogan & Hogan, 1989; Lanyon & Goodstein, 2004; Mikulay & Goffin, 1998; Ones, Viswesvaran, & Schmidt, 1993). Identifying whether job applicants have the propensity for such behavior is important because

> acts such as theft, drug and alcohol abuse, lying, insubordination, vandalism, sabotage, absenteeism, and assaultive actions are elements of a large syndrome that we call organizational delinquency. To call this a syndrome suggests that employees who steal are likely to engage in other delinquent acts as well. (Hogan & Hogan, 1989, p. 273)

Related to this, the Personnel Decisions Incorporated (1985) Employment Inventory contains scales that measure trouble with authority, hostility, and thrill seeking, and the Reliability Scale of the Hogan Personnel Selection Series (Hogan & Hogan, 1986, 1989) measures hostility to authority, thrill seeking, and social insensitivity. Clearly, these instruments were not designed to predict future instances of insidious workplace behavior. Further work is needed to validate instruments for this purpose. In this regard, job interviews may serve as a basis for exploring whether individuals possess a psychological predisposition toward both overt and covert forms of aggression. As suggested in detail elsewhere (Mantell, 1994), job applicants can be asked about situations in which they believe they were treated unfairly and asked to describe how they responded. Since perceptions of injustice are so closely linked with anger and aggression/ retaliation (Harris, 1993; Torestad, 1990), a predisposition toward such perceptions may be predictive of aggression on the job. Situational interviews might be developed to test for beliefs and tacit assumptions that might lead to aggressive and abusive behavior. For example, in applicants being hired for management positions, their assumptions about human behavior, and what might or might not be appropriate managerial behavior (firm vs. abusive management), might reveal a propensity toward the use of coercion or manipulation.

Finally, regardless of the effectiveness of various screening techniques, many future perpetrators will make (or have already made) their way into the workplace. Under these circumstances, organizational insiders might already possess the means (wherewithal) to engage in various antisocial behaviors but not the knowledge, skill, or ability to engage in more prosocial alternatives. Providing people with such skills has been a central element in alternatives to violence (AVP) programs employed in schools, prisons, and community settings ("Anti-violence initiative at work in Allegheny County," 1995; Sloane, 2004). This includes, but is not limited to, improving communication and conflict management skills, enhancing interpersonal trust, and providing practical techniques for dealing with confrontational situations.

Another way in which employees may be provided with alternative means of dealing with dissatisfaction, frustration, and other work-related irritations and provocations can be derived from organizational justice literature in general (Greenberg, 1987, 1990, 1996) and procedural justice literature in particular (Deutsch, 1975; Leventhal, 1980; Leventhal, Karuza, & Fry, 1980; Thibaut & Walker, 1975). For example, providing employees with a fair process—one that is consistent in application, suppresses bias, bases decisions on accurate information, provides for redress, represents the interests of all concerned, and derives from moral and ethical standards (Leventhal et al., 1980). Other justice-derived means relate to the use of interpersonal justice, in showing sensitivity and concern for the outcomes that people receive, and informational justice, providing knowledge (explanations, accounts, rationale, etc.) about the process used to determine those outcomes (Greenberg, 1993a). Recently, attention has been focused on the development of training programs to foster organizational justice (Skarlicki & Latham, 2005).

These are just a few examples of how the consideration of means might prove useful in the design and implementation of prevention and management strategies. We have focused our discussion on means as it relates to wherewithal and not the method by which harm is visited upon a target. Clearly, metal detectors and other security devices can be used to ensure that certain means (i.e., methods) are unavailable to the actor, and we will make that case in a later discussion about opportunity. Now, however, we turn our attention to motive.

Motive

The list of potential motives, or motivating factors and forces, is limitless. Add to this the difficulty in identifying the presence, absence, or precise nature of a motive, and one can quickly understand the problems associated with the inclusion of this variable in any model of human behavior. This was particularly true in the aggression area, in which the debate about including intent as a defining characteristic raged for decades. But, as aggression researchers have generally concluded, the concept of intent (although problematic) is important in understanding the nature and prevention of aggression (Baron & Richardson, 1994; Berkowitz, 1993; Geen, 1991).

Beyond the aggression arena, the study of human motivation is critical to our understanding of behavior in work settings and our ability to shape (or at least influence) that behavior (Pinder, 2008). As noted previously, motive has played an explicit role in research related to revenge, sabotage, emotional abuse, social undermining, and abusive supervision. In those instances where intent has not been integrated into definitions or theoretical perspectives, this has often been for legal (as opposed to conceptual) reasons. For example, workplace bullying researchers have been concerned that if intent were included in a definition, targets, human resources staff, and legal professionals would need to establish intent on the part of the actor to successfully bring a charge, prosecute, and prevail in a case of bullying. Recently, some scholars in the workplace bullying arena have begun to broach this issue. In crafting what he calls the Healthy Workplace Bill, David Yamada (2004) created language that states, "an abusive work environment exists when the defendant, *acting with malice*, subjects the complainant to abusive conduct so severe that it causes tangible harm to the complainant" (italics added; p. 498).

It is our contention that the nature, presence, or absence of motive is of tremendous importance in the study, prevention, and management of all negative workplace behavior. In thinking about this issue, we are reminded of important research in the area of causal attribution. As suggested by Weiner (1974), people make attributions as to the achievement or failure of others based, in part, on whether they perceive the cause as internal (ability or effort) or external (related to task difficulty or luck). If, for example, you believe that an employee has not been productive because she or he lacked ability, the answer might be to provide training. Or, if you assess the problem as being due to a lack of effort, you might consider motivational strategies, such as pay-for-performance. In this example, what if you're wrong? What if you provide training but the problem is lack of motivation or task difficulty. Your efforts to improve this person's performance would be wasted. Similarly, in attempting to prevent or manage insidious (or overtly aggressive) workplace behavior, one must determine whether or not a motive exists and, if so, what—specifically—is motivating the behavior.

In the case of extreme or overt instances of aggression, there may be little mystery as to the triggering or motivating factor. The precipitating event and aggressive reaction might occur in close proximity to each other.

While this does not necessarily assure a causal connection, there are many instances in which there will be little doubt. For more insidious behaviors, a useful approach for uncovering motive—as well as establishing the intentionality of the act—may be found in the sabotage literature. In a very thoughtful chapter on the subject, Giacalone, Riordan, and Rosenfeld, (1997) suggested that managers must determine whether (1) the event was sabotage, (2) the perpetrator was an individual or a group, (3) the event was an isolated event or part of pattern, (4) there was provocation prior to the incident, (5) the target was an individual, work unit, or the entire organization, and (6) there was psychological damage in addition to property damage. We believe that these questions serve as a good approach to identifying the presence, absence, and nature of motive as well as establishing means and opportunity. For now, we will focus on the connection to motive.

Giacalone et al. (1997) also suggest some useful techniques for collecting data. This includes the use of sabotage logs (a central information file on suspected sabotage that captures data related to the six previous questions), archival review of extant data (human resources and equal employment opportunity data, results of employee surveys, interview data, etc.), ongoing surveys, and the use of a nominal group technique to brainstorm problem areas and possible responses to these problems.

These techniques may be used in whole or in part to explore issues of motive or motivating factors that may underlie a wide range of insidious behaviors. The important point is to be "data driven" or "evidence based" in identifying and responding to such behavior—or any other challenges you face at work (Pfeffer & Sutton, 2006a, 2006b; Rousseau, 2006; Waclawski & Church, 2002). There are a number of useful approaches in the organizational learning and organization development literatures, designed for surfacing motives, and testing tacit assumptions (Argyris & Schön, 1974; Schön, 1983). This organizational development approach has recently been applied to reducing workplace aggression and bullying (Yorks, Neuman, Kowalski, & Kowalski, 2007). We believe that these approaches may prove useful within an MM&O framework.

Rather than provide a list of potential motives, a truly futile task, we would like to address one in particular. That is, the degree to which organizational policies and practices encourage aggression. In what has been described as a dog-eat-dog culture, raises, promotions, and choice work assignments may be given to "aggressive" employees who focus on these ends, with little consideration of the means they use to obtain these ends.

In this sense, these individuals embrace (and are rewarded for embracing) characteristics associated with Machiavellianism (Christie & Geis, 1970). This would include such behaviors as being arrogant, eschewing moral principles and ethical codes of conduct, or manipulating others in a ruthless manner. Many of these "heavy-handed" tactics are lauded in the popular business press. For example, in discussing tough bosses, Abraham Zaleznik describes their management styles as a "penchant for psychological oppression—an especially sadistic way of making a point, say, or a bullying quality that can transform underlings into quivering masses of Jell-O" (Dumaine, 1993, p. 39). Related to this, Folger and Skarlicki (1998) found that tough times could produce tough bosses, by creating an environment in which managers feel a need to distance themselves from the unpleasant decisions that they have to make and the employees impacted by these decisions. Regardless of the cause, these managerial behaviors may become exemplars, quickly modeled by others seeking advancement and success.

It is discouraging to admit that such management tactics are still held in high regard, especially since they run counter to decades-old research in management (Argyris, 1960; Blake & Mouton, 1964; D. McGregor, 1960) as well as more recent research and practice in the area (Frost, 2003; Kramer, 2006; Sirota, Mischkind, & Meltzer, 2005). Couple this with the voluminous research in organizational justice, demonstrating consistent empirical connections between unfair treatment and lower levels of employee performance (and higher levels of insidious behavior), and the use of such tactics becomes even more puzzling. Nevertheless, such reward structures may certainly motivate the kinds of behaviors described elsewhere in this text.

We conclude this section by saying whether the behavior is motivated by perceptions of unfair treatment, fear, shame, greed, anger, jealousy, or ignorance, successful interventions must recognize and address these underlying motives.

Opportunity

As noted earlier, an action must be possible (capable of happening) as well as practical and feasible (readily or easily employed in meeting one's objective). Practical applications for the prevention of workplace violence and theft focus on the reduction or elimination of opportunity. As suggested earlier, in the case of workplace violence, the use of metal detectors is meant to deny perpetrators access to firearms, knives, and other weapons. Similarly, the process of having security guards escort fired employees (or layoff victims) out of the building is another attempt to deny these individuals the opportunity to "act out" on their way out. In terms of employee theft, the use of security cameras, sophisticated inventory control systems, badge readers, and electronic article surveillance (EAS) tags are all meant to discourage, reduce, or eliminate the opportunity to steal cash or merchandise. Similarly, electronic auditing of computer accounts, electronic performance monitoring of employees, and multiple levels of password protection are routinely used to prevent (limit access) or discourage (render impractical) the theft of time or intellectual property. Clearly, these procedures can be effective in preventing or discouraging acts of sabotage, too.

In terms of more insidious behavior, such as incivility, social undermining, abusive supervision, emotional abuse, and other nonphysical forms of aggression, it is often the case that organizations encourage these behaviors, as discussed in the section on motive. Also, it is often the case that organizations simply permit (i.e., turn a blind eye toward) these behaviors. As it relates to opportunity, there are several applications that come to mind.

First, there should be no opportunity for employees to say that they were unaware that a particular behavior was inappropriate. Consequently, codes of conduct and company policies must clearly define what is, and is not, acceptable. In this regard, much can be learned from research and practice in the sexual harassment area, in which such guidelines have been available for many years (*Policy Guidance on Current Issues of Sexual Harassment*, 1990). In fact, the hostile work environment standard, from the Equal Employment Opportunity Commission guidelines on sexual harassment, served as the basis for pending antibullying legislation drafted by Yamada (2004), and the Joint Commission on Accreditation of Healthcare Organizations (2008) recently issued guidelines to all healthcare workers on acceptable and unacceptable workplace behavior.

Drawing on these practices, employers can discourage mistreatment at work by taking all complaints seriously; issuing strong policy statements condemning such behavior; informing employees about the policy and their rights; developing and implementing a complaint procedure; establishing a response system; implementing training; counseling or disciplining perpetrators; and keeping thorough records of complaints, investigations, and actions taken.

In our research, we have found that the vast majority of mistreatment occurring in work settings goes unreported. As noted earlier, it would be unlikely that an employee would report mistreatment by a supervisor to that particular supervisor. Even if there were other mechanisms to report such abuse, fear of reprisals might discourage a formal complaint. Finally, there are few formal organizational mechanisms for reporting "having your feelings hurt" or being subjected to "hostile gestures" or "glaring." For these and other reasons, there must be other mechanisms in place to limit the opportunity to engage in hostile behavior.

The Workplace Stress and Aggression Project, from which the data for this chapter were drawn, incorporated such practices in various interventions to reduce workplace aggression (Kowalski, Harmon, Yorks, & Kowalski, 2003; Neuman, 2004; Yorks et al., 2007). Two components lay at the heart of our process: (1) the systematic collection of anonymous survey data and (2) an attempt to change the nature of the conversations people have with one another in day-to-day interactions. Our process involved sensitizing individuals (throughout the organizational hierarchy) to the nature, prevalence, and potential impact of workplace aggression (based on our survey data and organizational performance measures) and the establishment of ground rules for interpersonal behavior, and the reinforcement of those rules in daily interactions. Preliminary data, collected over a 2-year period, demonstrated significant reductions in workplace aggression for 32 of the 60 aggressive behaviors captured by our questionnaire (53.3%) in 10 pilot (experimental) facilities, whereas for the 15 comparison (control) facilities, significant improvement occurred for 5 (8.3%) of the same 60 behaviors. This difference in improvement between groups of facilities was significant, $t(23) = 2.5$, $p = .02$ (Neuman & Keashly, 2005). In short, the individuals in our pilot facilities were reinforced for employing collaborative, nonthreatening, prosocial behaviors and, when breaches occurred, individuals were confronted in a constructive way and counseled about their unacceptable behavior. Importantly, we are not suggesting the elimination of conflict, which is often desirable, but the elimination of hostile and abusive behaviors by making their use impractical and unfeasible.

The Interaction of Means, Motive, and Opportunity in Practice

As discussed earlier, there is overlap (and interaction) between means, motive, and opportunity. This was clearly evidenced in our discussion about contentious work cultures and climates. For example, the encouragement and discouragement of dog-eat-dog behavior speaks both to motive (reinforcement and punishment) and opportunity (practicality and feasibility). As another example, when focusing on revenge, we clearly are talking about motivated behavior and so one approach to prevention would involve removing the factors that created that motive. In the case of an employee being fired for poor performance, a review of the "facts" might reveal a poor selection process, lack of training, or poor compensation practices. Any or all of these problems might lead to the dismissal of an employee. Or, an act of revenge might result from the insensitive way in which a person is severed from the organization (or marched, unceremoniously, from the building). In this case, the organization might consider its tactics in handling dismissals. In any of these cases, intervening earlier in the process might eliminate or, at least, diminish the intensity of a motive for revenge. Failing to intervene in these earlier stages, we might explore the means with which revenge could be implemented (e.g., computer sabotage) and simply remove the opportunity for revenge by that means (changing passwords when people leave the organization—willingly or unwillingly).

In the case of any motivated behavior, insidious or otherwise, we believe that an examination of means, motive, and opportunity may prove useful in identifying problems and designing and implementing interventions. Also, as suggested earlier, a more explicit focus on means, motive, and opportunity may help researchers better define the many constructs associated with negative workplace behavior, establish boundary conditions for these constructs, and develop strategies for the prevention and management of related behaviors. In sum, presenting the MM&O framework was our motive for contributing to this text, this chapter serves as a means to that end, and we are pleased to have had the opportunity.

REFERENCES

Adams, A., & Crawford, N. (1992). *Bullying at work*. London, England: Virago.

Andersson, L. M., & Pearson, C. M. (1999). Tit-for-tat? The spiraling effect of incivility in the workplace. *Academy of Management Review, 24*, 452–471.

Anfuso, D. (1994). Deflecting workplace violence. *Personnel Journal, 73*, 66–77.

Anti-violence initiative at work in Allegheny County. (1995). *Executive Report*, 13.

Aquino, K., Tripp, T. M., & Bies, R. J. (2001). How employees respond to personal offense: The effects of blame attribution, victim status, and offender status on revenge and reconciliation in the workplace. *Journal of Applied Psychology, 86*, 52–59.

Argyris, C. (1960). *Understanding organizational behavior.* Homewood, IL: Dorsey.

Argyris, C., & Schön, D. A. (1974). *Theory in practice: Increasing professional effectiveness.* Oxford, England: Jossey-Bass.

Ashforth, B. (1994). Petty tyranny in organizations. *Human Relations, 47,* 755–777.

Averill, J. R. (1982). *Anger and aggression: An essay on emotion.* New York, NY: Springer Verlag.

Baron, R. A., & Neuman, J. H. (1996). Workplace violence and workplace aggression: Evidence on their relative frequency and potential causes. *Aggressive Behavior, 22,* 161–173.

Baron, R. A., & Neuman, J. H. (1998). Workplace aggression—The iceberg beneath the tip of workplace violence: Evidence on its forms, frequency, and targets. *Public Administration Quarterly, 21,* 446–464.

Baron, R. A., Neuman, J. H., & Geddes, D. (1999). Social and personal determinants of workplace aggression: Evidence for the impact of perceived injustice and the Type A Behavior Pattern. *Aggressive Behavior, 25,* 281–296.

Baron, R. A., & Richardson, D. R. (1994). *Human aggression* (2nd ed.). New York, NY: Plenum.

Berkowitz, L. (1993). *Aggression: Its causes, consequences, and control.* Philadelphia, PA: Temple University Press.

Bies, R. J., & Tripp, T. M. (1996). Beyond distrust: Getting even and the need for revenge. In R. M. Kramer & T. Tyler (Eds.), *Trust in organizations* (pp. 246–260). Thousand Oaks, CA: Sage.

Bies, R. J., & Tripp, T. M. (1998a, August). Doing justice: The motivational dynamics of revenge. In A. M. O'Leary-Kelly & D. P. Skarlicki, Chairs, *Advances in organizational justice theories: The motivation to engage in dysfunctional behavior.* Symposium conducted at the meeting of the Academy of Management, San Diego, CA.

Bies, R. J., & Tripp, T. M. (1998b). Two faces of the powerless: Coping with tyranny in organizations. In R. M. Kramer & M. A. Neale (Eds.), *Power and influence in organizations* (pp. 203–219). Thousand Oaks, CA: Sage.

Bies, R. J., & Tripp, T. M. (2005). The study of revenge in the workplace: Conceptual, ideological, and empirical issues. In S. Fox & P. E. Spector (Eds.), *Counterproductive work behavior: Investigations of actors and targets* (pp. 65–82). Washington, DC: American Psychological Association.

Bies, R. J., Tripp, T. M., & Kramer, R. M. (1997). At the breaking point: Cognitive and social dynamics of revenge in organizations. In R. A. Giacalone & J. Greenberg (Eds.), *Antisocial behavior in organizations* (pp. 18–36). Thousand Oaks, Ca: Sage.

Blake, R. R., & Mouton, J. S. (1964). *The managerial grid.* Houston, TX: Gulf.

Bureau of Labor Statistics. (2008). *Workplace injury and illness summary.* Retrieved October 23, 2008, from http://www.bls.gov/news.release/osh.nr0.htm

Bureau of Labor Statistics. (2009). *Census of fatal occupational injuries in 2008.* Retrieved October 11, 2009 from, http://www.bls.gov/news.release/cfoi.nr0.htm

Bushman, B. J., Bonacci, A. M., Pedersen, W. C., Vasquez, E. A., & Miller, N. (2005). Chewing on it can chew you up: Effects of rumination on triggered displaced aggression. *Journal of Personality and Social Psychology, 88,* 969–983.

Buss, A. H. (1961). *The psychology of aggression.* New York, NY: John Wiley.

Cal/OSHA guidelines for workplace security. (1995, March 30). Retrieved October 23, 2008 from http://www.dir.ca.gov/dosh/dosh%5Fpublications/worksecurity.html

Christie, R., & Geis, F. L. (1970). *Studies in Machiavellianism.* New York, NY: Academic Press.

Claravall, L. (1996). Healthcare violence: A nursing administration perspective. *Journal of Nursing Administration, 26,* 118–122.

Conte, C. (1993, June 15). Mounting violence prompts some moves to improve workplace security. *Wall Street Journal,* p. 1.

Coombs, T. W., & Holladay, S. J. (2004). Understanding the aggressive workplace: Development of the Workplace Aggression Tolerance Questionnaire. *Communication Studies, 55,* 481–497.

Cortina, L. M., Lonsway, K. A., Magley, V. J., Freeman, L. V., Collinsworth, L. L., Hunter, M., & Fitzgerald, L. F. (2002). What's gender got to do with it? Incivility in the federal courts. *Law and Social Inquiry, 27,* 235–270.

Cortina, L. M., & Magley, V. J. (2009). Patterns and profiles of response to incivility in the workplace. *Journal of Occupational Health Psychology, 14,* 272–288.

Cortina, L. M., Magley, V. J., Williams, J. H., & Langhout, R. D. (2001). Incivility in the workplace: Incidence and impact. *Journal of Occupational Health Psychology, 6,* 64–80.

Crino, M. D. (1994). Employee sabotage: A random or preventable phenomenon? *Journal of Managerial Issues, 6*(3), 311–330.

Coyne, I., Seigne, E., & Randall, P. (2000). Predicting workplace victim status from personality. *European Journal of Work and Organizational Psychology, 9,* 335–349.

Davenport, N., Schwartz, R. D., & Elliott, G. P. (1999). *Mobbing: Emotional abuse in the American workplace.* Ames, IA: Civil Society.

Deutsch, M. (1975). Equity, equality, and need: What determines which value will be used as the basis for distributive justice? *Journal of Social Issues, 31,* 137–149.

Donnerstein, E., & Hatfield, E. (1982). Aggression and inequity. In J. Greenberg & R. L. Cohen (Eds.), *Equity and justice in social behavior* (pp. 309–336). New York, NY: Academic Press.

Duffy, M. K., Ganster, D. C., & Pagon, M. (2002). Social undermining in the workplace. *Academy of Management Journal, 45,* 331–351.

Duffy, M. K., Shaw, J. D., Scott, K. L., & Tepper, B. J. (2006). The moderating roles of self-esteem and neuroticism in the relationship between group and individual undermining behavior. *Journal of Applied Psychology, 91,* 1066–1077.

Dumaine, B. (1993, October 18). America's toughest bosses. *Fortune, 128,* 39–42, 44, 48, 58.

Einarsen, S., Aasland, M. S., & Skogstad, A. (2007). Destructive leadership behaviour: A definition and conceptual model. *Leadership Quarterly, 18,* 207–216.

Einarsen, S., Hoel, H., Zapf, D., & Cooper, C. L. (Eds.). (in press). Bullying and harassment in the workplace: Developments in theory, research, and practice (2nd ed.). London, England: CRC Press.

Einarsen, S., & Skogstad, A. (1996). Bullying at work: Epidemiological findings in public and private organizations. *European Journal of Work and Organizational Psychology, 5,* 185–201.

Escartín, J., Rodríguez-Carballeira, A., Zapf, D., Porrúa, C., & Martín-Peña, J. (2009). Perceived severity of various bullying behaviours at work and the relevance of exposure to bullying. *Work & Stress, 23,* 191–205.

Feshbach, S. (1964). The function of aggression and the regulation of aggressive drive. *Psychological Review, 71,* 257–272.

Folger, R., & Skarlicki, D. P. (1998). When tough times make tough bosses: Managerial distancing as a function of layoff blame. *Academy of Management Journal, 41,* 79–87.

Forrester, K. (2002). Aggression and assault against nurses in the workplace: Practice and legal issues. *Journal of Law and Medicine, 9,* 386–391.

Fox, S., & Spector, P. E. (Eds.). (2005). *Counterproductive work behavior: Investigations of actors and targets.* Washington, DC: American Psychological Association.

Frost, P. J. (2003). *Toxic emotions at work.* Boston, MA: Harvard Business School Press.

Gaudin, S. (2006). Cybersaboteur sentenced. *Information Week, 22.*

Geddes, D. (1994). *The relationship between negative feedback and increased organizational aggression.* Paper presented at the meeting of the Academy of Management, Dallas, TX.

Geddes, D., & Baron, R. A. (1997). Workplace aggression as a consequence of negative performance feedback. *Management Communications Quarterly, 10,* 433–454.

Geen, R. G. (1991). *Human aggression.* Pacific Grove, CA: Brooks/Cole.

Giacalone, R. A., & Greenberg, J. (Eds.). (1997). *Antisocial behavior in organizations.* Thousand Oaks, CA: Sage.

Giacalone, R. A., Riordan, C. A., & Rosenfeld, P. (1997). Employee sabotage: Toward a practitioner-scholar understanding. In R. A. Giacalone & J. Greenberg (Eds.), *Antisocial behavior in organizations* (pp. 109–129). Thousand Oaks, CA: Sage.

Greenberg, J. (1987). A taxonomy of organizational justice theories. *Academy of Management Review, 12,* 9–22.

Greenberg, J. (1990). Organizational justice: Yesterday, today, and tomorrow. *Journal of Management, 16,* 399–432.

Greenberg, J. (1993a). The social side of fairness: Interpersonal and informational classes of organizational justice. In R. Cropanzano (Ed.), *Justice in the workplace: Approaching fairness in human resource management* (pp. 79–102). Hillsdale, NJ: Lawrence Erlbaum Associates.

Greenberg, J. (1993b). Stealing in the name of justice: Informational and interpersonal moderators of theft reactions to underpayment inequity. *Organizational Behavior and Human Decision Processes, 54,* 81–103.

Greenberg, J. (1994). Restitution and retaliation as motives for inequity-induced pilferage. Unpublished manuscript, Ohio State University, Columbus.

Greenberg, J. (1996). *The quest for justice on the job: Essays and experiments.* Thousand Oaks, CA: Sage.

Greenberg, J. (1997). The STEAL motive: Managing the social determinants of employee theft. In R. A. Giacalone & J. Greenberg (Eds.), *Antisocial behavior in organizations* (pp. 85–108). Thousand Oaks, CA: Sage.

Greenberg, J., & Alge, B. J. (1998). Aggressive reactions to workplace injustice. In R. W. Griffin, A. M. O'Leary-Kelly, & J. M. Collins (Eds.), *Dysfunctional behavior in organizations: Violent and deviant behavior* (Vol. 23 Part A, pp. 83–117). Stamford, CT: JAI Press.

Griffin, R. W., & O'Leary-Kelly, A. M. (Eds.). (2004). *The dark side of organizational behavior.* San Francisco, CA: Jossey-Bass.

Grover, S. L. (1993). Lying, subterfuge, and deceit: A model of dishonesty in the workplace. *Organization Science, 4,* 478–495.

Grover, S. L. (1997). Lying in organizations. In R. Giacalone & J. Greenberg (Eds.), *Antisocial behavior in organizations* (pp. 68–84). Thousand Oaks, CA: Sage.

Grover, S. L. (2005). The truth, the whole truth, and nothing but the truth: The causes and management of workplace lying. *Academy of Management Executive, 19,* 148–157.

Harris, M. B. (1993). How provoking! What makes men and women angry? *Aggressive Behavior, 19,* 199–211.

Hartup, W. W. (1974). Aggression in childhood: Developmental perspectives. *American Psychologist, 29,* 336–341.

Harvey, P., Stoner, J., Hochwarter, W., & Kacmar, C. (2007). Coping with abusive supervision: The neutralizing effects of ingratiation and positive affect on negative employee outcomes. *Leadership Quarterly, 18,* 264–280.

Hoel, H., Cooper, C. L., & Faragher, B. (2001). The experience of bullying in Great Britain: The impact of organizational status. *European Journal of Work and Organizational Psychology, 10,* 443–466.

Hoel, H., Rayner, S., & Cooper, C. L. (1999). Workplace bullying. In C. L. Cooper & I. T. Robertson (Eds.), *International review of industrial and organizational psychology* (Vol. 14, pp. 195–229). New York, NY: John Wiley.

Hogan, J., & Hogan, R. (1986). *Hogan personnel selection series manual.* Minneapolis, MN: National Computer Systems.

Hogan, J., & Hogan, R. (1989). How to measure employee reliability. *Journal of Applied Psychology, 74,* 273–279.

Hornstein, H. A. (1997). *Brutal bosses and their prey: How to identify and overcome abuse in the workplace.* New York, NY: Riverhead Books.

How to predict and prevent workplace violence. (2005, April). *HR Focus, 82*(4), 10–11.

Joint Commission on Accreditation of Healthcare Organizations. (2008). *Behaviors that undermine a culture of safety.* Sentinel Event Alert, 40. Retrieved July 9, 2008, from http://www.jointcommission.org/SentinelEvents/SentinelEventAlert/sea_40.htm

Keashly, L. (1998). Emotional abuse in the workplace: Conceptual and empirical issues. *Journal of Emotional Abuse, 1,* 85–117.

Keashly, L., & Jagatic, K. (2003). By any other name: American perspectives on workplace bullying. In S. Einarsen, H. Hoel, D. Zapf, & C. L. Cooper (Eds.), *Bullying and emotional abuse in the workplace: International perspectives on research and practice* (pp. 31–61). London, England: Taylor & Francis.

Keashly, L., & Neuman, J. H. (2002, August). Exploring persistent patterns of workplace aggression. In P. J. Moberg, Chair, *Workplace abuse, aggression, bullying, and incivility: Conceptual and empirical insights.* Symposium conducted at the meeting of the Academy of Management, Denver, CO.

Keashly, L., & Nowell, B. (in press). Workplace bullying, conflict and conflict resolution. In S. Einarsen, H. Hoel, D. Zapf, & C. L. Cooper (Eds.), *Workplace bullying: Development in theory, research, and practice* (2nd ed.). London, England: CRC Press.

Keashly, L., Trott, V., & MacLean, L. M. (1994). Abusive behavior in the workplace: A preliminary investigation. *Violence and Victims, 9,* 341–357.

Koonin, M., & Green, T. M. (2004). The emotionally abusive workplace, *Journal of Emotional Abuse, 4,* 71–79.

Kowalski, R., Harmon, J., Yorks, L., & Kowalski, D. (2003). Reducing workplace stress and aggression: An action research project at the U.S. Department of Veterans Affairs. *Human Resource Planning, 26,* 39–53.

Kramer, R. M. (1994). The sinister attribution error: Paranoid cognition and collective distrust in organizations. *Motivation and Emotion, 18,* 199–230.

Kramer, R. M. (2006). The great intimidators. *Harvard Business Review, 84,* 88–96.

Kulas, J. T., McInnerney, J. E., DeMuth, R. F., & Jadwinski, V. (2007). Employee satisfaction and theft: Testing climate perceptions as a mediator. *Journal of Psychology, 141,* 389–402.

Lanyon, R. I., & Goodstein, L. D. (2004). Validity and reliability of a pre-employment screening test: The Counterproductive Behavior Index CBI. *Journal of Business and Psychology, 18,* 533–553.

LeBlanc, M. M., & Barling, J. (2005). Understanding the many faces of workplace violence. In S. Fox & P. E. Spector (Eds.), *Counterproductive work behavior: Investigations of actors and targets* (pp. 41–63). Washington, DC: American Psychological Association.

Lee, A. S. (2001). An analysis of workplace bullying in the UK. *Personnel Review, 29,* 593–612.

Leventhal, G. S. (1980). What should be done with equity theory? In K. J. Gerneg, M. S. Greenberg, & R. H. Willis (Eds.), *Social exchange: Advances in theory and research* (pp. 27–55). New York, NY: Plenum.

Leventhal, G. S., Karuza, J., & Fry, W. R. (1980). Beyond fairness: A theory of allocation preferences. In G. Mikula (Ed.), *Justice and social interaction* (pp. 167–218). New York, NY: Springer-Verlag.

Levinson, H. (1978, May/June). The abrasive personality. *Harvard Business Review, 56,* 86–94.

Lewis, B. E. (2004). *Disgruntled former employees may use the Internet for revenge.* Retrieved May 25, 2004, from http://www.workforce.com/section/03/article/23/72/62.html

Lewis, H. B. (1971). *Shame and guilt in neurosis.* New York, NY: International Universities Press.

Leymann, H. (1990). Mobbing and psychological terror at workplaces. *Violence and Victims, 5,* 119–126.

Leymann, H. (1996). The content and development of mobbing at work. *European Journal of Work and Organizational Psychology, 5,* 165–184.

Lim, S. G. P., & Cortina, L. M. (2005). Interpersonal mistreatment in the workplace: The interface and impact of general incivility and sexual harassment. *Journal of Applied Psychology, 90,* 483–496.

Lutgen-Sandvik, P., & Sypher, B. (Eds.). (2009). *Destructive organizational communication: Processes, consequences and constructive ways of organizing.* London, England: Routledge.

Mantell, M. (1994, December 15). Workplace violence: There are effective ways to prevent it. *Boardroom Reports,* 1–2.

Matthiesen, S. B., & Einarsen, S. (2007). Perpetrators and targets of bullying at work: Role stress and individual differences. *Violence and Victims, 22,* 735–753.

Mayhew, C., & Chappell, D. (2002). An overview of occupational violence. *Australian Nursing Journal, 9,* 34–35.

McEwen, J. T. (1990, Summer). The growing threat of computer crime. *Detective,* 6–11.

McGregor, D. (1960). *The human side of enterprise.* New York, NY: McGraw-Hill.

McGregor, J., Hamm, S., & Kiley, D. (2007). Sweet revenge. *BusinessWeek, 4018,* 64–70.

McLean Parks, J. (1997). The fourth arm of justice: The art and science of revenge. In R. J. Lewicki, R. J. Bies, & B. H. Sheppard (Eds.), *Research on negotiation in organizations* (Vol. 6, pp. 113–144). Greenwich, CT: JAI Press.

McPhail, S. M. (1996, April). *A proposed taxonomy of workplace violence.* Paper presented at the meeting of the Society for Industrial and Organizational Psychology, San Diego, CA.

Merchant, J. A., & Lundell, J. A. (2001). Workplace violence intervention research workshop, April 5–7, 2000, Washington, DC: Background, rationale, and summary. *American Journal of Preventive Medicine, 20,* 135–140.

Merriam-Websters Collegiate Dictionary (11th Ed.) (2003). Merriam-Webster Incorporated.

Micco, L. (1998, June). OSHA issues recommendations for improving night retail safety. *HR News, 17,* 13.

Mikulay, S. M., & Goffin, R. D. (1998). Measuring and predicting counterproductivity in the laboratory using integrity and personality testing. *Educational and Psychological Measurement, 58,* 768–790.

Mitchell, M. S., & Ambrose, M. L. (2007). Abusive supervision and workplace deviance and the moderating effects of negative reciprocity beliefs. *Journal of Applied Psychology, 92,* 1159–1168.

Mullen, E. A. (1997). Workplace violence: Cause for concern or the construction of a new category of fear. *Journal of Industrial Relations, 39,* 21–32.

Neuman, J. H. (2004). Injustice, stress, and aggression in organizations. In R. W. Griffin & A. M. O'Leary-Kelly (Eds.), *The dark side of organizational behavior* (pp. 62–102). San Francisco, CA: Jossey-Bass.

Neuman, J. H., & Baron, R. A. (2005). Aggression in the workplace: A social psychological perspective. In S. Fox & P. E. Spector (Eds.), *Counterproductive work behavior: Investigations of actors and targets* (pp. 13–40). Washington, DC: American Psychological Association.

Neuman, J. H., & Baron, R. A. (in press). Social antecedents of bullying: A social interactionist perspective. In S. Einarsen, H. Hoel, D. Zapf & C. L. Cooper (Eds.), *Bullying and Harassment in the workplace: Developments in theory, research and practice* (2nd ed.). London, England: CRC Press.

Neuman, J. H., & Keashly, L. (2004, April 4). Development of the Workplace Aggression Research Questionnaire (WAR-Q): Preliminary data from the Workplace Stress and Aggression Project. In R. J. Bennett & C. D. Crossley, Chairs, *Theoretical advancements in the study of anti-social behavior at work.* Symposium conducted at the meeting of the Society for Industrial and Organizational Psychology, Chicago, IL.

Neuman, J. H., & Keashly, L. (2005, August). Reducing aggression and bullying: A long-term intervention project in the U.S. Department of Veterans Affairs. In J. Raver, Chair, *Workplace bullying: International perspectives on moving from research to practice.* Symposium conducted at the meeting of the Academy of Management, Honolulu, HI.

Ones, D. S., Viswesvaran, C., & Schmidt, F. L. (1993). Comprehensive meta-analysis of integrity test validities: Findings and implications for personnel selection and theories of job performance. *Journal of Applied Psychology* (Monograph), *78,* 679–703.

Pearson, C. M., Andersson, L. M., & Wegner, J. W. (2001). When workers flout convention: A study of workplace incivility. *Human Relations, 54,* 1387–1420.

Peek-Asa, C., Runyan, C. W., & Zwerling, C. (2001). The role of surveillance and evaluation research in the reduction of violence against workers. *American Journal of Preventive Medicine, 20,* 141–148.

Penhaligon, N. L., Louis, W. R., & Restubog, S. L. D. (2009). Emotional anguish at work: The mediating role of perceived rejection on workgroup mistreatment and affective outcomes. *Journal of Occupational Health Psychology, 14,* 34–45.

Personnel Decisions Incorporated. (1985). *Development and validation of the PDI Employment Inventory.* Minneapolis, MN: Author.

Pfeffer, J., & Sutton, R. I. (2006a). Evidence-based management. *Harvard Business Review, 84,* 62–75.

Pfeffer, J., & Sutton, R. I. (2006b). *Hard facts, dangerous half-truths, and total nonsense: Profit from evidence-based management.* Boston, MA: Harvard Business School Press.

Pinder, C. C. (2008). *Work motivation in organizational behavior* (2nd ed.). New York: Psychology Press.

Policy guidance on current issues of sexual harassment. (1990). Retrieved January 26, 2004, from http://www.eeoc.gov/policy/docs/currentissues.html

Purdy, M. (1994, February 14). Workplace murders provoke lawsuits and better security. *New York Times*, pp. A1, B5.

Quine, L. (1999). Workplace bullying in NHS community trust: Staff questionnaire survey. *British Medical Journal, 318,* 228–232.

Rayner, C., & Hoel, H. (1997). A summary review of literature relating to workplace bullying. *Journal of Community and Applied Social Psychology, 7,* 181–191.

Rayner, C., Hoel, H., & Cooper, C. L. (2002). *Workplace bullying: What we know, who is to blame, and what can we do?* London, England: Taylor & Francis.

Richman, J. A., & Rospenda, K. M. (2005). Harassment and discrimination. In J. Barling, M. Frone, & E. K. Kelloway (Eds.), *The handbook of workplace stress* (pp. 149–188). Thousand Oaks, CA: Sage.

Richman, J. A., Rospenda, K. M., Nawyn, S. J., Flaherty, J. A., Fendrich, M., Drum, M. L., & Johnson, T. P. (1999). Sexual harassment and generalized workplace abuse among university employees: Prevalence and mental health correlates. *American Journal of Public Health, 89,* 358–363.

Robinson, S. L., & Bennett, R. J. (1995). A typology of deviant workplace behaviors: A multi-dimensional scaling study. *Academy of Management Journal, 38,* 555–572.

Roland, E., & Idsøe, T. (2001). Aggression and bullying. *Aggressive Behavior, 27,* 446–462.

Roscigno, V. J., Lopez, S. H., & Hodson, R. (2009). Supervisory bullying, status inequalities and organizational context. *Social Forces, 87,* 1561–1589.

Rousseau, D. M. (2006). Is there such a thing as "evidence-based management"? *Academy of Management Review, 31,* 256–269.

Salin, D. (2005). Workplace bullying among business professionals: Prevalence, gender differences and the role of organizational politics. *PISTES*. Retrieved January 30, 2009, from http://www.pistes.uqam.ca/v7n3/pdf/v7n3a2en.pdf

Scheff, T. J. (1987). The shame-rage spiral: A case study of an interminable quarrel. In H. B. Lewis (Ed.), *The role of shame in symptom formation* (pp. 109–149). Hillsdale, NJ: Lawrence Erlbaum Associates.

Schön, D. A. (1983). *The reflective practitioner: How professionals think in action* New York: Basic Book Inc.

Seigne, E., Coyne, I., Randall, P., & Parker, J. (2007). Personality traits of bullies as a contributory factor in workplace bullying: An exploratory study. *International Journal of Organization Theory and Behavior, 10,* 118–132.

Simonowitz, J. A. (1995). Violence in health care: A strategic approach. *Nurse Practitioner Forum, 6,* 120–129.

Sirota, D., Mischkind, L. A., & Meltzer, M. I. (2005). *The enthusiastic employee: How companies profit by giving workers what they want*. Upper Saddle River, NJ: Pearson Education.

Skarlicki, D. P., & Latham, G. P. (2005). How can training be used to foster organizational justice. In J. Greenberg & J. A. Colquitt (Eds.), *Handbook of organizational justice* (pp. 499–522). Mahwah, NJ: Lawrence Erlbaum Associates.

Sloane, S. D. (2004). Research into the effectiveness of an alternative to violence program in a prison system, *Dissertation abstracts International: Section B Sciences and Engineering, 64*(8-B), 4019.

Slora, K. B., Joy, D. S., Jones, J. W., & Terris, W. (1991). The prediction of on-the-job violence. In J. W. Jones (Ed.), *Preemployment honesty testing: Current research and future directions* (pp. 171–183). Westport, CT: Quorum.

Slora, K. B., Joy, D. S., & Terris, W. (1991). Personnel selection to control employee violence. *Journal of Business and Psychology, 5,* 417–426.

Spector, P. E. (1997). The role of frustration in antisocial behavior at work. In R. A. Giacalone & J. Greenberg (Eds.), *Antisocial behavior in organizations* (pp. 1–17). Thousand Oaks, CA: Sage.

Tahmincioglu, E. (2001, August 1). Vigilance in the face of layoff rage: Employer miscues can breed retaliation. *New York Times,* pp. C1, C6.

Tahmincioglu, E. (2004, April 25). In health and social services, a more violent workplace. *New York Times,* p. 1.

Tangney, J. P., Burggraf, S. A., & Wagner, P. E. (1995). Shame-proneness, guilt-proneness, and psychological symptoms. In J. P. Tangney & K. W. Fischer (Eds.), *Self-conscious emotions: The psychology of shame, guilt, embarrassment, and pride* (pp. 343–367). New York, NY: Guildford Press.

Tangney, J. P., Wagner, P., Fletcher, C., & Gramzow, R. (1992). Shamed into anger? The relation of shame and guilt to anger and self-reported aggression. *Journal of Personality and Social Psychology, 62,* 669–675.

Tangney, J. P., Wagner, P. E., Burggraf, S. A., Gramzow, R., & Fletcher, C. (1991, June). *Children's shame-proneness, but not guilt-proneness, is related to emotional and behavioral maladjustment.* Paper presented at the meeting of the Society for Research in Child Development, Seattle, WA.

Tangney, J. P., Wagner, P. E., & Gramzow, R. (1996). Relation of shame and guilt to constructive versus destructive responses to anger across the lifespan. *Journal of Personality and Social Psychology, 70,* 797–809.

Tedeschi, J. T., & Felson, R. B. (1994). *Violence, aggression, and coercive actions.* Washington, DC: American Psychological Association.

Tepper, B. J. (2000). Consequences of abusive supervision. *Academy of Management Journal, 43,* 178–190.

Tepper, B. J. (2007). Abusive supervision in work organizations: Review, synthesis, and research agenda. *Journal of Management, 33,* 261–289.

Thibaut, J., & Walker, L. (1975). *Procedural justice: A psychological analysis.* Hillsdale, NJ: Lawrence Erlbaum Associates.

Torestad, B. (1990). What is anger provoking: A psychophysical study of perceived causes of anger. *Aggressive Behavior, 16,* 9–26.

Tripp, T. M., & Bies, R. J. (1997). What's good about revenge? The avenger's perspective. In R. J. Lewicki, R. J. Bies, & B. H. Sheppard (Eds.), *Research on negotiation in organizations* (Vol. 6, pp. 145–160). Greenwich, CT: JAI Press.

Tripp, T. M., Bies, R. J., & Aquino, K. (2002). Poetic justice or petty jealousy? The aesthetics of revenge. *Organizational Behavior and Human Decision Processes, 89,* 966–984.

Tripp, T. M., Bies, R. J., & Aquino, K. (2007). A vigilante model of justice: Revenge, reconciliation, forgiveness, and avoidance. *Social Justice Research, 20,* 10–34.

Twale, D. J., & De Luca, B. M. (2008). *Faculty incivility: The rise of the academic bully culture and what to do about it.* San Francisco, CA: Jossey-Bass.

University of Iowa Injury Prevention Research Center. (2001). *Workplace violence: A report to the nation.* Retrieved February 2001, from http://www.public-health.uiowa.edu/iprc/NATION.PDF

Waclawski, J., & Church, A. H. (2002). Introduction and overview of organization development as a data-driven approach for organizational change. In J. Waclawski & A. H. Church (Eds.), *Organizational development: A data-driven approach to organizational change* (pp. 3–26). San Francisco, CA: Jossey-Bass.

Weiner, B. (1974). *Achievement motivation and attribution theory.* Morristown, NJ: General Learning Press.

Whittington, R., Shuttleworth, S., & Hill, L. (1996). Violence to staff in a general hospital setting. *Journal of Advanced Nursing, 24,* 326–333.

Wicker, F. W., Payne, G. C., & Morgan, R. D. (1983). Participant descriptions of guilt and shame. *Motivation and Emotion, 7,* 25–39.

Winstanley, S., & Whittington, R. (2004). Aggressive encounters between patients and general hospital staff: Staff perceptions of the context and assailants' levels of cognitive processing. *Aggressive Behavior, 30,* 534–545.

Yamada, D. C. (2004). Crafting a legislative response to workplace bullying. *Employee Rights and Employment Policy Journal, 8,* 475–521.

Yorks, L., Neuman, J. H., Kowalski, D. R., & Kowalski, R. (2007). Lessons learned from a five-year project within the Department of Veterans Affairs: Applying theories of interpersonal aggression and organizational justice to the development and maintenance of collaborative social space. *Journal of Applied Behavioral Science, 43,* 352–372.

Zapf, D., & Einarsen, S. (2003). Individual antecedents of bullying: Victims and perpetrators. In S. Einarsen, H. Hoel, D. Zapf, & C. L. Cooper (Eds.), *Bullying and emotional abuse in the workplace: International perspectives in research and practice* (pp. 165–184). London, England: Taylor & Francis.

Zellars, K. L., Tepper, B. J., & Duffy, M. K. (2002). Abusive supervision and subordinates' organizational citizenship behavior. *Journal of Applied Psychology, 87,* 1068–1076.

Zillmann, D. (1979). *Hostility and aggression.* Hillsdale, NJ: Lawrence Erlbaum Associates.

3

Two Images of Workplace Sabotage

Mark A. Seabright, Maureen L. Ambrose,
and Marshall Schminke

> I worked on Bank of America's payroll program, interfacing a clumsy old in-house system. … Because I was restricted in the amount of work I was allowed to do, I was having a lot of problems implementing the system. It was a real pain in the ass. Bank of America started being pushy because I wasn't getting the work done as fast as they wanted me to. When the higher-ups in the bank wanted to know what was going on, the computer supervisor said I was incapable of doing the job. They put all the blame on me because they didn't want the bosses to know how shitty their computer system really was. They made me look really bad, then went a step further and stopped paying me. I got so pissed off at them that I planted a logic bomb in the system, a kind of electronic "F**k you!" … The next time the payroll system started running, it slowly started disappearing. Once it started failing, all the other programs started deleting themselves. The logic bomb had a chain reaction effect. It started out small, but then all of a sudden the entire system was corrupted.
>
> —Lazlo
> *Programmer (as Quoted in Sprouse, 1992, p. 24)*

Lazlo's tale of workplace deviance captures the dominant image of sabotage, the caricature of the "'mad saboteur' who, overwhelmed by the trials and tribulations of everyday organizational life, explodes in a self-indulgent moment of destruction" (Jermier, 1988, p. 128). This view permeates popular accounts of sabotage in the workplace, and it is common to academic treatments as well. The image of the mad saboteur presents a particular characterization of the causes, emotions, goals, and forms of sabotage, categories that we emphasize in this chapter. Its prototypic features are employee mistreatment as a fundamental cause, anger or outrage as the emotional reaction, and a motive that is primarily expressive, whether it is to vent anger or to exact revenge. The type of sabotage that results from these conditions is a single, extreme act of deviance that demands attention.

But this image only captures one type of sabotage; by itself, it presents a rather narrow and stilted view of the phenomenon. In contrast, consider this vignette involving Otis, a letter carrier:

> I've been a letter carrier for eleven years. ... I take a lot of liberties when I deliver the mail. A lot of the time I play god as far as deciding what mail is important and what's not. I'll go out of my way to deliver any letter or postcard. I'll handle checks with kid gloves. I don't consider bills important, and junk mail is definitely not a priority. Magazines are a low priority because I usually want to read them first. ... On my route there are a lot of houses on hills that aren't that easy to get to. If there's just a bill and nothing else for one of those houses, I'll usually decide they don't want it that day. I'll deliver it the next day when they get more mail. I think most carriers will skip houses if it doesn't seem worth their time or effort. (Sprouse, 1992, p. 91)

Otis's story presents a very different image of sabotage. The provocation has more to do with power and control than it does with being wronged; the concomitant affect is more positive; and the motive is instrumental (aimed at changing the work or the work situation) rather than expressive (aimed at venting anger or exacting revenge). What is most striking, though, is that Otis's story captures a more subtle form of sabotage than that represented by the image of the mad saboteur. Unlike the one-time, major, and overt characteristics of Lazlo's behavior, Otis's insidious variant is ongoing, and it is relatively minor and covert.

Insidious sabotage has received little attention in either the popular press or the academic literature, for self-evident reasons. Because it is relatively covert, it is likely to go unnoticed by management and by researchers, and because it is relatively minor, it would seem to be less damaging or costly than extreme acts of sabotage. But these reasons for neglecting the topic of insidious sabotage are shortsighted. Because it is ongoing, the cumulative effect of the relatively minor acts of insidious sabotage may be even more damaging or costly than a single, extreme act of sabotage. Because it is covert, management is unable to respond to present acts or prevent future occurrences, thereby enabling the sabotage to continue unabated and perpetuating the underlying conditions that foster deviance. And because it is subtle, recurrent, and uncensored, insidious sabotage is likely to gradually lower the normative threshold for workplace deviance of all forms, whereas a single, extreme act of sabotage is likely to be rejected as aberrant and idiosyncratic. For all of these reasons, although less provocative, insidious sabotage may be as, or even more, organizationally significant than the mad saboteur form.

The purpose of this chapter is to contrast these two types of sabotage and, more specifically, to shed light on the relatively neglected insidious form. As suggested by the preceding discussion, we characterize insidious sabotage as ongoing, minor, and covert. Most of the chapters in this book add the qualification that insidious deviance targets individuals, but because sabotage behavior is far more likely to target organizations than individuals, as we elaborate later, our treatment of insidious sabotage includes acts that are intended to harm the organization as well as those targeted at individuals. Thus, one of the contributions of this chapter is to offer a different take on what is meant by insidious deviance, to extend the concept to behavior targeted at organizations.

In the following sections, we briefly define workplace sabotage and present a model of the causes, motives, and types of sabotage behavior. We then describe a study that examines the main features of this model and discuss the implications of our findings.

THE CONCEPT OF WORKPLACE SABOTAGE

Although definitions of sabotage uniformly state that it involves intentional behavior that is damaging to the organization, there is less agreement about its scope. Some definitions present a narrow conception of sabotage, limiting it to property destruction (Edwards & Scullion, 1982; Klein, Leong, & Silva, 1996; Spector, 1975). This view, although uncommon in the sabotage literature, is often adopted in general treatments of the subject. For example, Robinson and Bennett's (1995, 1997) typology of workplace deviance equates sabotage with property deviance. At the other extreme, some definitions are so broad that they become synonymous with negative workplace behavior (Brown, 1977; Dubois, 1979). For example, Dubois (1979) defined sabotage as any organizationally directed act that lowers the quantity or quality of production, including "destroying machines and products, arson, theft, all-out strikes when production is completely stopped, going slow, working to rule, working without enthusiasm, absenteeism, high labour turnover, avoidance of employment, refusal to work in production industries, starting work later and retiring earlier" (p. 17).

We adopt a middle ground (e.g., Crino, 1994; Crino & Leap, 1989; Giacalone, Riordan, & Rosenfeld, 1997; Jermier, 1988; LaNuez & Jermier, 1994; Taylor & Walton, 1971) by defining sabotage as *employee behavior intended to damage a company's property or products, impair its reputation, or subvert its processes.* Typical examples include destroying equipment, stopping production, working slowly, lowering product quality, bad-mouthing the company, and modifying work processes (DiBattista, 1991; Dubois, 1979; Edwards & Scullion, 1982; Giacalone & Rosenfeld, 1987; Graham, 1993; Molstead, 1986; Taylor & Walton, 1971; Thompson, 1983; Tucker, 1993; Zabala, 1989).

This definition helps to clarify several aspects of sabotage behavior and to position it within the mix of related concepts: workplace deviance (Robinson & Bennett, 1995, 1997), antisocial behavior (Giacalone & Greenberg, 1997; Robinson & O'Leary-Kelly, 1998), and organizational retaliation behavior (Skarlicki & Folger, 1997), to name a few (see Robinson & Greenberg, 1998, for a thorough list and review). First, the target of sabotage is the organization. Unlike workplace deviance, antisocial behavior, and organizational retaliation behavior, sabotage does not typically directly target individuals. When individuals are involved, it is as indirect targets, as means to inflict harm on the organization or to subvert its operations. Our study of workplace sabotage (Ambrose, Seabright, & Schminke, 2002) supports this claim. We found that only 22% of the sabotage vignettes in Sprouse's (1992) *Sabotage in the American Workplace* involved individual targets, but more important, 81% of these resulted in greater harm to the organization than to individuals.

Second, although intentional, sabotage is not necessarily intentionally harmful (Robinson & Greenberg, 1998). As the definition indicates, the purpose of sabotage ranges from inflicting harm (e.g., damaging property to get even for mistreatment, similar to organizational retaliation behavior) to subverting operations (e.g., altering processes in order to facilitate the work). In this particular way, sabotage is a broader construct than organizational retaliation behavior or other conceptualizations that limit their focus to behaviors that intentionally inflict harm on the organization (Robinson & Greenberg, 1998). Much of the sabotage literature, especially the recent literature, characterizes sabotage as a rational tactic to manage one's work environment (Analoui, 1995; DiBattista, 1996; Jermier, 1988; LaNuez & Jermier, 1994), rather than as an act of vengeance or affective expression. Jermier (1988), for example, has argued that sabotage is a form of labor resistance that attempts to alter the power dynamics in the workplace; "it is practiced strategically to contain exploitation and tactically to win issues" (p. 129). Harm that results from this form of sabotage may be purposeful, but subjectively justifiable as a means to achieve a greater good, as in "principled sabotage" (Jermier, 1988; Watson, 1971), or it may be an inadvertent consequence of attempts to facilitate the work, help coworkers, or better the organization (DiBattista, 1991; Edwards & Scullion, 1982; Giacalone & Rosenfeld, 1987; Taylor & Walton, 1971). As Bennett (1998, p. 229) has noted, "the goal of 'corrective' deviance is therefore not to intentionally cause harm; rather, harm may be an unintended consequence."

Third, sabotage varies along several dimensions: perpetrator (individual/ collective), severity (minor/major), visibility (overt/covert), and recurrence (one time/ongoing). The definition of sabotage does not restrict its domain to the widely held image of sabotage as an individual act of major, overt, one-time deviance. Like the concepts of deviance and antisocial behavior, sabotage can be committed by individuals or by groups, and it ranges from extreme, one-time occurrences to subtle, ongoing acts. In this way, sabotage is more inclusive than organizational retaliation behavior, which emphasizes minor, covert ways of striking back at the organization.

A MOTIVATIONAL MODEL OF SABOTAGE

In this section, we explore why sabotage occurs and, more specifically, why it occurs in the extreme versus the insidious form. Our approach to this question is to focus on the core motivational processes that lead to sabotage. We propose that motivation mediates the relationship between the causal conditions that trigger sabotage and the particular form that it takes (see Robinson & Bennett, 1997, for a similar formulation for workplace deviance). This formulation is a bare-bones model of workplace sabotage; it does not incorporate individual differences, structural constraints, or normative pressures (Robinson & Greenberg, 1998). We leave these refinements to future work.

We begin by reviewing the causes of sabotage identified in the literature. Next we consider the motives of the saboteur. Specifically, we identify two components of motive: affect (positive/negative) and goal (instrumental/ expressive). We use these two components to derive a typology of saboteurs' motives. Finally, we examine the forms of sabotage behavior, contrasting the extreme versus the insidious variants.

Our model posits that certain work conditions or experiences, such as injustice or powerlessness, influence the saboteur's motives and that, in turn, these motives affect the particular form of sabotage that results. Specifically, we suggest that the experience of injustice triggers the negative affect and expressive goals that lead to extreme acts of sabotage, whereas powerlessness triggers the relatively positive affect and instrumental goals that drive insidious sabotage.

Causes of Sabotage

The sabotage literature identifies five types of causes: injustice, powerlessness, frustration, facilitation of work, and boredom/fun (Crino & Leap, 1989; DiBattista, 1991, 1996; Edwards & Scullion, 1982; Giacalone & Rosenfeld, 1987; Harris & Ogbonna, 2009; Hollinger & Clark, 1982; Mangione & Quinn, 1975; McLean Parks & Kidder, 1994; Molstad, 1986; Sieh, 1987; Spector, 1975, 1997; Storms & Spector, 1987; Taylor & Walton, 1971; Zabala, 1989). We used these categories in our prior research (Ambrose et al., 2002; Seabright, Ambrose, & Schminke, 2000) to assess the antecedent conditions of the sabotage behavior reported in Sprouse's (1992) *Sabotage in the American Workplace.* We found that injustice was the most common cause of sabotage (59.8%), followed by powerlessness (19.7%), boredom/fun (10.7%), frustration (6.6%), and facilitation of work (1.6%). We review each type of cause in the following.

Injustice

Injustice, or an employee's belief that that he or she (or someone else) has been treated unfairly, is a frequently cited cause of sabotage (Crino, 1994; Crino & Leap, 1989; DiBattista, 1991, 1996; Harris & Ogbonna, 2009; Neuman & Baron, 1998; Robinson & Bennett, 1997; Skarlicki & Folger, 1997; Sieh, 1987; Skarlicki, van Jaarsveld, & Walker, 2008; Tucker, 1993). An employee who feels unjustly treated may try to even the score by committing sabotage. As Crino (1994, p. 315) has observed, an employee who has been "shown disrespect, passed over for promotion, given additional responsibilities with no pay increase, denied adequate resources to do the job, or didn't receive what he or she considered adequate credit for work performed from co-workers or management" fits the profile of the classic disgruntled saboteur.

Research on workplace deviance provides indirect support for this claim. Studies have shown that perceived injustice is related to various forms of deviance, including theft (Greenberg, 1990, 1993), vandalism (DeMore, Fisher, & Baron, 1988), aggression (Baron, Neuman, & Geddes, 1999), and organizational retaliation behavior (Skarlicki & Folger, 1997). Many of these studies have also shown that certain types, or combinations, of injustice— distributive (fairness of outcomes), procedural (fairness of procedures), or interactional (fairness of personal treatment)—are more likely to lead to deviant behavior. Skarlicki & Folger (1997), for example, found that all three of these types of injustice interacted in their effect on organizational retaliation behavior. Low levels of distributive justice predicted retaliation only when there was also low procedural and interactional justice.

Our research examined whether the injustice also plays a significant role in workplace sabotage (Ambrose et al., 2002). We found that perceived injustice was the most common cause of sabotage among the vignettes in Sprouse's (1992) *Sabotage in the American Workplace*. We also found that the types of injustice (distributive, procedural, and interactional) had an additive effect on the severity of the sabotage behavior, rather than individual or interactive effects. The magnitude of the sabotage was a function of the number of types of injustice, not which type or which combination of types. One explanation for the difference between our results and those of Skarlicki and Folger (1997), other than the difference in constructs, is that they focused on deviance frequency, whereas we focused on deviance severity.

Powerlessness

Powerlessness stems from a lack of freedom or autonomy (Bennett, 1998). Sabotage that results from powerlessness is an effort to attain control for its own sake. It involves trying to change the nature of work or the inducements–contributions equation to achieve a nonsanctioned end (i.e., something that benefits the person or workgroup, not the organization). Examples include wildcat strikes to enhance a bargaining position or breaking machinery to gain unscheduled breaks. Empirical research suggests that individuals who feel powerless may engage in sabotage (Bennett, 1998; DiBattista, 1991) and that such destructive behavior can increase individuals' sense of control (Allen & Greenberger, 1980). Some researchers identify powerlessness as a source of injustice (Bennett, 1998), creating a potential source of confusion between powerlessness and injustice as sabotage provocations. However, to maintain the conceptual distinction between these two, we confine our conceptualization of the power motive to acts aimed at obtaining control, rather than regaining justice.

Frustration

Organizational frustration is defined as an interference with goal attainment or goal maintenance (Spector, 1978). In this case, it is the emotional state of frustration that drives the sabotage. For example, anger over inadequate resources to do the job may lead to a cathartic destruction of property (Taylor & Walton, 1971). As with powerlessness, research demonstrates that sabotage is related to organizational frustration (Chen & Spector, 1992; Spector, 1975; Storms & Spector, 1987; Taylor & Walton, 1971). However, some clarification may be needed to distinguish between frustration and other possible motives. For example, researchers also have recognized that powerlessness can be frustrating (Bennett, 1998, p. 228) and that injustice can elicit frustration (Brown & Herrnstein, 1975). However, we conceptualize frustration as the motive for sabotage only if it is the blocking of goals per se that drives the act. Frustration is not the underlying motive if the employee is frustrated as the result of something else (e.g., powerlessness or injustice). In such cases, the source of the frustration (powerlessness or injustice) would be the motive for sabotage.

Facilitation of Work

Research demonstrates that facilitation of work, or attempting to make the work process easier to accomplish, can be a cause of sabotage (Bensman & Gerver, 1963; Taylor & Walton, 1971). However, it is important to distinguish between facilitation of work and related concepts like power. Power generally involves breaking the rules, whereas facilitation of work involves bending the rules. Power is any effort to change or restructure the work to achieve a personal or nonsanctioned end. It restructures social relationships, but does not necessarily make the work easier (Taylor & Walton, 1971). Facilitation of work involves nonsanctioned means to achieve sanctioned ends. The classic example of work facilitation is the use of a "tap" in airplane manufacturing (Taylor & Walton, 1971). A tap is a steel screw that rethreads a nut so that a misaligned bolt will fit. In the short run, this makes work easier, but in the long run employees know that it weakens the strength of the connection and may therefore be detrimental to the organization. Although many efforts to facilitate work are innocuous or perhaps even beneficial, these efforts lead to sabotage in cases such as this when individuals ease the work process at a cost (or potential cost) to the organization.

Boredom/Fun

Boredom/fun is identified as the motive for sabotage when the primary goal of the activity is to cut boredom, generate excitement, or have fun. "Changing the time on the punch clock, or pulling the fire alarm may add just the right level of excitement to an otherwise boring day" (Crino, 1994, p. 317). Research indicates that employees may engage in sabotage in an effort to alleviate boredom or entertain themselves or their coworkers (Crino, 1994; DiBattista, 1991; Giacalone & Rosenfeld, 1987; Harris & Ogbonna, 2009; Taylor & Walton, 1971).

Motivation of Saboteurs

Research examining what motivates deviant behavior tend to emphasize either affective states (e.g., Allen & Greenberger, 1980; Allred, 1999; Berkowitz, 1998; Bolin & Heatherly, 2001; Fox, Spector, & Miles, 2001; Hollinger & Clark, 1982; Mangione & Quinn, 1975; Spector, 1975) or cognitive processes (e.g., Aquino, Tripp, & Bies, 2001; Greenberg & Alge, 1998; Martinko, Gundlach, & Douglas, 2002; O'Leary-Kelly, Griffin, & Glew, 1996). Although some work behaviors may be more affect driven, and others may be more cognition driven (Weiss & Cropanzano, 1996), it seems unlikely that there would be much variation in the relative importance of affect and cognition between different types of deviant behavior. And there is evidence that workplace deviance is both, if not equally, affect and cognition driven (Lee & Allen, 2002). In a survey study, Lee and Allen (2002) directly assessed the relative importance of job affect and job cognitions in predicting workplace deviance among a sample of registered nurses. They found that when job affect was represented by both a general mood (positive affect) and a discrete emotion (hostility) measure, job affect and job cognition played equally important roles in predicting workplace deviance.

This line of reasoning suggests that sabotage is likely to be both affect and cognition driven. More specifically, we propose that the motivation of the saboteur is a function of both affect (positive/negative) and goal state (instrumental/expressive). Our view of the affective component of the saboteur's motivation is generic; we define it as the general moods or emotions (Lee & Allen, 2002; Weiss & Cropanzano, 1996) that are experienced prior to the sabotage event. Our take on the cognitive component, though, is more specific to the context of workplace sabotage. We suggest that the fundamental choice that determines the intentions of the saboteur is between instrumental and expressive goals, as defined later.

Affect

Several studies suggest that negative affect contributes to sabotage. Mangione and Quinn (1975) reported a significant negative correlation between job satisfaction and self-reports of counterproductive behavior (including working badly or damaging property on purpose), but only for the subsample composed of men 30 years old or older. Hollinger and Clark (1982) found that both global and specific measures of job satisfaction were negatively related to property and production deviance; unlike Mangione and Quinn (1975), controlling for age did not substantively alter these findings. In a study of work stressors and aggression, Chen and Spector (1992) reported that job dissatisfaction and feelings of anger were associated with sabotage behavior. And more recently, Fox et al. (2001) found that negative affect mediated the relationship between job stressors (including perceived injustice) and counterproductive work behavior. Their study lends support to the structure of our formulation about the causes, motives, and types of sabotage behavior.

This literature, however, doesn't delimit the role of negative affect in sabotage behavior. Although injustice and frustration have been shown to lead to negative moods and emotions (Fox et al., 2001; Spector, 1978, 1997; Weiss, Suckow, & Cropanzano, 1999), the affective consequences of other antecedents to sabotage are less clear. Similarly, negative affect may drive extreme acts of sabotage, but it is not necessarily associated with more insidious forms. Thus, we propose that some types of provocations (e.g., injustice and frustration) are more likely to lead to negative affect than others (e.g., facilitation of work and fun) and that, in turn, negative affect is more likely to result in some types of sabotage (major/one time/overt) than others (minor/ongoing/covert).

Conversely, positive affect may play a role in some types of sabotage. The best example of this is "sabotage as fun" (Taylor & Walton, 1971) or mischief (Giacalone & Rosenfeld, 1987; Thompson, 1983). Thompson (1983), for example, described workers in a beef processing plant deliberately cutting chunks out of pieces of meat and sometimes throwing them at coworkers, just for the fun of it. He noted that "the workers practically made a game out of doing forbidden things simply to see if they could get away with it" (p. 231). Positive affect may also accompany efforts to facilitate the work or to assert power or control. Edwards and Scullion (1982) described an example of functional sabotage in which piece-rate workers in a British components factory maximized their earnings by cutting their machines' cycle times; rather than being embittered or destructive for its own sake, these workers were simply taking advantage of an opportunity to bend the production rules in their favor. Together, these hints from the literature indicate that some antecedent conditions, such as fun and facilitation of work, support positive affect. These examples also suggest that positive affect is likely to contribute to relatively subtle forms of sabotage.

Goal State

Several authors have noted that the motives for sabotage, or for deviance in general, can represent either instrumental or expressive goals (Dubois, 1979; Edwards & Scullion, 1982; Robinson & Bennett, 1997; Taylor & Walton, 1971). Instrumental sabotage is "aimed at a limited or total transformation of the present situation," whereas expressive sabotage is "not out to achieve any practical result for its perpetrators, but expresses a wish to castigate the management, a protest against injustice, a rejection of accepted values" (Dubois, 1979, p. 60). Robinson and Bennett (1997) advanced a similar distinction in their model of workplace deviance. They proposed that an instrumental motivation attempts to correct for a perceived disparity by "repairing the situation, restoring equity, or improving the current situation," whereas an expressive motivation reflects a need to "vent, release, or express one's feelings of outrage, anger or frustration"

(p. 16). We suggest, however, that an expressive motivation is not limited to negative affect; it can be affectively neutral or positive, as in "sabotage as fun" (Taylor & Walton, 1971). More generally, we view affect and goal state as orthogonal aspects of motivation. That is, instrumental and expressive goals can be accompanied by either positive or negative affect (cf. Lee & Allen, 2002).

We propose that powerlessness and facilitation of work lead to instrumental goals, whereas injustice, frustration, and boredom/fun lead to expressive goals. Both Taylor and Walton (1971) and Edwards and Scullion (1982) have described attempts to assert control or to facilitate the work process as "utilitarian" forms of sabotage because they focus on changing some feature of the job context. Perceived injustice, on the other hand, can lead to desires to get back at the organization (Greenberg, 1996; Skarlicki & Folger, 1997), and frustration can result in hostile aggression (Berkowitz, 1989; Spector, 1978, 1997). And on a more positive affective note, boredom/fun can lead to expressions of mischief (Giacalone & Rosenfeld, 1987; Taylor & Walton, 1971; Thompson, 1983).

Moreover, we would expect an instrumental motivation to lead to more subtle forms of sabotage than an expressive motivation. The success of an instrumental goal depends upon getting away with, and holding on to, changes to the work situation that benefit the saboteur. This requires being both efficacious and covert; and minor, ongoing acts of sabotage provide a strategy for achieving both objectives. An expressive goal, on the other hand, operates by a different logic. Its success depends upon making a point, to oneself or to others. While avoiding punishment or other negative personal consequences, this implies that grand, open acts of sabotage are inherently more expressive.

Typology of Sabotage Motives

Table 3.1 displays a typology of sabotage motives based on affect (positive/negative) and goal state (instrumental/expressive). The benefit of this typology is that it articulates the relationships among seemingly disparate types of motives (e.g., mischief versus labor resistance), and it brings attention to relatively neglected ones (i.e., opportunism). The combination of negative affect and an expressive goal fits the image of the *mad saboteur* who seeks revenge for perceived mistreatment (Crino & Leap, 1989; DiBattista, 1991; Dubois, 1979; Giacalone & Rosenfeld, 1987; Taylor

TABLE 3.1

Types of Sabotage Motives

	Goal State	
Affect	**Expressive**	**Instrumental**
Negative	"Mad saboteur"	Labor resistance
Positive	Diversion	Opportunism

& Walton, 1971). The same affect, but in conjunction with an instrumental goal, drives sabotage as a form of *labor resistance* (Crino & Leap, 1989; Dubois, 1979; Jermier, 1988; LaNuez & Jermier, 1994; Taylor & Walton, 1971; Zabala, 1989). The combination of positive affect and an expressive goal incites *diversion* (Crino & Leap, 1989; DiBattista, 1991; Giacalone & Rosenfeld, 1987; Taylor & Walton, 1971; Thompson, 1983), whereas the motive associated with the same positive affect and an instrumental goal can be described as *opportunism*.

Of these four motives, opportunism has received the least attention in the sabotage literature. It subsumes efforts to facilitate the work (Edwards & Scullion, 1982; Taylor & Walton, 1971) as well as broader efforts to take advantage of the work situation in ways that enhance the power and control of the saboteur. And it contrasts with sabotage as labor resistance (Jermier, 1988), even though they both pursue instrumental aims. Whereas labor resistance focuses on preventing or redressing perceived losses (negative affect), opportunism seeks to promote possible gains (positive affect).

This typology also highlights the range of sabotage motives. The mad saboteur versus opportunism captures the contrast that we presented in the beginning of the chapter between Lazlo, the angry programmer, and Otis, the making-out letter carrier. Following our earlier comments, we expect mad saboteur motives (negative affect and expressive goals) to lead to extreme acts of sabotage and opportunistic motives (positive affect and instrumental goals) to lead to more subtle forms of sabotage.

Types of Sabotage

The two images of sabotage, the extreme and the insidious, vary along three dimensions: severity (minor/major), recurrence (one time/ongoing), and visibility (overt/covert). Severity, or the magnitude of the harm, captures a fundamental distinction between types of deviant behavior (Robinson & Bennett, 1995). Recurrence refers to the dynamic character of the sabotage behavior, and visibility indicates whether management became aware of the sabotage or of the identity of the saboteur. Insidious sabotage, by definition, is minor, ongoing, and covert, whereas the more extreme form is major, one time, and overt.

We are able to assess some aspects of this model using data from our prior study of workplace sabotage (Ambrose et al., 2002) and supplementing it with additional data from the same source (Sprouse, 1992). We describe this study next.

AN EXPLORATORY STUDY OF THE CAUSES, MOTIVES, AND TYPES OF SABOTAGE

Method

Procedure

The 132 accounts of workplace sabotage described in the book *Sabotage in the American Workplace: Anecdotes of Dissatisfaction, Mischief, and Revenge* (Sprouse, 1992) provided the data for the study. These accounts are self-reports, typically 200 to 800 words in length, from individuals interviewed by Sprouse. To identify subjects he distributed fliers, placed ads in newspapers, and received referrals from friends and friends of friends. The sample, therefore, is one of convenience; it may not be representative of sabotage in general.

After initial training, three raters independently coded each account. The training used 10 of the 132 sabotage vignettes to clarify the construct definitions and the procedures (see Ambrose et al., 2002, for more detail). The raters then coded the remaining 122 vignettes on six dimensions:

1. The main cause or antecedent condition of the sabotage ($0 = $ no, $1 = $ yes for each cause: injustice, powerlessness, frustration, facilitation of work, boredom/fun, or other)
2. The affective state of the saboteur prior to the sabotage (1 to 5 scale, with 5 being positive)
3. The goal of the sabotage ($0 = $ instrumental, $1 = $ expressive)

4. The severity of the sabotage (based on the 8-point scale representing seriousness or harmfulness on the x-axis of Robinson and Bennett's (1995) Figure 1 (pp. 562–563)

5. Whether the target or management became aware of the sabotage (1 = yes, 2 = no, 3 = don't know/missing)

6. Whether the target or management became aware of the identity of the saboteur (1 = yes, 2 = no, 3 = don't know/missing)

To round out the data for the present study, the authors coded the 122 vignettes on an additional dimension: recurrence of the sabotage (0 = one time, 1 = ongoing).

We assessed interrater agreement with Cronbach's alpha for the two variables with interval scales (affect and severity) and with Rust and Cooil's (1994) proportional reduction in loss (PRL) coefficient for the remaining categorical variables. The reliabilities ranged from .70 to .99, indicating acceptable interrater agreement for each of the variables.

Results

We analyzed the results using either linear regression or logistic regression, depending on whether the dependent variable was interval (affect and severity) or categorical (cause, goal, identify sabotage, identify saboteur, and recurrence). All of the models were statistically significant ($p < .05$).

The Relationship Between Causes and Motives

First, we explored the effect of the antecedent conditions (injustice, powerlessness, frustration, facilitation of work, and boredom/fun) on the saboteur's motivation (affect and goal state). Initial analysis regressing affect on all five causes revealed significant multicollinearity, that is, variance inflation factors (VIFs) above 10 (Ryan, 1997) for the two central causes, injustice and powerlessness. Given the exploratory nature of this study, our solution was simply to assess the relationship between each of the causal condition variables and the two dimensions of motivation (affect and goal state) with a separate model.

The results indicated a significant relationship between three of the five causes (powerlessness, injustice, and boredom/fun) and the affect of the saboteur. Powerlessness and boredom/fun were associated with more posi-tive affect ($\beta = .22$, $p < .05$, and $\beta = .52$, $p < .01$, respectively), and injustice was associated with more negative affect ($\beta = -.47$, $p < .01$). Power and boredom/fun were also related to the goals of the saboteur. Power was associated with instrumental goals ($b = -2.19$, χ^2 (1) $= 13.07$, $p < .01$), and boredom/fun was associated with expressive goals ($b = 1.91$, χ^2 (1) $= 9.34$, $p < .01$). Cross-tabulations showed that 93% of the sabotage events caused by power led to instrumental goals, versus only 55% for the sabotage events caused by the other antecedents. Similarly, 77% of the sabotage events caused by boredom/fun led to expressive goals, versus only 33% for the other sabotage events.

The Relationship Between Motives and Types of Sabotage

Next, we explored the effect of the motivation of the saboteur, as character-ized by affect and goals, on our three dimensions of sabotage type: sever-ity, recurrence, and visibility. The results indicated a significant relationship between goal state and the severity of the sabotage ($\beta = .25$, $p < .01$), but not between affect and sabotage severity ($\beta = .09$, n.s.). Instrumental goals were associated with relatively minor forms of sabotage. Further, the results showed that affect and goal state were both related to sabotage recurrence ($b = .99$, χ^2 (1) $= 8.08$, $p < .01$, and $b = -1.57$, χ^2 (1) $= 12.93$, $p < .01$, respectively). Positive affect and instrumental aims were associated with ongoing forms of sabotage. Cross-tabulations showed that 84% of instrumental motives led to sabotage recurrence, versus only 52% for expressive motives. Last, the results indicated a significant relationship between the affect of the sabo-teur and both of our measures of visibility—management's awareness of the sabotage ($b = .65$, χ^2 (1) $= 4.34$, $p < .05$) and management's awareness of the identity of the saboteur ($b = 1.11$, χ^2 (1) $= 10.13$, $p < .01$)—but only a marginal relationship between goal state and management's awareness of the sabotage or saboteur ($b = -.74$, χ^2 (1) $= 2.72$, $p < .10$, and $b = -.75$, χ^2 (1) $= 2.72$, $p < .10$, respectively). Positive affect, and possibly instrumental goals, was associated with more covert acts of sabotage. Cross-tabulations showed that 51% of expressive goals led to management's awareness of the sabotage, versus 34% for instrumental goals. Similarly, 49% of expressive goals led to an aware-ness of the identity of the saboteur, versus 31% for instrumental goals.

Thus, in the main, the results supported our predictions. That is, insidi-ous sabotage appears to represent a distinct form of sabotage behavior, precipitated by powerlessness (as opposed to injustice) and motivated by positive affect and instrumental goals (rather than negative affect and expressive goals).

Limitations

Our unusual source of data poses some distinct limitations. Sprouse's (1992) sampling procedure and the self-report methodology may have biased the type of sabotage accounts that were collected and the information that they contained. He only sampled individuals who admitted to engaging in sabotage and who agreed to be interviewed; the accounts are purely retrospective, and they only reflect the saboteur's perspective of the events. The results need to be interpreted in light of these limitations. However, the likely direction of any potential bias is informative. The journalistic nature of Sprouse's collection suggests a bias in favor of extreme acts and exaggerated accounts of sabotage. Our data source is likely to have underrepresented the frequency of insidious sabotage, and it may have provided a conservative test of our model.

DISCUSSION

The purpose of this chapter has been to provide a more nuanced view of workplace sabotage. In particular, we have argued that sabotage can be insidious, in contrast to the more commonly held view of sabotage as an extreme act of deviance. We proposed a model explaining why sabotage occurs in the insidious versus the extreme form. We argued that causes such as injustice trigger the negative affect and expressive focus that leads to extreme acts of sabotage, whereas antecedents such as powerlessness trigger the relatively positive affect and instrumental focus that drives insidious sabotage. The results of our exploratory study generally supported this framework.

Our analysis and findings suggest some conclusions about the unique features of insidious sabotage. It revolves around issues of power and control, rather than justice. It is motivated by the instrumental goal of changing the work or the work situation to the advantage of the saboteur. But, more specifically, it seems to relate to situations framed as achieving gains, rather than as recouping losses. The fact that the concomitant affect is relatively positive (although this wasn't found to predict sabotage severity) implies that it is not a response to an aversive organizational experience. The insidious saboteur is seeking ways to make out, not get even.

This perspective on sabotage suggests that more attention needs to be given to the role of power and control in workplace deviance. Considerable work has examined the relationship between justice and deviance (e.g., Ambrose et al., 2002; Baron et al., 1999; DeMore et al., 1988; Greenberg, 1993; Skarlicki & Folger, 1997), but the topic of power and deviant behavior has been relatively neglected (see Allen & Greenberger, 1980, and Bennett, 1998, for notable exceptions). This difference in theoretical emphasis may reflect the fact that injustice is especially relevant to major forms of deviance (cf. Skarlicki & Folger, 1997), which, until recently, have been the focus of the deviance literature. But our work suggests that power, rather than justice, is central to insidious sabotage. If this generalizes to other types of insidious deviance, the development of this relatively new line of research requires a better understanding of the role of power and control in deviant behavior.

For example, our work suggests that it is important to distinguish between reactions to a loss of power and efforts to gain power. The existing literature on power and deviance is limited to the former type of "powerlessness" (e.g., Allen & Greenberger, 1980; Bennett, 1998), whereas we have found the latter type to be especially relevant to insidious sabotage. The difference may be related to what Higgins (1998, 2000) refers to as regulatory focus, that is, the ways that people approach goal attainment. Higgins distinguished between two fundamental orientations: a promotion focus, which is concerned with the presence or absence of positive outcomes; and a prevention focus, which is concerned with the presence or absence of negative outcomes. This distinction could prove useful in developing a better understanding of the role of power in deviant behavior. A prevention focus may contribute to relatively major types of deviance, whereas a promotion focus may result in more subtle acts.

Our treatment of insidious sabotage has important practical implications. The obvious suggestion is to empower employees or to enhance their sense of control as a way to prevent insidious types of sabotage. Empowerment may provide employees with the same sense of control that can be achieved through deviant means, but it is less damaging and costly to the organization because it limits the scope to legitimate outcomes (Bennett, 1998). In a study of empowerment and deviance, Bennett (1998) found that the introduction of empowered work teams at a shipping company's distribution center reduced various types of employee deviance, including the number of customer claims, warning letters, and grievances.

Our focus in this chapter has been on the antecedents of insidious sabotage—both its likely causes and the motives they elicit. Future research might examine how the consequences of insidious sabotage differ from those of extreme acts of sabotage. As we noted earlier in this chapter, the low-level (and often covert) nature of insidious sabotage makes it less likely to draw the attention of management. Thus, insidious saboteurs are more likely to continue their behavior unfettered. While it may be tempting to assume this low-level sabotage is harmless, we argue against such temptation. Although insidious sabotage might be less salient to organizations, the cumulative effect of the sabotage may have serious impact. Edwards and Scullion (1982), for example, have shown that workers' persistent, opportunistic efforts to modify the work process can erode product quality. Recognizing the full impact of insidious sabotage, though, requires properly accounting for the indirect and recurring nature of the accompanying costs.

Additionally, it is important to consider the effect of insidious sabotage not just on the organization, but on its members as well. A single, extreme act of sabotage is likely to be salient to both management and employees. Action is likely to be taken and the act will be labeled as aberrant and idiosyncratic. However, because insidious sabotage is subtle, recurring, and likely to be ignored by the organization, it is also likely to become acceptable within the work group. This acceptability may then gradually lower the normative threshold for workplace deviance of all forms. Much like incivility spirals (Andersson & Pearson, 1999; Pearson & Porath, 2004), insidious sabotage may spiral into more frequent and more serious forms of sabotage.

Despite its theoretical and practical significance, little attention has been given to insidious sabotage. We hope that by identifying this important phenomenon and providing a foundation for understanding the organizational dynamics associated with it, this chapter will provide a starting point for future research.

NOTE

A preliminary version of this chapter was presented at the 2000 meeting of the Academy of Management Meeting, Toronto, Ontario, Canada.

REFERENCES

Allen, V. L., & Greenberger, D. B. (1980). Destruction and perceived control. In A. Braun & J. E. Singer (Eds.), *Advances in environmental psychology* (Vol. 2, pp. 85–109). New York, NY: Academic.

Allred, K. G. (1999). Anger and retaliation: Toward an understanding of impassioned conflict in organizations. In R. J. Bies, R. J. Lewicki, & B. H. Sheppard (Eds.), *Research on negotiation in organizations* (Vol. 7, pp. 27–58). Greenwich, CT: JAI.

Ambrose, M. L, Seabright, M. A., & Schminke, M. (2002). Sabotage in the workplace: The role of organizational injustice. *Organizational Behavior and Human Decision Processes, 89,* 947–965.

Analoui, F. (1995). Workplace sabotage: Its styles, motives, and management. *Journal of Management Development, 14,* 48–65.

Andersson, L. M., & Pearson, C. M. (1999). Tit for tat? The spiraling effect of incivility in the workplace. *Academy of Management Review, 24,* 452–471.

Aquino, K., Tripp, T. M., & Bies, R. J. (2001). How employees respond to personal offense: The effects of blame attribution, victim status, and offender status on revenge and reconciliation in the workplace. *Journal of Applied Psychology, 86,* 52–59.

Baron, R. A., Neuman, J. H., & Geddes, D. (1999). Social and personal determinants of workplace aggression: Evidence for the impact of perceived injustice and the Type A behavior pattern. *Aggressive Behavior, 25,* 281–296.

Bennett, R. J. (1998). Perceived powerlessness as a cause of employee deviance. In R. W. Griffin, A. O'Leary-Kelly, & J. M. Collins (Eds.), *Dysfunctional behavior in organizations, Part A: Violent and deviant behavior* (pp. 221–239). Greenwich, CT: JAI.

Bensman, J., & Gerver, I. (1963). Crime and punishment in the factory: The function of deviancy in maintaining the social system. *American Sociological Review, 28,* 588–598.

Berkowitz, L. (1989). Frustration-aggression hypothesis: Examination and reformulation. *Psychological Bulletin, 106,* 59–73.

Berkowitz, L. (1998). Affective aggression: The role of stress, pain, and negative affect. In R. G. Geen & E. Donnerstein (Eds.), *Human aggression: Theories, research, and implications for social policy* (pp. 49–72). San Diego, CA: Academic.

Bolin, A., & Heatherly, L. (2001). Predictors of employee deviance: The relationship between bad attitudes and bad behavior. *Journal of Business and Psychology, 15,* 405–418.

Brown, G. (1977). *Sabotage: A study in industrial conflict.* Nottingham, England: Spokesman Books.

Brown, R., & Herrnstein, R. J. (1975). *Psychology.* Boston, MA: Little, Brown.

Chen, P. Y., & Spector, P. E. (1992). Relationships of work stressors with aggression, withdrawal, theft and substance use: An exploratory study. *Journal of Occupational and Organizational Psychology, 65,* 177–184.

Crino, M. D. (1994). Employee sabotage: A random or preventable phenomenon? *Journal of Managerial Issues, 6,* 311–330.

Crino, M. D., & Leap, T. L. (1989, May). What HR managers must know about employee sabotage. *Personnel, 5,* 31–38.

DeMore, S. W., Fisher, J. D., & Baron, R. M. (1988). The equity-control model as a predictor of vandalism among college students. *Journal of Applied Social Psychology, 18,* 80–91.

DiBattista, R. A. (1991). Creating new approaches to recognize and deter sabotage. *Public Personnel Management, 20,* 347–352.

DiBattista, R. A. (1996). Forecasting sabotage events in the workplace. *Public Personnel Management, 25,* 41–52.

Dubois, P. (1979). *Sabotage in industry.* Harmondsworth, England: Penguin.

Edwards, P. K., & Scullion, H. (1982). *The social organization of industrial conflict: Control and resistance in the workplace.* Oxford, England: Basil Blackwell.

Fox, S., Spector, P. E., & Miles, D. (2001). Counterproductive work behavior (CWB) in response to job stressors and organizational justice: Some mediator and moderator tests for autonomy and emotions. *Journal of Vocational Behavior, 59,* 291–309.

Giacalone, R. A., & Greenberg, J. (1997). *Antisocial behavior in organizations.* Thousand Oaks, CA: Sage.

Giacalone, R. A., Riordan, C. A., & Rosenfeld, P. (1997). Employee sabotage: Toward a practitioner-scholar understanding. In R. A. Giacalone & J. Greenberg (Eds.), *Antisocial behavior in organizations* (pp. 109–129). Thousand Oaks, CA: Sage.

Giacalone, R. A., & Rosenfeld, P. (1987). Reasons for employee sabotage in the workplace. *Journal of Business and Psychology, 1,* 367–378.

Graham, L. (1993). Inside a Japanese transplant: A critical perspective. *Work and Occupations, 20,* 147–173.

Greenberg, J. (1990). Employee theft as a reaction to underpayment inequity: The hidden cost of pay cuts. *Journal of Applied Psychology, 75,* 561–568.

Greenberg, J. (1993). Stealing in the name of justice: Informational and interpersonal moderators of theft reactions to underpayment inequity. *Organizational Behavior and Human Decision Processes, 54,* 81–103.

Greenberg, J. (1996, April). *What motivates employee theft? An experimental test of two explanations.* Paper presented at the annual meeting of the Society for Industrial-Organizational Psychology, San Diego, CA.

Greenberg, J., & Alge, B. J. (1998). Aggressive reactions to workplace injustice. In R. W. Griffin, A. O'Leary-Kelly, & J. M. Collins (Eds.), *Dysfunctional behavior in organizations, Part A: Violent and deviant behavior* (pp. 83–117). Greenwich, CT: JAI.

Harris, L. C., & Ogbonna, E. (2009). Service sabotage: The dark side of service dynamics. *Business Horizons, 52,* 325–335.

Higgins, E. T. (1998). Promotion and prevention: Regulatory focus as a motivational principle. In M. E. Zanna (Ed.), *Advances in experimental social psychology* (Vol. 30, pp. 1–46). New York, NY: Academic.

Higgins, E. T. (2000). Making a good decision: Value from fit. *American Psychologist, 55,* 1217–1230.

Hollinger, R., & Clark, J. (1982). Employee deviance: A response to the perceived quality of the work experience. *Work and Occupations, 9,* 97–114.

Jermier, J. M. (1988). Sabotage at work: The rational view. In S. B. Bachrach (Ed.), *Research in the sociology of organizations* (Vol. 6, pp. 101–134). Greenwich, CT: JAI.

Klein, R. L., Leong, G. B., & Silva, J. A. (1996). Employee sabotage in the workplace: A bio-psychosocial model. *Journal of Forensic Sciences, 41*, 52–55.

LaNuez, D., & Jermier, J. M. (1994). Sabotage by managers and technocrats: Neglected patterns of resistance at work. In J. M. Jermier, D. Knights, & W. R. Nord (Eds.), *Resistance and power in organizations* (pp. 219–251). London, England: Routledge.

Lee, K., & Allen, N. J. (2002). Organizational citizenship behavior and workplace deviance: The role of affect and cognitions. *Journal of Applied Psychology, 87*, 131–142.

Mangione, T. W., & Quinn, R. P. (1975). Job satisfaction, counterproductive behavior, and drug use at work. *Journal of Applied Psychology, 60*, 114–116.

Martinko, M. J., Gundlach, M. J., & Douglas, S. C. (2002). Toward an integrative theory of counterproductive work behavior: A causal reasoning perspective. *International Journal of Selection and Assessment, 10*, 36–50.

McLean Parks, J., & Kidder, D. L. (1994). "Till death do us part …": Changing work relationships in the 1990s. In C. L. Cooper & D. M. Rousseau (Eds.), *Trends in organizational behavior* (Vol. 1, pp. 111–136). New York, NY: Wiley.

Molstad, C. (1986). Choosing and coping with boring work. *Urban Life, 15*, 215–236.

Neuman, J. H., & Baron, R. A. (1998). Workplace violence and workplace aggression: Evidence concerning specific forms, potential causes, and preferred targets. *Journal of Management, 24*, 391–419.

O'Leary-Kelly, A. M., Griffin, R. W., & Glew, D. J. (1996). Organization-motivated aggression: A research framework. *Academy of Management Review, 21*, 225–253.

Pearson, C. M., & Porath, C. (2004). On incivility, its impact, and direction for future research. In R. W. Griffin & A. M. O'Leary-Kelly (Eds.), *The dark side of organizational behavior* (pp. 403–425). San Francisco, CA: Jossey-Bass.

Robinson, S. L., & Bennett, R. J. (1995). A typology of deviant workplace behaviors: A multidimensional scaling study. *Academy of Management Journal, 38*, 555–572.

Robinson, S. L., & Bennett, R. J. (1997). Workplace deviance: Its definition, its nature, and its causes. In R. J. Lewicki, R. J. Bies, & B. H. Sheppard (Eds.), *Research on negotiation in organizations* (Vol. 6, pp. 3–28). Greenwich, CT: JAI.

Robinson, S. L., & Greenberg, J. (1998). Employees behaving badly: Dimension, determinants and dilemmas in the study of workplace deviance. In C. L. Cooper & D. M. Rousseau (Eds.), *Trends in organizational behavior* (Vol. 5, pp. 1–30). New York, NY: Wiley.

Robinson, S. L., & O'Leary-Kelly, A. M. (1998). Monkey see, monkey do: The influence of work groups on the antisocial behavior of employees. *Academy of Management Journal, 41*, 658–672.

Rust, R. T., & Cooil, B. (1994). Reliability measures for qualitative data: Theory and implications. *Journal of Marketing Research, 31*, 1–14.

Ryan, T. P. (1997). *Modern regression methods.* New York, NY: Wiley.

Seabright, M. A., Ambrose, M. L., and Schminke, M. (2000, August). *Two images of workplace sabotage: Hot and cold deviance.* Paper presented at the annual meeting of the Academy of Management, Toronto, Ontario, Canada.

Sieh, E. W. (1987). Garment workers: Perceptions of inequity and employee theft. *British Journal of Criminology, 27*, 174–190.

Skarlicki, D. P., & Folger, R. (1997). Retaliation in the workplace: The roles of distributive, procedural, and interactional justice. *Journal of Applied Psychology, 82*, 434–443.

Skarlicki, D. P., van Jaarsveld, D. D., & Walker, D. D. (2008). Getting even for customer mistreatment: The role of moral identity in the relationship between customer interpersonal injustice and employee sabotage. *Journal of Applied Psychology, 93*, 1335–1347.

Spector, P. E. (1975). Relationships of organizational frustration with reported behavioral reactions of employees. *Journal of Applied Psychology, 60*, 635–637.

Spector, P. E. (1978). Organizational frustration: A model and review of the literature. *Personnel Psychology, 31*, 815–829.

Spector, P. E. (1997). The role of frustration in antisocial behavior at work. In R. A. Giacalone & J. Greenberg (Eds.), *Antisocial behavior in organizations* (pp. 1–17). Thousand Oaks, CA: Sage.

Sprouse, M. (1992). *Sabotage in the American workplace: Anecdotes of dissatisfaction, revenge, and mischief.* San Francisco, CA: Pressure Drop Press.

Storms, P. L., & Spector, P. E. (1987). Relationship of organizational frustration with reported behavioral reactions: The moderating effect of perceived control. *Journal of Occupational Psychology, 60,* 227–234.

Taylor, L., & Walton, P. (1971). Industrial sabotage: Motives and meanings. In S. Cohen (Ed.), *Images of deviance* (pp. 219–245). London, England: Penguin.

Thompson, W. E. (1983). Hanging tongues: A sociological encounter with the assembly line. *Qualitative Sociology, 6*, 215–237.

Tucker, J. (1993). Everyday forms of employee resistance. *Sociological Forum, 8*, 25–45.

Watson, B. (1971). Counter-planning on the shop floor. *Radical America, 5*(3), 77–85.

Weiss, H. M., & Cropanzano, R. (1996). Affective events theory: A theoretical discussion of the structure, causes, and consequences of affective experiences at work. In B. M. Staw & L. L. Cummings (Eds.), *Research in organizational behavior* (Vol. 18, pp. 1–74). Greenwich, CT: JAI.

Weiss, H. M., Suckow, K., & Cropanzano, R. (1999). Effects of justice conditions on discrete emotions. *Journal of Applied Psychology, 84*, 786–794.

Zabala, C. A. (1989). Sabotage at General Motors' Van Nuys assembly plant, 1975–83. *Industrial Relations Journal, 20*, 16–32.

4

Getting Even for Interpersonal Mistreatment in the Workplace: Triggers of Revenge Motives and Behavior

David A. Jones

For many people, the term *workplace revenge* conjures up images of industrial sabotage and of workers "going postal." Indeed, a growing number of researchers have sought to understand the more extreme forms of "misbehavior" in organizations (Vardi & Weitz, 2004), such as violence (Folger & Baron, 1996), theft (Greenberg, 1990a; Shapiro, Treviño, & Victor, 1995), vandalism (DeMore, Fisher, & Baron, 1988), and sabotage (Analoui, 1995). However, these highly dramatic behaviors represent only the tip of the iceberg and are relatively infrequent. Some of the less extreme forms of interpersonal behavior in the workplace that violate norms of social conduct are much more common (e.g., public humiliation, belittling comments; Baron & Neuman, 1996, 1998). Moreover, individuals who experience interpersonal mistreatment can experience an intense desire to strike back, and they often do.

Interpersonal mistreatment in the workplace is potentially costly and damaging to organizations and the individuals who work in them. For instance, victims[1] of bullying (Hoel, Rayner, & Cooper, 1999) and incivility (Lim & Cortina, 2005) in the workplace have been found to suffer detrimental psychological and physical health outcomes, such as depression, psychological strain, and psychosomatic symptoms (e.g., nausea). In turn, organizations incur the financial costs associated with turnover, decreases in productivity, and general withdrawal that results from these reactions (e.g., Cortina, Magley, Williams, & Langhout, 2001; Pearson, Andersson, & Porath, 2000). As chronicled in this book, researchers have turned to studying behaviors that, together, fall under the rubric of what Edwards and Greenberg (Chapter 1, present volume) dubbed insidious workplace behavior (IWB), which includes actions that are often perceived as an attack on a victim's dignity. Such transgressions are usually low in intensity, to the point of being subtle and covert, although sometimes they are blatantly hostile. The targets of IWB tend to experience interpersonal mistreatment on a frequent basis. Over time, I argue, the victims of IWB can reach a breaking point at which they respond by wanting to harm the transgressor.

In this chapter, I begin by distinguishing between revenge motives and behavior. In the second section, I present results from a descriptive study in which I examined revenge from the perspective of avengers— that is, individuals who claim to have engaged in revenge at work. I use these results to illustrate theoretical assertions developed in the remainder of the chapter. In the third section, I explore why some individuals experience IWB, yet neither experience a strong desire for revenge, nor strike back. Following this, I focus on how a history of being a target of IWB increases the likelihood that individuals make hostile attributions about subsequent mistreatment events, and I explain the role of such attributions in the revenge process. Subsequently, I present a framework specifying the characteristics of mistreatment events that act as breaking points for revenge—the point at which individuals switch from more passively tolerating mistreatment to having a deep-seated desire to harm the transgressor. Specifically, I argue that events that violate or threaten important psychological needs relating to the very reasons why people care about justice can trigger a desire for revenge. Through their revenge, individuals can potentially repair the needs that were damaged or threatened by the mistreatment. I conclude by exploring practical implications for managers.

DISTINGUISHING BETWEEN REVENGE MOTIVES AND REVENGE BEHAVIOR

In this chapter, I distinguish between the psychological desire for revenge (i.e., the revenge motive) and acts of revenge (i.e., revenge behavior). Here, I define each construct and discuss why this distinction is useful for understanding revenge processes over time.

Revenge Motives

Definitions of revenge (e.g., Stuckless & Goranson, 1992) state that an avenger's actions are motivated by a psychological desire to harm the transgressor deemed responsible for mistreatment—I refer to this desire as the *revenge motive*. Workplace fairness scholars argue that employees who perceive interpersonal treatment as disrespectful or unfair can experience feelings of anger that sometimes simmer until they explode into a deep-seated desire for revenge (Bies & Tripp, 1996; Folger & Skarlicki, 1998; McLean Parks, 1997; Sheppard, Lewicki, & Minton, 1992; Skarlicki & Folger, 1997). Likewise, researchers who study incivility (Andersson & Pearson, 1999) and insults (Gabriel, 1998) argue that such experiences motivate revenge. The relationship between perceived mistreatment and the revenge motive is explained by widely held norms of negative reciprocity—the endorsement of the eye-for-an-eye principle (e.g., Blau, 1964; Eisenberger, Lynch, Aselage, & Rohdieck, 2004). Indeed, individuals who feel mistreated often believe that getting even is morally justified (Tripp & Bies, 1997). Later in this chapter, I review more specific motives for revenge, such as identity restoration (Aquino & Douglas, 2003).

Revenge Behavior

Whereas the revenge motive refers to the psychological desire to inflict harm, revenge behavior refers to victims' actions that are intended to inflict harm in return for some perceived wrongdoing (Stuckless & Goranson, 1992). Aquino, Tripp, and Bies (2001) expand upon the notion of harm to include victims' intent to inflict damage, injury, discomfort, or punishment to the parties deemed responsible for the harming.[2]

I distinguish between revenge motives and revenge behavior for several reasons. First, victims of mistreatment may be motivated to seek revenge, but they do not do so because, for example, they lack sufficient opportunity (Jones, 2004). Moreover, motives for revenge can be fulfilled without retaliating, such as when justice is served through other means (e.g., through organizational mechanisms or the offender's self-punishment; see Tripp, Bies, & Aquino, 2007). Second, as I will illustrate later, a considerable amount of time may elapse between the desire for revenge and its behavioral enactment. Sometimes, as the saying goes, revenge is a dish best served cold. This notion highlights the possibility that revenge motives can be placated before they manifest themselves in behavior. Third, distinguishing between revenge motives and behavior provides conceptual clarity about the types of behavior that constitute revenge. In short, revenge behavior, or retaliation, refers to any behavior that is motivated by a desire to harm an individual, group, or other social entity in return for some perceived offense (Stuckless & Goranson, 1992).

When the desire-to-harm criterion for defining revenge is applied, the size of the research literature on workplace revenge is much smaller than it may appear. Although there are several theoretical perspectives pertaining to revenge in organizations (e.g., Allred, 1999; Andersson & Pearson, 1999; Folger & Skarlicki, 1998; McLean Parks, 1997; Tripp et al., 2007), data-driven research is scarce. For instance, researchers have used the term *retaliation* to explain relationships between perceived mistreatment and some type of antisocial or counterproductive behavior (e.g., Blader, Chang, & Tyler, 2001; Shaw, Wild, & Colquitt, 2003; Skarlicki & Folger, 1997; Townsend, Phillips, & Elkins, 2000), and researchers have found positive relationships between perceived mistreatment and responses that look and smell like revenge (e.g., vandalism; DeMore et al., 1988). However, although revenge motives may underlie some of these relationships, no evidence for underlying revenge motives was presented in these studies. Demonstrating evidence for underlying revenge motives is important because other competing mechanisms may explain these relationships (e.g., equity restoration without any intent to harm a transgressor[3]). In this chapter, I focus on the data-driven studies for which evidence for revenge motives was shown.

At least three kinds of evidence have been presented in research from which there is some basis for inferring that the workplace behaviors under examination were motivated by intentions to harm a transgressor. First, one study showed that attitudes toward revenge moderated the relationship between experiencing threats to one's identity and antisocial behavior, such that the relationship was stronger among people with more favorable attitudes toward revenge (Aquino & Douglas, 2003). This finding suggests that the antisocial behavior in this study was motivated, at least in part, by a desire for revenge. Similarly, Mitchell and Ambrose (2007) demonstrated evidence for underlying revenge motives by showing that negative reciprocity beliefs (see Eisenberger et al., 2004; Perugini, Gallucci, Presaghi, & Ercolani, 2003) moderated the relationship between abusive supervision and deviant behavior directed toward one's supervisor, such that this relationship was stronger among individuals who more strongly endorsed negative reciprocity norms.

Second, some researchers have measured revenge motives and behavior directly. Aquino et al. (2001), for example, found that blame attributions were related to revenge behavior. These authors measured revenge behavior using items that referred specifically to an intent to harm (e.g., "I tried to hurt them"; see also Aquino, Tripp, & Bies, 2006; Bradfield & Aquino, 1999). In Jones (2009) I measured desires for revenge using items reflecting retaliatory intentions and the expected utility of revenge—whether the benefits of revenge are worth the potential costs. Results showed that the relationship between perceived injustice from one's supervisor (i.e., interpersonal injustice) and counterproductive behavior directed toward that supervisor was partially mediated by desires for revenge against that same entity. Similarly, the relationship between perceived injustice from the organization (i.e., procedural injustice) and counterproductive behavior directed toward it was partially mediated by desires for revenge against the organization.

A third type of evidence for an underlying revenge motive comes from first-person accounts about revenge. Results from interview studies show that some individuals experience anger and claim to find ways to settle the score when they feel mistreated at work (Allred, 1995; Bies & Tripp, 1996; Tripp & Bies, 1997; Tripp, Bies, & Aquino, 2002, Study 1). Barclay, Skarlicki, and Pugh (2005) made use of both qualitative and quantitative data in their study of revenge: They administered surveys to measure various constructs and coded qualitative data from layoff victims who were asked about whether they did anything to get even (for a similar measurement approach, see Skarlicki, Barclay, & Pugh, 2008, Study 1). Barclay et al. (2005) found that perceived injustice related positively to emotions like anger and hostility, mediated by attributions of blame, and that blame attributions predicted the degree of retaliation, which ranged from no retaliation to major acts of revenge. Using yet another approach, Ambrose, Seabright, and Schminke (2002) analyzed a published collection of first-person accounts of workplace sabotage and found that responses to unfair treatment from organizational authorities were most often motivated by revenge.

In sum, these three forms of evidence show that some employees do engage in behavior to get their revenge for perceived mistreatment. As I discuss in this chapter, these studies also highlight the roles of anger and attributions of blame in the revenge process. Building upon this background, I now present the results from interviews I conducted among individuals who claimed to have engaged in revenge at work. As I will show, these interviews reveal that the avengers typically experienced repeated incidents of mistreatment before having any desire for revenge. About a year later, on average, these individuals were the victims of a single mistreatment event that triggered their desires, or motives, for revenge. These individuals then engaged in one or more acts of revenge, typically several weeks or months after the mistreatment event.

A STUDY OF FIRST-PERSON ACCOUNTS OF REVENGE IN THE WORKPLACE

Here, I describe analyses among a subsample from a study I conducted to describe workplace revenge from the perspectives of avengers. In so doing, I hope to pave the way for theory and research questions to be developed inductively.

A Focus on Avengers

I developed a structured interview using a modified grounded theory approach (Glasser & Strauss, 1967). Grounded theory involves the development of content categories while the researcher analyzes qualitative data. The method allows for the use of theory to develop categories and interpret the data, but the emphasis is on building theory through the analyses. In the modified approach used here, relatively greater emphasis was placed on existing theory to develop the initial questions and coding categories. The interview script was finalized after modifying the initial script based on prestudy interviews conducted with personal acquaintances.

Participants, whose characteristics are described later, were recruited through postings on Internet message boards and through snowball sampling. Participants were required to view a Web page describing the steps taken to maintain confidentiality and anonymity, and they provided their consent and phone number through e-mail. All records of names and phone numbers were destroyed after each interview. Interviews were conducted via telephone and ranged from 45 to 120 minutes. Participants' responses were typed as they spoke.

At the beginning of each interview, I defined revenge to participants in a manner that highlighted the intent-to-harm criterion. I provided examples of revenge behavior and emphasized that "for your actions to be considered as revenge, you must have wanted your actions to harm someone or something in the workplace." I then asked participants if they had a particular situation they wanted to discuss. Usable data were obtained from 30 individuals (out of 33) who told a story in which they characterized their behavior as motivated by revenge.

After participants told their stories I conducted the semistructured interview. In some cases, I asked follow-up questions to clarify responses or to seek additional information. In addition to the interview questions, I asked participants to provide ratings of several statements. For these statements, I defined the range of response options and read anchor descriptions.

Avengers Who Experienced a History of Insidious Workplace Behavior

All but one of the 30 participants described their revenge motive as a response to a single transgression that stood out in their minds. For 20 avengers, a single interpersonal offense triggered their revenge motives after a history of conflict with, or mistreatment from, the same transgressor. In the following, I describe in more detail how I identified these 20 individuals, who are the focus of the present chapter.

Mistreatment History

I asked participants to choose one of five options that best described the offense they experienced and the context in which it occurred. Among the 30 participants, 9 individuals selected "One major incident without much prior mistreatment or conflict," 14 selected "One major incident after minor mistreatment or conflict," 6 selected "One major incident after major mistreatment or conflict," 1 selected "Several major incidents and no single one stands out," and nobody selected "Other." Thus, 21 individuals (70%) claimed that there was a history of mistreatment or conflict before one or more major incidents occurred.

Mistreatment From an Interpersonal Source

Among the 21 individuals who experienced prior mistreatment, 20 experienced mistreatment from an interpersonal source, which was the same source whom they blamed for the subsequent mistreatment event that prompted their revenge motive. The exception was one individual who blamed the mistreatment event on the company rather than on a specific individual.

Among these 20 individuals, 70% blamed their immediate supervisors for the mistreatment event, including 4 individuals who blamed the owner of a small business who was also their supervisor. Among the remaining 6 individuals, 2 of them blamed a general manager, 1 person blamed a subordinate, 1 person blamed a supervisor of other individuals in the organization, 1 person blamed a head of human resources, and 1 person blamed a manager who created the schedule of work hours. Two individuals who blamed their supervisors placed additional blame on one of their coworkers for the mistreatment event.

Subsample Characteristics

Among the 20 avengers who are the focus of the present chapter, 13 were women (65%) and 7 were men (35%). Their education levels varied, including 30% who had an undergraduate degree and 45% who had some kind of postgraduate training. At the time of the mistreatment event, their mean age was 27.60 years, but this varied considerably ($SD = 9.10$ years) and was skewed toward older individuals. The median age was 29 years. At the time of the mistreatment event, participants were working in a variety of jobs and industries, including retail or sales (33%), professional or consulting (17%), service (12%), manufacturing or production (6%), government (6%), manual labor (6%), research (6%), education (6%), health care (6%), and other (6%).

At the time of the interview, most participants (90%) were employed with an average tenure of 21.42 months ($SD = 28.64$), ranging from 5 months to 10.5 years. On average, participants reported having 13.80 years ($SD = 10.93$) of lifetime work experience.

A Closer Look at the History of Mistreatment

Among the 20 participants, 70% characterized the prior mistreatment as minor and 30% characterized it as major. The perceived mistreatment occurred for as long as 9 years prior to the mistreatment event that the avengers described as the trigger of their revenge motives; the mean length of prior mistreatment was about 1 year (12.79 months, $SD = 24.93$). Over 70% of these individuals experienced prior mistreatment for one month or longer.

Because the study was not designed to assess IWB, I did not ask participants about the characteristics of the mistreatment history, other than about the information presented herein. Nonetheless, some individuals described the history of mistreatment while telling their revenge story prior to the semistructured interview. Next are two quotes that pertain to the history of IWB that occurred prior to the mistreatment event that prompted revenge motives and behavior. Other examples are provided throughout this chapter.

In the words of a 29-year-old social worker:

> That stands out as the time when I really was mad and that's what I responded to, but it is really just another example of the relationship. She was always quick to point out when I did something wrong and would be critical in an unnecessarily disrespectful way. A lot of it was subtle and this incident I spoke about made it obvious: She didn't care about me.

A 26-year-old university researcher stated:

> He was being very curt with me. I would hear back from his subordinates things that he would say about me. Insinuations about possible revenge against me and other little things. Then it progressed to the silent treatment. He spoke to another supervisor about me negatively. I felt unfairly treated. I was worried about the potential for him to take things further. I was frustrated at my inability to resolve the situation maturely. When the main thing happened, I felt vengeful. I wanted to hurt him.

As these two quotes suggest, the avengers in this study experienced interpersonal mistreatment before being the victims of an acute event that triggered their desires for revenge.

Mistreatment Events as Breaking Points: Triggers of Revenge Motives

Among the 20 participants, 19 claimed that a single mistreatment event stood out in their minds as the event that provoked their revenge motives. The remaining participant claimed to have experienced many major events but stated, "There was definitely a time, though, when it all became just too much. It was like it crossed a line." Participants explicitly talked about their revenge motives and behavior in causal terms, suggesting that their revenge was a response to a single mistreatment event.

During all interviews, I tried to summarize the nature of the mistreatment event to capture its essence until participants confirmed its accuracy. Some participants had already provided a succinct summary of the mistreatment event during their revenge story and I read it back to them to ensure accuracy. In other cases, I asked participants to describe the essence of the mistreatment or offense in a phrase or a few words.

Many of the mistreatment events were about issues relating to organizational justice. I draw upon the justice literature to interpret these results for several reasons. First, perceptions of injustice have been linked theoretically and empirically with other IWB constructs such as incivility (Andersson & Pearson, 1999) and abusive supervision (Zellars, Tepper, & Duffy, 2002). Second, some mistreatment events were largely unrelated to IWB but were captured well by justice constructs (e.g., procedural justice). Third, scholars have argued for the importance of using a justice framework to understand workplace revenge (e.g., Bies & Tripp, 2001; Skarlicki & Folger, 1997; Tripp et al., 2007). Fourth, individuals who engage in revenge often frame it in justice terms (Hogan & Emler, 1981) and rationalize their actions by invoking principles of justice (Bies & Tripp, 1996). The data supported this notion. Among the avengers discussed herein, the average rating of the unfairness of the mistreatment event was almost 8 on a 9-point scale ranging from 1 (*it had nothing to do with unfairness*) through 5 (*somewhat unfair*) to 9 (*extremely unfair*) ($M = 7.90$, $SD = 1.50$). Eighteen individuals (90%) responded to this item using 7 or higher, and they often used words like *unfair* to describe their experience (e.g., "I felt unfairly treated by my direct supervisor," "It was a fairness issue," and "It was unfair").

Table 4.1 summarizes the types of mistreatment events that triggered revenge motives. Fourteen of the mistreatment events (70%) specifically related to one of four types of justice recognized by fairness scholars (e.g., Colquitt, 2001). Specifically, six mistreatment events were about procedural justice (the perceived fairness of decision-making procedures; Lind & Tyler, 1988) and distributive justice (the perceived fairness of outcomes; Homans, 1961). One mistreatment event related to informational justice (Greenberg, 1993; Shapiro, Buttner, & Barry, 1994), and seven events related to interpersonal justice (Bies & Moag, 1986). Six other mistreatment events were not directly related to these justice constructs.

Revenge Behavior

Most participants did not engage in revenge immediately after the mistreatment event. There was an average of about 3 weeks between the mistreatment event and revenge behavior ($M = 22.21$ days, $SD = 50.08$).

TABLE 4.1

Frequency of Categories and Specific Types of Mistreatment
Events That Triggered Revenge Motives

Categories and Specific Types of Mistreatment Events	Number of Cases
Procedural and distributive injustice	6 (total)
Unfair termination	3
Unfair scheduling processes and decisions	2
Unfair denial of bonus pay	1
Interpersonal and informational injustice	8 (total)
Accusation indicating disrespect	2
Rudeness and disrespect	2
Inadequate explanation for missing pay	1
Disrespectful use of foul language	1
Disrespectful of victim's abilities	1
Lack of concern for victim's well-being	1
Other	6 (total)
Damage to victim's reputation	2
Mistreatment of a coworker	2
Sexual harassment	1
Failure to act on concern	1

Note: $N = 20$

Table 4.2 displays the various types of revenge behavior. Most revenge behaviors were targeted directly toward the perceived perpetrator of mistreatment (e.g., sabotaging the target's work or career, damaging the target's reputation). Some actions were not aimed directly at the perpetrator of mistreatment but were, according to the participants, intended to harm the transgressor (e.g., giving discounts to customers when the target was the owner of a small business). Thus, virtually all of the revenge behavior was targeted toward another individual, rather than reflecting displaced aggression (Dollard, Doob, Miller, Mowrer, & Sears, 1939).

The interviews showed that some individuals engaged in several different types of revenge behavior and engaged in revenge frequently over a considerable period of time. Five individuals engaged in a single act of revenge in response to the mistreatment event. However, among the remaining 15 avengers, the average number of separate revenge acts was 119.60 ($SD = 144.30$), ranging from 6 to 445 acts of revenge, and 12 of

TABLE 4.2

Frequency of Categories and Specific Types of Revenge Behavior

Categories and Specific Types of Revenge Behavior	Number of Cases	Percent of Cases
Harming a target's reputation and career	11 (total)	55% (total)
Bad-mouthing target's reputation to others in the industry	4	20%
Bad-mouthing target's reputation to coworkers	3	15%
Bad-mouthing target's reputation to customers	2	10%
Badmouthing target's reputation to someone with authority	2	10%
Other actions directed against a target	13 (total)	65% (total)
Sabotaging target's career	3	15%
Bad-mouthing to get target fired	1	5%
Telling target's manager to encourage punishment	2	10%
Sabotaging target's work	2	10%
Encouraging customers to file complaints about target	1	5%
Acting disrespectfully to target in front of others	1	5%
Encouraging others to undermine target's power	1	5%
Acting less unfriendly to target	1	5%
Withdrawing other work promised to the target	1	5%
Financial benefit to avenger	7 (total)	35% (total)
Stealing product or money—under $1000	5	25%
Stealing product or money—over $1000	1	5%
Lying about hours worked	1	5%
Withdrawal behavior	2 (total)	10% (total)
Taking long breaks	1	5%
Purposely wasting time	1	5%
Other actions	4 (total)	20% (total)
Giving unauthorized discounts to customers	1	5%
Making long-distance phone calls	1	5%
Quitting without giving notice during a busy time	2	10%

Note: $N = 20$.

these avengers engaged in multiple types of revenge. As implied by these numbers, some individuals engaged in revenge on a frequent basis. For instance, 5 individuals engaged in a specific type of revenge about once a week, 4 engaged in a type a few times a week, 3 engaged in a type every other day, 1 engaged in a type every day, and 1 individual engaged in a type of revenge more than once daily. For 10 different types of revenge, one or more people engaged in it 50 or more times (e.g., badmouthing the target's reputation to others in the industry), including 5 revenge behaviors that were performed by one or more people 150 or more times (e.g., giving unauthorized discounts to customers, sabotaging the target's work). On average, individuals engaged in revenge for about six months ($M = 179.20$ days) but sometimes much longer ($SD = 309.58$ days). Thus, most revenge responses were ongoing, rather than isolated occurrences.

Discussion of General Findings

These interview findings highlight the role of IWB in the revenge process. Although the findings are subject to various limitations inherent in interview data (e.g., socially desirable responding and fallible memories) and the sampling strategy (e.g., a self-selected sample that may not represent the population of avengers), some consistent and noteworthy themes were present, which I use to illustrate some of the theoretical assertions I develop later.

Among the full sample ($N = 30$), two-thirds were the target of ongoing interpersonal mistreatment that, presumably, chipped away at their dignity (i.e., IWB). In all of these cases, the avengers claimed their revenge motive began in earnest after a single mistreatment event that stood out in their minds. Much like the history of IWB experienced by the victims, often, the mistreatment events that led to revenge motives were about issues relating to being treated with a lack of dignity and respect. Most avengers responded to the mistreatment event not through a single retaliatory action but, rather, through performing a number of revenge behaviors over time. Thus, these data suggest that, at least for these avengers, revenge processes unfolded over time and in a manner that was not always described well by strict tit-for-tat exchanges (Andersson & Pearson, 1999). Rather than striking back each time they felt mistreated, on average these avengers experienced mistreatment or conflict for about a year without retaliating and, when they eventually did, they tended to engage in repeated acts of revenge. Thus, it seems there is something about particular mistreatment events that can trigger an intense desire for revenge that is often not fulfilled by a single retaliatory action.

In each of the next three parts of this chapter, I explore one of three general questions that pertain to these findings: (1) Why might people who demonstrate a willingness to engage in revenge refrain from revenge during a prior period in which they experienced interpersonal mistreatment?

(2) Is there something about a history of IWB that makes revenge in response to a single mistreatment event more likely? (3) What is it about particular mistreatment events that push individuals to want to harm someone despite having experienced prior mistreatment that did not lead to a strong desire for revenge? These three questions organize and guide my review of the literature on workplace revenge and my attempt to contribute to theory development.

EXPERIENCING INSIDIOUS WORKPLACE BEHAVIOR BUT REFRAINING FROM REVENGE

On average, participants in the interview study reported in this chapter experienced IWB for over a year before they experienced a single mistreatment event that prompted them to seek revenge. Given that reciprocal exchanges occur during conflict in organizations (Pearson et al., 2000), it is not surprising that these individuals eventually engaged in revenge. What is more interesting, from both theoretical and practical perspectives, is that these individuals experienced IWB for some time *without* engaging in revenge. Why might some individuals who eventually engage in revenge refrain from doing so during a significant period in which they felt mistreated? Bies and Tripp (1998; Tripp & Bies, 1997) suggest that some people refrain from revenge because they believe that the transgressor will nonetheless "get what's coming to them," they do not want to waste time and energy seeking revenge, or because they are unable to think of an appropriate response. I now discuss five additional possibilities.

Behavioral Control

Bies and Tipp (1998) reported that some individuals refrained from revenge because they did not believe there was good opportunity to strike back. In Jones (2004), I found empirical support for this notion. Specifically, a measure of perceived control (i.e., the perceived opportunity for revenge; e.g., "If I was mistreated by my immediate supervisor, there are many ways I could get back") accounted for a significant proportion of variance in counterproductive behavior beyond that of other predictors (e.g., demographics, perceived norms about revenge).

Fearing Negative Consequences

Perceived power differences between victims and transgressors may constrain victims' desires to get even because they fear negative repercussions and reprisal from transgressors (Bies & Tripp, 1998). Research shows that people are less willing to seek revenge against more powerful targets (Aquino et al., 2001). Consistent with this notion, all but one avenger from the interview study reported here experienced IWB from a higher ranking individual (e.g., an immediate supervisor or other manager), which is acknowledged to be a clear indicator of social status in organizations (Aquino & Douglas, 2003). Thus, these avengers may have been reluctant to strike back at those individuals who have control over valued outcomes (e.g., promotion opportunities, continued employment). For example, one avenger stated, "I knew I had to be careful because he was more powerful than me and could ruin my career." When asked about power differences, the average response among avengers was 7.48 ($SD = 2.44$) on a 9-point scale ranging from 1 (*the target of my revenge was less powerful than me*) through 5 (*... equal in power*) to 9 (*... much more powerful than me*). Thus, victims' desires to get even can be constrained when they are less powerful and they fear reprisal from transgressors.

Relationship Maintenance

People may also refrain from revenge behavior while suffering a history of IWB because they want to maintain positive working relationships with transgressors with whom they will continue to interact (Aquino, Grover, Goldman, & Folger, 2003) and they depend upon to conduct their work (Allred, 1999). As such, some people may seek reconciliation to maintain a relationship even while feeling resentment and anger toward a transgressor (Tripp et al., 2007). In the interview study reported here, the single participant in a managerial position stated, "I knew we had to work together. I thought I could turn it around and channel that energy." Seventy percent of the participants stated they intended to continue working in their organizations at the time of their revenge (which was, on average, about a year after the initial IWB). It appears, then, that most of the participants intended to remain in contact with the perpetrator of IWB and, therefore, might have refrained from exacting revenge to maintain positive and productive working relationships.

Forgiveness

Researchers have explored why some individuals refrain from retaliating in response to mistreatment, forgiving the transgressor instead (Aquino et al., 2001, 2003, 2006; Bies, Tripp, & Kramer, 1997; Bradfield & Aquino, 1999). Some of these studies show that people are more likely to forgive harm-doers when they hold the harm-doers less at blame for their mistreatment. As I will suggest shortly, it may often take repeated incidents of IWB before individuals begin to make strong attributions of malicious intent. Other theory and research suggests that forgiveness offers individuals a means of restoring a sense of justice, especially when they are less powerful and, therefore, more reluctant to engage in revenge (Bies & Tripp, 1996; Tripp et al., 2007).

Victims also may forgive transgressors for multiple acts of mistreatment particularly when those victims have higher propensities to forgive. In this connection, one study found that an agreeableness scale, which included a forgiveness facet, was negatively related to behaviors like theft and vandalism (Lee, Ashton, & de Vries, 2005). This suggests that forgiveness may represent a coping strategy that placates the desire for revenge (Aquino et al., 2001). Moreover, some individuals may prefer to forgive than to seek revenge because forgiveness is an easier, less effortful act.[4]

Impression Stability

Another possible reason why individuals experience IWB for some time without retaliating comes from a recent model that explains how perceptions of fairness change over time (Jones & Skarlicki, 2010). These writers argue that, once formed, perceptions of fairness about a social entity (e.g., a manager) are highly resistant to change. Their model predicts that a manager's behavior is often interpreted in keeping with the perceiver's prior impression of that manager, including when the manager's behavior is ambiguous (which is usually the case with respect to IWB; Andersson & Pearson, 1999; Vardi & Weitz, 2004). Experimental research has demonstrated such biased information processing effects on fairness judgments and revenge behavior (Jones & Skarlicki, 2005). This notion is also consistent with the tendency for some individuals who experience mistreatment to give perpetrators the benefit of the doubt (Bies & Tripp, 1996). Thus, when IWB is committed, victims interpret their mistreatment in keeping with their prior perceptions of the transgressors. If their prior perceptions are positive, or even slightly negative instead of blatantly hostile, they may conclude that the mistreatment is not aversive enough to warrant revenge.

Jones and Skarlicki (2010) propose that before established perceptions of fairness about an entity can change, individuals often must experience repeated examples of behavior that runs counter to their prior perceptions to reduce the certainty of those perceptions. Thus, among individuals who initially do not have highly negative perceptions of their managers, for example, repeated incidents of mistreatment may be necessary before victims switch from believing their managers are something other than very bad people to believing their managers are extremely unfair and exploitive. Such personalistic attributions for perceived mistreatment are a key component of the revenge process (e.g., Bies et al., 1997), which I discuss next.

HOW INSIDIOUS WORK BEHAVIOR FACILITATES HOSTILE ATTRIBUTIONS FOR MISTREATMENT EVENTS

Why might a history of IWB increase the likelihood that an acute mistreatment event triggers revenge motives? Some researchers suggest that acts of revenge tend not to be committed in response to isolated events, but rather, in response to a repeated pattern of prior mistreatment (Bies et al., 1997; Morrill, 1992). Among the 27 avengers I interviewed who blamed an individual for the mistreatment event, 74% (who comprised the subsample analyzed in the present chapter) claimed to have experienced a history of mistreatment by the same offender. This finding raises an interesting question that I explore next. Namely, why might a history of IWB create conditions in which a single interpersonal transgression provokes intense revenge motives?

The Limits of Forgiveness

Bradfield and Aquino (1999) note that revenge and forgiveness can be viewed as alternative coping strategies for dealing with interpersonal mistreatment. Forgiveness, however, has limits insofar as individuals who experience repeated mistreatment may find limited coping benefits in forgiveness when transgressors had repeatedly demonstrated their willingness to attack their dignity. Thus, individuals may seek revenge as a problem-focused strategy to cope with their subsequent mistreatment. For example, Table 4.2 shows that some avengers engage in actions that may deter future mistreatment (Carlsmith, Darley, & Robinson, 2002; e.g., telling the target's manager about the offense to encourage punishment) or that are intended to remove the transgressors from the work environment (e.g., bad-mouthing to get the target fired).

IWB and Hostile Attributions

Folger and Skarlicki (1998) argued that the mistreatment events relating to interpersonal insensitivity are particularly likely to lead to revenge (see also, Jones, 2009). It is easier for individuals to assign blame and intentionality for transgressions perpetrated by people, rather than by organizations or other group-level entities (Folger & Cropanzano, 1998, 2001). In this section, I review research and theory on the attributions individuals make for interpersonal mistreatment, and I argue that a history of experiencing IWB facilitates the ease with which individuals make hostile attributions for subsequent mistreatment events that are then seen as intentional and morally reprehensible.

Sense Making to Understand Mistreatment

Negative events that violate expectations and norms of social conduct trigger efforts to explain and understand why those events occurred (for a review, see Jones & Skarlicki, 2010). In particular, individuals who experience negative events are motivated to impute responsibility by assessing whether an actor (e.g., a supervisor) or external source is responsible for the event. In some cases, individuals attribute the event to mitigating circumstances (e.g., "She is just having a bad day"; Bies & Tripp, 1996), but if victims perceive that a transgressor's actions are intentional and within his or her control (e.g., Folger & Cropanzano, 1998), they hold the transgressor accountable and interpret his or her actions as a personal attack (Bies, 2001). Negative emotions become intensified when a transgressor is held accountable for mistreatment (Allred, 1999), especially morally reprehensible mistreatment, which motivates people to seek revenge (Bies & Tripp, 1996; Folger, Cropanzano, & Goldman, 2005).

Attributions in the Revenge Process

A few empirical studies demonstrate that attributions of blame play an important role in workplace revenge. Aquino et al. (2001), for example, found that blame attributions were related positively to revenge behavior. Bradfield and Aquino (1999) likewise found support for a model in which blame for interpersonal mistreatment was related to thoughts about revenge, which in turn, predicted revenge behavior. More recently, Barclay et al. (2005) found that the relationship between perceptions of unfairness and emotions like anger and hostility were mediated by attributions of blame, and that the relationship between blame and retaliation was mediated by anger and hostility.

Researchers using qualitative methodologies also have concluded that attributions of blame and malicious intent are associated with revenge motives and behavior. For example, people who experience negative interpersonal treatment tend to make overly personalistic attributions (Bies & Tripp, 1996; Bies et al., 1997). This is in keeping with the so-called sinister attribution error (Kramer, 1994) in which people are inclined to attribute malicious intent to those who have mistreated them.

Taken together, this shows that attributions of blame and sinister intent play an important role in the revenge process. Beyond this, however, scholars have discussed the specific processes through which these attributions are made. Folger and his associates have offered a conceptualization of attribution-like processes in response to perceived injustice that, I suggest, can be applied to interpersonal mistreatment more broadly. Specifically, fairness theory (Folger & Cropanzano, 1998, 2001; Folger et al., 2005) proposes that when individuals experience a potentially aversive event, such as interpersonal mistreatment, they seek answers to three fundamental questions:

1. *Would* an alternative event have felt better (i.e., was the event injurious)?
2. *Could* the agent have acted differently (i.e., did the agent act with intent)?
3. *Should* the agent have acted differently (i.e., did the event violate norms for moral conduct)?

Folger and Cropanzano (1998, 2001) propose that individuals make these judgments through a process of counterfactual thinking in which they engage in mental simulations comparing the mistreatment to imagined alternatives to determine whether some other treatment would have felt better, and could and should have resulted instead. For instance, individuals might compare the injurious interpersonal treatment they experienced to more favorable treatment from another manager and conclude that the offender could have acted differently. Likewise, individuals also might compare the mistreatment they encountered to normative codes of social conduct and conclude that the transgressor should have acted differently, yet chose otherwise. When an individual believes that an agent could and should have refrained from interpersonal mistreatment, anger and resentment result, as well as a desire for revenge. Folger and Skarlicki (1998) emphasized that it is not the degree of experienced harm on its own that motivates punishment of a transgressor, but the belief that the transgressor's actions are intentional and morally repugnant.

IWB and Hostile Attributions of Mistreatment Events

Earlier, I asserted that a history of being a target of IWB facilitates attributions of hostile intent of a subsequent mistreatment event. At the heart of this assertion is a temporal dynamic that may best be understood through a theoretical lens that accounts for perceptions of mistreatment over time. Earlier, I introduced such a model (Jones & Skarlicki, 2010) that delineates how individuals' perceptions of *entity* fairness (e.g., "My supervisor is not entirely fair and trustworthy") can color their interpretations of *events* relating to fair and unfair treatment (e.g., "The way my supervisor behaved was disrespectful"). To the extent that a history of IWB influences the certainty of a negative perception of the transgressor, this perception may bias a victim's interpretations of subsequent events, thereby making attributions of hostile intent more likely.

According to Jones and Skarlicki (2010), employees are highly motivated to make sense of unexpected events relating to fair and unfair treatment in the workplace. In response to expectancy-violating events that are unfavorable, individuals engage in counterfactual thinking to make judgments about controllability and moral culpability (Folger & Cropanzano, 1998), as well as other sense-making activities that facilitate these judgments. Couched in these terms, victims may interpret a history of IWB as evidence that the mistreatment event was controllable (as opposed to a one-time event that may be attributed to external causes) and immoral (because the transgressor demonstrated repeated willingness to violate established norms of moral conduct).

I noted that an actor's intent underlying interpersonal mistreatment is often ambiguous (e.g., Andersson & Pearson, 1999; Bies et al., 1997).

I argue that a history of IWB reduces this ambiguity when individuals interpret subsequent events. Specifically, when individuals experience a more serious mistreatment event, the history of IWB affects attributions of controllability and moral culpability. In other words, repeated experiences with IWB increases the likelihood individuals assume unprincipled acts are due to malicious intent, whereas in the absence of an IWB history, such intent cannot be readily assumed.

In this connection, consider the following quote from the interviews examined herein in which a 29-year-old sales person's request for time off was declined by a manager responsible for scheduling. This avenger concluded that the transgressor was motivated by malicious intent, which I suggest was facilitated by the history of IWB.

> We had a waiting list for days off. First come, first served type of thing. Somehow I got the shaft. I got the good impression that she did it knowing I wanted to go. She never told me I couldn't go until two days beforehand. She had a vendetta against me.

Other avengers made personalistic attributions for the mistreatment event in the same breath with which they mentioned a history of IWB. One 35-year-old manager stated:

> Before this happened, she did a lot of other things. She would make weekly requests for unreasonable stuff that I couldn't do. She propped me up for difficult positions that couldn't happen, then held me to failure. She was always talking about me to others. She was evil, difficult, manipulative, and backstabbing. She was a saboteur. I wanted bad things to happen to her.

One final example is significant because the avenger tied personalistic attributions to the IWB history that precipitated the mistreatment event. In response to receiving demeaning treatment in front of other coworkers, this 27-year-old power line technician stole $6,000 from the owner of the business and destroyed important paper work.

> He treated all of us with absolutely no respect. One day someone was complaining and he said, "Oh you guys don't know how easy you have it. Monkeys could do this job." This guy was verbally aggressive to his employees and unfair in many ways. When he humiliated me in front of everyone, it enraged me that he could be such an ignorant, nonunderstanding, pigheaded a**hole. Low-down, dirty, rotten pr**k.

These quotes illustrate that revenge in response to a single mistreatment event often occurred after a history of IWB, which likely facilitated personalistic attributions and beliefs about malicious intent. These findings also suggest that, rather than viewing a revenge episode as beginning with a triggering event (e.g., Andersson & Pearson, 1999), researchers should expand the scope of revenge episodes to include the potential history of perceived mistreatment that may affect underlying attributions of transgressors' motivation for subsequent events.

MISTREATMENT EVENTS AS BREAKING POINTS: TRIGGERS OF REVENGE

What characteristics of mistreatment events incite individuals to engage in revenge? On average, the avengers in the interview study presented in this chapter experienced IWB for about a year before experiencing a single mistreatment event, which, according to them, spawned their first earnest desires for revenge. Building on this, I now address a key question: What is it about particular mistreatment events that trigger a revenge motive?

Breaking Points for Revenge Motives

Theory suggests that interpersonal mistreatment in the workplace can lead to a tipping point (Andersson & Pearson, 1999) at which victims decide to strike back (Folger & Skarlicki, 1998; Kinney, 1995; Morrill, 1992). Indeed, some of the previously presented quotes from the interviews I conducted illustrate how a single act of mistreatment was, in the avengers' minds, the breaking point that triggered their revenge motive. Other quotes from the avengers I interviewed further illustrate this breaking point phenomenon: "There was already tension before that. This was the straw that broke the camel's back," "I was completely disillusioned and it took that one thing to set me off," "That's when I started acting back. Up until then it was only little things," "That was the one event that drew the line in the sand," and "But this was the one thing that triggered everything."

To describe this breaking point phenomenon, Andersson and Pearson (1999) used a metaphor: The point at which heat turns water into steam. Folger and Skarlicki (1998) used a different metaphor: The point at which heat causes a kernel of corn to pop. These metaphors are informative because they point to three characteristics of the revenge process.

1. Heat is an important part of these metaphorical processes, much like anger is an important part of the breaking point for revenge (e.g., Allred, 1999).
2. Like the fundamental shift from water to steam, or from a corn kernel to popcorn, the breaking point represents a fundamental shift from accepting mistreatment passively to having an active desire to strike back.
3. Although a physicist could determine the conditions under which both phenomena occur, it would be difficult for a casual observer to predict the precise point at which water changes to steam, or a kernel changes to popcorn—the scientific understanding of workplace revenge is currently somewhere between the metaphorical physicist and the casual observer.

Although researchers understand some factors that relate to the breaking point, they are unable to predict it with precision. Now, I review theory and research bearing on the breaking point and add to these ideas to help move researchers toward the physicist end of the metaphorical continuum.

Blame and Anger in the Triggering Process

Earlier I reviewed research and theory demonstrating that attributions of blame and hostile intent are important determinants of how revenge motives are triggered (e.g., Barclay et al., 2005; Bies et al., 1997; Bradfield & Aquino, 1999; Folger & Skarlicki, 1998). Among the avengers discussed in this chapter, the average rating of how certain they were about who was to blame for the mistreatment event was high—an 8.05 (SD = 1.70) on a 9-point scale.

Anger in response to blame also plays a key role in revenge (Allred, 1999; Barclay et al., 2005; Bies & Tripp, 1996; Folger & Skarlicki, 1998). The important role of anger in revenge is reflected in the data analyzed in this chapter: the average rating of anger at the time of the mistreatment event was 7.80 (SD = 1.03) on a scale ranging from 1 (*not angry at all*) through 5 (*somewhat angry*) to 9 (*very angry*). Before individuals were asked to rate their anger, they were asked to describe their emotions at the time of the offense. Fifteen individuals (75%) explicitly stated anger or angry and the remaining five mentioned related emotions (e.g., upset). A key question, however, is: About precisely what are avengers angry? That is, what is it about some offenses that compel people to seek revenge? To address this question I present a framework based largely on Cropanzano, Byrne, Bobocel, and Rupp's (2001) multiple-needs model of justice and its application to changes in fairness perceptions (Jones & Skarlicki, 2010).

A Multiple-Needs Approach to Understanding Triggers of Revenge

Jones and Skarlicki (2010) propose that perceptions about whether someone is a fair or unfair person can change when that person behaves in a highly unexpected way, which prompts individuals to engage in sense making to understand the unexpected behavior. In the context of how revenge motives are triggered, the relevant perception change involves shifting from a positive perception to a highly negative one, or shifting from a negative perception to an extremely negative one. Given that attributions of blame and malicious intent play a key role in the revenge process, a shift from any previous perception to believing that a person is highly exploitive, malicious, or even evil, may be predictive of the breaking point at which victims want to retaliate.

Jones and Skarlicki (2010) assert that fairness perceptions are most likely to change in response to events that *violate expectations* of interpersonal conduct in contexts that are highly *important* to people. Two aspects of this assertion are worthy of further comment: the roles of unexpected behavior and event importance in perception change processes. The first aspect is that a perception that a person is fair can change through processes triggered by behavior that *shockingly* violates the perceiver's preexisting perceptions. Indeed, violated expectations for fair treatment can lead to revenge (Jones & Skarlicki, 2005). Among the avengers I interviewed, when asked to describe their emotions at the time of the major offense, several individuals referred to some degree of surprise (e.g., confused, betrayed, disappointed, and surprised; see also Bies & Tripp, 2002). Behavior that is shockingly reprehensible can lead individuals to conclude that the transgressor is an inherently "bad" person who deserves to be punished.

The opening assertion in the preceding paragraph also highlighted the role of *event importance* in perception-change processes. Perceptions of fairness are more likely to change to the extent that expectancy-violating events are perceived as important (Jones & Skarlicki, 2010). Drawing upon Cropanzano et al.'s (2001) multiple-needs model, which is described next, Jones and Skarlicki (2010) suggest that events—mistreatment events in the context of this chapter—are important to the extent they violate or threaten people's core psychological needs, which makes salient the very reasons why people care about justice.

The Multiple-Needs Model

Williams (1997) developed a multiple-needs model to understand social ostracism, proposing that four fundamental needs underlie most social behavior. Applying this model to organizational justice, Cropanzano et al. (2001) linked these needs to three models that explain why justice matters to people: the instrumental, relational, and moral virtues models.

The first need discussed by Williams (1997), the need for *control*, relates to the desire to predict and manage social interactions. Cropanzano et al. (2001) linked the control need to the instrumental model of justice (Tyler, 1987), noting that justice is important to people because, in the long run, it affects self-interest over which people desire control. The need to *belong* relates to the desire to form meaningful interpersonal relationships. Cropanzano et al. (2001) linked belonging needs to the relational model of justice (Tyler & Lind, 1992), which specifies that justice is important to people because it sends messages about their worth and standing within groups. Cropanzano et al. (2001) also linked the relational justice model to the need for *self-esteem*—the desire to hold oneself in positive regard—given that justice communicates information about group standing thereby affecting self-esteem (Tyler & Lind, 1992). Finally, the need for *meaningful existence* refers to the need for individuals to find meaning in their lives and feel a sense of worth. Cropanzano et al. (2001) noted that the search for personal meaning includes *moral purpose* (Becker, 1973), which is the term I will use for this need. Cropanzano et al. (2001) linked the need for moral purpose to the moral virtues, or deontic, model (Folger et al., 2005), which emphasizes that people care about justice because it relates to widely shared beliefs about the moral obligation to treat others with dignity and respect. Hereafter, I use the term *justice motives* when referring to reasons why justice matters and, hence, the reasons why people are motivated to respond to injustice (e.g., relational justice motives, deontic justice motives).

Based on the multiple-needs model (Cropanzano et al., 2001) and its application to perception-change processes (Jones & Skarlicki, 2010), I suggest that the extent to which a mistreatment event violates or threatens core psychological needs and arouses the associated justice motives will determine the likelihood the event will act as a breaking point—a fundamental shift in how individuals perceive and react to a transgressor. Through this perception-change process, the transgressor is transformed into a malicious person who deserves to be punished. Viewing offenders in this way frees victims from the moral chains that may otherwise prevent them from striking back. Moreover, through their revenge, individuals can attempt to repair damaged needs and address the justice concerns aroused by the offense.

Reconciling the Multiple-Needs Model With the Interview Findings

Cropanzano et al. (2001) noted that the four psychological needs and their associated justice motives are often interrelated. For example, an individual who experiences belittling treatment from a supervisor in front of his or her coworkers might experience intense feelings of injustice because the supervisor's behavior in this example affects multiple needs and arouses multiple justice motives. Specifically, the supervisor's behavior may (1) threaten belonging and self-esteem needs, arousing relational justice motives; (2) be perceived as morally reprehensible, affecting the need for moral purpose and arousing deontic justice motives; and (3) threaten the victim's tangible self-interest if the treatment is believed to be indicative of future exploitation by the supervisor, thereby affecting the need for control and arousing instrumental justice motives.

My subjective interpretations of some avengers' statements from the interview data suggest that the multiple-needs framework (Cropanzano et al., 2001) is useful for identifying triggers of revenge motives. However, my analyses suggest the correspondence between psychological needs and justice motives may not be as straightforward as Cropanzano et al. (2001) suggest. This is understandable given that, as Cropanzano et al. (2001) recognize, needs and associated justice motives are highly interrelated, as illustrated by the example in the preceding paragraph. Moreover, there is no reason to believe the statements by avengers reflect all of their needs and motives affected by mistreatment events. In the following sections, I use quotes from the interview study to illustrate how this multiple-needs perspective is useful for understanding the characteristics of events that trigger revenge motives.

Events That Threaten Control Needs as Triggers of Revenge

In this section, I examine how events that violate or threaten control needs and that arouse instrumental and other motives (e.g., power restoration) can propel people to seek revenge to address the affected needs or satisfy the associated motive.

Control Needs and Instrumental Motives

Some mistreatment events arouse instrumental justice motives because the events affect individuals' tangible self-interests (e.g., unfair performance appraisal systems that affect compensation). Such events may be taken as indicative of future unfairness, thereby creating uncertainty and a lack of control over the attainment of important outcomes (e.g., pay or promotion). In response, individuals may engage in revenge in their attempts to restore perceptions of control (Bies et al., 1997). This is in keeping with the classic frustration–aggression hypothesis, which long has been accepted by psychologists (Dollard et al., 1939).[5] Among the avengers I interviewed, four of them mentioned frustration when asked about their emotions in response to the offense that triggered their revenge motives. Research has shown that frustration resulting from the interruption of goal pursuit is associated with counterproductive workplace behavior (e.g., Fox & Spector, 1999), which may to some extent reflect motives for revenge among individuals who wish to regain psychological control.

A second way in which revenge can address threats to the need for control and instrumental justice motives is through deterrence. Some avengers view their revenge as legitimate responses that defend their self-interests (Bies & Tripp, 1998). Some retaliatory actions protect individuals' future self-interests (economic or otherwise) by deterring future mistreatment (Carlsmith et al., 2002) or by removing the transgressor from the work environment entirely. In the interview data, three individuals stated they engaged in revenge, at least in part, with the hope of removing the transgressor from the work environment by getting him or her fired.

The aforementioned mechanisms described may explain why certain events are associated with revenge. Specifically, Bies and Tripp (1996) suggested that violations of an organization's formal rules can motivate revenge. I suggest here that underlying this observation is a process through which individuals seek revenge to regain control and address instrumental justice motives through deterrence or the prevention of future mistreatment. Consider the following quote from a 28-year-old real estate agent:

> She offered me a bonus program, and I did what she asked to qualify for it. She forgot to clear it in advance with the head office and I didn't receive it. She did other stuff before that, but when she messed with my pay … So I sabotaged her job with the company and it worked. I knew that I could benefit myself if she was out of the way, but I also wanted to get back at her in a bad way.

Control Needs and Power Restoration Motives

In addition to the link between the need for control and instrumental motives (Cropanzano et al., 2001), events that violate the need for control may instigate related power restoration motives. Victims of mistreatment often report feelings of helplessness and paralysis (Bies & Tripp, 2005) and research suggests that retaliation is mitigated when other opportunities for power restoration are present (Cropanzano & Baron, 1991). Moreover, people are especially likely to seek revenge against more powerful targets when they believe that formal mechanisms in the organization are incapable of punishing wrongdoers (Aquino et al., 2006; Tripp et al., 2007), suggesting that people seek control and power through revenge when they believe justice will not be served through other means.

Relating to power restoration motives, when asked what he or she had hoped to achieve through revenge, one avenger from the interview study responded with "to gain power." In describing his revenge motive, another avenger stated, "I felt I couldn't be complete until I had done this; until I had made him feel somewhat along the lines of how bad he made me feel." Another avenger responded to the question, "How did you feel after the revenge?" by saying, "More powerful."

Links Between Control Needs and Other Needs and Motives

Events that attack individuals' power and status are thought to motivate revenge (Bies & Tripp, 1996), particularly among victims who perceive they have less status than the transgressor (Bies et al., 1997). Thus, among people for whom power and status are central to their identities, events that threaten their power and status may violate self-esteem and belonging needs, and arouse relational justice motives.

Several avengers from the interview study made comments in which the roles of control and self-esteem needs, and relational and power restoration motives, were apparent. For example, a 21-year-old sales person seemed to relate the needs for control and self-esteem to the motive to restore a sense of power through revenge.

> He made me feel humiliated. It would be nice to make him feel the same way without causing him too much suffering. Just like a flawless victory. Doing something that screws him. Something where I'm the obvious victor.

Other accounts from avengers demonstrated that they viewed revenge as the only means available to restore a sense of control about their reputation or status. For example, comments from a 35-year-old head of a public relations department (quoted earlier) appeared to be motivated to seek revenge to protect his or her reputation among other group members.

> I tried to exhaust the official means, but because she was a union employee I couldn't do anything. I felt like a lame duck. She could persecute and ruin my reputation and I couldn't do anything about it. My only recourse was truly childish by getting back at her and retaliating ... I told select people things that I knew would bury her. My retaliation was strategic.

The preceding quotes illustrate my assertion that mistreatment events that affect individuals' control needs and that arouse instrumental and power restoration motives can trigger desires for revenge. Some quotes suggested that events that violate control needs can simultaneously relate to self-esteem needs and relational justice motives, which I focus on next.

Events That Threaten Belonging and Self-Esteem Needs as Triggers of Revenge

A well-established trigger for revenge is an attack on an individual's identity—an event that damages his or her self-esteem and perceived standing within a group. Such events arouse relational justice motives because people are motivated to maintain positive self-images and favorable social identities

(Tyler & Lind, 1992). Aquino and Douglas (2003) argued that when an event threatens an individual's identity, he or she is motivated to defend against the threat. Retaliation can restore individuals' self-esteem and status within groups that may have been damaged by mistreatment (Bies & Tripp, 1996; Bies et al., 1997; Tripp & Bies, 1997). Moreover, when individuals experience an attack on their identities, it grants them victim status (Andersson & Pearson, 1999), offering justification for their revenge motives and behavior. Striking back in response to an attack on one's self-worth also helps save face (Pearson et al., 2000) and can fortify an individual's identity as a person who will not tolerate mistreatment (Tedeschi & Nesler, 1993). Consistent with these arguments, identity threats have been found to predict antisocial behavior (e.g., "Saying or doing something to purposely hurt other coworkers while at work"), especially among lower status employees (Aquino & Douglas, 2003). As I show next, findings from the interview study appear to reflect these points.

Self-Esteem Needs and Relational Motives

Events that violate belonging needs may often threaten an individual's sense of worth and standing within a group, thereby also violating self-esteem needs. When I asked the 20 avengers to describe their emotions at the time of the mistreatment event, 6 individuals mentioned emotions that were related to self-esteem: 2 stated humiliated, 1 stated embarrassed, and 3 stated hurt or damaged self-esteem. On a scale from 1 (*not humiliated at all*) to 5 (*moderately humiliated*) to 9 (*extremely humiliated*), the mean rating of humiliation in response to the mistreatment event was 4.63. However, there was considerable variability ($SD = 3.21$), with 50% of the avengers rating the item as moderately humiliated or higher.

Belonging and Self-Esteem Needs and Relational Motives

The avengers I interviewed described several mistreatment events that appeared to violate their need to belong thereby arousing relational justice motives. These mistreatment events included attacks on individuals' perceived worth and status, public ridicule, and reputation damage. Some individuals might retaliate in response to such events through actions intended to lower the transgressor's reputation within a group to restore a sense of justice (McLean Parks, 1997). Reflecting this, one avenger I interviewed stated, "I just wanted to damage his reputation like he damaged mine."

Public ridicule and humiliation can provoke revenge (Morrill, 1992) and this was evident in some of the mistreatment events described by the avengers from the interview study. A 27-year-old power line technician who was quoted earlier stated:

> I felt like punching him in the face. He humiliated me in front of the guys. That was the worst thing. He was disrespectful to everyone but he never really singled anyone out like he did to me that time.

In one case, a 55-year-old nurse interpreted the mistreatment event as an attack on his or her worth as an employee. This individual's revenge behavior resulted in the termination of the transgressor's employment contract thereby potentially raising the status of the victim whose job responsibilities increased as a result. This individual stated:

> I basically felt that my talents were being wasted. I can still see that little a**hole's face with his legs crossed, saying "I just don't think a nurse can give an injection." It was so disrespectful. He didn't respect me professionally.

The preceding quotes suggest that mistreatment events that violate belonging and self-esteem needs and that arouse relational justice motives are powerful triggers of revenge. In the next section, I explore how a fourth need—the need for moral purpose—and the associated deontic justice motive might also be a powerful trigger of the desire for revenge.

Events That Threaten the Need for Moral Purpose as Triggers of Revenge

Some individuals view revenge as a moral imperative—that is, revenge rights a wrong (Bies & Tripp, 1996; McLean Parks, 1997; Tripp & Bies, 1997). Retaliating also might help people maintain their beliefs in a just world (Lerner, 1980) by causing something "bad" to happen to a "bad" person (Bies et al., 1997). Indeed, people punish harm-doers because they want them to suffer, not merely to deter them from committing harmful acts in the future (Carlsmith et al., 2002).

Folger and Skarlicki (1998) discussed the so-called social covenant: People deserve to be treated with respect and dignity, and violating this covenant is the "ultimate universal affront" (p. 69). These authors used the term *moralistic aggression* to describe the tendency for avengers to feel morally justified and to believe that it is socially acceptable to right a wrong by punishing transgressors. Other scholars have discussed the *deontic response*: Violations of moral principles are met with strong emotional responses, and revenge is an end in itself because harm-doers who are guilty of moral misconduct should be punished (Folger et al., 2005). Indeed, interview studies have shown that people often justify their acts of revenge on moral grounds (Bies & Tripp, 1996; Tripp & Bies, 1997).

Moral Purpose Needs and Deontic Motives

The findings from the interview study are consistent with these morality-based perspectives. The avengers were asked if their revenge was justified and responded on a scale ranging from 1 (*not justified*) to 5 (*moderately justified*) to 9 (*very justified*). The mean rating was 6.58 ($SD = 2.67$). Seventy-five percent of the avengers responded using 5 or higher and 50% responded using 8 or 9. When asked how they felt after their revenge, three individuals said "justified" and two said "vindicated." A clear example of a mistreatment event that represented a moral violation that triggered revenge motives involved a case of sexual harassment. This 29-year-old veterinary clinic employee stated:

> After I fumed and thought about it, I thought "screw them, I don't care any more." I never felt guilty. I thought, "Ha ha, I'm getting my revenge." I'm making them lose money. They don't deserve [to make money] because they are bad people. I felt very justified.

Moral Purpose Needs and Prosocial Motives

Interview studies have shown that some individuals' acts of revenge are simultaneously prosocially motivated (Bies & Tripp, 1996; Tripp & Bies, 1997). In the data analyzed in the present chapter, several avengers claimed their intent to harm the transgressors was also motivated by prosocial concerns about helping other people or their organization. During the interviews, I asked the avengers to describe potential motives for their behavior other than their intent to harm. Consistent with the notion that revenge acts can at once be intended to harm the transgressor and to stop perceived wrongdoing (Miceli & Near, 1997), five individuals stated they also wanted to prevent the abuse of others and three individuals also wanted to change the work environment to make it more positive for everyone. Next, I provide a few illustrative quotes from these avengers.

Some acts of revenge were done, in part, to protect others from future mistreatment, including customers and clients. For example, one avenger stated, "They had overcharged people for things and I felt sorry for them. I purposely did not enter things to save the client money but at the same time to hurt the company." Another avenger said, "Part of my motivation was to prevent people from getting ripped off. The company doesn't offer what they purport to offer. They're crooks. Part of it was that." Another avenger stated a motive to help medical patients: "I felt he wasn't good for the patients. He touched some people inappropriately and he asked them things he shouldn't have. By getting rid of him, the patients would benefit. I would benefit, too."

Research suggests that some acts of revenge are motivated, in part, by people's desires to help their organization (Bies & Tripp, 1998). Illustrating this, one avenger who was interviewed claimed that his or her actions were intended to help the company. A 25-year-old employee working in the publishing industry sought revenge against a coworker who was "bad for the company." Another avenger stated about the transgressor, "I also wasn't happy that he was ripping off [the company] by taking money in fees that should have gone to [the company]." Although it is unknown whether such allegedly prosocial motives were genuine motivators of revenge or merely self-justifications for revenge behavior, many of these avengers claimed to believe they were doing the right thing.

Moral Purpose Needs and Deontic Motives: Third-Party Revenge

Third-party observers have been shown to react to injustice experienced by others (e.g., Skarlicki, Ellard, & Kelln, 1998). Two of the avengers from the interview study did not personally experience the mistreatment event, yet they retaliated nonetheless. One avenger, a 29-year-old health consultant, drew upon notions of deservingness (see Ellard & Skarlicki, 2002) and stated the following:

> This one incident with this girl was just a blip one afternoon but it was more intense than the others. His conduct was unbecoming in the workplace and as a person. I was incensed because people don't deserve to be treated that way. Like they're 10 year olds. Treat them as adults. These actions threw it over the top.

The preceding quotes illustrate that morally charged mistreatment events arouse deontic justice motives that trigger desires for revenge. Some acts of revenge appeared to be simultaneously motivated by prosocial concerns, such as to protect other coworkers or customers. In some cases, individuals sought revenge in response to the mistreatment of others; these avengers believed that they were righting a wrong through their revenge.

Mistreatment Events as Breaking Points for Revenge: Concluding Comments

The multiple-needs framework (Cropanzano et al., 2001) proved useful for explaining the characteristics of events that act as breaking points for revenge and for providing a unified framework for organizing existing theory and findings that speak to the triggers of revenge. Although subject to my interpretation, data from the interview study appeared to be highly consistent with this framework. I showed that events that violate or threaten psychological needs and that arouse justice motives appeared to trigger desires for revenge. Expanding the multiple-needs model (Cropanzano et al., 2001), I introduced additional motives for revenge—power restoration and prosocial motives—and I linked these to the needs for control and moral purpose, respectively.

This framework about triggers of revenge motives incorporates previous theory about sources of provocation (Bies & Tripp, 2005, p. 70) and extends this theory by clarifying the underlying psychological mechanisms. Bies and Tripp (2005) identified three sources of provocation: (a) goal obstruction that causes revenge in response to frustration (which relates to control needs and instrumental and power restoration motives); (b) violations of rules, social norms, and promises (which relate to needs for control and moral purpose, and instrumental, deontic, and prosocial motives), and (c) status and power derogation (which relate to self-esteem and belonging needs, and relational motives). In short, events that threaten important needs and arouse specific justice motives trigger desires for revenge because, through revenge, individuals can attempt to restore or protect the needs that were damaged or threatened, and to address the justice motives that were aroused.

Drawing upon Jones and Skarlicki's (2010) model of fairness-perception change in response to specific events, I argued that the processes through which revenge motives are triggered include a fundamental shift in how individuals view the transgressors—this fundamental shift explains why individuals might passively accept IWB for some time before experiencing a single event that triggers their desires for revenge. Jones and Skarlicki (2009) proposed that events that violate important psychological needs and arouse justice motives are most likely to trigger sense-making efforts that can lead to perception change. In the context of revenge, when sense-making about such events lead to attributions of blame and intentional ill will it can result in a new perception of the transgressor as highly exploitive, unfair, and even as a "bad" person. When individuals perceive transgressors in these terms, they are motivated to seek revenge in an attempt to address affected needs and fulfill various justice motives.

In future research on revenge, progress may be achieved by testing the multiple-needs perspective developed herein. Advances might also be achieved by more clearly conceptualizing the temporal dynamics of mistreatment over time to understand how perceptions of social entities affect individuals' interpretations of acute mistreatment events and how these perceptions can shift to being extremely negative (Jones & Skarlicki, 2010).

IMPLICATIONS FOR MANAGERIAL PRACTICE

The analyses presented in this chapter suggest a number of implications for managerial practice. Almost all the avengers I interviewed engaged in revenge in response to mistreatment by their manager. As such, I focus on actions that managers can take to minimize the extent they are blamed for unfavorable events and ameliorate revenge motives if managers are blamed.

Understanding Perceived Mistreatment

To prevent and manage perceived mistreatment, managers must be able to recognize the types of mistreatment victims perceive as particularly damaging. The interview findings presented in this chapter showed that most acts of revenge occurred in response to perceived injustice. Thus, managers who receive training in the principles of organizational justice (Greenberg, 2006; Skarlicki & Latham, 2005) will be better equipped to identify, prevent, and manage events that are potentially perceived as unfair. Managers also can learn to manage attributions through social accounts, a notion that I discuss later.

The multiple-needs framework developed herein for understanding triggers of revenge also may be useful for developing managers' awareness about perceived mistreatment. Specifically, managers could be trained to understand how events can affect or threaten important psychological needs (control, belonging, self-esteem, and moral purpose). Once managers are able to recognize why some mistreatment events are perceived as particularly egregious, they may be better able to avoid committing them, and better equipped to address affected needs if mistreatment occurs, as I discuss later.

Changing Negative Perceptions

Drawing upon a model of justice perceptions over time (Jones & Skarlicki, 2010), I argued that avengers who experience a history of IWB are likely to draw upon this information when judging subsequent mistreatment from the same transgressors. As a result, avengers are more likely to blame these transgressors for the mistreatment and to view the events as violating norms for moral conduct, which are two conditions associated with revenge (Folger & Skarlicki, 1998). Thus, managers need to prevent IWB from occurring and, accordingly, should heed the advice presented elsewhere in this book.

Moving beyond the prevention of IWB, managers armed with the ability to recognize events that trigger revenge motives may come to realize that their reputation may be tarnished due to their past actions. The avengers from the interview study claimed they experienced interpersonal mistreatment for just over a year, on average, prior to the mistreatment event that prompted their desires for revenge. Thus, there appears to be a "window of opportunity" during which time managers could prevent mistreatment from escalating into a desire for revenge by changing negative perceptions about their character.

Jones and Skarlicki (2010) outline how managers can change people's negative perceptions of them. They argue that repeated incidents of shockingly high levels of fair treatment and concern for human dignity are often needed to reduce the certainty of negative perceptions, thereby making those perceptions more malleable. Thus, managers who wish to change negative perceptions about their character need to make a concerted effort to repeatedly engage in actions that demonstrate fairness and respectful treatment. As I discuss later, managers may be able to prompt individuals to reconsider the nature of their character by apologizing and expressing remorse for harm done, and communicating how their ways have changed.

It may be difficult for managers to actively manage their reputations because they often are the bearers of bad news. Next, I focus on how managers can manage attributions for unfavorable events to lessen the likelihood that they are blamed, thereby reducing revenge motives or preventing them entirely.

Managing Attributions: Providing Causal Accounts for Mistreatment Events

The degree to which transgressors are blamed for mistreatment is consistently implicated in revenge processes (e.g., Barclay et al., 2005). Analyses of the interview data showed that avengers were highly certain about who was to blame for mistreatment and that they often made highly personalistic attributions. With this in mind, managing attributions of blame should be effective in reducing revenge motives in response to acute events (Bradfield & Aquino, 1999).

Research on causal accounts has shown that explanations can be used to manage attributions by deflecting blame away from offenders (Bies, 1987), which can mitigate perceived unfairness (Shaw et al., 2003) and retaliation (Jones & Skarlicki, 2005). Thus, when possible, and presumably when true, managers should provide causal explanations that convince perceivers that unfavorable events were beyond their reasonable control and due to external causes. Managers need to provide accounts that are perceived as adequate, such as by explaining the specific rationale for a decision, and they need to do so in a sincere manner (Bobocel & Zdaniuk, 2005).

Some of the mistreatment events in the interview study presented in this chapter were ones in which the transgressors may have been able to deflect blame by providing explanations. For instance, six mistreatment events concerned issues relating to procedural justice and distributive justice (e.g., unfair scheduling processes and decisions). Managers could have explained the rationale for these decisions in ways that made it clear that any harm was not motivated by malicious intent, thereby reducing attributions of blame and the resulting revenge motives. Another avenger actually described the mistreatment event as a situation in which his or her manager did not provide an explanation about a portion of pay that the avenger felt was owed; this is a clear case in which an explanation for the pay discrepancy may have prevented the revenge motive from occurring. On a related note, I asked the last nine avengers I interviewed what could have been done, if anything, to remove their desire for revenge; three of these individuals claimed that an explanation from the transgressor about why the event happened would have been sufficient.

Thus, in some cases, causal accounts might be effective for placating the desire for revenge. However, other mistreatment events, particularly those that involve assaults on individuals' dignity, may not easily be "explained away," perhaps because the transgressors' control over such actions is undeniable. In these cases, I argue, managers may benefit from acknowledging the harm and addressing the needs that were affected by the mistreatment.

Addressing Needs Affected by Mistreatment Through Apologies

I suggested in the previous paragraph that there is sometimes little room to deflect blame for some mistreatment events, such as those relating to disrespectful treatment, which comprised at least 35% of the mistreatment events experienced by the avengers in the interview study presented in this chapter. In such cases, managers should admit responsibility for the harm done and attempt to address the needs that were affected. This suggestion is consistent with Conlon and Murray (1996), who argued that apologies in which the account-giver takes responsibility for the mistreatment are effective when the victims have already attributed clear blame for the event.

In the interview study, an average of three weeks elapsed between the start of revenge motives and their behavioral manifestations. This finding is suggestive of a second window of opportunity during which time managers can attempt to "fix what's broken." Moreover, the desire for revenge can endure for several months or longer (Bies & Tripp, 1996), as evidenced by my finding that avengers engaged in multiple acts of revenge for, on average, about six months. Thus, managers might benefit from taking steps that address the revenge motive even months after mistreatment events occur.

The multiple-needs perspective presented in this chapter suggests that the desire for revenge may be reduced by addressing the underlying justice motives through repairing the needs that were threatened or violated. Theory suggests that forgiveness relates positively to fulfillment of the "justice gap"—the discrepancy between current and desired outcomes (Exline, Worthington, Hill, & McCullough, 2003). Thus, victims may be more likely to forgive if actions are taken to restore the needs that were damaged to desired levels. In the remainder of this chapter, I explore how managers can begin the process of addressing violated needs through apologies.

Apologies

Conflict can be reduced by acknowledging victims' interpretations of mistreatment and by expressing regret (McLaughlin, Cody, & O'Hair, 1983). One way of doing this is deceptively simple, but quite effective—by apologizing for one's misdeeds. In fact, failing to respond to a perceived injustice can further enrage victims (Vidmar, 2000). By contrast, apologies symbolize a transgressor's effort to address injustice, thereby minimizing the victim's desire for revenge. Indeed, research has demonstrated that apologizing for harm done can help control victims' negative responses (Ohbuchi, Kameda, & Agarie, 1989). Among the nine avengers whom I asked what could have been done to remove or prevent their desires for revenge, three of them stated that the transgressor could have apologized or admitted that a mistake had been made.

Not all apologies, however, are created equal; apologies without substantive content can lead to greater perceptions of unfairness because the apologizer's honorable intent is questioned (Skarlicki, Folger, & Gee, 2004). Research on forgiveness (Exline & Baumeister, 2000) suggests that managers should apologize for mistreatment in a manner that admits responsibility, asks for forgiveness, and shows repentance by expressing guilt or sadness.

Beyond these more general recommendations, apologies can be used to begin the process of addressing the specific needs violated by mistreatment. Although tied to the multiple-needs model (Cropanzano et al., 2001), researchers should test the effectiveness of these strategies.

Addressing Control Needs

Apologizing can restore a sense of control to the victims of mistreatment because a sincere apology indicates that the transgressor is aware of, and sorry for, the harm done. Hence, an apology can send a signal that future mistreatment is unlikely to occur (Greenberg, 1990b). Managers should use apologies to address control needs and future-oriented instrumental justice motives by including statements that indicate that their ways have changed (e.g., "I promise not to treat you this way again"). Relating to power restoration motives that underlie some revenge, apologizing can also restore a sense of power because victims may feel like they achieved a small victory when transgressors admit fault. Thus, managers might give victims of interpersonal mistreatment such a victory when possible (e.g., "You were right to be upset. I was in the wrong here").

Addressing Self-Esteem and Belonging Needs

Apologies also might be used to restore victims' sense of identity and worth that was damaged by mistreatment, which is considered an essential step toward forgiveness (Hampton, 1988). When apologizing for this type of mistreatment, managers should emphasize an employee's worth to the work group or organization. Managers could address relational motives and belonging needs by apologizing publicly in front of other group members or by taking other steps to show publicly that the employee is a valued group member. Furthermore, expressing remorse is a way of demonstrating interpersonal sensitivity (Greenberg, 1994), and managers who do so send a signal that they are now treating their victims with the dignity and respect they deserve.

Addressing Morality-Related Needs

Some apologies also might help address morality-based needs and deontic motives for justice; that is, the desire to punish morally reprehensible people. Individuals who experience disrespectful treatment often want to show others that it is not them, but rather the transgressor, who deserves contempt (Novaco, 1976). Managers might satisfy this need by providing sincere apologies in which they admit moral culpability and show remorse for it. Doing so might help convince victims that the transgressors' actions were isolated and do not represent their character (Schlenker, 1980).

Apologies that contain expressions of regret and remorse—what Bies (1987) termed penitential accounts—may be highly effective for reducing revenge motives. When managers express remorse for the harm done, it provides a "down payment" toward restoring justice and promotes forgiveness

(O'Malley & Greenberg, 1983). In particular, the expression of remorse and repentance may help satisfy avengers' desires to punish transgressors because remorse implies some degree of self-punishment; to the extent justice is served by the transgressor, the victim may have less need to seek revenge. Folger et al. (2005) discussed moral remedies—actions by the transgressor that are intended to satisfy the victim's desire to punish. Thus, managers who feel a sense of remorse might reduce their victims' desires to punish by communicating self-punishment (e.g., "I've been beating myself up over this and I really regret what I did"). In other words, justice can be restored when transgressors demonstrate feelings like guilt and remorse (O'Malley & Greenberg, 1983). Managers also might consider making public apologies for widely known mistreatment, especially when the mistreatment violates shared norms for moral conduct, to address revenge motives among third-party observers. In short, apologies might offer managers an effective tool for managing moral outrage and reducing motives for revenge.

ACKNOWLEDGMENT

I gratefully acknowledge constructive comments from the editor, Jerald Greenberg, and Sarah A. Carroll on earlier drafts of this chapter.

NOTES

1. The term *victim* is used in this chapter to denote individuals who *perceive* they were the target of mistreatment and this term is not intended to convey any position about which individuals might be in the right or wrong or who may have objectively committed the first offense. Similarly, the term *transgressor* is used to denote the individual(s) a victim perceives as responsible for the perceived mistreatment.
2. In Bies and Tripp's analyses of their interview findings (e.g., 1996), they conceptualize revenge responses more broadly than in the present chapter, including responses like forgiveness or doing nothing. I restrict my use of the term *revenge* to an individual's conscious intent to cause harm.
3. Providing evidence of people's intent to harm is important to demonstrate when making inferences about revenge behavior because other mechanisms can explain relationships between perceived mistreatment and behaviors that appear to be motivated by a desire for revenge. For instance, some individuals who engage in vandalism or

sabotage may be motivated primarily by thrill seeking, or individuals who engage in theft might be motivated primarily by greed or equity restoration. In some cases when other motives are dominant, perceived mistreatment may provide a convenient justification for the behavior to help reduce cognitive dissonance (Festinger, 1957) or to manage third-party attributions.

4. I thank the editor for this point.
5. I thank the editor for this point.

REFERENCES

Allred, K. G. (1995). *Judgment, anger, and retaliation: A new perspective on non-cooperation in organizations.* Unpublished doctoral dissertation, University of California, Los Angeles.

Allred, K. G. (1999). Anger driven retaliation: Toward an understanding of impassioned conflict in organizations. In R. J. Bies, R. J. Lewicki, & B. H. Sheppard (Eds.), *Research on negotiations in organizations* (Vol. 7, pp. 27–51). Greenwich, CT: JAI Press.

Ambrose, M. L., Seabright, M. A., & Schminke, M. (2002). Sabotage in the workplace: The role of organizational injustice. *Organizational Behavior and Human Decision Processes, 89,* 947–965.

Analoui, F. (1995). Workplace sabotage: Its styles, motives and management. *Journal of Management Development, 14,* 48–65.

Andersson, L. M., & Pearson, C. M. (1999). Tit for tat? The spiraling effect of incivility in the workplace. *Academy of Management Review, 24,* 452–471.

Aquino, K., & Douglas, S. (2003). Identity threat and antisocial behavior in organizations: The moderating effects of individual differences, aggressive modeling, and hierarchical status. *Organizational Behavior and Human Decision Processes, 90,* 195–208.

Aquino, K., Grover, S. L., Goldman, B., & Folger, R. (2003). When push doesn't come to shove: Interpersonal forgiveness in workplace relationships. *Journal of Management Inquiry, 12,* 209–216.

Aquino, L., Tripp, T. M., & Bies, R. J. (2001). How employees respond to personal offense: The effects of blame, attribution, victim status, and offender status on revenge and reconciliation in the workplace. *Journal of Applied Psychology, 86,* 52–59.

Aquino, K., Tripp, T. M., & Bies, R. J. (2006). Getting even or moving on? Power, procedural justice, and types of offense as predictors of revenge, forgiveness, reconciliation, and avoidance in organizations. *Journal of Applied Psychology, 91,* 653–668.

Barclay, L. J., Skarlicki, D. P., & Pugh, S. D. (2005). Exploring the role of emotions in injustice perceptions and retaliation. *Journal of Applied Psychology, 90,* 629–643.

Baron, R. A., & Neuman, J. H. (1996). Workplace violence and workplace aggression: Evidence on their relative frequency and potential causes. *Aggressive Behavior, 22,* 161–173.

Baron, R. A., & Neuman, J. H. (1998). Workplace aggression—The iceberg beneath the tip of workplace violence: Evidence on its forms, frequency, and targets. *Public Administration Quarterly, 21,* 446–464.

Becker, E. (1973). *The denial of death.* New York, NY: The Free Press.

Bies, R. J. (1987). The predicament of injustice: The management of moral outrage. In L. L. Cummings & B. M. Staw (Eds.), *Research in organizational behavior* (Vol. 9, pp. 289–319). Greenwich, CT: JAI Press.

Bies, R. J. (2001). Interactional (in)justice: The sacred and the profane. In J. Greenberg & R. Cropanzano (Eds.), *Advances in organizational behavior* (pp. 89–118). Palo Alto, CA: Stanford University Press.

Bies, R. J., & Moag, J. S. (1986). Interactional justice: Communications criteria of fairness. In R. Lewicki, M. Bazerman, & B. Sheppard (Eds.), *Research on negotiation in organizations* (Vol. 1, pp. 43–55). Greenwich, CT: JAI Press.

Bies, R. J., & Tripp, T. (1996). Beyond distrust: "Getting even" and the need for revenge. In R. M. Kramer & T. Tyler (Eds.), *Trust in organizations* (pp. 246–260). Thousand Oaks, CA: Sage.

Bies, R. J., & Tripp, T. (1998). Revenge in organizations: The good, the bad, and the ugly. In R. W. Griffin, A. O'Leary-Kelly, & J. Collins (Eds.), *Dysfunctional behavior in organizations: Vol. 1. Violent behaviors in organizations.* (pp. 49–68). Greenwich, CT: JAI Press.

Bies, R. J., & Tripp, T. (2001). A passion for justice: The rationality and morality of revenge. In R. Cropanzano (Ed.), *Justice in the workplace: From theory to practice* (Vol. 2, pp. 197–208). Mahwah, NJ: Lawrence Erlbaum Associates.

Bies, R. J., & Tripp, T. M. (2002). Hot flashes, open wounds: Injustice and the tyranny of its emotions. In S. Gilliland, D. Steiner, & D. Skarlicki (Eds.), *Emerging perspectives on managing organizational justice* (pp. 203–23). Greenwich, CT: JAI Press.

Bies, R. J., & Tripp, T. M. (2005). The study of revenge in the workplace: Conceptual, ideological, and empirical issues. In S. Fox & P. E. Spector (Eds.), *Counterproductive work behavior: Investigations of actors and targets* (pp. 65–81). Washington, DC: American Psychological Association.

Bies, R. J., Tripp, T. M., & Kramer, R. M. (1997). At the breaking point: Cognitive and social dynamics of revenge in organizations. In R. A. Giacalone & J. Greenberg (Eds.), *Anitsocial behavior in organizations* (pp. 18–36). Thousand Oaks, CA: Sage.

Blader, S. L., Chang, C., & Tyler, T. R. (2001). Procedural justice and retaliation in organizations: Comparing cross-nationally the importance of fair group processes. *International Journal of Conflict Management, 12,* 295–311.

Blau, P. M. (1964). *Exchange and power in social life.* New York, NY: Wiley.

Bobocel, D. R., & Zdaniuk, A. (2005). How can explanations be used to foster organizational justice? In J. Greenberg & J. A. Colquitt (Eds.), *Handbook of organizational justice* (pp. 469–498). Mahwah, NJ: Lawrence Erlbaum Associates.

Bradfield, M., & Aquino, K. (1999). The effects of blame attributions and offender likeableness on forgiveness and revenge in the workplace. *Journal of Management, 25,* 607–631.

Carlsmith, K. M., Darley, J. M., & Robinson, P. H. (2002). Why do we punish? Deterrence and just desserts as motives for punishment. *Journal of Personality and Social Psychology, 83,* 284–299.

Colquitt, J. A. (2001). On the dimensionality of organizational justice: A construct validation of a measure. *Journal of Applied Psychology, 86,* 386–400.

Conlon, D. E., & Murray, N. M. (1996). Customer perceptions of corporate responsiveness to product complaints: The role of expectations. *Academy of Management Journal, 39,* 1040–1056.

Cortina, L. M., Magley, V. J., Williams, J. H., & Langhout, R. D. (2001). Incivility at the workplace: Incidence and impact. *Journal of Occupational Health Psychology, 6,* 64–80.

Cropanzano, R., & Baron, R. A. (1991). Injustice and organizational conflict: The moderating role of power restoration. *International Journal of Conflict Management, 2,* 5–26.

Cropanzano, R., Byrne, Z. S., Bobocel, D. R., & Rupp, D. E. (2001). Moral virtues, fairness heuristics, social entities, and other denizens of organizational justice. *Journal of Vocational Behavior, 58,* 164–201.

DeMore, S. W, Fisher, J. D., & Baron, R. M. (1988). The equity-control model as a predictor of vandalism among college students. *Journal of Applied Social Psychology, 18,* 80–91.

Dollard, J., Doob, L. W., Miller, N. E., Mowrer, O. H., & Sears, R. R. (1939). *Frustration and aggression.* New Haven, CT: Yale University Press.

Eisenberger, R., Lynch, P., Aselage, J., & Rohdieck, S. (2004). Who takes the most revenge? Individual differences in negative reciprocity norm endorsement. *Personality and Social Psychology Bulletin, 30,* 787–799.

Ellard, J. H., & Skarlicki, D. P. (2002). A third-party observer's reactions to employee mistreatment: Motivational and cognitive processes in deservingness assessments. In S. W. Gilliland, D. D. Steiner, & D. P. Skarlicki (Eds.), *Emerging perspectives on managing organizational justice: Vol. 2. Research in social issues in management* (pp. 133–158). Greenwich, CT: Information Age Publishing.

Exline, J. J., & Baumeister, R. F. (2000). Expressing forgiveness and repentance. In M. E. McCullough, K. I. Pargament, & C. E. Thoresen (Eds.), *Forgiveness: Theory, research, and practice* (pp. 133–155). New York, NY: Guilford Press.

Exline, J. J., Worthington, E. L., Hill, P., & McCullough, M. E. (2003). Forgiveness and justice: A research agenda for social and personality psychology. *Personality and Social Psychology Review, 7,* 337–348.

Festinger, L. (1957). *A theory of cognitive dissonance.* Evanston, IL: Row, Peterson.

Folger R., & Baron, R. A. (1996). Violence and hostility at work: A model of reactions to perceived injustice. In G. R. Van den Bos & E. Bulatao (Eds.), *Violence on the job: Identifying risks and developing solutions* (pp. 51–85). Washington, DC: American Psychological Association.

Folger, R., & Cropanzano, R. (1998). *Organizational justice and human resource management.* Thousand Oaks, CA: Sage.

Folger, R., & Cropanzano, R. (2001). Fairness theory: Justice as accountability. In J. Greenberg & R. Cropanzano (Eds.), *Advances in organizational behavior* (pp. 1–55). Palo Alto, CA: Stanford University Press.

Folger, R., Cropanzano, R., & Goldman, B. (2005). What is the relationship between justice and morality? In J. Greenberg & J. A. Colquitt (Eds.), *Handbook of organizational justice* (pp. 215–245). Mahwah, NJ: Lawrence Erlbaum Associates.

Folger, R., & Skarlicki, D. P. (1998). A popcorn metaphor for employee aggression. In R. W. Griffin, A. O'Leary-Kelly, & J. M. Collins (Eds.), *Dysfunctional behavior in organizations: Violent and deviant behavior* (Vol. 1, pp. 43–81). Greenwich, CT: JAI Press.

Fox, S., & Spector, P. E. (1999). A model of work frustration-aggression. *Journal of Organizational Behavior, 20,* 915–931.

Gabriel, Y. (1998). An introduction to the social psychology of insults in organizations. *Human Relations, 51,* 1329–1354.

Glasser, B. G., & Strauss, A. L. (1967). *The discovery of grounded theory.* Chicago, IL: Aldine.

Greenberg, J. (1990a). Employee theft as a reaction to underpayment inequity: The hidden cost of pay cuts. *Journal of Applied Psychology, 75,* 561–568.

Greenberg, J. (1990b). Looking fair vs. being fair: Managing impressions of organizational justice. In B. M. Staw & L. L. Cummings (Eds.), *Research in organizational behavior* (Vol. 12, pp. 111–157). Greenwich, CT: JAI Press.

Greenberg, J. (1993). The social side of fairness: Interpersonal and informational classes of organizational justice. In R. Cropanzano (Ed.), *Justice in the workplace: Approaching fairness in human resource management* (pp. 79–103). Hillsdale, NJ: Erlbaum.

Greenberg, J. (1994). Using socially fair treatment to promote acceptance of a work site smoking ban. *Journal of Applied Psychology, 79,* 288–297.

Greenberg, J. (2006). Losing sleep over organizational injustice: Attenuating insomniac reactions to underpayment inequity with supervisory training in interactional justice. *Journal of Applied Psychology, 91*(1), 58–69.

Hampton, J. (1988). Forgiveness, resentment, and hatred. In J. G. Murphy & J. Hampton (Eds.), *Forgiveness and mercy* (pp. 35–87). New York, NY: Cambridge University Press.

Hoel, H., Rayner, C., & Cooper, C. L. (1999). Workplace bullying. In C. L. Cooper & I. T. Robertson (Eds.), *International review of industrial and organizational psychology* (Vol. 14, pp. 195–230). New York, NY: Wiley.

Hogan, R., & Emler, N. P. (1981). Retributive justice. In M. J. Lerner & S. C. Lerner (Eds.), *The justice motive in social behavior* (pp. 125–143). New York, NY: Plenum Press.

Homans, G. C. (1961). *Social behavior: Its elementary forms.* New York, NY: Harcourt, Brace.

Jones, D. A. (2004). Counterproductive work behavior toward supervisors and organizations: Injustice, revenge, and context. In D. H. Nagao (Ed.), *Best paper proceedings of the sixty-fourth annual meeting of the Academy of Management* [CD], ISSN 1543-8643.

Jones, D. A. (2009). Getting even with one's supervisor and one's organization: Relationships among types of injustice, desires for revenge, and counterproductive work behaviors. *Journal of Organizational Behavior, 30,* 525–542.

Jones, D. A., & Skarlicki, D. P. (2005). The effects of overhearing peers discuss an authority's reputation for fairness on reactions to subsequent treatment. *Journal of Applied Psychology, 90,* 363–372.

Jones, D. A., & Skarlicki, D. P. (2010). *How perceptions of fairness can change: A dynamic model of organizational justice.* Unpublished manuscript.

Kinney, J. A. (1995). *Violence at work.* Englewood Cliffs, NJ: Prentice Hall.

Kramer, R. M. (1994). The sinister attribution error. *Motivation and Emotion, 18,* 199–231.

Lee, K., Ashton, M. C., & de Vries, R. E. (2005). Predicting workplace delinquency and integrity with the HEXACO and five-factor models of personality structure. *Human Performance, 18,* 179–197.

Lerner, M. J. (1980). *The belief in a just world: A fundamental delusion.* New York: Plenum Press.

Lim, S., & Cortina, L. M. (2005). Interpersonal mistreatment in the workplace: The interface and impact of general incivility and sexual harassment. *Journal of Applied Psychology, 90,* 483–496.

Lind, E. A., & Tyler, T. R. (1988). *The social psychology of procedural justice.* New York: Plenum Press.

McLaughlin, M. L., Cody, M. J., & O'Hair, H. D. (1983). The management of failure events: Some contextual determinants of accounting behavior. *Human Communication Research, 9,* 208–224.

McLean Parks, J. M. (1997). The fourth arm of justice: The art and science of revenge. In R. J. Lewicki, R. J. Bies, & B. H. Sheppard (Eds.), *Research on negotiation in organizations* (Vol. 6, pp. 113–144). Greenwich, CT: JAI Press.

Miceli, M. P., & Near, J. P. (1997). Whistle-blowing as antisocial behavior. In R. A. Giacalone & J. Greenberg (Eds.), *Antisocial behavior in organizations* (pp. 130–149). Thousand Oaks, CA: Sage.

Mitchell, M. S., & Ambrose, M. L. (2007). Abusive supervision and workplace deviance and the moderating effects of negative reciprocity beliefs. *Journal of Applied Psychology, 92,* 1159–1168.

Morrill, C. (1992). Vengeance among executives. *Virginia Review of Sociology, 1,* 51–76.

Novaco, R. W. (1976). The functions and regulation of the arousal of anger. *American Journal of Psychiatry, 133,* 1124–1128.

Ohbuchi, K., Kameda, M., & Agarie, N. (1989). Apology as aggression control: Its role in mediating appraisal of and response to harm. *Journal of Personality and Social Psychology, 56,* 219–227.

O'Malley, M., & Greenberg, J. (1983). Sex differences in restoring justice: The down payment effect. *Journal of Research in Personality, 17,* 174–185.

Pearson, C. M., Andersson, L. M., & Porath, C. L. (2000). Assessing and attacking workplace incivility. *Organizational Dynamics, 29,* 123–137.

Perugini, M., Gallucci, M., Presaghi, F., & Ercolani, A. P. (2003). Reciprocity. *European Journal of Personality, 17,* 251–283.

Schlenker, B. R. (1980). *Impression management: The self-concept, social identity, and interpersonal relations.* Monterey, CA: Brooks/Cole.

Shapiro, D. L., Buttner, E. H., & Barry, B. (1994). Explanations: What factors enhance their perceived adequacy? *Organizational Behavior and Human Decision Processes, 58,* 346–368.

Shapiro, D. L., Treviño, L. K., & Victor, B. (1995). Correlates of employee theft: A multidimensional justice perspective. *International Journal of Conflict Management, 6,* 404–414.

Shaw, J. C., Wild, E., & Colquitt, J. A. (2003). To justify or excuse?: A meta-analytic review of the effects of explanations. *Journal of Applied Psychology, 88,* 444–458.

Sheppard, B. H., Lewicki, R. J., & Minton, J. W. (1992). *Organizational justice: The search for fairness in the workplace.* New York, NY: Macmillan.

Skarlicki, D. P., Barclay, L. J., & Pugh, S. D. (2008). When explanations for layoffs are not enough: Employer's integrity as a moderator of the relationship between informational justice and retaliation. *Journal of Occupational and Organizational Psychology, 81,* 123–146.

Skarlicki, D. P., Ellard, J. H., & Kelln, B. R. C. (1998). Third-party perceptions of a layoff: Procedural, derogation, and retributive aspects of justice. *Journal of Applied Psychology, 83,* 119–127.

Skarlicki, D. P., & Folger, R. (1997). Retaliation in the workplace: The roles of distributive, procedural, and interactional justice. *Journal of Applied Psychology, 82,* 434–443.

Skarlicki, D. P., Folger, R., & Gee, J. (2004). When social accounts backfire: The exacerbating effects of a polite message or an apology on reactions to an unfair outcome. *Journal of Applied Social Psychology, 34,* 322–341.

Skarlicki, D. P., & Latham, G. P. (2005). How can training be used to foster organizational justice? In J. Greenberg & J. A. Colquitt (Eds.), *Handbook of organizational justice* (pp. 499–522). Mahwah, NJ: Lawrence Erlbaum Associates.

Stuckless, N., & Goranson, R. (1992). The Vengeance Scale: Development of a measure of attitudes toward revenge. *Journal of Social Behavior and Personality, 7,* 25–42.

Tedeschi, J. T., & Nesler, M. (1993). Grievances: Development and reactions. In R. Felson & J. T. Tedeschi (Eds.), *Aggression and violence: A social interactionist approach.* Washington, DC: American Psychological Association.

Townsend, J., Phillips, J. S., & Elkins, T. J. (2000). Employee retaliation: The neglected consequence of poor leader-member exchange relations. *Journal of Occupational Health Psychology, 5,* 457–463.

Tripp, T. M., & Bies, R. J. (1997). What's good about revenge? The avenger's perspective. In R. J. Lewicki, R. J. Bies, & B. H. Sheppard (Eds.), *Research on negotiation in organizations* (Vol. 6, pp. 145–160). Greenwich, CT: JAI Press.

Tripp, T. M., Bies, R. J., & Aquino, K. (2002). Poetic justice or petty jealousy? The aesthetics of revenge. *Organizational Behavior and Human Decision Processes, 89,* 966–984.

Tripp, T. M., Bies, R. J., & Aquino, K. (2007). A vigilante model of justice: Revenge, reconciliation, forgiveness, and avoidance. *Social Justice Research, 20,* 10–34.

Tyler, T. R. (1987). Conditions leading to value-expressive effects in judgments of procedural justice: A test of four models. *Journal of Personality and Social Psychology, 52,* 333–344.

Tyler, T. R., & Lind, E. A. (1992). A relational model of authority in groups. In M. P. Zanna (Ed.), *Advances in experimental social psychology* (Vol. 25, pp. 115–191). San Diego, CA: Academic Press.

Vardi, Y., & Weitz, E. (2004). *Misbehavior in organizations: Theory, research and management.* Mahwah, NJ: Lawrence Erlbaum Associates.

Vidmar, N. (2000). Retribution and revenge. In J. Sanders & V. L. Hamilton (Eds.), *Handbook of justice research in law* (pp. 31–63). New York, NY: Kluwer Academic.

Williams, K. D. (1997). Social ostracism. In R. M. Kowalski (Ed.), *Aversive interpersonal behaviors* (pp. 133–170). New York, NY: Plenum Press.

Zellars, K. L., Tepper, B. J., & Duffy, M. K. (2002). Abusive supervision and subordinates' organizational citizenship behavior. *Journal of Applied Psychology, 87,* 1068–1076.

5

Research on Workplace Incivility and Its Connection to Practice

Christine M. Pearson

> In working with others who have been uncivil to your colleagues, there's a great temptation to retaliate. If you don't get beyond that, the organization may unravel.
>
> **—Partner in a law firm**

We sense it before we can name it. Your boss rolls her eyes then sighs, "I already *told* you what I wanted"; your cubicle neighbor ignores your plea for assistance; your leader forgets to mention your name when boasting about his team. Incivility makes otherwise unremarkable interpersonal give-and-take conspicuous and memorable to us. Through others' uncivil body language, facial expressions, demeaning remarks, omissions and mindlessness, we size up the interaction and feel diminished. We absorb these cues through situations and behaviors embedded in very narrow slices of experience. We recognize in the instant a phenomenon that is called incivility.

This chapter is comprised of five sections. In the first, I summarize briefly the nature of incivility, including its definition and key characteristics. In the second, I provide an overview of conceptual underpinnings and empirical findings about workplace incivility. In the third, I describe incivility from the target's perspective, including emotional responses and behavioral consequences. In the fourth section, practical considerations and recommendations for the target are offered. The fifth section concludes with thoughts about future research opportunities.

INCIVILITY: WHAT IS IT? WHY SHOULD ANYONE CARE?

Incivility: Low intensity deviant (rude, discourteous) behavior with ambiguous intent to harm the target in violation of workplace norms for mutual respect. (Andersson & Pearson, 1999, p. 457)

Curiosity about incivility dates back to the Middle Ages (cf. the dicta of Erasmus and Christine de Pisan). Some claim that we are experiencing a techno-facilitated, multinational explosion of incivility. Popular books describe the prevalence, potential antecedents, and consequences of incivility in society (e.g., Caldwell, 1999; Carter, 1998; Forni, 2002, 2008; Truss, 2005). The construct of workplace incivility only recently has been introduced to organizational literature (e.g., Andersson & Pearson, 1999). Nonetheless, the relevance of the phenomenon has been validated in stories about this research published in more than 500 newspapers and periodicals spanning the United States, Western Europe, Canada, and Australia (Pearson, Andersson, & Porath, 2005).

Whereas civility signals self-control (Wilson, 1993), incivility signals carelessness. Work relationships are smoothed when we treat each other civilly (that is, with dignity, with regard to each other's feelings, with adherence to norms of mutual respect; Carter, 1998; Elias, 1982; Johnson, 1988; Morris, 1996), while incivility chafes relationships. Uncivil interactions promote disharmony and feed ill will (Andersson & Pearson, 1999) and cost individuals, teams, and organizations a great deal of money (Pearson & Porath, 2009). Incivility constitutes barbed interactions that have the potential to erode the very contexts in which they occur.

Classic sociological studies provide insight into the effects of incivility on targets and instigators, as well as on the context within which they interact. Following Goffman's (1967) work on interpersonal interactions, I note that when incivility occurs, interaction rituals are violated as norms are broken and rules of conduct are ignored. According to Goffman's observations, it seems reasonable to expect that incivility could impinge on individuals in two ways. First, the infraction could impact individuals directly by shattering obligations about how they are supposed to conduct themselves. Second, uncivil interactions could impact individuals indirectly by shattering expectations about how others are supposed to behave toward them. It also might be inferred that when incivility occurs, it signals asymmetry in the rules of conduct. According to Goffman's framework, it is conceivable that instigators of incivility, through their uncivil behaviors, are attempting to lead others to treat them differently. Studies, in fact, confirm this. When incivility occurs, there is an inherent conflict between the instigator's view of the right and wrong way to treat others and the target's view of the right and wrong way to be treated (Pearson, Andersson, & Wegner, 2001).

Turning our focus from the actors to the context, guiding parameters regarding incivility might be understood from the perspective of Parsons's classical theory of action (1959). Viewed through this lens, incivility would have the potential to disrupt three of the four systems of action identified by Parsons. Specifically, an uncivil interaction could shatter (1) cultural systems (i.e., the values and norms that direct and limit the types of interactions condoned among individuals), (2) social systems (i.e., actions between two or more individuals who are regulated by roles and role expectations), and (3) personality systems (i.e., the variety of actions that are organized within an individual). These systems provide a framework for conceptualizing the reach of damage that potentially may be sparked by incivility.

In more current research focused specifically on the issue of incivility, diverse disciplines seem to be converging (e.g., law, criminology, psychology, health care, public administration, and organization science). Legal research about incivility has examined the effects that the phenomenon can have on day-to-day conduct, including the potential negative impact on professionalism (e.g., Austin, 1988; Crain, 1997; Wegner, 1996). Scholarship from a legal perspective also offers an early glimpse into how incivility might escalate from the exchange of nasty words to physical violence (MacKinnon, 1994). Recent research related to criminology confirms the potential for escalation from uncivil words to violent deeds (Felson & Steadman, 1983). Psychological research offers insight into the effects of modeling as it may play out in imitative, escalating aggressive behavior (Bandura, 1983), the effect of social dominance on reactions to incivility (Cortina, Magley, Williams, & Langhout, 2002), as well as health consequences of direct and vicarious exposure (Lim, Cortina, & Magley, 2008; Miner-Rubino & Cortina, 2007).

As an interaction that conveys rudeness through the violation of social norms, it comes as no surprise that incivility can engender costs for the target. Whether using demeaning language and voice tone, slurring another's competence, brushing off requests, or disrupting a subordinate from completing a task, instigators' behaviors can upend the workplace experiences of their targets (Pearson, Andersson, & Wegner, 2001). But, can this phenomenon inflict additional burdens? Research has demonstrated that when uncivil interpersonal interactions occur at work, they are accompanied by greater aggression, higher turnover, lower productivity, and customer dissatisfaction (Connelly, 1994; Gonthier, 2002; Hutton & Gates, 2008; Lewis, 2000; Pearson et al., 2005; Pearson & Porath, 2009; Walters, 1994; Windsor, 1999). What begins as low-intensity negative interaction can lead to an upward spiral of aggression; what begins as an affront of ambiguous intent can lead to increasingly purposeful and harmful acts. Along the way, incivility can foster contempt and subvert organizational leadership (Andersson & Pearson, 1999). The effects of incivility are widespread.

Scholars have found that a substantial percentage of employees see themselves as targets of incivility (e.g., Cortina et al., 2001; Ehrlich & Larcom, 1994). As many as 25% of employees in a recent survey have reported witnessing incivility daily, whereas as many as 50% have claimed to be direct targets of incivility at least once per week (Pearson et al., 2005). In a study of the federal court system, Cortina and her colleagues (2002) found that nearly 66% of participants in their study had experienced incivility or harassment on the job. Theoretical underpinnings, earlier studies from disciplines outside business, and personal observation led us (with Porath at the University of Southern California, Andersson at Temple University, and Wegner at the University of North Carolina) to begin what has become a 10-year multiphased study of workplace incivility. The next section comprises a brief sampling of what we have learned through these explorations.

EXPLORING THE PHENOMENON OF INCIVILITY: A MULTIPHASED APPROACH

The goal of our research team has remained constant: to understand the phenomenon of incivility, including how it differs from other forms of counterproductive workplace behaviors, as well as its impact on organizations, targets, instigators, and others. To date, we have studied the uncivil experiences of more than 4,000 people. We have interviewed, surveyed, and observed workers, managers, professionals, and executives who witnessed, managed, or personally experienced workplace incivility from their fellow employees. Our samples have come from organizations in all industries, ranging from proprietorships of only 2 people to major organizations employing over 100,000.

Our studies of incivility have drawn from two conceptual perspectives—social interaction theory (Tedeschi & Felson, 1994) and social cognitive theory (Bandura, 1986). Consistent with social interaction theory, we conceptualize incivility as a dynamic exchange between individuals. By dynamic we mean that incivility is a process rather than a single event. Thus, unlike many other forms of counterproductive workplace behavior (e.g., homicide, vandalism), incivility can occur as multiple, spiraling acts over time. This frame allows us to consider the individual and interpersonal factors involved in uncivil encounters (Pearson et al., 2005). Consistent with social cognitive theory, we consider not only the person involved in the uncivil interaction, but also the environment in which the incivility occurs. We use social cognitive theory to hypothesize how target effects, such as status and gender, and environmental effects, such as organizational context and norms, affect target responses.

Phase 1: Qualitative Research on Targets' Experiences

As we devised our initial strategies for empirical exploration, these frameworks led us to believe that incivility likely would be influenced (and complicated) by the intricacies of interpersonal interaction, as well as by the context. Therefore, to capture an appropriately nuanced perspective of the phenomenon, we began our research using qualitative methods. We were seeking a multidimensional rendering of incivility that included thick descriptions of the behaviors, characteristics, and roles played by instigators and targets. Thus, we limited our first sample to individuals who personally had experienced workplace incivility and who were willing to discuss their responses to it, as well their perceptions of the instigator and the organization in which it occurred. Through interviews and focus groups, 670 participants across the United States contributed to the foundation of our database. During this initial effort, participants convinced us that incivility matters to employees and to the organizations in which they work. Participants revealed that incivility in their own environments caused organizational disruption, as well as negative consequences for

targets, instigators, and witnesses. Through vivid descriptions of participants' actual experiences, we came to appreciate how the relatively mild
behavioral roots of incivility and the ambiguity of intent that are characteristic of this phenomenon might result in negative consequences for
diverse stakeholders (Pearson et al., 2001).

Phase 2: Questionnaire Research on Targets' Responses

We followed our qualitative, thematic research by collecting survey data
from an initial sample of 775 respondents across industries, hierarchical status, and geographic locations within the United States. From these
respondents, we honed our understanding of the nature of incivility, as
well as the roles and characteristics of targets and instigators.

We uncovered gender and status differences, discovering, for example,
that target is a gender-blind role, that instigators tend to be male, and that
those of higher status are more likely to be instigators than targets. We also
found men to be much more likely to behave uncivilly toward someone of
lower status than someone of higher status, whereas women were equally
likely to be uncivil to superiors as to subordinates, but very unlikely to
behave uncivilly toward peers (Pearson, 2001). From this initial investigation, we learned that incivility led to depletion of targets' work efforts as
a result not only of their purposeful decisions, but also of their concerns
about future interactions with instigators.

Phase 3: Experiences of Managers of Incivility

Next, we conducted extensive, in-depth interviews with people whose
professions required them to manage incivility on a daily basis; law
enforcement officers, attorneys, judges, and inner-city emergency medical
professionals contributed to this phase of our research. These individuals
provided insight into the evolution of incivility, based on their own observations and experiences of escalation. We learned, for example, that incivility can escalate between instigators and targets and that it can cascade
throughout and beyond the organization in which it originates.

In the simplest form of give-and-take, incivility ricochets between instigators and targets without escalating. In tit-for-tat fashion, uncivil words
and deeds are simply reciprocated. In this form, incivility does not inten-
sify as barbs are exchanged. Nonetheless, the cumulative effect may erode

workplace norms as witnesses are exposed to repeated uncivil interactions. Incivility also can escalate between instigators and targets resulting in a chain reaction that spirals upward with increasing intensity. The initial, relatively mild signals of disrespect through uncivil words become aggressive. In rare cases, escalating incivility can end in physical violence. Incivility also can cascade as secondary spirals are set off when the behaviors of the original instigator are reenacted by new instigators and targets. Or, incivility can cascade when targets displace their reactions to others rather than retaliating directly against their instigators (Pearson, Andersson, & Porath, 2000).

The seasoned experts who participated in this phase of our research provided field evidence of the many varieties of contagion of incivility. According to their experiences, when an uncivil interaction occurs, targets and witnesses spread the phenomenon throughout the organization and beyond. Many other individuals can experience the effects of incivility if the original occurrence of incivility is modeled through similar behavior toward new targets at work and at home (Pearson et al., 2000).

Phase 4: In-Depth Analyses of Professionals' Responses

To test findings to this point, we conducted our next phase of research via a multiple-day learning forum to which we invited a select group of executives and professionals who were experts on the topic of incivility. All participants were attempting to curtail incivility as part of their own work responsibilities. This phase of our research allowed us to test and enrich the practical relevance and resonance of what we were learning. Collectively, we deepened our understanding of and appreciation for the challenges of managing incivility within an organization.

During this phase, we heard a new perspective of instigators. Specifically, the instigators of incivility were characterized as often being cunning participants in the uncivil encounters, capable of creating a self-reinforcing cycle in which they could enact uncivil words and deeds with little or no threat of retribution. Experts who participated in the learning forum underscored the importance of establishing and maintaining organizational expectations about mutual respect. They also shared examples of holistic approaches needed for curtailing workplace incivility (cf. Pearson & Porath, 2005). This phase reinforced the notion that incivility is difficult to detect and to curtail because uncivil encounters often occur outside the purview of more powerful people who might be willing and able to manage them. These studies reveal a rich perspective of the impact of incivility on targets, including targets' emotional and behavioral responses, the next topic.

FROM THE RECEIVING END: THE TARGET'S PERSPECTIVE

To contribute to the integration of research and practice, our recent research focuses on emotional and behavioral responses to incivility. In particular, we study outcomes for those on the receiving end of incivility, that is, the targets. Here I begin by offering a brief rationale in support of this perspective.

Emotional reactions express judgments about situations in which individuals find themselves (Averill, 1978). When negative situations occur at work (e.g., through incivility), it stands to reason that employees will respond in terms of their emotional reactions. Supporting this perspective, Harlos and Pinder (2000) demonstrated that employees who purposefully are intimidated or degraded by superiors or other organizational authority figures experience negative emotions. Scholars also have underscored the importance of understanding this perspective in calling for investigation of specific types of events that upset and stir employees' emotions (e.g., Basch & Fisher, 2000). We believe that an uncivil encounter could comprise an emotionally stirring event. With this in mind, we have been assessing the relationship between incivility and emotional consequences. Our efforts proved worthwhile. We have learned, for example, that incivility provokes emotional responses. Specifically, our data confirm that targets who perceive greater incivility tend to experience greater emotional responses (Porath & Pearson, 2005).

Emotional Consequences

Emotional consequences can be provoked at work and they can interrupt work activities (George & Brief, 1996). Psychological studies regarding emotion are complemented by an emergent literature focused on emotion as related to the workplace (e.g., Ashforth & Humphrey, 1995; Brief & Weiss, 2002; Felblinger, 2008; Fineman, 2000; Hochschild, 1983; Rafaeli & Sutton, 1987).

This body of work suggests that emotions not only accompany work experiences, but also precede and follow such experiences. More precisely, scholars have contended that negative emotions precede, accompany, and follow unjust experiences at work (Harlos & Pinder, 2000).

We wondered whether negative emotional responses might accompany targets' experiences of incivility. We were drawn, in particular, to examine potential relationships between experienced incivility and what are commonly considered primary negative emotions: anger, fear, and sadness (Ekman, 1980; Ekman & Friesen, 1975; Izard, 1971). We believed this perspective could be particularly important because very little organizational research has examined the stimuli or effects of fear and sadness (Brief & Weiss, 2002; Harlos & Pinder, 2000; Pinder, 1997). The discussion that follows attempts to highlight what we are learning regarding the negative emotions of anger, fear, and sadness as related to incivility, as well as what we are learning about the potential behavioral consequences that may accompany these emotions, and their impact.

Regarding Anger

Anger is an emotional response to a perceived misdeed (Averill, 1983), energized by an offense or an injury for which another is viewed as responsible (Greenspan, 1988; Lazarus & Lazarus, 1994). This emotional state signals that something needs to change (Ekman, 2003). Anger commonly is aroused by insult, denigration, personal offense (Ekman, 2003), and disrespect (Miller, 2001), but it can be provoked by virtually any potential harm if that harm is appraised as unjustifiable (Averill, 1978).

Anger Is Common in the Workplace

It is understandable the anger is common in the workplace given that some consider the workplace one of the most interpersonally frustrating contexts within which individuals interact (Allcorn, 1994; Bensimon, 1997). Evidence of the workplace origins of anger can be as common as coworkers spoiling their colleagues' efforts or superiors blocking subordinates' needs or hampering their goal-directed behaviors (Pinder, 1997). Potential links between anger and intentional deprivation are clear. But, we were intrigued to learn whether anger also occurs when the intent of the deprivation is ambiguous, as in incivility. We found that when incivility occurs, the target is likely to experience anger (Porath & Pearson, 2005). Further, we confirmed an association between anger and some forms of incivility that might be considered depriving to the target. For example, we discovered that targets of incivility experience anger when their identities are threatened or challenged and when their self-esteem has been damaged (Porath, Overbeck, & Pearson, 2008).

Regarding Fear

Fear occurs when someone senses impending evil or feels threatened that danger lurks (de Becker, 1997; Greenspan, 1988). Fear is a protective emotional state, enabling us to react to threats of physiological or psychological danger or pain (Ekman, 2003). Literature is rapidly emerging regarding fear in society (e.g., Clarkson, 2002; Glassner, 1999; Lerner, 2004), but only scant organizational research has examined fear in the workplace (Brief & Weiss, 2002; Harlos & Pinder, 2000; Pinder, 1997). The limited studies of work-related fear have examined two issues: (1) the effects of fear as a control mechanism to maintain the organizational hierarchy (e.g., Fineman & Sturdy, 1999); and (2) the outcome of fear when a dramatic negative event occurs, such as homicide, terrorism, or intimate partner violence (e.g., Barling, Rogers, & Kelloway, 2001; Dietz, Robinson, Folger, Baron, & Schulz, 2003; Reeves, 2004). Some of these studies confirm that fear in the workplace is fostered by dramatic deviance (e.g., workplace homicide or domestic violence). Our interest was in ascertaining whether there might be a relationship between workplace fear and the relatively mild deviance of incivility. Our findings confirm that people who experience greater incivility also experience greater levels of fear (Porath & Pearson, 2005).

Regarding Sadness

Sadness is an emotional state triggered by loss, often accompanied by a sense of helplessness (Ekman, 2003). Sadness and grief seem to have virtually no place in organizational literature. The few exceptions regard the ways in which organizations should deal with death in the workplace (e.g., Stein & Winokuer, 1989) and the ways in which sadness can be a reflection of perceived organizational powerlessness (e.g., Roseman, Dhawan, Rettek, & Naidu, 1995). Scant research has examined potential relationships between sadness and workplace deviance. We were intrigued to test whether sadness might relate to the relatively mild interpersonal deviance of workplace incivility. Our rationale was as follows. When targets experience incivility, their expectations are shattered and their routines are disrupted. Disruption of routines and expectations can beget isolation and humiliation, which can beget sadness (Tedeschi & Felson, 1994; Vogel & Lazare, 1990). Additionally, targets may perceive loss when incivility occurs, whether through damage to their social networks or to their relationships with instigators (Pearson et al., 2001). Sadness can accompany a sense of loss (Ekman, 2003; Parry, 1990). Therefore, it seemed reasonable that any of these negative outcomes of incivility could be accompanied by feelings of sadness. Our data confirmed that targets who experience greater incivility experienced greater degrees of sadness (Porath & Pearson, 2005).

Each of these empirical confirmations regarding emotional consequences of incivility enriches organizational research about counterproductive behavior at work. As a next step, our keen interest in practical application led us to expand our perspective by examining the behavioral impact when anger, fear, or sadness are experienced in relation to incivility. We discovered varied behavioral outcomes that have the potential to be counterproductive for the target, the instigator, and the organization. Those outcomes are summarized next in regard to anger, fear, and sadness.

Behavioral Outcomes, Potential Consequences

When Targets Are Angry

When people are angry, they are likely to seek retribution (Allred, 2000). Responses to anger may include aggressive behavior—whether direct, indirect, or displaced—and nonaggressive behavior (Averill, 1983). In organizational studies, for example, employees' anger has been linked to aggressive behaviors, such as theft (Chen & Spector, 1992), revenge (Skarlicki & Folger, 1997), and physical violence (Folger & Skarlicki, 1998).

When we examined the actions of angry targets of incivility we found predictable behaviors. When anger is experienced in relation to incivility, targets seek direct retribution at their instigators. They attempted to achieve this by threatening and belittling the instigator. Additionally, targets claimed that they stole important belongings from their instigators and harmed their instigators' property. Targets who were angered also tended to aggress indirectly against their instigators. For example, angered targets spread negative rumors about their instigators, intentionally avoided them, and withheld information they needed (Porath & Pearson, 2005).

As to potential consequences, each of these behaviors by angered targets has negative effects on instigators, whether by spoiling instigators' reputations or perceived character, or by limiting instigators' access to resources. These reactions also have the potential to cause negative organizational consequences. At the least, they would comprise equivocal reciprocal incivility. At the most, they could trigger escalation. Either outcome has the potential to negatively affect coworkers, witnesses, and the surrounding work environment.

When Targets Are Fearful

Fear reduces self-efficacy (Bandura, Reese, & Adams, 1982). Fearful employees lose self-confidence, become depleted, harbor doubts about their career futures, and withdraw emotionally from work and relationships (Harlos & Pinder, 2000). When targets of incivility experience fear, we found that they aggressed against their instigators (as do angry targets), but fearful targets did not aggress directly. Rather, when fear accompanies incivility, retribution by targets toward their instigators was covert. Instead of demeaning or threatening the instigator in person, fearful targets belittled their instigators behind their backs. Rather than confronting their instigators (as some angry targets do), fearful targets avoided their instigators and withheld useful information from them (Porath & Pearson, 2005). Further, when fear accompanies targets' perceptions of incivility, targets displace their negative reactions on their organizations. They reduce efforts that they otherwise would make on behalf of their organizations. Our data confirm that fearful targets intentionally do the following: (1) decrease the amount of work effort they put forth, (2) reduce the quantity of time they put into their work, and (3) diminish the quality of the work they produce (Porath & Pearson, 2005). Fearful targets also displace their fear by turning to others. Abundant evidence of the tendency to seek social support when fearful can be found in clinical psychological research involving subjects as diverse as long-term health care providers (Uphold & Mkanta, 2005), patients awaiting coronary surgery and parents of emotionally disturbed children (Scharer, 2005). We have found that targets of incivility also seek social support, often among friends outside of work. At home, they may attempt to reduce their bad feelings by turning to friends and family for relief. At work, targets may displace their fear by decreasing their assistance to coworkers and customers and, thus, reducing their organizational citizenship behaviors (Organ & Lingl, 1995; Porath & Pearson, 2005).

These actions of fearful targets can have negative effects on the targets themselves, their friends and family members, coworkers, their organizations, and their instigators. By reducing or diminishing their contributions to the workplace (whether through time, effort, or quality), the organization suffers. If reductions are noticed by high-ranking organizational officials, the target's performance reputation may suffer as a result. With the targets' reductions of work efforts and citizenship behaviors, coworkers and team members may be burdened with additional workloads that would otherwise have been shared by the target. Instigators may find themselves lacking information, resources, or assistance that would previously have been shared by their fearful targets. In some of our earliest studies we learned, for example, that as many as 25% of targets intentionally decreased their work efforts and 33% reduced their commitment when incivility occurred (Pearson et al., 2000). Further, almost all targets spread the word of their uncivil treatment to others, including colleagues or friends and family members outside the workplace (Pearson, 2001). In this manner, the reputations of instigators and their organizations may be tarnished.

When Targets Are Sad

Sadness causes a loss of energy and enthusiasm. Those who are sad often believe that nothing can be done to set the situation right (Smith & Ellsworth, 1985). Extreme sadness can lead to withdrawal (Parry, 1990). We were curious to learn whether sad targets of workplace incivility withdrew. When we analyzed the behavioral responses, we found a dramatic consequence. Those who experienced greater sadness as a result of incivility were more likely to leave their jobs than those who experienced less sadness (Porath & Pearson, 2005).

Exit may be the most negative effect of workplace incivility. From a practical, purely economic perspective, the fully loaded costs of replacing employees have been estimated at 1.5 to 2.5 times the position salary or an average of $50,000 per exiting employee as measured across all jobs and industries in the United States (Cascio, 2000). When an employee exits because of incivility, the organizational impact is more than financial. Targets who exit because of incivility tend not to report that justification as cause for departure. As a result, this consequence of incivility eludes documented organizational memory. Also, target departures often occur some time after the uncivil encounter, so the temporal association between the instigator's actions and the target's response (of exiting) may also be missed by the organization. Therefore, when a target of incivility exits, the organization loses not only a valued employee, but also valuable insight about the high costs of the phenomenon of incivility.

Targets' Actions: Coping With Incivility

Elsewhere, we have detailed organizational recommendations about managing incivility based on such practices as setting zero-tolerance expectations, hiring for civility, collecting 360-degree feedback, heeding warning signals, removing instigators who repeatedly behave uncivilly, and others (e.g., Pearson et al., 2001, 2005; Pearson & Porath, 2004, 2005, 2009). Each of these tactics must emanate from high organizational levels. To achieve any of these recommendations requires the participation of actors with legitimate organizational power. But, many targets of incivility lack the hierarchical muscle to put these approaches into action or the political savvy to know how to do so. Nonetheless, when incivility occurs, these targets must cope.

To contend with incivility, targets may attempt to deal with the encounter and their emotional reactions by using various cognitive and behavioral means (Ekman, 1980). There is little guidance for targets attempting to do so and whatever sources there may be offer advice that is not based on sound research. Therefore, to address this gap, I turn to the practical matter of advising targets of incivility as to how to cope effectively. Initially, I offer a few recommendations that emerge from our understanding of incivility. Following this, I share observations based on the effective responses of targets who have participated in our studies.

Why Instigators Are Not Bullies and Why the Distinction Matters

There may be just cause for concern regarding a response that is prescribed all too often. Frequently, targets are urged to respond to workplace incivility much as a child might respond to an encounter with a schoolyard bully—that is, by confronting their instigators head-on (e.g., Marano, 1995; Namie & Namie, 2000; Schachner, 1999) For several reasons, however, this prescription is fundamentally flawed and potentially career threatening to the target. From a social interactionist perspective (Tedeschi & Felson, 1994), confronting an instigator is likely to escalate ill will and to foster future repercussions, rather than to cause that instigator to desist, as popular prescriptions promise. Further, as informed by social cognitive theory (Bandura, 1986), confronting instigators ignores not only the influence of the persons (a workplace instigator actually shares few characteristics with a schoolyard bully), but also the impact of the environment (sarcasm notwithstanding, playgrounds and organizations have very little in common). Whereas schoolyard playmates squabble among peers (albeit potentially varied in physique), the workplace target and instigator often command unequal organizational power; generally, as we have noted, the hierarchical balance tips in favor of the instigator. When an instigator holds greater legitimate power, by definition, that individual has greater access to resources and wider networks over which he or she can wield power (French & Raven, 1959). This leaves the lesser powered target highly vulnerable to greater abuse at the hands of the instigator.

To differentiate further between schoolyard bullying and workplace incivility, reaction to an affront in the schoolyard may attract the attention of a teacher or other supervisor, whereas when incivility occurs most targets find no such mediators in their work environments. Based on our studies, targets of incivility are well advised to resist the temptation to try to get even, whether through direct or indirect aggression. This recommendation is important for targets of equal or greater status than their instigators (given the escalating nature of incivility), and it is crucial for targets of lesser status (given inherent relative power differences).

Displacement and Associated Costs

It is important to keep in mind that targets often displace their reactions to workplace incivility. As noted, many targets redirect their negative responses to incivility on others. Coworkers may encounter angry targets who snap at subordinates, make wisecracks to their colleagues, or even model the very uncivil treatment they had received. At home, angry targets may be short tempered with their significant others; fearful targets may recount their experiences to family and friends; sad targets may withdraw. Initially, these reactions may seem less dangerous than aggressing directly against instigators, but they are far from innocuous, hence an additional recommendation to refrain from displacing incivility on others, guarding against the inherent costs of doing so.

Staying Put and Knowing Why

Most targets choose to remain in the environments in which they experienced incivility. These individuals should be clear about why they are staying and any expectations that may have driven this decision. Sometimes, uncivil behavior is chronic (Pearson et al., 2001). Therefore, a target who remains on the job should guard against potential repeated opportunities for incivility from the instigator. All too often, we have witnessed and heard about targets turning a blind eye to this possibility. Some believe that instigators will become enlightened and change their ways; often they do not. Others believe that if they just work a little harder to please their instigators, their relationship will improve, but usually it does not. Many hope that a powerful person in the organization will recognize the damaging nature of the instigator's behavior and take action to curtail it, but such resolution generally fails to occur. It is essential to remember that incivility is not within the sole control of the target. Rather, incivility emerges from the dynamics of social interaction. General advice for the target, then, is to exert control over context by avoiding opportunities to experience repeated incivility from instigators. This may mean avoiding interactions in isolation, for example. Sometimes, this decision necessitates detachment or departure.

Detaching for Resolution

Incivility can trigger detachment. Many targets pull away from their workplaces, as we have noted, whether by decreasing effort or attention (cf. Pearson et al., 2001, for targets' own examples). Some targets choose the ultimate workplace detachment: they leave their jobs. For the benefit of those faced with such decisions, I note that targets repeatedly report that an exit is implemented optimally through careful planning. Our studies have shown that many targets who exit remain in their jobs for months after the incivility. During this period, they invest time and effort to locate better work opportunities. In the interim, of course, targets retain the ability to time their exits by maintaining work performance standards.

Mustering Strength and Learning

Although experiences of incivility have been described to us as debilitating, dysfunctional, and confusing, we have also found ample evidence of targets who viewed their experiences, eventually, as sources of strength and learning. Despite the immediate negative emotional reactions, some targets have described their uncivil experiences as opportunities to assume and exert control through their reactions. For example, rather than reciprocating with incivility in ways that could foment into a spiral of escalation, some targets choose to release negative emotions by increasing their involvement in exercise and sports activities, hobbies, and other diversions. Some spend more quality time with their families (Pearson & Porath, 2004; Porath & Pearson, 2005). In hindsight, some targets even begin to see their uncivil encounters as crucibles or negative personal experiences through which they achieve transformation and personal growth (Bennis & Thomas, 2002).

Uncivil experiences can spark targets' adaptive capacities to transcend adversity. Many targets are quite insistent about having made a conscious choice to rise above their uncivil experiences (Pearson et al., 2001). They tell us that they achieved this by looking deeper within themselves and reflecting about the situation from a broader perspective. Some focused their reactions in the best interests of overall organizational welfare. Others became conscious of and conscientious about putting work into proper perspective. Specifically, they claimed that the uncivil encounter was the tipping point that caused them to reduce the significance of work in the overall scheme of their lives. Others told us that they turned to spiritual guidance to rise above the uncivil treatment, whether through prayer, meditation, or deep reflection about the Golden Rule (Pearson & Porath, 2003).

Uncivil encounters also can prompt targets to learn (Pearson et al., 2005). After experiencing incivility some told us that they read about topics such as relationship building, emotional intelligence, and conflict management to help them decipher what had happened to them and to increase their emotional and interpersonal savvy. Others sought counsel from experts in interpersonal interaction, such as human resources professionals and psychologists, so that they could better interpret their uncivil encounters. When incivility occurred, targets also turned to attorneys to learn how to protect themselves.

FUTURE RESEARCH DIRECTIONS

We turn, finally, to two potential directions for future investigation. Both seem to have the capacity to advance research, as well as to provide practical insight and application. Both require adapting new frames of reference.

Thin-Slicing the Reality of Incivility

In *Blink: The Power of Thinking without Thinking*, Malcolm Gladwell (2005) put forth engaging anecdotes and research findings regarding the pros and cons of *thin-slicing*, that is, releasing the power of our adaptive unconscious. It seems possible that the frame of thin-slicing could inform our understanding of workplace incivility, providing new perspectives into the phenomenon itself. When an uncivil encounter occurs, the tremors seem to reverberate in the unconscious. This narrow slice of experience often leaves targets and witnesses feeling offended without knowing precisely why. It is possible that the adaptive unconscious informs the triggering of incivility. Researchers might seek to uncover the extent to which the assumptions and behaviors of instigators and targets result from conscious versus unconscious attitudes. To what extent are instigators' or targets' judgments and behaviors driven by what they choose to believe versus immediate, automatic associations of which they may not even be aware? There is relevant evidence that bias can be conveyed and felt in subtle behaviors (e.g., proxemics, smiling, eye expressions) that are unconscious and diametrically opposed to the ways in which those who transmit bias would choose to feel (Greenwald, McGhee, & Schwartz, 1998). It is intriguing to consider whether these same mechanisms come into play during uncivil encounters.

Perhaps if we can learn to decode underlying snap judgments and first impressions (via knowledge about the adaptive unconscious, or the ability to thin-slice), we may better understand the roles of targets and instigators. We know that incivility often causes targets to experience difficulties in articulating and responding to offenses. Psychological scholars (e.g., Nisbett & Wilson, 1977) have suggested that responses to provocations through the adaptive unconscious make individuals' abilities to think and act highly susceptible to outside influences. Could phenomenological similarities of immediate (often escalating) experiences of incivility reflect some sort of debilitation through the adaptive unconscious? More specifically, could instigators' uncivil words and deeds reflect immediate, automatic, negative associations? Might these associations be conveyed by instigators to their targets in behaviors that occur beyond the instigator's own awareness?

A final comment on the usefulness of an adaptive unconscious framework regards the concept of *mindreading*, that is, putting oneself in the mind of someone else (Ekman, 1995). Mindreading allows us to adjust and update our perceptions of the intentions of others (Ekman, 1995; Ekman & Friesen, 1975). But, when emotions are aroused (as occurs in the case of incivility), our ability to mind read shuts down (Ekman, 1995). Arousal leaves us mind-blind. Therefore, our vision and thinking narrow, and our perspectives become rigid: in other words, we stop factoring data (Ekman, 1995). Is there a potential link here to the experiences of incivility such as might be viewed from the perspectives of both targets and instigators? Does an uncivil encounter provoke an autism by which either party may withdraw into himself or herself and become indifferent to reading external realities? With creative application, for example, by videotaping uncivil encounters and then thin-slicing facial indicators of emotion, adaptive unconscious may provide a provocative and useful means of reframing incivility.

When Values Collide: Incivility, Cultural Variance, Masking, and the Role of "Face"

It is logical to assume that culture and incivility will intermingle. After all, culture is the enactment of norms and values, and incivility is the violation of those norms. But how, precisely, do differences among cultures affect norms about incivility? Relevant research demonstrates that individual expectations can vary cross-culturally (e.g., Adler & Graham, 1989). How might expectations about what constitutes civil interaction vary among employees within an organization that crosses cultural boundaries? Certainly, organizations that seek civility in such operations (e.g., where diverse expectations about civil behavior exist) are challenged to define and manage "appropriate" norms. Cross-cultural exploration of incivility could offer practical insight, for example, by distinguishing effective practices.

Even within a common culture, our unconscious attitudes and related behaviors may misalign with our espoused, conscious values. What we say and do may contrast sharply with what we would prefer to do. When we experience negative reactions, we may choose to mask our true feelings, inhibiting or suppressing our negative emotional responses (Gross & Levenson, 1997). Or, our inadvertent behaviors (in response to negative encounters, for example) may unmask our authentic sentiments (Ekman & Friesen, 1975). When incivility occurs, such masking and unmasking may occur. Targets may mask their true negative reactions in an attempt to reset norms (that is, by ignoring their violation) or in an effort to save face for themselves or others (by voiding any effects of the affront). After incivility occurs, instigators may attempt to mask their true feelings (for example, in front of more powerful employees) to avoid repercussions.

If masking does occur in response to incivility, it would be interesting to examine whether this intentional hiding of feelings affects individual psychological or behavioral outcomes. Precedent for related effects have been documented in regard to interactions between employees and customers (e.g., Hochschild, 1983). But, what sorts of costs and benefits might be accrued by targets who mask negative emotional reactions to incivility? If masking occurs in response to incivility, then how are effects experienced by others in the organization and beyond? From a broader perspective, do organizations concerned with maintaining civility among their employees inadvertently signal the desirability of masking as related to individuals' experiences of incivility?

Finally, we might associate *masking* with *face*, as regards energy expended in efforts to save face for oneself or others (Goffman, 1959, 1967). It could be useful, both to researchers and to practitioners, to decipher ways in which incivility is conveyed and interpreted across cultures that vary with respect to the relative importance of face. How do behavioral indicators of incivility in Asia, for example, where face is paramount, compare to indicators in the United States or Western Europe, where face is less important? When incivility occurs, are the emotional responses of targets in these cultures similar? Or, how do the behaviors of instigators and targets in these cultures differ? When someone has been the target of incivility, is face lost? If expressing anger in organizations in Western cultures can increase one's power (as posited, for example, by Tiedens, 2001), does an outburst of anger from an instigator or an angry response from a target increase his or her organizational power? Is this outcome regarding power similar in Eastern cultures? Or, is it possible that in either or both cultures the disrespect of incivility causes loss of face for instigators instead of targets? The interaction between incivility and cultural values clearly is a complex and intriguing matter warranting future research.

CONCLUDING THOUGHTS

Within the past decade, organizational research has advanced our understanding of workplace incivility. Nonetheless, targets, instigators, organizations, and their related stakeholders have much to gain by further investigations of this all-too-common workplace phenomenon. A great deal of work lies ahead for those wishing to inform scholarship and assist people at all levels in organizations. Despite having named workplace incivility, we have only begun to decipher its essence and impact. I hope that these thoughts and observations will encourage additional researchers to embrace the challenge of better understanding workplace incivility.

REFERENCES

Adler, N. J., & Graham, J. L. (1989). Cross-cultural interaction: The international comparison fallacy. *Journal of International Business Studies, 20,* 515–537.

Allcorn, S. (1994). *Anger in the workplace: Understanding the causes of aggression and violence.* Westport, CT: Quorum.

Allred, K. G. (2000) Anger and retaliation in conflict: The role of attribution. In M. Deutsch & P. T. Coleman (Eds.), *Handbook of conflict resolution: Theory and practice* (pp. 236–255). San Francisco, CA: Jossey-Bass.

Andersson. L. M., & Pearson, C. M. (1999). Tit for tat? The spiraling effect of incivility in the workplace. *Academy of Management Review, 24,* 452–471.

Ashforth, B. E., & Humphrey, R. H. (1995). Emotion in the workplace: A reappraisal. *Human Relations, 48,* 97–125.

Austin, R. (1988). Employer abuse, worker resistance, and the tort of intentional infliction of emotional distress. *Stanford Law Review, 41,* 1.

Averill, J. R. (1978). Anger. In H. Howe & R. Dienstbier (Eds.), *Nebraska symposium on motivation.* Lincoln, NE: University of Nebraska Press.

Averill, J. R. (1983). Studies on anger and aggression: Implications for theories of emotion. *American Psychologist, 38,* 1145–1160.

Bandura, A. (1983). Psychological mechanisms of aggression. In R. G. Geen & E. I. Donnerstein (Eds.), *Aggression: Theoretical and empirical reviews* (pp. 1–40). San Diego, CA: Academic.

Bandura, A. (1986). *Social foundations of thought and action: A social cognitive theory.* Englewood Cliffs, NJ: Prentice-Hall.

Bandura, A., Reese, L., & Adams, N. E. (1982). Microanalysis of action and fear arousal as a function of differential levels of perceived self-efficacy. *Journal of Personality and Social Psychology, 43,* 5–21.

Barling, J., Rogers, A. G., & Kelloway, E. K. (2001). Behind closed doors: In-home workers' experience of sexual harassment and workplace violence. *Journal of Occupational Health Psychology, 6,* 255–269.

Basch, J., & Fisher, C. D. (2000). Affective events–emotions matrix: A classification of work events and associated emotions. In Ashkanasy, N. M., Hartel, C. E. J., & Zerbe, W. J. (Eds.), *Emotions in the workplace* (pp. 36–48). Westport, CT: Quorum Books.

Bennis, W. G., & Thomas, R. J. (2002, September). Crucibles of leadership. *Harvard Business Review,* 3–9.

Bensimon, H. (1997). What to do about anger in the workplace. *Training and Development, 51,* 28–32.

Brief, A. P., & Weiss, H. M. (2002). Organizational behavior: Affect in the workplace. *Annual Review of Psychology, 53,* 279–307.

Caldwell, M. (1999). *A short history of rudeness: Manners, morals and misbehavior in modern science.* New York, NY: St. Martin's.

Carter, S. (1998). *Civility: Manners, morals and the etiquette of democracy.* New York, NY: Harper Perennial.

Cascio, W. (2000). *Costing human resources* (4th ed.). Cincinnati, OH: South-Western.

Chen, P. Y., & Spector, P. E. (1992). Relationships of work stressors with aggression, withdrawal, theft, and substance abuse: An exploratory study. *Journal of Occupational and Organizational Psychology, 65,* 177–184.

Clarkson, M. (2002). *Intelligent fear: How to make fear work for you.* Toronto, Ontario, Canada: Key Porter Books.

Connelly, J. (1994, November 28). Have we become mad dogs in the office? *Fortune,* 197–199.

Cortina, L. M., Lonsway, K. L., Magley, V. J., Freeman, L. V., Collinsworth, L.L., Hunter, M., & Fitzgerald, L. F. (2002). What's gender got to do with it? Incivility in the federal courts. *Law and Social Inquiry, 27,* 235–270.

Cortina, L. M., Magley, V. J., Williams, J. H., & Langhout, R. D. (2001). Incivility in the workplace: Incidence and impact. *Journal of Occupational Health Psychology, 6,* 64–80.

Crain, M. (1997, February). *Legal issues surrounding "violence" in the workplace: Update and conceptualization.* Paper presented at the Festival of Legal Learning, UNC School of Law, Chapel Hill, NC.

de Becker, G. (1997). *The gift of fear.* Boston, MA: Little, Brown.

Dietz, J., Robinson, S. L., Folger, R., Baron, R. A., & Schulz, M. (2003). The impact of community violence and an organization's procedural justice climate on workplace aggression. *Academy of Management Journal, 46,* 317–326.

Ehrlich, H. J., & Larcom, B. E. K. (1994). *Ethnoviolence in the workplace.* Baltimore, MD: Center for the Applied Study of Ethnoviolence.

Ekman, P. (1980). Biological and cultural contributions to body and facial movement in the expression of emotions. In A. O. Rorty (Ed.), *Explaining emotions* (pp. 73–102). Berkeley, CA: University of California Press.

Ekman, P. (1995). *Telling lies: Clues to deceit in the marketplace, politics and marriage.* New York: Norton.

Ekman, P. (2003). *Emotions revealed.* New York, NY: Henry Holt & Company.

Ekman, P., & Friesen, W. V. (1975). *Unmasking the face.* Englewood Cliffs, NJ: Prentice Hall.

Elias, N. (1982). *The history of manners.* New York, NY: Pantheon.

Felblinger, D. M. (2008). Incivility and bullying in the workplace and nurses' shame responses. *Journal of Obstetric, Gynecologic, and Neonatal Nursing, 37,* 234–242.

Felson, R. B., & Steadman, H. J. (1983). Situational factors in disputes leading to criminal violence. *Criminology, 21,* 59–74.

Fineman, S. (2000). *Emotion in organizations* (2nd ed.). Thousand Oaks, CA: Sage.

Fineman, S., & Sturdy, A. (1999). The emotions of control: A qualitative exploration of environmental regulation. *Human Relations, 52,* 631–663.

Folger, R., & Baron, R. A. (1996). Violence and hostility at work: A model of reactions to perceived injustice. In G. R. VandenBos & E. Q. Bulatao (Eds.), *Violence on the job: Identifying risks and developing solutions* (pp. 51–85). Washington, DC: American Psychological Association.

Folger, R., & Skarlicki, D. P. (1998). A popcorn model of workplace violence. In R. W. Griffin, A. O'Leary-Kelly, & J. Colling (Eds.), *Dysfunctional behavior in organizations* (Vol. 1, 43–81). Greenwich, CT: JAI.

Forni, P. M. (2002). *Choosing civility: The 25 rules of considerate conduct.* New York, NY: St. Martin's Griffin.

Forni, P. M. (2008). *The civility solution: What to do when people are rude.* New York, NY: St. Martin's.

French, J. R. P., Jr., & Raven, B. (1959). The bases of social power. In D. H. Cartwright (Ed.), *Studies in social power* (pp. 150–167). Ann Arbor, MI: Institute for Social Research.

George, J. M., & Brief, A. P. (1996). Motivational agendas in the workplace: The effects of feelings on focus of attention and work motivation. In L. L. Cummings & B. M. Staw (Eds.), *Research in organizational behavior* (Vol. 18, pp. 75–109). Greenwich, CT: JAI.

Gladwell, M. (2005). *Blink: The power of thinking without thinking.* New York, NY: Little, Brown.

Glassner, B. (1999). *The culture of fear.* New York, NY: Basic Books.

Goffman, E. (1959). *The presentation of self in everyday life.* New York, NY: Doubleday.

Goffman, E. (1967). *Interaction ritual.* New York, NY: Pantheon.

Gonthier, G. (2002). *Rude awakenings: Overcoming the civility crisis in the workplace.* Chicago, IL: Dearborn Trade Publishing.

Greenspan, P.S. (1988). *Emotions and reasons: An inquiry into emotional justification.* New York, NY: Routledge.

Greenwald, A. G., McGhee, D. E., & Schwartz, J. L. K. (1998). Measuring individual differences in implicit cognition: The implicit association test. *Journal of Personality and Social Psychology, 74,* 1464–1480.

Gross, J. J., & Levenson, R. W. (1997). Hiding feelings: The acute effects of inhibiting negative and positive emotion. *Journal of Abnormal Psychology, 106,* 95–103.

Harlos, K. P., & Pinder, C. C. (2000). Emotion in the workplace. In S. Fineman, *Emotions in organizations* (2nd ed., pp. 255–276). Thousand Oaks, CA: Sage.

Hochschild, A. R. (1983). *The managed heart: Commercialization of human feeling.* Berkeley: CA: University of California Press.

Hutton, S., & Gates, D. (2008). Workplace incivility and productivity losses among direct care staff. *American Association of Occupational Health Nurses Journal, 56,* 168–175.

Izard, C. E. (1971). *The face of emotion.* New York, NY: Appleton-Century-Crofts.

Johnson, C. L. (1988). Socially controlled civility. *American Behavioral Scientist, 31,* 685–701.

Lazarus, R. S., & Lazarus, B. N. (1994). *Passion and reason: Making sense of our emotions.* New York, NY: Oxford University Press.

Lerner, H. (2004). *Fear and other uninvited guests.* New York, NY: HarperCollins.

Lewis, D. E. (2000, October 8). Working it out: From casual to rude. *Boston Globe,* J.-2.

Lim, S., Cortina, L. M., & Magley, V. J. (2008). Personal and workgroup incivility: Impact on work and health outcomes. *Journal of Applied Psychology, 93,* 95–107.

MacKinnon, C. (1994). *Only words.* New York, NY: Basic Books.

Marano, H. E. (1995, September 1). Big. Bad. Bully. *Psychology Today,* 50–68.

Miller, D. T. (2001). Disrespect and the experience of injustice. *Annual Review of Psychology, 52,* 527–553.

Miner-Rubino, K., & Cortina, L. M. (2007). Beyond targets: Consequences of vicarious exposure to misogyny at work. *Journal of Applied Psychology, 92,* 1254–1269.

Morris, J. (1996, Autumn). Democracy beguiled. *The Wilson Quarterly,* 24–35.

Namie, G., & Namie, R. (2000). *The bully at work: What you can do to stop the hurt and reclaim your dignity on the job.* Naperville, IL: Sourcebooks.

Nisbett, R. E., & Wilson, T. D. (1977). Telling more than we can know: Verbal reports on mental processes. *Psychological Review, 84,* 231–259.

Organ, D. W. & Lingl, A. (1995). Personality, satisfaction and organizational citizenship behavior. *Journal of Social Psychology. 135*(3), 339–350.

Parry, G. (1990). *Coping with crises.* London, England: British Psychological Society and Routledge.

Parsons, T. (1958). An approach to psychological theory in terms of the theory of action. In S. Koch (Ed.), *Psychology: A study of a science* (Vol. 3, pp. 321–340). New York, NY: McGraw-Hill.

Pearson, C. M. (2001). *Incivility in the workplace: An executive summary of findings.* London, Ontario, Canada: Richard Ivey School of Business, University of Western Ontario.

Pearson, C. M., Andersson, L. A., & Porath, C. L. (2000). Assessing and attacking workplace incivility. *Organizational Dynamics, 29*(2), 123–137.

Pearson, C. M., Andersson, L. A., & Porath, C. L. (2005). Workplace incivility. In S. Fox & P. E. Spector (Eds.), *Counterproductive work behavior* (pp. 177–200). Washington, DC: American Psychological Association.

Pearson, C. M., Andersson, L. A., & Wegner, J. A. (2001). When workers flout convention: A preliminary study of workplace incivility. *Human Relations, 54,* 1387–1420.

Pearson, C. M., & Porath, C. L. (2003, August). *Toxic stakeholders: The reach of workplace incivility.* Paper presented at the annual meeting of the Academy of Management, Seattle, WA.

Pearson, C., & Porath, C. (2004). On incivility, its impact and directions for future research. In R. Griffin & A. O'Leary-Kelly (Eds.), *The dark side of organizational behavior* (pp. 403–425). San Francisco, CA: Jossey-Bass.

Pearson, C. M., & Porath, C. L. (2005). On the nature, consequences and remedies of workplace incivility: No time for 'nice'? Think again. *Academy of Management Executive, 19,* 1–12.

Pearson, C. M., & Porath, C. L. (2009). *The cost of bad behavior: How incivility is damaging your business and what to do about it*. New York, NY: Portfolio.

Pinder, C. C. (1997). *Work motivation in organizational behavior*. Upper Saddle River, NJ: Prentice Hall.

Porath, C. L., & Pearson, C. M. (2005). *Status, anger, fear, action: The impact of structural force on emotional responses and behaviors of targets of workplace incivility*. Los Angeles: Marshall School of Business, University of Southern California.

Porath, C. L., Overbeck, J., & Pearson, C. M. (2008). Picking up the gauntlet: How individuals respond to status challenges. *Journal of Applied Social Psychology, 38*(7), 1945–1980.

Rafaeli, A., & Sutton, R. I. (1987). Expression of emotion as part of the work role. *Academy of Management Review, 12,* 23–37.

Reeves, C. A. (2004). When the dark side of families enters the workplace: The case of intimate partner violence. In R. W. Griffin & A. M. O'Leary-Kelly (Eds.), *The dark side of organizational behavior* (pp. 103–128). San Francisco, CA: Jossey-Bass.

Roseman, I. J., Dhawan, N., Rettek, S. I., & Naidu, R.K. (1995). Cultural differences and cross-cultural similarities in appraisals and emotional responses. *Journal of Cross-Cultural Psychology, 26*(1), 23–48.

Schachner, S. C. (1999). Taking a bully by the horns. *ABA Journal, 85,* 90–92.

Scharer, K. (2005, January–March) Internet social support for parents: The state of science. *Journal of Child & Adolescent Psychiatric Nursing, 18*(1), 26–35 (AN 16199770).

Skarlicki, D. P., & Folger, R. (1997). Retaliation in the workplace: The role of distributive, procedural and interactional justice. *Journal of Applied Psychology, 82,* 434–443.

Smith, C. A., & Ellsworth, P. C. (1985). Patterns of cognitive appraisal in emotions. *Journal of Personality and Social Psychology, 48,* 813–838.

Stein, A. J., & Winokuer, H. R. (1989). Monday mourning: Managing employee grief. In K. J. Doka (Ed.), *Disenfranchised grief: Recognizing hidden sorrow* (pp. 91–102). Lexington, MA: Lexington Books/D.C. Heath.

Tedeshi, J. T., & Felson, R. B. (1994). *Violence, aggression and coercive actions*. Washington, DC: American Psychological Association.

Tiedens, L. Z. (2001). Anger and advancement versus sadness and subjugation: The effect of negative emotion expression on social status conferral. *Journal of Personality and Social Psychology, 80,* 86–94.

Truss, L. (2005). *Talk to the hand: The utter bloody rudeness of the world today or six good reasons to stay home and bolt the door*. New York, NY: Gotham Books.

Uphold, C. R. & Mkanta, W. N. (2005, August). Use of healthcare services among persons living with HIV infection: State of the science and future directions. *AIDS Patient Care and STDs, 19*(8), 473–485.

Vogel, W., & Lazare, A. (1990). The unforgivable humiliation. *Contemporary Family Therapy, 12,* 139–151.

Walters, D. K. (1994, December 4). Read this story on rudeness: Now! *Los Angeles Times,* p. D1.

Wegner, J. W. (1996). Lawyers, learning and professionalism. *Cleveland State Law Review, 43,* 191–216.

Wilson, J. Q. (1993). *The moral sense*. New York, NY: Free Press.

Windsor, P. (1999, April 23). What do companies pay for workplace rudeness? *Washington Business Journal, 3.*

6

Sexist Humor in the Workplace: A Case of Subtle Harassment

Christie Fitzgerald Boxer and Thomas E. Ford

Humor is an integral part of interaction in the workplace. As Duncan, Smeltzer, and Leap (1990, p. 263) stated, "When a group of people are assembled to accomplish a task, there is always some form of joking behavior and work group humor." In fact, it has been suggested that humor is *embedded* in a group's culture (Fine, 1983; Fine & De Soucey, 2005; Sev'er & Ungar, 1997). Fine and De Soucey (2005) contended that through interaction and the development of ongoing relationships, groups naturally develop a joking culture—a set of shared humorous experiences or references—that provide a basis for further interaction. Similarly, Sev'er and Ungar (1997) proposed that humor in the workplace provides a basis for dynamic social interaction in which the humorist and the recipient negotiate changes in the social context according to their perceptions of the underlying meaning of the humor. As such, Sev'er and Ungar suggested that jokes themselves are not funny or offensive events. Rather, joking represents a *process* whereby the joke teller and audience interact with one another according to their respective understandings of the embedded meaning of the material.

Theorists have referred to humor in the workplace as a double-edged sword (e.g., Holmes & Marra, 2002; Malone, 1980; Meyer, 2000). As a basis for social interaction, it can have both invaluable and detrimental consequences for people at work.

On the one hand, humor helps people cope with stress and boredom (e.g., Roy, 1960), builds cohesion and solidarity among work groups (e.g., Fine & De Soucey, 2005; Kahn, 1989; Martineau, 1972), affords the expression of criticism and disagreement in a nonthreatening manner (e.g., Duncan et al., 1990; Ullian, 1976), and helps employees deal with organizational change (e.g., Ullian, 1976). It also can act as a social salve or lubricant when interactions become combative or oppositional (Fine & De Soucey, 2005; Pache, 1992;

Yedes, 1996). Joking signals a mind-set or interpretative frame that "rescues interactions from friction" (Fine & De Soucey, 2005, p. 9). Joking adds levity to disagreement and redefines it as nonserious or nonthreatening.

On the other hand, humor also can be used to divide organization members from one another (e.g., Fine & De Soucey, 2005), to isolate "outsiders" (e.g., Kanter, 1977), and to express underlying hostile attitudes (e.g., Brunner & Costello, 2002). Furthermore, in the case of sexist humor—that is, humor that denigrates, demeans, stereotypes, oppresses, or objectifies a person on the basis of his or her gender (LaFrance & Woodzicka, 1998; Sev'er & Ungar, 1997)—it can create a hostile work environment with long-term adverse consequences such as poor employee morale and even formal sexual harassment charges (e.g., Brunner & Costello, 2002; Hemmasi & Graf, 1998; Hemmasi, Graf, & Russ, 1994; LaFrance & Woodzicka, 1998).

Sexist humor is a particularly insidious form of workplace behavior. By communicating denigration through levity it can make ambiguous how one should interpret the message—and thus, whether it, indeed, is an objectionable form of harassment (Montemurro, 2003). Machan (1987, p. 218) astutely articulated this paradox suggesting that what is funny to one person may be "the height of bad taste to another."

Is sexist humor in the workplace sexual harassment or is it merely harmless entertainment? Why do men engage in sexist humor in the workplace? What are the consequences of sexist humor? For instance, how is it related to stereotypes and prejudice? Does it foster an organizational culture of tolerance of sexism? Does it really have adverse consequences for its targets? These are the overarching questions that guided our review of theory and empirical research for this chapter.

SEXIST HUMOR AS A SUBTLE FORM OF SEXUAL HARASSMENT

As we suggested earlier, sexist humor has been defined as humor that denigrates, demeans, stereotypes, oppresses, or objectifies a person on the basis of his or her gender (LaFrance & Woodzicka, 1998; Sev'er & Ungar, 1997). Although both women and men can be the targets of sexist humor, women are more likely to be targeted (e.g., Bell, McLaughlin, & Sequeira, 2002; Duncan et al., 1990; Fitzgerald, Shullman, et al., 1988; Pryor, 1995a, 1995b).

Also, given the hierarchical structure of organizations and the relative power disparities between men and women (Neitz, 1980; Sev'er & Ungar, 1997), women in the workplace are likely to be affected to a greater degree by denigration through humor. Thus, we focus our discussion of sexist humor only on humor that disparages women.

Sexist humor essentially trivializes the expression of sexism. Because humor communicates that its content is to be interpreted in a nonserious and noncritical mind-set, sexist humor can uniquely denigrate women while minimizing standard challenges or opposition that nonhumorous sexist communications likely would incur (e.g., Bill & Naus, 1992; Ford & Ferguson, 2004; Johnson, 1990). In fact, it often is difficult to distinguish between joking that naturally and appropriately occurs during the course of work interactions and joking that constitutes sexual harassment (Baird, Bensko, Bell, Viney, & Wood, 1995; Duncan et al., 1990; Hemmasi et al., 1994).

Defining Sexual Harassment

In 1980, the Equal Employment Opportunity Commission (EEOC) established a legal definition of sexual harassment, distinguishing between two types of unlawful discrimination: quid pro quo harassment and hostile environment harassment. Quid pro quo occurs when submission to sexual advances or requests for sexual favors is made a term of employment either implicitly or explicitly. Examples include an employer firing an employee for being sexually noncompliant or a manager promising a promotion to a subordinate in return for sexual favors. As these examples illustrate, quid pro quo harassment requires the perpetrator to have employment-related power over the victim.

Hostile environment harassment occurs when gender-based conduct either unreasonably interferes with one's work performance or creates an intimidating, hostile, or offensive work environment (EEOC, 1980, p. 74677). Unlike quid pro quo harassment, hostile environment harassment can be perpetrated by anyone with whom one interacts on the job, including supervisors, coworkers, and subordinates. Also, whereas quid quo pro harassment typically is directed at a single person, court rulings in sexual harassment claims (e.g., *Broderick v. Ruder*, 1988) have established that hostile work environment harassment involves the creation of an offensive atmosphere at work that can affect anyone or everyone in a particular work setting (Duncan et al., 1990; LaFrance & Woodzicka, 1998).

As Duncan et al. (1990, pp. 269–270) described, Title VII of the Civil Rights Act of 1964 guarantees employees "the right to work in an environment free of discriminatory intimidation, ridicule and insult." In the 1986 case of *Meritor Savings Bank v. Vinson*, the Supreme Court ruled that a hostile environment violates Title VII, thus supporting the EEOC's definition of hostile environment harassment as a form of sex discrimination. Furthermore, a number of judicial decisions in sexual harassment suits in the 1990s (e.g., the 1991 Clarence Thomas–Anita Hill hearings; the 1995 sexual harassment suit filed against Chevron Corporation) have established that patterns of behaviors such as lewd or sexist remarks, jokes, or teasing violate Title VII, and thus constitute forms of sexual harassment. Sexist jokes, then, can constitute sexual harassment, in particular, gender harassment—sex-related harassment that is not explicitly sexual (EEOC, 1993).

Research has shown that gender harassment in the form of sexist jokes and teasing is the most commonly experienced type of sexual harassment by women in the workplace (e.g., Fitzgerald et al., 1988; Gruber & Bjorn, 1986; Pryor, 1995a, 1995b). For example, Fitzgerald et al. (1988) surveyed 2,599 undergraduate and graduate students as well as faculty and staff at two universities. Among all participants, they found that gender harassment (e.g., suggestive stories or offensive jokes) was the most frequently reported experience of sexual harassment among five dimensions of sexual harassment assessed by their Sexual Experiences Questionnaire (SEQ). Over 31% of the female student respondents and 34% of the working women respondents reported experiencing some form of gender harassment, whereas only 15% of the students and 17% of the working women reported experiencing more serious forms of sexual harassment. Similarly, Pryor (1995a) used data from a survey of over 2,600 employees from a government agency and found that gender harassment in the form of sexual teasing and jokes was the most frequently experienced form of sexual harassment among women. Pryor (1995b) found that gender harassment (i.e., sexual teasing, sexist jokes) was the most common form of harassment reported among female military personnel. In fact, 82% of harassed military women experienced sexist joking in one form or another.

When Is a Joke Perceived as Sexual Harassment?

Sentiment over the use of sexist humor in public domains such as the workplace has become critical (Apte, 1987; Barker, 1994). Survey research indicates that the general public is increasingly defining sexist humor as a form of sexual harassment. In 1987, Terpstra and Baker found that only 20% of the respondents perceived sexist jokes and crude language as harassment. However, in 1995, Graf and Hemmasi surveyed 300 employees in both manufacturing and service industries and found that 57% of the respondents (including both men and women) considered sexist humor to be inappropriate in the workplace. In similar fashion, Frazier, Cochran, and Olson (1995) surveyed 4,000 university students, faculty, and staff, and found that a large majority of 71% viewed sexist jokes as sexual harassment.

Although a general consensus is growing that sexist humor in the workplace constitutes harassment, various factors influence the degree to which sexist jokes are perceived as harassment as opposed to merely harmless fun. These variables include gender, attitudes toward and identification with women, and the organizational status of the humorist.

Gender Differences

Perhaps not surprisingly, men and women often differ in their perceptions of sexist humor (Duncan et al., 1990; Hemmasi et al., 1994; Smeltzer & Leap, 1988). Johnson (1990) demonstrated that joke tellers and joke recipients (those hearing the jokes) interpret disparaging jokes differently. Joke tellers recognize that jokes do not reflect their true underlying attitudes. To a joke teller, then, a sexist joke may be considered "just a joke." In contrast, joke recipients tend to believe the jokes reflect to some degree the joke teller's true underlying sentiments. Thus, women as recipients of sexist jokes are less likely than men to perceive these same jokes as completely benign, without at least a kernel of hurtful intent. Bergmann (1986) offered a similar perspective. She maintained that when women are continually targeted by sexist and sexual humor, they do not interpret it as merely harmless fun, "an isolated event in which a woman is harmlessly teased or ridiculed" (p. 76). Rather, they interpret it as one instance among many in which others intentionally try to belittle or demean them.

Accordingly, research suggests that men view sexist humor as funnier and less offensive than women (e.g., Love & Deckers, 1989; Neuliep, 1987; Ryan & Kanjorski, 1998). Love and Deckers (1989), for instance, found that women rated sexist cartoons as being less funny than did men because they identified with the cartoon victim. Furthermore, women are more likely than men to view sexist jokes or remarks as constituting harassment (e.g., Bell et al., 2002; Frazier et al., 1995; Hemmasi & Graf, 1998; Smeltzer & Leap, 1988). Smeltzer and Leap (1988) found that women considered sexist humor in the workplace as being more inappropriate than did men. Similarly, Frazier et al. (1995) reported that 74% of the women they surveyed considered sexual jokes and teasing to be harassment, whereas only 47% of the men felt the same.

Interestingly, the amount of work experience women have appears to influence the likelihood that they will label their experiences as sexual harassment. Fitzgerald et al. (1988) administered their SEQ to female undergraduate and graduate students and working women in professional, semiprofessional, and blue-collar positions. One striking finding was that working women were more likely than the student samples to label their experiences as sexual harassment. Furthermore, female graduate students were more likely than undergraduates to label sexual harassment experiences as such. Perhaps with greater work experience, women develop clearer expectations about precisely what constitutes inappropriate conduct at work.

Attitudes Toward Women

Consistent with La Fave's vicarious superiority theory (La Fave, 1972; La Fave, Haddad, & Maesen, 1976/1996) and Zillmann and Cantor's (1972, 1976/1996) disposition theory, the differences in humor perceptions between men and women may be due more to gender attitudes than to biological sex (Hemmasi et al., 1994; Sev'er & Ungar, 1997). A central hypothesis of both theories that has received considerable empirical support is that the degree of amusement elicited by disparaging humor is related positively to the degree to which one holds negative attitudes toward the disparaged target (e.g., Cantor & Zillmann, 1973; La Fave, McCarthy, & Haddad, 1973; McGhee & Duffey, 1983; Wicker, Barron, & Willis, 1980).

In the context of sexist humor, there is substantial evidence suggesting that regardless of gender, people enjoy sexist humor insofar as they hold negative (i.e., sexist) attitudes toward women (e.g., Butland & Ivy, 1990; Ford, Johnson, Blevins, & Zepeda, 1999; Henkin & Fish, 1986; LaFrance & Woodzicka, 1998; Moore, Griffiths, & Payne, 1987). Greenwood and Isbell (2002) found that men and women high in hostile sexism—that is, antagonism toward women (Glick & Fiske, 1996)—were more amused by and less offended by "dumb blonde" jokes than were men and women low in hostile sexism. In similar fashion, Thomas and Esses (2004) found that men reported more enjoyment of female-disparaging jokes and a greater likelihood of telling those jokes insofar as they were high in hostile sexism.

Organizational Status of the Humorist

The interpretation of sexist humor in the workplace depends on the relative status of the humorist and the object of the humor. What is innocent horseplay coming from a coworker may be inappropriate sexual harassment coming from a supervisor. Hemmasi et al. (1994) found that the same sex-related jokes—either sexual or sexist—were more likely to be viewed as sexual harassment when told by a male supervisor than by a male coworker. Giuffre and Williams (1994) interviewed wait staff who worked with members of the same and opposite sex at a restaurant. Almost all of the respondents described their work environment as "highly sexualized" (p. 381). Sexist jokes, sexual innuendo, and teasing were commonplace. Three women and one man reported being sexually harassed by their manager. Interestingly, though, all four reported similar behaviors from their coworkers but did not label the behaviors as sexual harassment. Rather, they dismissed them as "only joking" (p. 384). Sexist joking and sexual teasing from coworkers were taken rather lightly, as innocuous or benign expressions of camaraderie. However, the same behaviors performed by a supervisor were taken seriously and labeled as sexual harassment.

The different reactions to sexist joking by coworkers and superiors may be due to different role expectations ascribed to them. People have conceptions of the prototypical instances of discrimination—behaviors that represent the "best" or "classic" examples of discrimination. Furthermore, instances that match these prototypes are more readily viewed as discrimination than those that do not (Baron, Burgess, & Kao, 1991; Inman & Baron, 1996; Inman, Huerta, & Oh, 1998). Relevant to perceptions of potential sexual harassment, men have traditionally occupied positions of power and authority, and sexual harassment often is viewed as an attempt to assert or maintain power and authority over women (Montemurro, 2003; Thacker & Ferris, 1991). Thus, a male superior denigrating a female subordinate likely conforms to common conceptions of the prototypical or classic case of sexual harassment. As a result, women are more likely to perceive sexual harassment in sexist jokes told by a superior than by a coworker. Ironically,

Pryor (1995b) reports, in a survey of military women, that sexual harassment was perpetrated most often by coworkers (45% of all cases).

Consistent with the prototype hypothesis, Inman and Baron (1996) found that instances of potential discrimination were more likely to be perceived as racism or sexism when perpetrators and targets were prototypical—that is, when they conformed to common notions of the classic instances of discrimination (e.g., Whites derogating Blacks, men derogating women). Rodin, Price, Bryson, and Sanchez (1990) similarly found that perpetrators of a discriminatory acts were seen as being more prejudiced if he or she belonged to an empowered group (e.g., Whites, men) compared to a less powerful group (e.g., Blacks, women).

Collectively, the findings described in this section highlight the need for managers—especially men—to be sensitive to the ways in which their joking may be interpreted. In fact, it would be prudent to advise managers to avoid sexually oriented comments altogether (Hemmasi et al., 1994).

WHY MEN ENGAGE IN SEXIST HUMOR AT WORK

Higher status members of organizations tend to tell jokes more often than lower status members and use humor to solidify or clarify their status or power (Coser, 1960; Hemmasi et al., 1994; Neitz, 1980; Smeltzer & Leap, 1988; Traylor, 1973). Traylor (1973) suggested that humor (disparaging or otherwise) defines social groupings or social rankings and clarifies status differences among group members. Telling disparaging jokes can be viewed as an aggressive act. As such, it is reserved for those higher in organizational or cultural status (Neitz, 1980). Given the sexual stratification of most organizations and society more generally, it is not surprising that men are more likely to initiate sexist jokes. Hemmasi et al. (1994) found that both male and female employees at a variety of organizations considered sexist jokes to be more offensive than neutral jokes, sexual jokes, or jokes that disparaged men. Men, however, were far more likely than women to tell those sexist jokes at work.

Men appear to engage in sexist joking at work for psychological reasons. Berger (1987) identified four types of theories bearing on why humor attempts are or are not perceived as funny: psychoanalytic theories, superiority theories, incongruity theories, and cognitive theories. These theories differ with respect to their relative emphases on the social context and the structure of humor content in the elicitation of amusement. Incongruity and cognitive theories emphasize the irony and surprise of humor content (e.g., Attardo, 1993; Berger, 1987; Raskin, 1985; Suls, 1972). In contrast, superiority theories, most notably, La Fave's vicarious superiority theory (La Fave, 1972; La Fave et al., 1976/1996) and Zillmann and Cantor's (1972, 1976/1996) disposition theory suggest that the origins and functions of humor are grounded in antagonistic relationships between humorists and the objects of their jokes. Superiority theories, then, most directly address why men engage in sexist humor at work.

According to superiority theories, amusement results from a sudden feeling of superiority or triumph one feels from the recognition of the infirmities or misfortunes of others. Essentially, amusement results from the enhancement of self-esteem of the individual or in-group derived from a "downward social comparison" (Wills, 1981) with disliked others or members of an out-group. Accordingly, superiority theories most directly and fully address disparaging forms of humor such as sexist humor (for thorough reviews of superiority theories and their origins, see Ford & Ferguson, 2005; Gruner, 1997; Keith-Spiegel, 1972; Morreall, 1983; Zillmann & Cantor, 1976/1996).

In response to a threat to personal identity or social identity—that part of a person's self-concept that is derived from social group memberships (Tajfel & Turner, 1986)—one might initiate disparaging humor as a means of self-enhancement. Consistent with this idea, theorists have argued that disparaging humor may enhance one's social identity (e.g., Bourhis, Gadfield, Giles, & Tajfel, 1977; Martineau, 1972; Meyer, 2000; Ruscher, 2001). Martineau (1972), for example, suggested that disparaging humor enhances the solidarity of the in-group—that is, the degree to which members identify with the group. In addition, Bourhis et al. (1977) suggested that disparaging humor is a mechanism by which people attain positive distinctiveness from out-groups, allowing them to maintain positive social identities—feelings of superiority over out-groups. They proposed that "anti-out-group humor can, through out-group devaluation and denigration, be a creative and potent way of asserting in-group pride and distinctiveness from a dominant out-group" (p. 261).

The use of sexist humor as a means of self-enhancement in response to threats to social identity can be readily observed in organizations. For example, Kahn (1989) provided an example of sexist humor recorded by a consultant to a bank. The consultant observed that the main work area consisted of tellers, most of whom were women; supervisors, comprised mostly of men; and one manager, a woman who recently was promoted from supervisor. One day, a woman teller accidentally short-circuited a computer system that monitored the bank's transactions. As a result of this incident, many jokes were told throughout the organization about females' alleged inferiority with technology. At a subsequent meeting, a female secretary accidentally unplugged a slide projector with her foot as she walked by. A male supervisor joked to his colleagues about a "woman's touch," which elicited laughter from other supervisors. The consultant hypothesized that the male supervisors resented the woman, who had been promoted to manager, and that this resentment was expressed in the jokes about the teller and the secretary. According to superiority theories, the sexist jokes at the bank could have functioned as a means of self-enhancement for the male supervisors whose social identities were threatened because a woman was promoted to manager over them. The jokes provided male supervisors with a means of reasserting in-group pride and distinctiveness from the women who allegedly were "so incompetent that they could not use the computer without jamming it, and so clumsy that they could not walk across a room without tripping over a cord." Because they, themselves, "could never be so incompetent," the jokes allowed the men to feel superior.

In addition to the psychological function of self-enhancement, men may engage in sexist humor at work to maintain formal organizational power over women (e.g., Brunner & Costello, 2002; Gruber & Bjorn, 1986; Kahn, 1989; Montemurro, 2003; Mulkay, 1988; Sev'er & Ungar, 1997). Montemurro (2003), for example, argued that workplace hierarchies long have been dominated by men, and that sexist humor in the workplace maintains and reinforces this male-dominated structure, while perpetuating the view of women as "second class citizens" (p. 434). Brunner and Costello (2002) similarly suggested that sexist humor supports existing patriarchal structures within organizations and perpetuates the domination of women by hindering their advancement.

Although sexist humor may appear innocent and harmless, it communicates underlying sexist attitudes and stereotypical assumptions about women in the workplace. For example, female tellers in the bank described by Kahn (1989) believed their male supervisors viewed them through the stereotypical lens of female technological inferiority and that this restricted their access to challenging responsibilities involving the bank's computer system. Moreover, the consultant noted that male supervisors might have engaged in sexist joking—either purposely or unconsciously—to communicate their resistance to the promotion of women to positions of control and authority (Kahn, 1989). Thus, sexist joking could have functioned in this bank to maintain formal organizational power imbalances between men and women. This example illustrates that humor, as a medium of communication, is instrumental in preserving existing power structures. Because of its levity and consequent interpretative ambiguity, humor provided a less blatantly hostile, more "socially acceptable" way for male supervisors to communicate sexist sentiments and resistance to women in positions of control and authority.

Organizations or work groups in which women are a sizable minority are especially high-risk settings for gender-harassing behaviors (Kanter, 1977). Indeed, women who lack organizational power because of their minority status or because they hold low status jobs are most likely to be objects of sexist jokes and other forms of sexual harassment (e.g., Gruber & Bjorn, 1986). Pryor (1995b) found, for example, that more than 65% of harassed women in the military reported that there were more men than women in their workplaces.

In her classic study of gender composition in organizations, Kanter (1977) examined the experiences of women who had token status (i.e., one in which women comprised no more than 15% of the employees) at an organization described by the pseudonym "Indsco." In the presence of token women, Indsco men engaged in "boundary heightening," that is, they exaggerated their common qualities as men (the in-group) as well as the ways in which women (the out-group) deviated from them. For example, men told sexist jokes (e.g., raunchy, "farmer's daughter" jokes) and engaged in "locker room humor" as ways of excluding and isolating women as outsiders. By forcing exposure to sexist humor upon the token women, Indsco men simultaneously degraded the organization's women and asserted their dominance and power over them.

THE CONSEQUENCES OF SEXIST HUMOR

We propose that sexist humor in the workplace is a subtle form of harassment that can have deleterious consequences for women in organizations as well as their organizations in toto. In this section, we review theoretical and empirical literature on the effects of sexist humor on stereotypes about and prejudice toward women and on organizational culture. We also consider how women respond to sexist humor in the workplace.

The Relationship Between Sexist Humor and Gender Stereotypes and Prejudice

Sexist humor, itself, is a subtle expression of prejudice, a means of communicating shared stereotypes and antagonistic attitudes toward women. For men in the organizations studied by Kanter (1977) and by Kahn (1989) to "get" the sexist jokes circulated around their respective offices, they had to share knowledge of certain demeaning stereotypes.

Sexist joking certainly is a means of transmitting negative stereotypes and hostile sentiments toward women. It clarifies for group members that demeaning stereotypes and prejudiced attitudes are shared aspects of group culture. However, one may ask whether sexist joking creates negative stereotypes or makes people more prejudiced toward women. Research on the effects of reciting and hearing a variety of types of disparaging humor addresses this question.

Reciting disparaging jokes has been shown to negatively affect the joke teller's attitudes and stereotypes toward the group that is the object of the humor. Hobden and Olson (1994) found that reciting jokes that disparaged lawyers led participants to report a more negative attitude toward lawyers. Maio, Olson, and Bush (1997) likewise found that Canadian participants who recited humor material that disparaged Newfoundlanders reported a more negative stereotypical representation of them. As Hobden and Olson (1994) suggested, both self-perception theory (Bem, 1972) and cognitive dissonance theory (Festinger, 1957) can account for these findings. According to self-perception theory, the negative remarks participants make about a social group could provide information to people about their own attitudes toward the group, thereby leading them to hold negative attitudes and stereotypes. Alternatively, according to cognitive dissonance theory, participants' negative remarks could be inconsistent with their attitudes, thus creating cognitive dissonance. Participants might have changed their attitudes and stereotypes to fit their remarks thereby reducing cognitive dissonance. According to these explanations, the negative consequences of reciting disparaging humor does not implicate any unique effects of humor as a medium of communication apart from the disparaging content.

The effects of exposure to disparaging humor are less intuitive. Olson, Maio, and Hobden (1999) conducted three experiments designed to test the unique effects of exposure to disparaging humor. They exposed participants either to humor disparaging men, humor disparaging lawyers, neutral humor, nonhumorous statements disparaging men, or nonhumorous statements disparaging lawyers. They then measured the content and accessibility of stereotypes about, and attitudes toward, men and lawyers. Across the 3 experiments, they performed a total of 83 analyses, only one of which revealed a significant effect of exposure to disparaging humor relative to exposure to neutral humor or nonhumorous disparagement. In general, exposure to disparaging humor simply did not affect the content or accessibility of stereotypes about and attitudes toward the disparaged groups relative to nonhumorous disparaging statements or neutral humor.

Although Olson et al. (1999) found no effects of exposure to disparaging humor, they did not address empirically two issues that are relevant for interpreting their findings. First, Olson et al. did not measure individual differences in prejudice toward the disparaged groups prior to completing the studies. Therefore, it is possible that disparaging humor could affect stereotypes of out-groups for people who are highly prejudiced toward that group. Second, Olson et al. measured the effects of disparaging humor on stereotypes and attitudes toward groups that were high in status or social power (e.g., men, lawyers). They concluded that disparaging humor might affect only the recipients' stereotypes and attitudes when the disparaged group is relatively disadvantaged or low in status (e.g., women).

Addressing these two issues, Ford, Wentzel, and Lorion (2001) demonstrated that, even among men high in hostile sexism—that is, men who had antagonistic attitudes toward women (Glick & Fiske, 1996)—exposure to sexist humor did not affect the evaluative content of men's stereotypes about women relative to nonhumorous disparagement or to neutral humor. Collectively, then, Olson et al. (1999) and Ford et al. (2001) provide no evidence that exposure to disparaging humor uniquely affects stable knowledge structures, such as stereotypes and attitudes toward social groups.

Sexist Humor Fosters an Organizational Culture of Tolerance of Sexism

Although exposure to disparaging humor may not affect internal sources of self-regulation (i.e., attitudes and stereotypes), it can have negative social consequences. Ryan and Kanjorski (1998), for example, found that, among men, enjoyment of sexist humor was correlated positively with acceptance of rape myths and endorsement of adversarial sexual beliefs. In addition, Ford (2000, Experiment 1) exposed men and women, who scored either high or low in hostile sexism, to sexist jokes (e.g., "A man and a woman were stranded in an elevator and they knew they were gonna die. The woman turns to the man and says, 'Make me feel like a woman before I die.' So he takes off his clothes and says, 'Fold them!'"), sexist statements (e.g., "I just think that a woman's place is in the home and that it's a woman's role to do domestic duties, such as laundry, for her man"), or to neutral jokes. Then, participants read a vignette in which a male supervisor treated a new female employee in a patronizing manner. The supervisor communicated low performance expectations and addressed the female employee using a pet name suggesting a level of romantic intimacy that is inappropriate and potentially threatening in the workplace. After reading the vignette, participants rated the offensiveness of the supervisor's remarks and how critical they were of his remarks. Exposure to sexist jokes led to greater tolerance of the supervisor's sexist remarks in comparison to exposure to neutral jokes or to comparable nonhumorous disparagement, but only for participants scoring high in hostile sexism.

Similarly, Ford et al. (2001) exposed men who were high and low in hostile sexism to either sexist jokes, sexist statements, or neutral jokes. Participants then read the "sexist supervisor" vignette used by Ford (2000, Experiment 1). As they read the vignette, participants were asked to imagine that they were the depicted supervisor, and thus had behaved in a sexist manner themselves. Participants then rated how they would feel about themselves. Upon exposure to sexist jokes, men who were high in hostile sexism anticipated feeling less self-directed negative affect (e.g., guilt, shame) than did men who were low in hostile sexism. Furthermore, men who were high in hostile sexism anticipated feeling less self-directed negative affect upon exposure to sexist jokes than upon exposure to non-humorous sexist statements or to neutral jokes. In contrast, men who were low in hostile sexism reported no differences in anticipated feelings of negative affect upon exposure to sexist jokes, to sexist statements, or to neutral jokes. Taken together, Ford (2000) and Ford et al. (2001) suggest that, among people who have relatively prejudiced attitudes toward women, exposure to sexist humor increases personal tolerance of other instances of discrimination against women.

To explain these findings, Ford and Ferguson (2004) proposed a prejudiced norm theory. According to this conceptualization, sexist humor (and other forms of disparaging humor) changes the "rules" in a given context that dictate appropriate reactions to discrimination against members of the disparaged group. That is, for people with relatively sexist attitudes, it expands the bounds of appropriate conduct, creating a perceived local norm of tolerance of sex discrimination. Sexist humor circulated through an organization, then, can create a culture of tolerance of discrimination against women.

Prejudiced norm theory contends that, as a medium of communication, humor undermines the seriousness with which the underlying message should be interpreted. Humor activates a conversational rule of levity—to switch from the usual serious mind-set to a playful or noncritical mind-set for interpreting the underlying message (Attardo, 1993; Berlyne, 1972; Mannell, 1977; McGhee, 1972; Sev'er & Ungar, 1997; Ziv & Gadish, 1990). As a result, derision of social groups under the guise of humor may go unchallenged and uncriticized (e.g., Bill & Naus, 1992). Indeed, by making light of the expression of prejudice, disparaging humor communicates an implicit normative standard that, in this context, one need not be critical of discrimination against the disparaged group. Instead, the message is sent that it is acceptable in this context to treat such discrimination in a more light-hearted manner.

Furthermore, the recipient's (i.e., the person to whom a joke is told) response to disparaging humor contributes to whether the humor will succeed in creating this implicit norm of tolerance of discrimination. If receivers accept the humor—that is, switching to a noncritical mindset—they tacitly consent to a shared understanding (a social norm) that it is acceptable in this context to make light of discrimination against the disparaged group. That is, humor indicates a shared interpretation of its underlying message to the extent that the receiver approves of it (Fine, 1983). Others have made similar arguments regarding the communication of socially unacceptable sentiments through humor (e.g., Emerson, 1969; Francis, 1988; Khoury, 1985).

The humor recipient, however, may reject the conversational rule to switch to a noncritical mind-set for interpreting the underlying derision. Specifically, the recipient may think it's inappropriate to make light of the expression of prejudice (Apte, 1987; Barker, 1994; Mannell, 1977; Sev'er & Ungar, 1997), and thus challenge (reject) the normative standard implied by the humor (Attardo, 1993; Francis, 1988). The recipient's opposition to the disparaging humor and its implied meta-message suggests there is not a shared understanding that it is acceptable to make light of discrimination against the targeted group. The recipient's rejection of the disparaging humor, then, prevents the construction of a shared norm of tolerance of discrimination. As a result, the broader nonprejudiced standards of conduct should not be displaced by the disparaging humor, and instances of discrimination still should be perceived as socially inappropriate. In keeping with this hypothesis, Ford (2000, Experiments 2 and 3) found that the activation of a noncritical mind-set was necessary for sexist humor to increase tolerance of a sexist event. When participants high in hostile sexism interpreted sexist jokes in a serious or critical manner the effect of exposure to sexist humor on tolerance of a sexist event was nullified.

The recipient's level of prejudice toward the disparaged group affects acceptance or approval of disparaging humor and, thus, the humor's effect on perceptions of normative tolerance of discrimination as well as personal tolerance of discrimination. Highly prejudiced people are less likely to have well-internalized nonprejudiced convictions (Devine, Monteith, Zuwerink, & Elliot, 1991; Devine, Plant, Amodio, Harmon-Jones, & Vance, 2002; Monteith, Devine, & Zuwerink, 1993). Consequently, they should be less likely to challenge or reject disparaging humor and its implicit meta-message that discrimination need not be taken seriously. As we noted earlier, many studies have found that people who have sexist attitudes are inclined to be accepting of and more amused by sexist humor (e.g., Butland & Ivy, 1990; Henkin & Fish, 1986; LaFrance & Woodzicka, 1998; Moore et al., 1987). Because of their greater acceptance of disparaging humor, prejudiced people should be more likely to perceive a norm of tolerance of discrimination against a disparaged group. Supporting this hypothesis, Ford et al. (2001) found that relative to men low in hostile sexism, men high in hostile sexism acknowledged greater tolerance of sexism in their immediate contexts upon being exposed to sexist humor.

Finally, people high in prejudice are not only likely to perceive a norm of tolerance of discrimination upon exposure to disparaging humor, they also are inclined to use that norm as a guide for regulating social judgment. Ford et al. (2001) found that for men high in hostile sexism, a perceived norm of tolerance of sexism mediated the effect of exposure to sexist humor on tolerance of a sexist event. For men high in hostile sexism, exposure to sexist humor created a perceived norm of tolerance of sexism, and they used that norm as a guide for evaluating a separate sexist event.

Prejudiced norm theory, then, implies that sexist humor is an important medium through which an organization's normative structure may be changed. For people with relatively sexist attitudes, sexist humor in the workplace can inhibit critical reactions to sexist behavior, creating a perceived organizational norm of tolerance of sexism. Consistent with this idea, Hemmasi and Graf (1998) reported that the more frequently people hear sexist jokes, the less inappropriate they judge them to be. As they put it, "Apparently, greater exposure to such materials in the workplace (a) desensitizes employees to the question of material inappropriateness; it must be alright if everyone else is doing it, and/or (b) sends the signal to them that the behavior is condoned by the organization" (p. 456).

According to contemporary models of prejudice (e.g., Crandall & Eshleman, 2003; Gaertner & Dovidio, 1986), such a normative climate of tolerance of discrimination fosters the perpetration of discriminatory behavior. By replacing the usual nonsexist norms in a given situation with a norm of tolerance of discrimination against women, sexist humor essentially justifies a wider range of negative responses toward women. Thus, for men with relatively sexist attitudes, sexist humor may create a climate in which they can release their usually suppressed prejudice (Crandall & Eshleman, 2003). Consequently, within such climates sexist men would be likely to engage in subtle forms of discrimination against women upon exposure to sexist humor. Ford, Boxer, Armstrong, & Edel, (2008, Experiment 2) tested this hypothesis. They asked male students to recommend funding cuts to various student organizations after they had viewed either sexist humor video clips or neutral humor video clips. After exposure to the sexist humor clips, men who were high in hostile sexism cut significantly more funding from a women's organization than did men who were low in hostile sexism.

This pattern of results was ameliorated in the neutral humor condition. These findings demonstrate the role of sexist humor as a "releaser" of prejudice toward women and illustrates that exposure to sexist humor can have real consequences for behavior. In this context, sexist behavior could easily be rationalized as falling within the bounds of social acceptability. Sexist humor trivializes derision of women and implies a normative standard that sexism need not be taken seriously in the immediate context.

How Women Respond to Sexist Humor in the Workplace

To this point, we have examined the consequences that sexist humor can have for women in organizations as well as for organizational cultures as a whole. We now turn our attention to the related matter of how women respond, emotionally and behaviorally, to sexist humor in the workplace.

Emotional Reactions

Does sexist joking in the workplace have adverse emotional effects on women or is it merely a benign nuisance? LaFrance and Woodzicka (1998) demonstrated that gender harassment in the form of sexist joking can create serious emotional distress for women.

LaFrance and Woodzicka (1998) examined women's emotional responses to sexist jokes. Female undergraduates listened to an audiotape of a man telling either seven sexist jokes or seven attorney jokes. After this, LaFrance and Woodzicka measured self-reported reactions to the jokes and facial expressions in response to each joke, providing an index of automatic (i.e., spontaneous, uncontrolled) emotional reactions. The findings demonstrate that hearing sexist jokes had adverse emotional effects on women. Specifically, participants reported feeling more disgusted, angry, and surprised in response to sexist jokes than to nonsexist jokes. Also, their nonverbal facial expressions revealed negative affective reactions. Compared to women hearing jokes about attorneys, women hearing sexist jokes were more likely to roll their eyes, displaying feelings of contempt, and to cover their mouths with their hand, showing signs of embarrassment.

Further analyses revealed that participants' levels of hostile sexism (Glick & Fiske, 1996) and their degrees of identification with women moderated their emotional responses to sexist jokes. Specifically, women higher in hostile sexism gave higher amusement and funniness ratings to the sexist jokes. Hostile sexism also predicted automatic affective reactions to sexist jokes: Women higher in hostile sexism displayed more genuine smiling in response to sexist jokes. In addition, level of identification with women was associated negatively with their reports of amusement and the funniness of the sexist jokes. As levels of identification with women increased, women rated sexist jokes as being less funny and less amusing. Level of identification with women also was related positively to displays of frowning facial expressions associated with sadness. In sum, women who endorse nonsexist attitudes or who identify strongly with women have especially adverse emotional reactions to the disparagement of women as communicated in sexist jokes (LaFrance & Woodzicka, 1998).

LaFrance and Woodzicka (1998) demonstrated important emotional reactions women have toward sexist humor. Importantly, other research conducted in actual workplace settings corroborates their findings. For example, Fitzgerald and Swan (1995) noted that gender harassment operates cumulatively to create psychological stress for victims (and a hostile work environment) in much the same way that frequent hassles (e.g., time pressures and interpersonal difficulties) create stress. Although any given joke or sexist remark in itself might not create much stress, repeated exposure to such harassment over time may create substantial psychological discomfort (e.g., Crull, 1982; Gutek & Koss, 1993; LaFrance & Woodzicka, 1998). Pryor (1995b) reported that a survey conducted by the U.S. Merit Systems Protection Board (USMSPB) in 1981 found that 21% of women who experienced gender-harassing behaviors (e.g., sexist or sexual joking/teasing) reported having emotional and physical problems as a result. Gutek and Koss (1993) similarly reported that women often experienced self-blame, anxiety, depression, anger and disillusionment in response to gender-harassing behaviors. In addition, gender-harassed women also experienced lower levels of job satisfaction and motivation.

The organizational status of the harasser influences the degree to which women experience emotional problems as well as negative attitudes toward the organization. These problems are more pronounced when the harasser is a supervisor as opposed to a coworker, subordinate, or other member of the organization. Indeed, one of the most important factors influencing the psychological reactions of the harassed woman is whether the harasser possesses some sort of organizational power over her (Pryor, 1995b).

Women's organizational status also affects their emotional reactions to gender harassment. High status can act as a buffer against the emotional effects of harassment. Pryor's (1995b) study indicated that women of higher military rank experienced fewer negative emotional reactions to sexually harassing behaviors than their lower ranked counterparts. Their higher organizational status presumably provided more avenues for redress. However, harassed women of all military ranks experienced considerable emotional distress insofar as they believed that reporting the harassment formally would be ineffective in stopping it.

Pryor's (1995a) survey of over 2,600 government employees examined some of the reasons why gender harassment in the workplace bothers or distresses women. Female employees were asked to rate their agreement with nine statements regarding why harassing behavior might affect them negatively in the workplace (e.g., "the behaviors I observed were unprofessional," "the person who did these things was trying to exploit his or her power over me"). Most women indicated that there were multiple reasons why gender-harassing behaviors at work bothered them. However, the most popularly expressed reason (75%) was that such behaviors violated their expectations of professionalism in the workplace—expectations that do not include sexist joking. Furthermore, women were particularly offended by sexist joking by a male superior because it violated expectations of professionalism to a greater degree than the same behavior by a male coworker, and also because it was seen as an abuse of power. In fact, 26% of the female employees reported that exploitation of power was a reason why sexist behavior at work was distressing.

Behavioral Responses

Women often respond to gender harassment in a passive manner, such as by ignoring it, going along with it, laughing it off, reinterpreting it as innocuous, pretending not to notice, and blaming themselves (Gruber, 1989; Gruber & Bjorn, 1986; Gutek & Koss, 1993; Pryor, 1995b; Swim & Hyers, 1999). Jensen and Gutek (1982), for instance found that 25% of harassed women attributed their victimization internally, to something they did themselves. In keeping with this, and out of fear of retaliation, women often avoid such assertive strategies as directly challenging their harassers (Gruber, 1989). Furthermore, women generally refrain from using formal organizational channels as a means of redress because they perceive their organizations as unable to protect them adequately from retaliation (e.g., Collins & Blodgett, 1981; Gruber, 1989; USMSPB, 1981). Gutek (1985) revealed that only 18% of harassed women reported incidents of sexual harassment to individuals in positions of authority, and Gruber and Bjorn (1982) found that only 7% did so. Similarly, Pryor (1995b) stated that only 10% of harassed women took any formal actions whatsoever against their harassers.

Women may respond to gender and sexual harassment in passive manners because they are highly visible minorities in male-dominated workplaces or because they have relatively lower job status or job skills in their organizations (Gruber & Bjorn, 1986). Thus, women's lower levels of organizational power may preclude anything other than passive responses to incidents of sexual harassment, particularly without fear of retaliation

(Fitzgerald & Swan, 1995). Indeed, retaliation is a legitimate fear. Women who report sexual harassment receive lower job evaluations, are denied promotions, and sometimes even are fired (Loy & Stewart, 1984). In studies of sexual harassment described by Fitzgerald and Swan (1995), women who filed formal complaints reported that it "only made things worse" (p. 123). Gruber (1989) reported that women are unlikely to respond to sexual harassment in assertive or confrontational manners because such actions often are discouraged by the cultures of their organizations. In such cultures, women are likely to believe that their complaints will not be handled in serious, sympathetic, and professional manners.

Women also may fail to confront or to report gender harassment because such actions are inconsistent with expectations to comply with the stereotypical role of women as passive and polite (Ruscher, 2001). For many women, it may seem inappropriate to do anything but endure or tolerate harassing jokes and remarks by male coworkers or superiors. Thus, women may perceive the most appropriate and organizationally adaptive strategy for dealing with gender harassment is to ignore it, laugh it off, or deny that it is a problem. At the Indsco corporation described by Kanter (1977), women were expected to accept the joking without challenge or criticism. When they objected, male colleagues criticized them for lacking a sense of humor. Furthermore, women reported being "tested" by men who would tell sexist jokes in their presence and observe their reactions. Women who accepted the jokes were accepted as loyal "honorary in-groupers," whereas women who objected were ridiculed for having "no sense of humor." Such women risked being labeled according to negative stereotypes, such as "women's libber" or "iron maiden," and were shunned by their male colleagues.

Corroborating Kanter's case study findings, Dodd, Giuliano, Boutell, and Moran (2001) reported that, in an experimental setting, men disliked a woman who confronted a sexist remark more than a woman who reacted passively. When faced with sexist jokes or other gender-harassing behaviors, women must weigh the possibility of social reprisals into their decisions of how to respond. Not surprisingly, many women find it easier simply to "go along with" sexist jokes than to risk negative sanctions from workplace colleagues by speaking out against them (Kanter, 1977; Montemurro, 2003).

Beyond fear of reprisals, the interpretative ambiguity of sexist humor also may discourage assertive responses. It can compromise a woman's understanding of how best to respond. Sexist jokes trivialize gender harassment (Montemurro, 2003). Thus, although women may find sexist jokes offensive, they might not know whether a particular sexist joke constitutes a degree of harassment sufficiently serious to warrant assertive, formal responses. Montemurro (2003) asserts further that the trivialization of gender harassment is reinforced by the "humorous" portrayal in television sitcoms of gender harassment in the workplace. By portraying gender harassment as funny and not to be taken seriously, television shows trivialize it, thereby contributing to the ambiguity women may experience when deciding how to interpret and respond to demeaning sexist jokes.

MANAGERIAL IMPLICATIONS

Sexual harassment affects not only victims, but their organizations as well (Gutek & Koss, 1993; Schaefer & Finegold, 1995). The possible costs of sexual harassment to organizations include the obvious legal liabilities, as well as low employee morale, loss of loyalty to the organization, and reduced productivity (Schaefer & Finegold, 1995). In 1981, the USMSPB noted that sexual harassment levies a substantial cost to organizations, both directly in terms of turnover (10% of women victims quit their jobs), absenteeism and medical costs, and indirectly, in terms of victims' lowered motivation, distraction, and loss of commitment to their organizations (Gutek & Koss, 1993; Schaefer & Finegold, 1995).

Sexist humor, in particular, diminishes cohesiveness among coworkers (Duncan, 1982). Specifically, it fosters competition and discourages teamwork among men and women. In a context of sexist humor, which demeans women, men and women can have difficulty relating to one another as equals free of disrespect, resentment, and antagonism. Sexist humor also may reinforce status differences between men (the joke tellers) and women (objects of sexist jokes) thereby perpetuating power imbalances between them (Duncan, 1982; Sev'er & Ungar, 1997).

This evidence should not be taken to suggest that organizations should completely avoid or suppress all humor. After all, humor in the workplace can foster positive working relationships. It contributes to relationship building among colleagues; it allows employees to communicate disagreement in a nonthreatening manner, and it fosters group cohesiveness and solidarity (Duncan, 1982; Holmes & Marra, 2002; Martineau, 1972). Only when humor is used to disparage a group of people or to create a hostile work environment does it become problematic.

How, then, can organizations avoid sexual harassment while maintaining an atmosphere that allows for collegial humor? We now consider several possibilities.

Acknowledge Deleterious Effects

To begin, leaders need to recognize that sexist humor is not merely harmless fun. It has deleterious effects on women and their organizations. Managers need to appreciate the difficulty women have in determining whether sexist joking or teasing constitutes harassment. They need to know that women's emotional reactions to being demeaned and disrespected affect their motivation, morale, and job satisfaction. Finally, managers need to recognize that women have fears about reporting harassment (e.g., negative job evaluations, demotions, being labeled according to a negative stereotype). Understanding women's experiences enables managers to deal effectively and sensitively with harassment claims (Cabrera & Kleiner, 1992). For example, awareness of the emotional and behavioral effects sexist humor has on women can help managers appreciate the seriousness of sexist humor and help shape their intervention strategies. Managers can communicate their awareness of the harmfulness of sexist humor and other forms of gender harassment by taking swift, decisive action when such incidents are reported, and by holding harassers accountable for their behavior (Schaefer & Finegold, 1995).

Encourage Normative Change and Set Clear Guidelines

Managers cannot merely react to individual instances of sexist humor or other harassing behaviors as they occur. Prejudiced norm theory asserts that when men engage in sexist joking with impunity, an implicit norm of tolerance of sex discrimination may emerge and guide their actions toward women and their reactions to sex discrimination. If permitted, sexist humor can shape the culture of organizations in ways that have deleterious effects for women. Thus, it is critical that managers create proactively a normative culture of zero tolerance of sexist humor and other behaviors that contribute to sex discrimination (Schaefer & Finegold,

1995). They also must formally educate employees about organizational policies regarding sexual harassment (Schaefer & Finegold, 1995).

With this in mind, the National Alliance to Nurture the Aged and the Youth (NANAY) recommended that organizations establish guidelines for appropriate workplace humor. For example, it should be free of sexual suggestion or offense, and it never should come at the expense of someone else (NANAY, 2002). Humor at the expense of others is an aggressive act that relegates the object of humor to a subservient, inferior status (Neitz, 1980). Workplace humor should allow men and women to laugh together and should come at the expense of neither. Such humor can only occur in a climate of equality and mutual respect between men and women with neither gender attempting to assert superiority over the other (Neitz, 1980).

Efforts to create organizational cultures that are intolerant of sexist jokes and other forms of harassment have positive effects on women's responses to harassing behaviors and their attitudes toward their organization. Culbertson and Rodgers (1997), for instance, found that Navy women reported satisfaction with and commitment to the Navy as a whole to the extent that they perceived officers as being strongly committed to taking sexual harassment policies seriously (e.g., by taking swift and appropriate action to incidents of sexual harassment).

Taken together, we advocate that managers participate in "harassment awareness and prevention" workshops. Workshops should educate managers about different types of sexual harassment and how harassment affects victims and their organizations. In particular, workshops should bring to light the not-so-obvious effects of seemingly innocuous sexist humor on women and their organizations. Furthermore, managers should be trained in how to respond to harassment claims and in how to identify developing harassment situations (e.g., situations in which women are reluctant to report incidents of sexist joking). Workshops also should provide ideas for how managers can initiate and maintain a culture of zero tolerance for sex discrimination.

CONCLUSION

We have examined the capacity of sexist humor to function as a subtle form of sexual harassment in the workplace. Research overwhelmingly demonstrates that sexist humor in the workplace is indeed a form of gender harassment and not merely harmless entertainment (Bergmann, 1986; Duncan et al., 1990; Fitzgerald et al., 1988; Frazier et al., 1995; Gruber & Bjorn, 1982; Kanter, 1977; Pryor, 1995a, 1995b). Although humor in the workplace may have positive functions, sexist humor clearly does not. Humor that trivializes sex discrimination should be avoided to promote a friendly and supportive workplace environment for all employees. Sexism communicated through humor should be treated seriously to minimize harmful consequences to both victims and organizations.

Sexist humor's harmful consequences extend beyond the workplace. Not only does sexist humor maintain an imbalanced "sexist social order" (Crawford, 2000, p. 220), it also might increase the propensity of sexist men to commit sexual violence against women. Viki, Thoma, and Hamid (2008) found that sexist men reported a greater propensity to commit sexually violent acts against women upon exposure to sexist jokes than they did upon exposure to neutral jokes.

Sexist humor derives power to trivialize sexism and foster a normative climate of tolerance of sex discrimination from the ambiguity of society's attitudes toward women. The blatant sexism and open discrimination that existed prior to the civil rights movement of the 1960s and the feminist movement of the 1970s has been largely replaced by subtle, more complex forms of sexism such as "ambivalent sexism" (Glick & Fiske, 1996), "modern sexism" (Swim, Aikin, Hall, & Hunter, 1995), and "neo-sexism" (Tougas, Brown, Beaton, & Joly, 1995). These contemporary models suggest that attitudes toward women have become ambivalent, containing both positive and negative components. That is, many Americans consciously espouse egalitarian values and nonprejudiced attitudes while possessing negative sentiments toward women.

As a result of this ambivalence, society does not consider sexism as being completely unacceptable as it might prejudice toward dentists or boy scouts. On the other hand, society does not treat sexism as being completely acceptable and free to be expressed openly as it might prejudice toward criminals or White supremacy groups (Crandall & Ferguson, 2005). Sexism is in an in-between state of acceptability—it is in what Crandall and Ferguson (2005) refer to as a state of shifting social acceptability. That is, sexism is shifting from being completely acceptable to being completely unacceptable. Thus, sexism is conditional. It must be suppressed under most circumstances. However, it may be released, if immediate social norms justify its expression (Crandall & Eshleman, 2003). Sexist humor creates such norms.

We are optimistic that society's attitudes toward women will continue to become egalitarian. As they do, sexism will shift from being conditional to being completely unacceptable. And when this occurs, sexist humor will seem as inappropriate and passé as jokes about African Americans or Irish immigrants seem now.

REFERENCES

Apte, M. L. (1987). Ethnic humor versus "sense of humor": An American sociocultural dilemma. *American Behavioral Scientist, 30*, 27–41.

Attardo, S. (1993). Violation of conversational maxims and cooperation: The case of jokes. *Journal of Pragmatics, 19*, 537–558.

Baird, C. L., Bensko, N. L., Bell, P. A., Viney, W., & Woody, W. D. (1995). Gender influence on perceptions of hostile environment sexual harassment. *Psychological Reports, 77*, 79–82.

Barker, K. (1994). To be PC or not to be? A social psychological inquiry into political correctness. *Journal of Social Behavior and Personality, 9*, 271–281.

Baron, R. S., Burgess, M. L., & Kao, C. F. (1991). Detecting and labeling prejudice: Do female perpetrators go undetected? *Personality and Social Psychology Bulletin, 17*, 115–123.

Bell, M. P., McLaughlin, M. E., & Sequeira, J. M. (2002). Discrimination, harassment, and the glass ceiling: Women executives as change agents. *Journal of Business Ethics, 37*, 65–76.

Bem, D. J. (1972). Self-perception theory. In L. Berkowitz (Ed.), *Advances in experimental social psychology* (Vol. 6, pp. 1–62). San Diego, CA: Academic Press.

Berger, A. A. (1987). Humor: An introduction. *American Behavioral Scientist, 30*, 6–15.

Bergmann, M. (1986). How many feminists does it take to make a joke? Sexist humor and what's wrong with it. *Hypatia, 1*, 63–80.

Berlyne, D. E. (1972). Humor and its kin. In J. H. Goldstein & P. E. McGhee (Eds.), *The psychology of humor* (pp. 43–60). New York, NY: Academic Press.

Bill, B., & Naus, P. (1992). The role of humor in the interpretation of sexist incidents. *Sex Roles, 27*, 645–664.

Bourhis, R. Y., Gadfield, N. J., Giles, H., & Tajfel, H. (1977). Context and ethnic humor in intergroup relations. In A. J. Chapman & H. C. Foot (Eds.), *It's a funny thing, humor* (pp. 261–265). Elmsford, NY: Pergamon Press.

Broderick v. Ruder, 46 FEB Cases 1272 (1988).

Brunner, P. W., & Costello, M. L. (2002, Spring). *Where's the joke? The meaning behind sexual humor. Advancing Women in Leadership.* http://www.advancingwomen.com/awl/spring2002/BRUNN%7E37.HTM

Butland, M. J., & Ivy, D. K. (1990). The effects of biological sex and egalitarianism on humor appreciation: Replication and extension. *Journal of Social Behavior and Personality, 5*, 353–366.

Cabrera, N., & Kleiner, B. H. (1992). Understanding and dealing with the problem of sexual harassment in the workplace. *Women in Management Review, 7*, 16–20.

Cantor, J. R., & Zillmann, D. (1973). Resentment toward victimized protagonists and severity of misfortunes they suffer as factors in humor appreciation. *Journal of Experimental Research in Personality, 6,* 321–329.

Collins, E. G. C., & Blodgett, T. B. (1981, March/April). Sexual harassment: Some see it, some won't. *Harvard Business Review,* 77–95.

Coser, R. L. (1960). Laughter among colleagues: A study of the social functions of humor among the staff at a mental hospital. *Psychiatry, 23,* 81–95.

Crandall, C. S., & Eshleman, A. (2003). A justification-suppression model of the expression and experience of prejudice. *Psychological Bulletin, 129,* 414–446.

Crandall, C. S., & Ferguson, M. A. (2005, September). *Prejudice and prejudices: Resistance to social change is at the heart of prejudice.* Paper presented at the conference Looking Toward the Future: Discrimination and Prejudice in the 21st Century, Madison, WI.

Crawford, M. (2000). Only joking: Humor and sexuality. In C. Travis & J. White (Eds.), *Sexuality, society, and feminism* (pp. 213–236). Washington, DC: American Psychological Association.

Crull, P. (1982). Stress effects of sexual harassment on the job: Implications for counseling. *American Journal of Orthopsychiatry, 52,* 539–543.

Culbertson, A., & Rodgers, W. (1997). Improving managerial effectiveness in the workplace: The case of sexual harassment of navy women. *Journal of Applied Social Psychology, 27,* 1953–1971.

Devine, P. G., Monteith, M. J., Zuwerink, J. R., & Elliot, A. J. (1991). Prejudice with and without compunction. *Journal of Personality and Social Psychology, 60,* 817–830.

Devine, P. G., Plant, E. A., Amodio, D. M., Harmon-Jones, E., & Vance, S. L. (2002). The regulation of explicit and implicit racial bias: The role of motivations to respond without prejudice. *Journal of Personality and Social Psychology, 82,* 835–848.

Dodd, E. H., Giuliano, T. A., Boutell, J. M., & Moran, B. E. (2001). Respected or rejected: Perceptions of women who confront sexist remarks. *Sex Roles, 45,* 567–577.

Duncan, W. J. (1982). Humor in management: Prospects for administrative practice and research. *Academy of Management Review, 7,* 136–142.

Duncan, W. J., Smeltzer, L. R., & Leap, T. L. (1990). Humor and work: Applications of joking behavior to management. *Journal of Management, 16,* 255–278.

Emerson, J. P. (1969). Negotiating the serious import of humor. *Sociometry, 32,* 169–181.

Equal Employment Opportunity Commission. (1980). Guidelines on discrimination because of sex. *Federal Register, 45,* 74676–74677.

Equal Employment Opportunity Commission. (1993). Notice of proposed rule making: Guidelines on harassment based on race, color, religion, gender, national origin, age, or disability. *Federal Register, 58,* 51266–51269.

Festinger, L. (1957). *A theory of cognitive dissonance.* Stanford, CA: Stanford University Press.

Fine, G. A. (1983). Sociological approaches to the study of humor. In P. E. McGhee & J. H. Goldstein (Eds.), *Handbook of humor research* (pp. 159–181). New York, NY: Springer-Verlag.

Fine, G. A., & De Soucey, M. (2005). Joking cultures: Humor themes as social regulation in group life. *Humor: International Journal of Humor Research, 18,* 1–22.

Fitzgerald, L. F., Shullman, S. L., Bailey, N., Richards, M., Swecker, J., Gold, Y., ... Weitzman, L. (1988). The incidence and dimensions of sexual harassment in academia and the workplace. *Journal of Vocational Behavior, 32,* 152–175.

Fitzgerald, L. F., & Swan, S. (1995). Why didn't she just report him? The psychological and legal implications of women's responses to sexual harassment. *Journal of Social Issues, 51,* 117–138.

Fitzgerald, L. F., Weitzman, L. M., Gold, Y., & Ormerod, M. (1988). Academic harassment: Sex and denial in scholarly garb. *Psychology of Women Quarterly, 12,* 329–340.

Ford, T. E. (2000). Effects of sexist humor on tolerance of sexist events. *Personality and Social Psychology Bulletin, 26,* 1094–1107.

Ford, T. E., Boxer, C. F., Armstrong, J., & Edel, J. R. (2008). More than just a joke: The prejudice-releasing function of sexist humor. *Personality and Social Psychology Bulletin 32,* 159–170.

Ford, T. E., & Ferguson, M. A. (2004). Social consequences of disparagement humor: A prejudiced norm theory. *Personality and Social Psychology Review, 8,* 79–94.

Ford, T. E., & Ferguson, M. A. (2005). *Disparagement humor: A theoretical and empirical review of psychoanalytic, superiority, and social identity theories. Humor: International Journal of Humor Research, 21*(3), 283–312.

Ford, T. E., Johnson, F. J., Blevins, J., & Zepeda, C. (1999, August). *Effects of the gender of the joke-teller upon perceptions of offensiveness of sexist jokes.* Paper presented at the annual meeting of the American Sociological Association, Chicago, IL.

Ford, T. E., Wentzel, E. R., & Lorion, J. (2001). Effects of exposure to sexist humor on perceptions of normative tolerance of sexism. *European Journal of Social Psychology, 31,* 677–691.

Francis, R. G. (1988). Some sociology of humor: The joke. *International Social Science Review, 63,* 431–446.

Frazier, P. A., Cochran, C. C., & Olson, A. M. (1995). Social science research on lay definitions of sexual harassment. *Journal of Social Issues, 51,* 21–37.

Gaertner, S. L., & Dovidio, J. F. (1986). The aversive form of racism. In J. F. Dovidio & S. L. Gaertner (Eds.), *Prejudice, discrimination and racism* (pp. 61–89). San Diego, CA: Academic Press.

Giuffre, P. A., & Williams, C. L. (1994). Boundary lines: Labeling sexual harassment in restaurants. *Gender and Society, 8,* 378–401.

Glick, P., & Fiske, S. T. (1996). The ambivalent sexism inventory: Differentiating hostile and benevolent sexism. *Journal of Personality and Social Psychology, 70,* 491–512.

Graf, L. A., & Hemmasi, M. (1995, November). Risqué humor: How it really affects the workplace. *HR Magazine, 40,* 64–67.

Greenwood, D., & Isbell, L. M. (2002). Ambivalent sexism and the dumb blonde: Men's and women's reactions to sexist jokes. *Psychology of Women Quarterly, 26,* 341–350.

Gruber, J. E. (1989). How women handle sexual harassment: A literature review. *Sociology and Social Research, 74,* 3–9.

Gruber, J. E., & Bjorn, L. (1986). Women's responses to sexual harassment: An analysis of sociocultural, organizational, and personal resource models. *Social Science Quarterly, 67,* 814–826.

Gruner, C. R. (1997). *The game of humor: A comprehensive theory of why we laugh.* New Brunswick, NJ: Transaction Publishers.

Gutek, B. (1985). *Sex and the workplace.* San Francisco, CA: Jossey-Bass.

Gutek, B., & Koss, M. P. (1993). Changed women and changed organizations: Consequences of and coping with sexual harassment. *Journal of Vocational Behavior, 42,* 1–21.

Hemmasi, M., & Graf, L. (1998). Sexual and sexist humor in the work place: Just "good fun" or sexual harassment? *Proceedings of Decision Sciences Institute* (pp. 455–457). Las Vegas, NE: DSI.

Hemmasi, M., Graf, L. A., & Russ, G. S. (1994). Gender-related jokes in the workplace: Sexual humor or sexual harassment? *Journal of Applied Social Psychology, 24,* 1114–1128.

Henkin, B., & Fish, J. M. (1986). Gender and personality differences in the appreciation of cartoon humor. *Journal of Psychology, 120,* 157–175.

Hobden, K. L., & Olson, J. M. (1994). From jest to antipathy: Disparagement humor as a source of dissonance-motivated attitude change. *Basic and Applied Social Psychology, 15,* 239–249.

Holmes, J., & Marra, M. (2002). Over the edge? Subversive humor between colleagues and friends. *Humor: International Journal of Humor Research, 15,* 65–87.

Inman, M. L., & Baron, R. S. (1996). Influence of prototypes on perceptions of prejudice. *Journal of Personality and Social Psychology, 70,* 727–739.

Inman, M. L., Huerta, J., & Oh, S. (1998). Perceiving discrimination: The role of prototypes and norm violation. *Social Cognition, 16,* 418–450.

Jensen, I., & Gutek, B. A. (1982). Attributions and assignment of responsibility for sexual harassment. *Journal of Social Issues, 38,* 121–136.

Johnson, A. M. (1990). The "only joking" defense: Attribution bias or impression management? *Psychological Reports, 67,* 1051–1056.

Kahn, W. (1989). Toward a sense of organizational humor: Implications for organizational diagnosis and change. *Journal of Applied Behavioral Science, 25,* 45–63.

Kanter, R. M. (1977). Numbers: Minorities and majorities. In *Men and women of the corporation* (pp. 206–242). New York, NY: Basic Books.

Keith-Spiegel, P. (1972). Early conceptions of humor: Varieties and issues. In J. H. Goldstein & P. E. McGhee (Eds.), *The psychology of humor* (pp. 4–39). New York, NY: Academic Press.

Khoury, R. M. (1985). Norm formation, social conformity, and the confederating function of humor. *Social Behavior and Personality, 13,* 159–165.

La Fave, L. (1972). Humor judgments as a function of reference groups and identification classes. In J. H. Goldstein and P. E. McGhee (Eds.), *The psychology of humor* (pp. 195-210). New York, NY: Academic Press.

La Fave, L., Haddad, J., & Maesen, W. A. (1996). Superiority, enhanced self-esteem, and perceived incongruity humor theory. In A. J. Chapman & H. C. Foot (Eds.), *Humor and laughter: Theory, research and applications* (pp. 63–91). New York, NY: Wiley. (Original work published 1976)

La Fave, L., McCarthy, K., & Haddad, J. (1973). Humor judgments as a function of identification classes: Canadian vs. American. *Journal of Psychology, 85,* 53–59.

LaFrance, M., & Woodzicka, J. A. (1998). No laughing matter: Women's verbal and nonverbal reactions to sexist humor. In J. Swim & C. Stangor (Eds.), *Prejudice: The target's perspective* (pp. 61–80). San Diego, CA: Academic Press.

Love, A. M., & Deckers, L. H. (1989). Humor appreciation as a function of sexual, aggressive, and sexist content. *Sex Roles, 20,* 649–654.

Loy, P. H., & Stewart, L. P. (1984). The extent and effects of sexual harassment of working women. *Sociological Focus, 17,* 31–43.

Machan, D. (1987). What's black and blue and floats in the Monongahela River? *Forbes, 140,* 216–220.

Maio, G. R., Olson, J. M., & Bush, J. (1997). Telling jokes that disparage social groups: Effects on the joke-teller's stereotypes. *Journal of Applied Social Psychology, 27,* 1986–2000.

Malone, P. B. (1980). Humor: A double-edged tool for today's managers. *Academy of Management Review, 5,* 357–360.

Mannell, R. C. (1977). Vicarious superiority, injustice, and aggression in humor: The role of the playful "judgmental set." In A. J. Chapman & H. C. Foot (Eds.), *It's a funny thing, humor* (pp. 273–276). Elmsford, NY: Pergamon Press.

Martineau, W. H. (1972). A model of social functions of humor. In J. H. Goldstein & P. E. McGhee (Eds.), *The psychology of humor* (pp. 101–125). New York: Academic Press.

Meritor Savings Bank v. Vinson, 106 S. Ct. 2399 (1989).

Meyer, J. C. (2000). Humor as a double-edged sword: Four functions of humor in communication. *Communication Theory, 10,* 310–331.

McGhee, P. E. (1972). On the cognitive origins of incongruity humor: Fantasy assimilation versus reality assimilation. In J. H. Goldstein & P. E. McGhee (Eds.), *The psychology of humor* (pp. 61–79). New York, NY: Academic Press.

McGhee, P. E., & Duffey, N. S. (1983). Children's appreciation of humor victimizing different racial groups: Racial-ethnic differences. *Journal of Cross-Cultural Psychology, 14,* 29–40.

Monteith, M. J., Devine, P. G., & Zuwerink, J. R. (1993). Self-directed versus other-directed affect as a consequence of prejudice-related discrepancies. *Journal of Personality and Social Psychology, 64,* 198–210.

Montemurro, B. (2003). Not a laughing matter: Sexual harassment as "material" on workplace-based situation comedies. *Sex Roles, 48,* 433–445.

Moore, T. E., Griffiths, K., & Payne, B. (1987). Gender, attitudes towards women, and the appreciation of sexist humor. *Sex Roles, 16,* 521–531.

Morreall, J. (1983). *Taking laughter seriously.* Albany, NY: State University of New York.

Mulkay, M. (1988). *On humor: Its nature and its place in modern society.* Oxford, United Kingdom: Basil Blackwell.

National Alliance to Nurture the Aged and the Youth. (2002). A little workplace humor might get people back on track. Retrieved July 20, 2005, from http://www.nanay.com/News%20Update/April%202002/Humor.htm

Neitz, M. J. (1980). Humor, hierarchy, and the changing status of women. *Psychiatry, 43,* 211–223.

Neuliep, J. W. (1987). Gender differences in the perception of sexual and nonsexual humor. *Journal of Social Behavior and Personality, 2,* 345–351.

Olson, J. M., Maio, G. R., & Hobden, K. L. (1999). The (null) effects of exposure to disparagement humor on stereotypes and attitudes. *Humor: International Journal of Humor Research, 12,* 195–219.

Pache, I. (1992). Maybe there is some anger behind that laughter: Humor and laughter in a multi-cultural women's group. *Working Papers on Language, Gender & Sexism, 2,* 87–97.

Pryor, J. B. (1995a). The phenomenology of sexual harassment: Why does sexual behavior bother people in the workplace? *Consulting Psychology Journal: Practice and Research, 47,* 160–168.

Pryor, J. B. (1995b). The psychosocial impact of sexual harassment on women in the U.S. military. *Basic and Applied Social Psychology, 17,* 581–603.

Raskin, V. (1985). *Semantic mechanisms of humor.* Boston, MA: Reidel.

Rodin, M. J., Price, J. M., Bryson, J. B., & Sanchez, F. J. (1990). Asymmetry in prejudice attribution. *Journal of Experimental Social Psychology, 26,* 481–504.

Roy, D. F. (1960). "Banana time": Job satisfaction and informal interaction. *Human Organization, 18,* 158–168.

Ruscher, J. B. (2001). *Prejudiced communication: A social psychological perspective.* New York, NY: Guilford Press.

Ryan, K. M., & Kanjorski, J. (1998). The enjoyment of sexist humor, rape attitudes, and relationship aggression in college students. *Sex Roles, 38,* 743–756.

Schaefer, A. G., & Finegold, M. A. (1995, February). Creating a harassment-free workplace. *Risk Management,* pp. 53–56.

Sev'er, A., & Ungar, S. (1997). No laughing matter: Boundaries of gender-based humour in the classroom. *Journal of Higher Education, 68*, 87–105.

Smeltzer, L. R., & Leap, T. L. (1988). An analysis of individual reactions to potentially offensive jokes in work settings. *Human Relations, 41*, 295–304.

Suls, J. M. (1972). A two-stage model for the appreciation of jokes and cartoons: An information-processing analysis. In J. H. Goldstein & P. E. McGhee (Eds.), *The psychology of humor* (pp. 81–100). New York, NY: Academic Press.

Swim, J. K., Aikin, K. J., Hall, W. S., & Hunter, B. A. (1995). Sexism and racism: Old-fashioned and modern prejudices. *Journal of Personality and Social Psychology, 68*, 199–214.

Swim, J. K., & Hyers, L. L. (1999). Excuse me—what did you just say?!: Women's public and private responses to sexist remarks. *Journal of Experimental Social Psychology, 35*, 68–88.

Tajfel, H., & Turner, J. C. (1986). The social identity theory of intergroup behavior. In W. G. Austin & S. Worchel (Eds.), *Psychology of intergroup relations* (pp. 7–24). Chicago, IL: Nelson-Hall.

Terpstra, D. E., & Baker, D. D. (1987). A hierarchy of sexual harassment. *Journal of Psychology, 121*, 599–605.

Thacker, R. A., & Ferris, G. R. (1991). Understanding sexual harassment in the workplace: The influence of power and politics within the dyadic interaction of harasser and target. *Human Resource Management Review, 1*, 23–37.

Thomas, C. A., & Esses, V. M. (2004). Individual differences in reactions to sexist humor. *Group Processes and Intergroup Relations, 7*, 89–100.

Traylor, G. (1973). Joking in a bush camp. *Human Relations, 26*, 479–486.

Tougas, F., Brown, R., Beaton, A. M., & Joly, S. (1995). Neosexism: Plus ça change, plus c'est pareil. *Personality and Social Psychology Bulletin, 21*, 842–849.

Ullian, J. A. (1976). Joking at work. *Journal of Communication, 26*, 129–133.

U.S. Merit Systems Protection Board. (1981). *Sexual harassment in the federal workplace: Is it a problem?* Washington, DC: U.S. Government Printing Office.

Viki, G. T., Thoma, M., & Hamid, S. (2008). *Why did the woman cross the road? The effect of sexist humor on men's self-reported rape proclivity.* Unpublished manuscript, University of Kent, Canterbury, Kent, UK.

Wicker, F. W., Barron, W. L., III, & Willis, A. C. (1980). Disparagement humor: Dispositions and resolutions. *Journal of Personality and Social Psychology, 39*, 701–709.

Wills, T. A. (1981). Downward comparison principles in social psychology. *Psychological Bulletin, 90*, 245–271.

Yedes, J. (1996). Playful teasing: Kiddin' on the square. *Discourse and Society, 7*, 417–438.

Zillmann, D., & Cantor, J. R. (1996). A disposition theory of humor and mirth. In A. J. Chapman & H. C. Foot (Eds.), *Humor and laughter: Theory, research and applications* (pp. 93–116). New York, NY: Wiley. (Original work published 1976)

Ziv, A., & Gadish, O. (1990). The disinhibiting effects of humor: Aggressive and affective responses. *Humor: International Journal of Humor Research, 3*, 247–257.

7

Lying to Bosses, Subordinates, Peers, and the Outside World: Motivations and Consequences

Steven L. Grover

In Thomas Hardy's (1927) novel *Far from the Madding Crowd*, an army officer named Troy shows off his swordsmanship to a young lady named Bathsheba by removing a caterpillar from her dress with his saber. The following conversation ensues:

> "But you said before beginning that it was blunt and couldn't cut me!"
> "That was to get you to stand still, and so make sure of your safety. The risk of injuring you through your moving was too great not to force me to tell you a fib to escape it."
> She shuddered. "I have been within an inch of my life, and didn't know it!"
> "More precisely speaking, you have been within half an inch of being pared alive two hundred and ninety-five times."
> "Cruel, cruel, 'tis of you!"
> "You have been perfectly safe, nevertheless. My sword never errs." And Troy returned the weapon to the scabbard. (Hardy, 1927, p. 146)

Lying is perhaps one of the most common insidious behaviors, and this example illustrates many of the issues surrounding lying. Troy lies to the young lady in a way that he portrays as being in her own interest so that she doesn't get "pared alive two hundred and ninety five times." However, telling this lie may have longer term consequences for his reputation and her trust in him, even though he has used the tactic of lying to smooth out a momentary situation in an expedient manner. Like Troy, many of us experience the need if not to lie then to alter how honest we are on a daily basis. Nearly everyone has told the occasional lie or discovered at other times that they have been victims of lies. Nevertheless, the term *lying* carries negative connotations, and when challenged to think of when they have lied, many people are put off by the term. In keeping with the theme of this volume, this chapter examines small everyday lies, what they are, and why they occur.

Lying has been defined as making a statement that one knows to be false, and theorists further distinguish between lies of concealment and lies of deceit (Bok, 1978; Ekman, 1985). Concealment, often called lying by omission, involves leading someone to believe something that is false without actually making an untrue statement. Direct deceit is making a statement one knows to be false. I discuss several different types of insidious lies, including (1) white lies, the fibs that lubricate social discourse; (2) lies that come from being placed in difficult situations; (3) lies used as negotiation tactics; and (4) lies that promote self-esteem or group-esteem. As this list suggests, there are many different reasons for telling lies and situations in which lies are told. In fact, most people find it extremely challenging to be perfectly truthful throughout their careers (Grover, 2005).

In this chapter I will explore lying to various audiences, because how and when we lie to people depends on our relationships with the people involved. The causes, consequences, and prevalence of lying should differ, for example, between our trusted friends and colleagues and business customers with whom we are negotiating. Therefore, I separately explore lying to a number of different audiences, including subordinates, superiors, peers, and customers. In doing so, I draw on social science literature to consider the reasons one might lie.

LYING TO SUBORDINATES

The first audience I discuss is subordinates. People lie to subordinates for several reasons. With the privilege of rank comes a certain obligation for discretion; high status often brings with it access to information that sometimes cannot be revealed to subordinates. As such, bosses may find themselves sometimes needing to conceal information from their subordinates even if they do not need to make untrue statements.

Confidential Information

Keeping confidences often involves concealing information. After all, there are secrets that bosses know and are expected to keep quiet. Performance evaluations and subsequent pay reviews are events about which bosses might not be completely honest for fear of triggering invidious comparisons. Because people have a tendency to compare themselves to others, performance evaluations often include, at least from the subordinate's viewpoint, some comparison with coworkers. Consider, for example, a boss who is engaged in evaluating the performance of average workers and their outstanding colleagues. The boss stands to benefit little by explicitly highlighting this negative comparison because the lower performers may not be as capable as the higher performers. In fact, making comparisons can be counterproductive because people do not have accurate self-perceptions: If compared to a higher performing individual, then one might experience negative inequity, potentially creating anger and reducing performance. To avoid this, some bosses will refocus such discussion on the individual and shy away from comparisons with others. But it's easy to imagine some subordinates asking bosses for "honest" evaluations—ones that are never forthcoming. "Tell me, is X really better at this than me?" or "Is X really a better worker than I am?" Because blunt honesty may provoke negative reactions, managers may choose to refocus the discussion, such as on the present worker's needs and goals. Alternatively, a manager might answer such questions by smoothing over actual performance differences by saying something like, "Both you and X are comparable employees although X performed better on this occasion." In either case, the boss may be seen as deceiving the employee to some degree.

Bosses also need to keep personal confidences. Since front-line managers are the first port of call in all personal (and potentially troubling) human resource issues, they are privy to information that should not be shared. Preserving privacy under such conditions often is considered one of the manager's primary job responsibilities. For example, in a manufacturing plant with which I am familiar, managers knew that a restructuring was being planned that was going to result in layoffs. In some cases the managers even knew well in advance who was going to be laid off. However, this information was not shared for fear of the consequent social problems and interference with daily plant activities that might have resulted if managers revealed what they knew.

Sometimes confidences are among managers' fiduciary responsibilities. By keeping confidences managers stand to protect their organizations financially. In the building industry, for example, a particular project might make a very large profit, although this is likely to be kept secret because it benefits no one for this information to be revealed. The customer or client will feel bad, and perhaps cheated, if the information leaks out and lands on his or her lap. Assuring secrecy, then, may require either telling subordinates partial truths or concealing information from them altogether.

Leader Integrity

Honesty and lying are likely to have reputational effects on bosses (Palanski & Yammarino, 2009). The leadership literature recently has shifted toward examining what has come to be called "authentic leadership" (Bass & Steidlmeier, 1999) or "ethical leadership" (Brown, Treviño, & Harrison, 2005; Treviño, Hartman, & Brown, 2000), part of which involves telling the truth (Grover & Moorman, 2004). Kouzes and Posner (2002) have found that honesty is the attribute of leaders most desired by their subordinates and followers. Grover and Moorman (2004) suggest that followers attribute honesty to leaders who consistently tell the truth, but paradoxically leaders cannot always tell the truth (Grover, 2005). As a result, subordinates engage in attribution processes based on the frequency with which the truth is told, the circumstances of deceit (was it justified?), and the length of their relationships with their leaders. This attribution process is continual, and Moorman and Grover (2004) theorize that people are inclined to follow leaders whom they believe to be honest.

While there is abundant theory that honest leaders will have better leadership outcomes, scant empirical evidence has been collected. One of the exceptions to the empirical paucity is a study showing that political leaders are perceived more positively when they tell the truth than when they lie (Grover & Hunt, 2005). Additionally, this process is mediated by trust, which means that being truthful promotes trust and, in turn, trust elevates perceptions of leaders. Moreover, people trust truthful leaders and rate them positively as a result. Therefore, being truthful would seemingly be a good policy for leaders. However, this relation of truthfulness and positive perception of leaders only holds under certain circumstances.

One of the circumstances that affects these leaders' honesty results is the degree to which one agrees with the leader in the first place. Tresna Hunt and I found that people reject dishonest leaders who hold values inconsistent with their own, but that they tend to forgive dishonest leaders who hold values similar to themselves (Grover & Hunt, 2006). We examined this issue in a political context. When the political leader in question led a party whose values were similar to participants' values, leader dishonesty in the form of lying had no effect on trust or satisfaction. However, leaders who held disparate values from the participant were trusted much less after they lied, and they also were rated much more negatively. Presumably, people are more forgiving of those who hold values that are similar to their own.

Values and ethical leadership may be virtually inseparable, and the discussion of right and wrong gets muddied in the discussions of ethical leadership. Becker (1998) created a simplified notion of integrity by defining it as behaving according to a justifiable set of principles. Such a characterization sidesteps the need to state the ethical principles. They only have to be "morally justifiable." Becker (1998) used Ayn Rand's objectivist philosophy to illustrate the idea, which led to an individual benefit maximization approach. However, the core idea was that people with integrity behave in a highly consistent manner according to *some* principles. Bass and Steidlmeier (1999) extend this notion of integrity somewhat to include responding to what one intuitively knows is right in their notion of authentic leadership. They also reject the notion that people can lead in inspirational, "transformational" ways unless they believe it to be ethical. Leading in an ethical manner appears to affect followers via a mechanism of shared values. For example, Brown and Treviño (2006) found that authentic leadership led subordinates to feel they had values congruent with the leader. Additionally, they found less behavioral deviance in work groups that had more inspirational, value-laden leadership. Avolio and Gardner (2005) reviewed the literature on positive forms of leadership, finding that multiple studies revealed a greater connection between leaders and followers when leaders led from a clear base of identifiable values.

In summary, research on lying by supervisors has shown that leaders and managers are in a difficult position with regard to truthfulness. On the one hand, the nature of managerial work requires leaders to keep confidences and to hold secret information. On the other hand, leaders who lie are perceived negatively. This creates a conundrum. One way out of this paradox suggested by contemporary leadership theory is for leaders to stick to a clear set of values. If leaders behave consistently over time in service to a set of values, then the people who are drawn to that value-based mission in the first place might overlook the occasional misrepresentation, concealment, or deception. The people who were not drawn to the leader's mission may be disgruntled, but they were less instrumental to goal accomplishment in any event.

LYING TO BOSSES

People lie to their bosses and to others of higher rank in their organizations for many reasons. In fact, more research has investigated lying to bosses than to other targets (e.g., Grover & Hui, 2005; Schweitzer, Ordonez, & Douma, 2004; Umphress, Ren, Bingham, & Gogus, 2009). Lying to one's boss may be one of the most ubiquitous types of lying.

The person doing the lying is subservient in the boss–subordinate power relationship. The boss in this case has legitimate power, reward power, and coercive power over subordinates. This power dynamic colors the manner in which people lie upward in their organizations. Subservient people lie to get themselves out of trouble. The role conflict theory of lying characterizes this as an attempt to resolve the conflicting nature of different demands that are placed on a person (Grover, 1993a). Suppose, for example, that a person has two bosses who make incompatible demands on him or her. The resulting conflict may prompt some people to extract themselves from such situations by lying.

Sometimes conflicting demands are placed on individuals by the boss or by the organization, making the target of the lies more difficult to discern. For example, who is the intended audience of the fabricated data on a hospital chart? There are several audiences, of course, depending on who reads the chart. The fabricator is lying to the patient, other medical professionals, colleagues, and even to the hospital itself. Lying on a patient chart illustrates that when we are talking about lying we are talking about communication. Any form of communication can differ in level of honesty, regardless of its form.

The distortions that we have come to call lies can be reactions to the complications and contradictions of our work lives. I found that nurses lie on medical charts when there is conflicting information over what the nurse should be doing (Grover, 1993b). People in nursing, like those in nearly any occupation, have conflicting ideas about how their enterprises should function. Nurses are asked to do lots of different things, and the requests come from many different people, including bosses (head nurses or charge nurses), doctors, hospital administrators, and, of course, patients. Sometimes these demands conflict, and a way of dealing with it is to do one thing instead of another and then lie about it.

An example of role conflict is difference of opinion over the frequency and timing of taking vital signs. The nurse might believe vital signs need to be taken less often than the doctor orders. One way of dealing with this difference of opinion would be for the nurse to take the vital signs when the nurse thinks it is appropriate and then to misreport it in the chart or lie orally to the doctor. Let's consider another example. Nurses in neonatal intensive care units may have doctors' orders to administer a certain amount of formula to babies to prevent necrotizing enterocolitis. However, nurses find babies are still hungry after being fed and feed the babies extra formula but record in their chart that they had given only the prescribed amount. Without passing judgment on this medical matter, this example illustrates how well-intentioned people may lie to avoid creating trouble.

Performance Reporting

Lying by subordinates to their superiors may involve misreporting performance because incentives commonly support inflating one's performance. One way of looking at this self-presentation is to regard it as impression management. Whenever one seeks a job or a promotion, or is involved in a performance evaluation, one is invited implicitly (at least, in Western society) to inflate one's accomplishments (Gilmore & Ferris, 1989; Kacmar, Delery, & Ferris, 1993). As a minimum we are encouraged to present ourselves in a positive light. A personal example illustrates this point: My university evaluates full professors on a biennial basis. We are asked to evaluate ourselves on dimensions such as teaching, research, and leadership. Although we provide documentation and a statement concerning each of these areas, we also are asked to rate our performance on each dimension using a scale anchored at below satisfactory, satisfactory, above satisfactory, well above satisfactory, or outstanding. The last time we did this, we were asked explicitly by our dean not to be modest and to present ourselves in a positive light. This is an explicit example of a direct suggestion (or pressure) to inflate one's performance. (Perhaps my university is like Lake Woebegone, where all the children—or professors—are above average.)

The corporate world is filled with programs aimed at getting people to work at high levels of productivity. Whether called goal setting (Locke & Latham, 1990), stretch goals (Kerr & Landauer, 2004), performance management (Kanungo & Mendonca, 2002; McDavid & Hawthorn, 2006), excellence or six sigma, such programs endeavor to raise peoples' performance levels. Nearly everyone's performance improves to some degree from one year to the next as their skills improve and as technologies and support structures come to their aids. However, when the chance for performance self-reporting presents itself, how honest are people? Certainly, people are likely to lie to authorities when lying is consistent with their self-interests. Combine the self-interest incentives with the conflict pressures suggested above and lying may skyrocket. Two studies comparing these pressures with the incentive to lie found that both influence lying. People are inclined to lie when it benefits them and when they are pressured to do so. Furthermore, these are separate factors that have additive effects (Grover & Hui, 1994, 2005). Many goal-setting programs therefore include two different motivations to lie.

Lying also increases as a function of goal difficulty. Schweitzer et al. (2004), for example, found that people are more likely to lie about their performance when attempting to achieve difficult goals than easy ones. More interestingly, they also found that people were most likely to lie when they had nearly accomplished the difficult performance goal. These findings suggest that people stretch the truth when it is so close to reality as to require very little stretching.

Schweitzer and Hsee (2002) refer to this stretching as elasticity in another study. Some things are more elastic than others, in their terms, because some things have a greater uncertainty. People are more likely to lie about issues that harbor uncertainty because they can get away with it. Moreover, people are generally less likely to lie about issues that are countable and the information is readily available. For example, a builder asked to estimate or quote a building construction cost may be working with elastic or inelastic information. A highly complex building that is entirely new and different from previous projects will have much more uncertainty in its estimated costs than a small building of a type built in the past. One might compare my university's new library building (large, complex, unusual design) to a new discount store (a straightforward replication of previous work) as two projects with uncertain and certain costs, respectively. Uncertain information, therefore, provides further foundation for lying.

These various examples of lying to people in positions of higher power (e.g., one's boss or the organization as a whole) occur because people have opportunities and pressure to do so. In Schweitzer and colleagues' (2004) study, for example, the levels of goal attainment were set by an authority figure (the experimenter), and participants responded to the situation. Because humans have rational choice, it would be unfair to characterize people who have to lie as pawns. Indeed, some people told the truth about their performance when they had not met the goal (Schweitzer et al., 2004). Also, in my nursing study, most people told the truth (Grover, 1993b). It is apparent, however, that people are highly responsive to social systems when they lie to the power elite.

LYING TO PEERS

Analyzing peers as the audience of lies removes the power differential that permeated my analysis of lies to subordinates and superiors. Maintaining social relationships, compared to maintaining the social order, underpins lying to peers in everyday encounters.

The "little white lie" is an example of the type of lying that maintains social relationships with peers. The primary motivation for this type of dishonesty is to maintain the self-esteem of both the liar and his or her intended audience. At the simplest level, we maintain others' self-esteem, and thus relationships, by telling them things that make them feel better even if they are untrue. The classic example is "you look nice this morning," a statement that does not have to be grounded completely in a solid and impermeable truth. It's possible that the speaker doesn't really mean this, but this doesn't matter given that his or her statement stands to make the other person feel better. This deception can serve valuable instrumental purposes. For example, if you boost a person's feelings about himself or herself shortly before that person is to make an important presentation to a client, then you may be behaving instrumentally by elevating his or her confidence, which potentially may improve the quality of his or her presentation.

Colleagues or peers also can make one another feel better by helping one another interpret the complex world around them (Weick, 2001). People working together within an organization often share information about, and interpretations of, what is happening in their organizations. For example, a new department head recently was appointed at my university. One of the first things he did was chat with each individual lecturer about the following year's teaching schedule. Afterward, in a number of different situations, these individuals compared their experiences and dramatized the event to make sense of it. This sense-making process included telling one another about their perceptions of what was said in these meetings. Although I don't want to suggest that anyone lied intentionally, the process of sharing this information made it possible to reveal things that were not said in the meeting (concealment), comparing experiences so as to verify the truth. For example, if a colleague reports that he or she is uneasy with a new supervisor and is threatened, then coworkers might be reluctant to characterize their interactions with the new supervisor in more positive terms. The point here is that people respond to one another and send messages and tell stories to promote social cohesion. The process of saying things that seek to boost the esteem of others may be regarded as a prosocial form of lying (McLeod & Genereux, 2008). Thus, lies can be considered positive as well as negative. Most lies to peers that help boost self-esteem probably are not considered lies at all, rather as normal forms of social discourse.

Another reason people lie to peers is to benefit themselves and their own self-esteem through social comparisons. Because coworkers are likely to be similar to one another, they are likely to share information relevant to their job performance. In other words, we judge our own performance by comparing it to the performance of others (Luhtanen & Crocker, 1991; Wheeler, 1991). For example, members of a group of telemarketers soliciting charitable donations are likely to compare themselves to the others sitting around them making calls. By asking how much money others have generated they stand to learn about their own performance. Some people may be motivated to distort the information being shared in order to maintain a "one-up" position (Tannen, 1994). That is, some people may have a need to be the best within a work group and may distort information sharing to retain such a perceived position. This process may have a beneficial effect for the company by prompting others to try harder to match the performance standard.

LYING OUTSIDE THE ORGANIZATION

In the course of doing their jobs, many people in organizations must at some point communicate with people outside their organization, such as suppliers and customers. It seems reasonable to consider how honest employees are with these people and some of the reasons why they might lie to them. One of the most ubiquitous empirical sources for lying is the negotiation context. Specifically, there is a fair amount of literature investigating honesty in distributive negotiations, which are over a fixed pool of money or other resources (Lewicki, Saunders, & Barry, 2005). For example, negotiating for a used car would be considered a distributive negotiation if there is only one car in question and the buyer wants less money to spend, while the seller demands more money.

Purchasing agents' jobs are to negotiate deals to the advantage of their companies, and research suggests that they may not be honest in those negotiations. Aquino and Becker (2005), for example, asked MBA students to play the roles of either purchasing agents or suppliers in a negotiation exercise in which the purchasing agents had secret information that influenced the profitability of the deal for the supplier. Specifically, they were told that they would be purchasing a part for only 3 years instead of 8 as originally intended. This discrepancy was critical because a major capital investment had to be made in which the payoff period determined the price. During the negotiation, the suppliers always asked how long the contract would last and all but 2 out of nearly 100 purchasing agents lied.

That purchasing agents lie is probably not simply an artifact of the laboratory situation with MBA students. In a field study Robertson and Rymon (2001) found that 10% to 29% of practicing purchasing agents admit to deception. The agents in these situations reported using a variety of ways to deceive. The outright lie was less common than simply keeping information to oneself or leading another to believe something that was untrue.

When studying socially undesirable behavior such as lying, one always must be concerned that the respondents will not tell the truth to a researcher. Robertson and Rymon (2001) got around this problem by using a random response technique in which people answer sensitive questions honestly. The technique pairs questions together, a sensitive question of interest with a nonsensitive question. The following is an example of one of their sensitive questions: "Think back over all the transactions with your most recent supplier. Did you ever falsely impose time pressure on the seller to reach an agreement?" This question was paired with "the second to last digit of my home phone number is 5, 6, or 7." Participants are instructed to take a dollar bill out of their pockets and to look at the last digit of the serial number. If it is an odd number, they answer the first question; they answer the second question if it is an even number. The logic of this technique lies in the known probability of the nonsensitive question being true (e.g., "5, 6, or 7" represents 3 possibilities out of 10, or a probability of .30) and the known probability of having answered it (e.g., the probability is .50 of a digit on the dollar being odd). In this example an equal number of people answer the sensitive and nonsensitive questions. Therefore, deviations from the result of .30 can be attributed to the sensitive (unknown) answers. If the results were .40 instead of .30, then we would know that the frequency of the sensitive questions were .50 [(.3 × .5) + (.5 × .5) = .40] (Lensvelt-Mulders, Hox, Van Der Heijden, & Maas, 2005).

The bargaining situation itself may breed lying. In many Western societies, bargaining is characterized as a competitive endeavor that lacks clear rules (Murnighan, 1991). The combination of competition, procedural ambiguity, and self-interest is a clear recipe for deceit. Indeed, studies show that people in bargaining situations who believe they will not be caught lie when it benefits them to do so. For example, Boles, Croson, and Murnighan (2000) found that people lied to benefit themselves in rounds of repeated ultimatum bargaining games, but were less likely to do so when they were expected to have repeated interactions with the same person. Other studies show that people are more likely to lie in their own interest at the end of such games, when no retribution is possible from the other party, than in earlier rounds (Schweitzer & Croson, 1999).

Dishonesty with bargaining partners comes at a cost because people do not like to be lied to. Opponents of liars rate them negatively, have low trust in them, and punish them (Aquino & Becker, 2005; Boles et al., 2000; Sanchez-Pages & Vorsatz, 2007; Schweitzer & Croson, 1999). Some literature suggests that trust can be recovered when a person has been betrayed, but when betrayal is accompanied by a direct lie, trust cannot be recovered as successfully as when the lie took the form of concealment (Schweitzer, Hershey, & Bradlow, 2006). The research therefore supports the notion that lying in negotiation might be fairly common, but it affects long-term relationships negatively.

Customer Service

Customers are another important audience to whom employees may lie. I now address the honesty with which customer encounters are conducted and explore some of the reasons for dishonesty in such situations.

A study of flight attendants found that they told lies for a variety of reasons (Scott, 2003). Many of their lies were intended to make their lives easier. For example, flight attendants sometimes tell passengers that there are no more pillows when they simply do not feel like looking for them. Some lies to passengers were directed at smoothing flight operations and the security or comfort of passengers as a whole. To get an inebriated passenger off the plane instead of confronting the individual directly by saying "You're drunk, get off the plane," a flight attendant told the passenger there was a problem with her ticket that they had to fix at the desk. When the passenger stepped off the plane they sealed the door behind her, avoiding an ugly scene that may have upset other passengers. Flight attendants also reported making up "rules" that they felt "ought to be the rule," like not applying nail polish while inside the cabin.

The little white lies of customer service come partly from the nature of the role that service providers play. Flight attendants, hotel clerks, teachers, security guards, and police officers, for example, are in positions of authority when dealing with their constituents. A social expectation is placed on them to have answers ready and to establish policy, in essence, to make things run smoothly. They may use deceit or concealment to complete or fulfill that obligation. When such an individual lies, he or she may have in mind the interest of a larger group, or they may be lying or concealing information out of expediency. It is much easier to give a brief and plausible explanation to someone than it is to explain a complex situation. This accounts for why it is expedient for a flight attendant to lie by saying that there are no more pillows instead of telling the truth by explaining that he or she cannot look right now because there are more pressing things to do before taking off.

Sometimes, it is entirely beneficial to the audience *not* to hear the truth. An airplane full of passengers may not benefit from hearing the details of the potential mechanical problems that are causing a delay or a turnaround. Other times such fibs may protect the interests of other customers, such as disguising details of a sick (or dead) passenger in order to protect their privacy. Customer service workers also may lie to protect the image of their companies, again in their formal roles as their companies' representatives. Instead of telling customers that they cannot check into a hotel because the hotel doesn't staff enough housekeepers, the clerk might blame faceless and nameless (and presumably inconsiderate) guests who stayed beyond the required check-out time. Lies to customers are meant to smooth over the social process of the service encounter.

CONSEQUENCES

Although my examples of lies to customers involve little immediate consequence, their long-term consequences are noteworthy for several reasons. First, as lying becomes habituated most people engaging in them give them little thought. The flight attendant's lie about the pillows in the airplane, for example, is just one of many scripted lines that may be used in the course of doing that job. This suggests that lying becomes an automatic part of the job because it is an accepted norm. The message to the employee learning the job is clear: Lying appropriately is an accepted part of doing the job properly.

A second longer term consequence of habitual lying is its effects on the liar's self-concept. A dominant idea in social psychology is that much human behavior and cognition is designed to support a positive self-concept. For example, we rationalize our successes and failures in ways that make us feel better about ourselves. Another dominant idea in social psychology is that people hold multiple identities and that their behavior and ways of thinking are guided by efforts to support these identities (Tajfel, 1982). When thinking about moral behavior, people construct their identities in ways that support the belief that they are moral individuals (Aquino & Reed, 2002). People who have strong moral identities—those for whom being moral and compassionate is the key to their self-image—are likely to be negatively influenced by habituated lying because it challenges their self-image. Regardless of moral identity, however, there could be a long-term negative or dissonant influence of small, habituated lies. Specifically, over the longer term, employees may begin to blur the boundaries between right and wrong that go beyond the smoothing of some uncomfortable encounters.

A third long-term consequence of these small lies has to do with reputation (Ferris, Blass, Douglas, Kolodinsky, & Treadway, 2003; Ferris, Perrewe, Anthony, & Gilmore, 2000). When employees lie repeatedly to customers, they risk long-lasting negative effects on their customers. Eventually customers may begin to think that a particular company, as opposed to only the individual involved, cannot be trusted. At some point, nearly all customers realize they have been deceived. When the flight attendant makes up policies, at least some customers will ascertain that those policies are not in fact real, but rather fabrications of the unethical flight attendant. And, to the extent that customers believe that customer service personnel reflect on their companies, the reputation of the organization may become jeopardized. These sorts of insidious lies, which customers might hear repeatedly in many different forms over long periods of time, threaten to erode trust for both individuals and the companies they represent (Elangovan & Shapiro, 1998).

ADDITIONAL DETERMINANTS OF LYING

I have considered lies to different types of audiences, demonstrating that the type of audience may influence the nature and consequences of lies. In addition to the type of audience, additional characteristics of relationships also influence if and how people lie. These other characteristics include (1) the intimacy of the relationships, such as whether the audience member is a friend or a foe; (2) the level of trust between the parties; and (3) whether the individual is a member of an out-group or an in-group.

Relationship quality might be considered a combination of the level of intimacy and the positivity of that relationship. Honesty is likely to be a casualty of cantankerous relationships. People who are enemies are believed not to be entitled to the truth. Put differently, people may neutralize or justify lying to enemies or members of out-groups (Robinson & Kraatz, 1998). Enemies have not earned trust and the right of honesty, and a way to rationalize a person's unethical behavior is to castigate him or her—an action that is far easier if the party in question is a recognized enemy. On the other hand, close relationships may require diplomatic sorts of honesty.

Trust is defined as a willingness to make oneself vulnerable to another (Rousseau, Sitkin, Burt, & Camerer, 1998). People tend to believe, and therefore to trust, people who are honest (Mayer, Davis, & Schoorman, 1995). Lying reduces trust, and direct deceit has a more negative effect on trust than does concealment. Schweitzer and his colleagues (1999, 2006) suggest that there is a continuum of trust betrayal by lying. People feel more betrayed and are less likely to recover trust when they have been directly deceived, and therefore greater deception corresponds with lower trust recovery (Schweitzer et al., 2006).

The identity groups to which one belongs may also characterize relationships. People define their identities as members of groups (Tajfel, 1982), and they create images of their in-groups and out-groups by developing stories or stereotypes of members of both the in- and out-groups. People in general should value honesty to support an in-group compared to an out-group (Yamagishi & Yamagishi, 1994). Supporting or maintaining groups and group identities requires trust. In fact, trust is the very essence of a group: a number of people who trust one another.

To explore the issues of how intimacy, trustworthiness, and group identity influence truthfulness in interactions, I will in the following paragraphs overlay audience with these elements of relationship. The goal is to entertain the notion that there is a great variety of relationships within each of the audience categories that I have already discussed. The context around which a relationship is built has monumental bearing on the levels and types of honesty or dishonesty that are displayed.

Boss–Subordinate Relationships

The first type of audience and relationship that I want to explore is that of bosses and subordinates together. The leader–member exchange (LMX) literature has explored what it calls "relationship quality" extensively (Graen & Uhl-Bien, 1995). The typical LMX framework characterizes leaders as having limited resources to give subordinates, and therefore they distribute benefits under their control selectively based on the quality of relationship that the leader has with subordinates. Hence, the relationship can be explained as an exchange in which those pairs of supervisors and subordinates who have positive relationships exchange more than those pairs with low quality relationships. The nature of the exchange is that subordinates exert more effort in exchange for an increasingly favorable return of resources. High-quality relationships are marked by mutual positive affect, loyalty, professional respect, trust, and commitment. The LMX aspects of relationship quality have similarities with other concepts that have described truthfulness propensity in this chapter.

Having high-quality LMX relationships may result in a certain type of honesty between the two parties. However, the weakness of the LMX formulation in terms of honesty is that it is an exchange relationship. In the

LMX way of thinking bosses and subordinates afford each other honesty in a variety of forms. For example, bosses should be more forthcoming with confidential or political information to subordinates with whom they hold positive LMX relationships. This is part of the exchange: Getting important and potentially useful information in exchange for the benefits accrued to the boss. Confidential, political, and social information is exchanged in the subordinate-to-boss direction as well. Subordinates should generally be more likely to deliver information to bosses with whom they hold positive relationships. This extends especially to political information or social information, the type of thing that a subordinate comes across as part of a social network, and information that is potentially useful to bosses. In contrast to the partners who have positive LMX relationships, the other subordinates should be commensurately cautious with political and social information because disclosing it has not proved beneficial to them in the past, else they would have higher quality relationships already.

LMX relationships are by definition *exchange* relationships, which vary significantly from the relationships described at the beginning of this section as being characterized by intimacy and positivity. Some supervisors and subordinates have a highly positive relationship that might be much closer to friendship on the intimacy continuum. Pairs who hold bonds based on friendship are likely to be more honest in general with one another. Defining the relationship in terms of friendship changes the nature of the honesty compared to LMX because it shifts the motivation from honesty or dishonesty. Toward the friendship end of the intimacy continuum people with professional relationships have a motivation to reveal information in a benevolent fashion to the other party. Trust researchers highlight this notion of benevolence as a crucial part of the trust equation (Mayer et al., 1995). Similarly, both bosses and subordinates might conceal information that is harmful to the other party, suggesting a prosocial motivation for lying. For example, a boss might have information about a customer not liking a subordinate and choose not to reveal that information to the subordinate or even to actively conceal that information from the subordinate if it would have a negative effect on the subordinate. At the opposite end of the intimacy and positivity continuum, however, adversarial boss–subordinate pairs might seek out damaging information to offend or harm the other party.

A third way of clarifying the boss–subordinate relationship and the type of lying that may occur as a result is by group membership. Bosses and subordinates sometimes identify themselves together and other times very separately. For example, in settings where the bosses are called "the suits," it is not difficult to imagine a substantial perceptual distinction between the upper and lower levels of the organization. In such work groups the supervisor might be quite separate and the other members of the work group might think of themselves as a unit. Other times there may be a stronger affinity with the work group or unit compared to hierarchical level. In identity terms they may help define one another as members of the engineering section or the underwriting section, for example. Where the social identities of the bosses and the subordinates are similar, there is less psychological distinction between the bosses and the subordinates; hence, there should be greater cooperation and the type of lying or honesty should be consistent with the identity.

Peer Relationships

Truthfulness and honesty among peers bears similarities in terms of intimacy, trust, and social identity to supervisor–subordinate relationships. Not all peer relationships are identical. Some peer relationships are quite close and the trust upon which they are formed reflects a mutual self-disclosure. Should this trust be violated in close personal relationships by dishonesty or deceit, the consequences in the deterioration of the relationship are much more costly than for distant relationships.

One of the precursors to strong and close intimate relationships is the amount of time over which the relationship has been built. We are unsure of our relationship and relative standing and attraction to people when we first meet them. While we may have inklings about how much we like someone when we first meet, probably based on how similar we are, our knowledge of the other person and our relationship to that person becomes stronger over time. It's not that the relationship will become better; it's simply that we have very strong opinions about the quality of the relationship. There is greater certainty in relationships over time. For example, people who have been married a long time have few surprises of character to reveal to one another.

The length of time over which relationships are built relates to the cost of trust violations. Long, established relationships built on trust suffer a much greater blow than do relatively newly formed relationships. Trust, once violated, is difficult to rebuild in any circumstance (Schweitzer et al., 2006).

Moreover, we can make two predictions regarding longer and shorter peer relationships. The first prediction has to do with the likelihood of deceit. If the long-standing relationship is built on trust, then we expect that people are less likely to break that trust with deceit. Notice that I am making the distinction between long-standing relationships built on trust versus those in which trust is not a key ingredient. Sometimes peers in organizations learn to work with one another over years or decades, but they never build that trust for any of a variety of reasons, most likely of which is that the trust is not earned because one or neither party is willing to make themselves vulnerable to the other party. Therefore, the prediction that long-term, trusting relationships deter lying is in comparison to both untrusting long-term relationships and new relationships. People do not invest their energy and trust in new relationships. Because there is the possibility of deceit or other violations of trust, people in business organizations withhold trust in the early stages of relationships. This trust investment model is largely cognitive: People can rationally determine how much trust they have in a relationship and how much they are willing to invest. However, the prediction also reflects McAllister's (1995) affective component of trust. Part of the trust in long-term relationships is a feeling, a strong bond with the other person, and violation of this is not so much a violation to the other person as it is to oneself. People feel as though they are violating their own feelings if they deceive this affective trust. Therefore, emotional, affective reasons suggest that people are less likely to lie to those with whom they hold long-term positive relationships.

Social identity is another factor of honesty and dishonesty among peers. Some so-called peers are part of one's primary affinity group whereas others are in marginal groups and still others fall outside any affinity group. There are a number of different motivations for being more truthful with one's identity group than other groups. Some reasons are fairly pragmatic, such as the need to maintain a reputation. In order to function effectively in a host of different settings, one must have a reputation that allows one to interact with others. If other people do not trust the individual due to having been lied to in the past, then it cripples an individual's ability to get things done through other people. In cases where people can work independently, they potentially suffer alienation by being ostracized from any important social group when they violate the trust of the group by lying.

If we consider all the groups with whom we identify as dots on a circular chart, with groups that are closer to the center of that chart being our primary affiliation groups, then all of the identity issues should become more important toward the center of that chart. In the center then we should expect more honesty than at the periphery. Consider for a moment the types of honesty and dishonesty that might be expected. Going back to the definitions at the beginning of this chapter, there should be a great deal of honesty at the center of one's affinity chart. However, people are generally honest to people with whom they interact, even if they are at the outside or have nothing to do with one's identity groupings. What we should find is that the quality of information and the forthrightness with which we present ourselves diminishes at the periphery. People have a mutual allegiance to the members of their identity groups. They depend on them to tell the truth because the information they provide informs not only the technical work that is being done but also the social structure of the group. According to social information processing theory people learn all sorts of things about their jobs and how to do them by listening to and considering the information from the people around them (Salancik & Pfeffer, 1978). The quality of this information has an impact on what the group collectively thinks and does.

People might be dishonest to peers in a variety of ways depending on group membership or identification. Similar to high- and low-quality boss–subordinate relationships, people are expected to be more honest to salient identity group members than nonmembers or members of more peripheral groups. At the same time people might protect members of an in-group by providing prosocial lies or obfuscating information to in-group members in a way that supports the group. Out-group members, in contrast, are likely to be privy to less information and to lower quality information. This might take the form of outright deceitful lies to members of hostile out-groups that are portrayed as enemies. In fact, the group can use their social information processing—their sharing of information—to stereotype the out-group as evil and deserving of bad treatment, and not deserving of ordinary courtesy, ethical treatment, and honesty. Slightly more central to identity than hostile out-groups are members of groups that may be of tangential identity interest to the individual. These groups do not help form an individual's personal self-identity and, therefore, may engender neither outright lying nor prosocial lying. They are likely to hear lower quality information in which the quest of the truth is not so important. To illustrate, consider a conversation with someone from another department of your organization compared to someone from your own department. It might be critically important to talk through an issue with someone who is close to you. Your own department members may need some level of understanding, if not agreement, that is unnecessary with members of another department. For example, you might discuss a current political issue within your organization by simply gathering and sharing cursory information with someone from the other department, but need to clarify and expand your meanings with members of your own department. Part of the reason for this is that you will establish your own reputation more solidly the closer to home you are. People in out-groups, such as other departments of your organization, may have more of a thumbnail sketch of who you are and what you stand for. The point here is that people may not obfuscate or deliberately lie to members of tangential out-groups; rather, people put less effort into giving exact information and clarifications because they don't need to.

Relationships Outside the Organization

Finally, let's turn to honesty with members of the outside world. Relationships to the outside world can include a wide range of different encounters, typically including customers, professional colleagues, suppliers, or vendors. The range, of course, is much greater and could include the news media, package delivery service, or acquaintances from outside the organization. Again, the quality and type of relationship overlays the audience. Key to our understanding of honesty with the outside world is whether it is a long-term or temporary relationship. There are abundant studies in the bargaining literature to suggest that the longevity of the relationship affects a number of issues. Similar too to other audiences is that trust is a cornerstone of how honestly we might treat an external audience. Specifically, if the relationship is a long-term one, then deceit is less likely. For example, Boles et al. (2000) found that negotiators were more honest with bargaining opponents when they thought they would have to bargain with the same person again in the future.

The degree to which people outside the organization are members of one's identity group influences interactions outside the organization as well as inside the organization and maybe even more. The extremes between in-group and out-group are perhaps more pronounced with people outside the organization. For example, professional colleagues outside the organization may identify with a professional identity that makes them seem very close to oneself, even if they do in some technical way compete or work for organizations that compete (Wenger, 1998). For example, physicians with a specialty, such as obstetrics, know one another and may have fairly close relationships by virtue of sharing the same values and training about their craft. In fact, professionals who practice alone find their professional community important in order to learn and to process interpretations of their client encounters. At the opposite extreme, interacting with the outside world can be a completely foreign encounter with members of communities with which one has no identification. For example, a school principle forced to meet with local businesses in a partnering scheme may have little in common with the local business people. We therefore expect extremes in honesty to correspond with the extreme potential differences in-group identification of encounters outside the organization. In the very close type of group identity such as physicians who are meeting with a local association of physicians, we would expect a fair amount of honesty. People portray themselves in positive terms, and therefore they potentially hide or cover up issues that do not fit a positive self-presentation. For example, if a professional had made a mistake, then in retelling the story might choose to do so in a way that made the mistake appear to be a natural progression from the events or not a mistake at all. Therefore, we would expect a high degree of accurate information sharing among such a group, and this information sharing would be similar to, but not identical to, sharing with members of an in-group within an organization. The major difference between relationships inside the organization and outside, then, would be that the presentation of self would not be as constant outside as to members of the same organization. People we see every day can form more accurate pictures of ourselves than do people who are outside the organization and with whom we may interact on a more infrequent basis.

Outside groups can belong to the completely opposite end of the spectrum: Sometimes people interact with virtual enemies when dealing with the outside world. In belligerent bargaining between unions and management representatives, for example, the parties may think of each other in the most negative terms. If people are portrayed, therefore, as enemies, then there is no reason to expect the high level of honesty that would be afforded those whom we respect and trust. One reason for low levels of honesty would be the belief that the other party is not telling you the truth. If you have no expectation of the truth, then it is easy to justify lying or at least lower levels of truth from oneself.

This section has attempted to discuss some of the nuance of relationship and how it affects honesty to various audiences. Intimacy, trust, and group identity were chosen to exemplify a few variations in relationship intensity. The major point of this section is to demonstrate that there is a wide variety of relationships. At the extreme every relationship is unique, and this uniqueness influences how honest we are with one another.

SUMMARY AND PRACTICAL IMPLICATIONS

This chapter has focused the discussion of lying as an insidious act aimed at different types of audiences. Examining how people lie to different audiences elucidates the social psychological similarities and differences in how and why people lie in the workplace. The common reasons for lying were to smooth things out or to reduce conflict, and to lie in a way that benefits oneself. I have also identified a number of mostly negative consequences of lying, such as reduced trust and difficult long-term interactions. The environmental circumstances that encourage lying are prevalent, however, and people do lie with some frequency. This combination of negative effects and a host of environmental encouragement creates a conundrum. In the following section I make some practical suggestions intended to help people live with this conundrum.

Be Honest

The first recommendation is to be honest. Being honest instead of lying or perverting the truth has benefits. Honesty builds trust. Therefore, people who want to continue relationships over time need to be honest in order to establish the trust that makes interaction easier and cheaper. For example, trusting relationships are cheaper in business because fewer safeguards need to be included in the transaction with parties who are trusted. At the negative extreme everything needs to be checked and accounted for when dealing with untrustworthy parties, which is potentially costly in auditing and administrative expenses.

A second reason to be honest is that it is simpler. Lies breed more lies, and it takes much more cognitive work to remember lies and their implications.

When we are completely honest, without even shading for impression management, we don't have to remember what we have said before. Every concealment or deceit, on the other hand, needs to be cataloged to avoid detection and its consequences.

Third, we build reputations for honesty. People who tell the truth consistently can be trusted over the long run, and, in contrast, people who do not consistently tell the truth may be avoided. The benefits of being honest and building trust accrue exponentially. When we are in relationships that exist due to our previous honesty, then future relationships build on our being honest during that encounter.

Recover From Dishonesty

As noted at the outset it may not be that easy to be honest. People find themselves in positions where it is nearly impossible or severely difficult to remain honest all the time. Although the advice given is to remain honest, it seems prudent to consider here how to maximize benefit when honesty is not possible. First, consider the consequences of dishonesty previously noted. As stated in this chapter the consequences of dishonesty will vary with the audience and the relationship that is established with the recipient of lies. Since many lies are the result of conflicts over inability to perform multiple services simultaneously, the recipient of a lie might be chosen in a way that minimizes the damage. Moreover, when some deceit is necessary, then it might be best to choose the party carefully, perhaps the party with whom one has little relationship and will suffer minimal loss.

The type of lie also has an impact on perceptions. If people cannot avoid any type of dishonesty, then concealment might be better than direct deceit. Directly lying to people has an insulting emotional impact that will be difficult to turn around compared to concealment, which might be explained away. Additionally, explaining deceit will be a way to regain trust. People like explanations and feel treated fairly, even in the face of having been deceived, when they are given reasons for the lie. For example, when the boss has to conceal bad news for the sake of the company, the boss can regain trust and reestablish relationships with close colleagues or subordinates when it is explained in the aftermath that it was impossible to reveal that information due to legal or fiduciary reasons. Giving the reasons is more important to regaining trust than are the details of the reasons.

Be Aware

This chapter has identified that honesty is largely contextual: Our tendencies to lie or to tell the truth vary depending on the situations in which we find ourselves. Accordingly, we need to be aware of our own situations and how they influence our propensity to lie, and we need to be cognizant of the pressures and situations of the people around us. We can't be surprised when we are deceived, for example, because we have placed other people under extreme performance pressure. Therefore, we should be aware of the pressures we place on people and endeavor to make those pressures reasonably achievable. Furthermore, the consequences of not achieving goals, for example, should not be so overwhelming as to encourage dishonesty.

We also have to be aware of the setting in which we operate as potential recipients of dishonesty. One of the conclusions of this chapter based on bargaining research is that short-term relationships may encourage dishonesty because people need not be concerned about the long-term consequences. In short-term interactions, therefore, we should guard against dishonesty by providing the safeguards for dishonesty. It would be foolish to blindly trust, of course, and it only makes sense to look to the context to determine whether we are engaging in long-term interactions in which trust is a key ingredient or in a short-term encounter that will likely never happen again.

Question Truth

Last, and somewhat metaphysically, we might question what truth is at all. Truth is what people believe is correct, and therefore truth is subject to all kinds of human frailties, including cognitive limitations and being formed through social processes. Humans often don't know what the truth is; rather, they have an idea of what they believe to be true. This truth is formed by listening to and interacting with other people. The world is a complex place and we simplify it to fit our capabilities of understanding.

Given our limitations, therefore, my suggestion is both to take truth seriously and to acknowledge its limitations. This paradox is difficult to live with. On the one hand we don't know what is true and what is not. On the other we have to pay attention and determine ourselves to be as truthful as possible. Understanding this paradox, however, is liberating and informative. Understanding that other people are presenting information about the world as they see it can help us to appreciate perspectives that we might otherwise be tempted to label unethical or deceptive. Additionally, understanding the limitations of truth make the first suggestion in this section to be truthful easier to live by. We can be truthful to the best of our abilities as humans. We don't always know the truth, but can endeavor to present the world to other people in the most accurate way possible.

The opening quotation from *Far from the Madding Crowd*, illustrates a number of common issues surrounding lying in organizations. Troy lied to smooth over a more complex explanation, but he had ulterior motives as well. He was trying to generate positive esteem for himself by impressing Bathsheba. In the short term it worked because she married him, but the relationship was doomed with such deceit from the outset.

REFERENCES

Aquino, K., & Becker, T. E. (2005). Lying in negotiations: How individual and situational factors influence the use of neutralization strategies. *Journal of Organizational Behavior, 26,* 661–679.

Aquino, K., & Reed, A., II. (2002). The self-importance of moral identity. *Journal of Personality and Social Psychology, 83,* 1423–1440.

Avolio, B. J., & Gardner, W. L. (2005). Authentic leadership development: Getting to the root of positive forms of leadership. *Leadership Quarterly, 16,* 315–338.

Bass, B. M., & Steidlmeier, P. (1999). Ethics, character, and authentic transformational leadership behavior. *Leadership Quarterly, 10,* 181–217.

Becker, T. E. (1998). Integrity in organizations: Beyond honesty and conscientiousness. *Academy of Management Review, 23,* 154–161.

Bok, S. (1978). *Lying: Moral choice in public and private life.* Hassocks, England: Harvester Press.

Boles, T. L., Croson, R. T. A., & Murnighan, J. K. (2000). Deception and retribution in repeated ultimatum bargaining. *Organizational Behavior and Human Decision Processes, 83,* 235–259.

Brown, M. E., & Treviño, L. K. (2006). Socialized charismatic leadership, values congruence, and deviance in work groups. *Journal of Applied Psychology, 91,* 954–962.

Brown, M. E., Treviño, L. K., & Harrison, D. A. (2005). Ethical leadership: A social learning perspective for construct development and testing. *Organizational Behavior and Human Decision Processes, 97,* 117–134.

Ekman, P. (1985). *Telling lies: Clues to deceit in the marketplace, politics, and marriage.* New York, NY: W. W. Norton.

Elangovan, A. R., & Shapiro, D. L. (1998). Betrayal of trust in organizations. *Academy of Management Review, 23,* 547–566.

Ferris, G. R., Blass, F. R., Douglas, C., Kolodinsky, R. W., & Treadway, D. C. (2003). Personal reputation in organizations. In J. Greenberg (Ed.), *Organizational behavior: The state of the science* (2nd ed., pp. 211–246). Mahwah, NJ: Lawrence Erlbaum Associates.

Ferris, G. R., Perrewe, P. L., Anthony, W. P., & Gilmore, D. C. (2000). Political skill at work. *Organizational Dynamics, 28*, 25–37.

Gilmore, D. C., & Ferris, G. R. (1989). The effects of applicant impression management tactics on interviewer judgments. *Journal of Management, 15*, 557–564.

Graen, G. B., & Uhl-Bien, M. (1995). Relationship-based approach to leadership: Development of leader-member exchange (LMX) theory of leadership over 25 years: Applying a multi-level multi-domain perspective. *Leadership Quarterly, 6*, 219–247.

Grover, S. L. (1993a). Lying, deceit and subterfuge: A model of dishonesty in the workplace. *Organization Science, 4*, 478–495.

Grover, S. L. (1993b). Why professionals lie: The impact of professional role conflict on reporting accuracy. *Organizational Behavior and Human Decision Processes, 55*, 251–272.

Grover, S. L. (2005). The truth, the whole truth, and nothing but the truth: The causes and management of workplace lying. *Academy of Management Executive, 19*, 148–157.

Grover, S. L., & Hui, C. (1994). The influence of role conflict, role strength, and reward contingencies on lying behavior. *Journal of Business Ethics, 13*, 295–303.

Grover, S. L., & Hui, C. (2005). How job pressures and extrinsic rewards affect lying behavior. *International Journal of Conflict Management, 16*, 289–300.

Grover, S. L., & Hunt, T. (2005, July). *The effect of honesty on trust in and satisfaction with leader-subordinate relationships.* Paper presented at the meetings of the European Group on Organization Studies, Berlin, Germany.

Grover, S. L., & Hunt, T. (2006, August). *The impact of honesty and value congruence on leadership perceptions.* Paper presented at the annual meeting of the Academy of Management, Atlanta, Georgia.

Grover, S. L., & Moorman, R. H. (2004, July). *Leadership integrity: How honesty and consistency of leaders influence organisational conscience.* Paper presented at the meeting of the European Group on Organization Studies, Ljubljana, Slovenia.

Hardy, T. (1927). *Far from the madding crowd.* London, England: Macmillan.

Kacmar, M., Delery, J. E., & Ferris, G. R. (1993). Differential effectiveness of applicant impression management tactics on employment interview decisions. *Journal of Applied Social Psychology, 22*, 1250–1272.

Kanungo, R. N., & Mendonca, M. (2002). Employee withdrawal behavior: Role of the performance management process. In M. Koslowsky & M. Krausz (Eds.), *Voluntary employee withdrawal and inattendance: A current perspective* (pp. 71–94). New York, NY: Kluwer Academic/Plenum.

Kerr, S., & Landauer, S. (2004). Using stretch goals to promote organizational effectiveness and personal growth: General Electric and Goldman Sachs. *Academy of Management Executive, 18*, 134–138.

Kouzes, J. M., & Posner, B. Z. (2002). *The leadership challenge* (3rd ed.). San Francisco, CA: Jossey-Bass.

Lensvelt-Mulders, G. J., Hox, J. J., Van Der Heijden, P. G., & Maas, C. J. (2005). Meta-analysis of randomized response research: Thirty-five years of validation. *Sociological Methods & Research, 33*, 319–348.

Lewicki, R., Saunders, D. M., & Barry, B. (2005). *Negotiation.* Burr Ridge, IL: McGraw Hill/Irwin.

Locke, E. A., & Latham, G. (1990). *A theory of goal setting and task performance.* Englewood Cliffs, NJ: Prentice Hall.

Luhtanen, R., & Crocker, J. (1991). Self-esteem and intergroup comparisons: Toward a theory of collective self-esteem. In J. Suls & T. A. Wills (Eds.), *Social comparison: Contemporary theory and research* (pp. 211–234). Mahwah, NJ: Lawrence Erlbaum Associates.

Mayer, R. C., Davis, J. H., & Schoorman, F. D. (1995). An integration model of organizational trust. *Academy of Management Review, 20,* 709–734.

McAllister, D. J. (1995). Affect- and cognition-based trust as foundations for interpersonal cooperation in organizations. *Academy of Management Journal, 38,* 24–59.

McDavid, J. C., & Hawthorn, L. R. (2006). *Program evaluation and performance measurement: An introduction to practice.* Beverly Hills, CA: Sage.

McLeod, B. A., & Genereux, R. L. (2008). Predicting the acceptability and likelihood of lying: The interaction of personality with type of lie. *Personality and Individual Differences, 45,* 591–596.

Murnighan, J. K. (1991). *The dynamics of bargaining games.* Englewood Cliffs, NJ: Prentice Hall.

Palanski, M. E., & Yammarino, F. J. (2009). Integrity and leadership: A multi-level conceptual framework. *Leadership Quarterly, 20,* 405–420.

Robertson, D. C., & Rymon, T. (2001). Purchasing agents' deceptive behavior: A randomized response technique study. *Business Ethics Quarterly, 11,* 455–479.

Robinson, S. L., & Kraatz, M. S. (1998). Constructing the reality of normative behavior: The use of neutralization strategies by organizational deviants. In R. W. Griffin, A. M. O'Leary-Kelly, & J. M. Collins (Eds.), *Dysfunctional behavior in organizations* (pp. 203–220). Stamford, CT: JAI Press.

Rousseau, D. M., Sitkin, S. B., Burt, R. S., & Camerer, C. (1998). Not so different after all: A cross-discipline view of trust. *Academy of Management Review, 23,* 393–404.

Salancik, G. R., & Pfeffer, J. (1978). A social information processing approach to job attitudes and task design. *Administrative Science Quarterly, 23,* 224–253.

Sanchez-Pages, S., & Vorsatz, M. (2007). An experimental study of truth-telling in a sender-receiver game. *Games and Economic Behavior, 61,* 86–112.

Schweitzer, M. E., & Croson, R. T. A. (1999). Curtailing deception: The impact of direct questions on lies and omissions. *International Journal of Conflict Management, 10,* 225–248.

Schweitzer, M. E., Hershey, J. C., & Bradlow, E. T. (2005). *Promises and lies: Restoring violated trust.* Unpublished manuscript, University of Pennsylvania.

Schweitzer, M. E., & Hsee, C. K. (2002). Stretching the truth: Elastic justification and motivated communication of uncertain information. *The Journal of Risk and Uncertainty, 25,* 185–201.

Schweitzer, M. E., Ordonez, L., & Douma, B. (2004). The role of goal setting in motivating unethical behavior. *Academy of Management Journal, 47,* 422–432.

Scott, E. D. (2003). Plane truth: A qualitative study of employee dishonesty in the airline industry. *Journal of Business Ethics, 42,* 321–337.

Tajfel, H. (1982). *Social identity and intergroup relations.* New York, NY: Cambridge University Press.

Tannen, D. (1994). *Talking from 9 to 5: How women's and men's conversational styles affect who gets heard, who gets credit, and what gets done at work.* London, England: Virago Press.

Treviño, L. K., Hartman, L. P., & Brown, M. (2000). Moral person and moral manager: How executives develop a reputation for ethical leadership. *California Management Review, 42,* 128–142.

Umphress, E. E., Ren, L. R., Bingham, J. B., & Gogus, C. I. (2009). The influence of distributive justice on lying for and stealing from a supervisor. *Journal of Business Ethics, 86,* 507–518.

Weick, K. E. (2001). *Making sense of the organization.* Malden, MA: Blackwell.

Wenger, E. (1998). *Communities of practice: Learning, meaning and identity.* New York, NY: Cambridge University Press.

Wheeler, L. (1991). A brief history of social comparison theory. In J. Suls & T. A. Wills (Eds.), *Social comparison: Contemporary theory and research* (pp. 3–21). Mahwah, NJ: Lawrence Erlbaum Associates.

Yamagishi, T., & Yamagishi, M. (1994). Trust and commitment in the United States and Japan. *Motivation and Emotion, 18,* 129–166.

Section 3

Methodological Issues

8

Challenges and Recommendations in the Measurement of Workplace Incivility

Steve M. Jex, Jennifer L. Burnfield Geimer, Olga Clark, Ashley M. Guidroz, and Jennifer E. Yugo

In recent years, several well-publicized incidents of workplace homicide have greatly increased public awareness of violence and aggression in the workplace (e.g., U.S. Bureau of Labor Statistics, 2005) and even have been the subject of "dark" humor (e.g., "going postal"). It has also shown that the prevalence of nonfatal assaults in the workplace has increased considerably, particularly among employees in health care settings (U.S. Department of Health and Human Services, 2006). However, despite the seriousness of both fatal and nonfatal incidents, the fact remains that physical violence in organizational settings is rare.

What appears to occur with much greater frequency, however, is aggression and mistreatment that is not physical in nature. For example, Cortina, Magley, Williams, and Langhout (2001) reported that more than 70% of employees report being the victims of overt or "lower level" forms of aggression and mistreatment in the workplace on a daily basis (e.g., being interrupted while talking in a meeting, being the target of jokes because he or she is overweight, or being the subject of unfounded rumors about the employee's love life). Given this high prevalence, it is not surprising that low-level forms of mistreatment and aggression have been the focus of a great deal of research in recent years (Duffy, O'Leary-Kelly, & Ganster, 2003; Tepper, 2007).

Aside from the high frequency of occurrence, interest in relatively low-level forms of mistreatment is also driven by two other factors. First, it has been argued that instances of physical violence and aggression often result from the escalation of low-level conflicts (e.g., Pearson, Andersson, &

Wegner, 2001). A person being mistreated by his or her coworkers may respond by retaliating, which invites further mistreatment in response, and ultimately this "spiraling" process may lead to physical aggression. Given the relatively low frequency of physical aggression in organizations, this spiraling process has not received a great deal of empirical attention, although it has received some empirical support (Glomb & Liao, 2003). Second, it also has been argued, and shown empirically, that low-level forms of mistreatment have a negative effect on employees' physical health and psychological well-being, even if they do not escalate into more serious forms of violence (Bowling & Beehr, 2006). Mistreatment, thus, may be considered a potent organizational stressor that has potentially negative impact on employees and their organizations.

Perhaps the most common form of mistreatment in the workplace, and the focus of this chapter, is *workplace incivility*. According to Andersson and Pearson (1999), workplace incivility is defined as "low-intensity deviant behavior with ambiguous intent to harm the target, in violation of workplace norms for mutual respect. Uncivil behaviors are characteristically rude and discourteous, displaying a lack of regard for others" (p. 457). Given this definition, there obviously are many potential forms of incivility in the workplace. Examples of workplace incivility that frequently occur include acts of rudeness, such as ignoring someone who says hello, interrupting someone who is speaking, failing to return phone calls, and taking credit for work someone else has done. Most readers probably have experienced some of these behaviors at one time or another. Furthermore, there is evidence that employees who experience repeated acts of incivility are at greater risk for physical and mental health problems (Cortina et al., 2002) and are less productive (Pearson, Andersson, & Porath, 2005) than employees who do not experience high levels of incivility. Such individuals also are more likely to reciprocate acts of incivility, thereby leading to its escalation (Glomb & Liao, 2003). Given these potential negative effects of workplace incivility, it is critical to develop an accumulated knowledge base to understand its causes and potential preventive strategies.

Despite this need for more research, studying workplace incivility has proven to be a considerable challenge due, in large part, to measurement issues. This chapter will focus on what we believe to be the most important issues in the measurement of workplace incivility. Specifically, we begin by discussing the problem of defining workplace incivility. As we will show, a common operational definition of workplace incivility has proven to be elusive. We then shift to a discussion of the different perspectives from which workplace incivility has been measured. Indeed, incivility has been measured almost exclusively from the victim's perspective, yet much is to be gained by adopting other perspectives (e.g., the "perpetrator" of uncivil behavior, observers of the behavior). We then shift to a discussion of the difficulties of estimating the true level of incivility in organizations, such as differences in the interpretation of uncivil behavior, and social desirability effects. Finally, we conclude by offering suggestions regarding how to improve the measurement of workplace incivility.

DEFINING THE CONSTRUCT: WHAT IS WORKPLACE INCIVILITY?

A fundamental principle of psychological measurement is that variables must first be clearly defined to be accurately measured, particularly when measuring psychological variables that are conceptual in nature (Nunnally & Bernstein, 1994). Within the organizational sciences, most research focuses on variables that are abstract in nature (e.g., job satisfaction, organizational commitment) and thus no physical referent is available. Fortunately, many of the variables measured in organizational research have consensually accepted definitions. In these cases, although measurement certainly is important, it is generally not controversial.

In the case of workplace incivility, however, arriving at a common definition is more challenging. As we previously noted, Andersson and Pearson (1999) have provided the most commonly used definition. Unfortunately, there are several problems with this definition as the basis for construct measurement. First, their definition depends greatly on the subjective viewpoint of the person experiencing the uncivil behavior. For example, being interrupted in a meeting may be seen as rude and uncivil by only some people, but not all. Although we agree with Andersson and Pearson that there are some common societal and organizational norms governing how people treat one another, agreement on what those norms are is imperfect.

More recently, Zauderer (2002) defined workplace incivility as "disrespectful behavior that undermines the dignity and self-esteem of employees and creates unnecessary suffering, indicating a lack of concern for the well-being of others and contrary to how individuals expect to be treated" (p. 36).

This definition differs from Andersson and Pearson's (1999) by incorporating the victim's affective reactions. According to Zauderer's (2002) definition, but not Andersson and Pearson's (1999) definition, behavior is not considered uncivil unless the victim reacts negatively. These differences exist, subtle though they may be, and illustrate the challenges of creating an operational definition and ultimately a measure of incivility.

A second problem is that workplace incivility overlaps conceptually with other forms of interpersonal mistreatment, making it difficult to identify the unique qualities of incivility. Although, researchers agree that incivility is distinct from physical aggression and violence (Cortina et al., 2001; Pearson, Andersson, & Porath, 2000), considerably less distinctiveness exists among less serious forms of mistreatment. To illustrate this, Table 8.1 lists a number of forms of mistreatment appearing in the literature in the past 10 years. In addition to providing a definition of each, we also distinguish these with respect to (1) whether the perpetrator intends to harm his or her victim, (2) whether there is a clear power differential between perpetrators and victims, and (3) whether the definition requires repetition of the behavior over time.

As illustrated by the definitions in Table 8.1, workplace incivility is almost indistinguishable from most of the other forms of interpersonal mistreatment. The primary criteria that appear to differentiate incivility from these other forms are intent, power differential, and the repetitiveness of the behavior. Unfortunately, however, the subjectivity of these criteria makes them problematic. As an example, an act of rudeness from a coworker may appear to have no clear intent to harm the victim, although it may be purposive (if, for example, it is motivated to get the victim to resign). Power differences are not characteristic of incivility, although they do define other forms of mistreatment (e.g., bullying and mobbing). Based on this similarity, one may conclude that some instances of incivility also can be considered instances of bullying and mobbing. With regard to repetitiveness, Table 8.1 specifies that behavior need not recur to be considered workplace incivility, although, this is in fact a distinguishing criterion of bullying and mobbing. Again, this raises the issue of whether incivility is distinct from these two constructs and leads to the conclusion that in some cases it is not.

In summary, a fundamental challenge in measuring workplace incivility is the fact its definition defies precise measurement. Conceptual definitions proffered thus far are vague and leave considerable room for

TABLE 8.1

Distinguishing Between Forms of Interpersonal Mistreatment

Construct	Definitions Cited in the Literature	Harmdoer's Intention to Cause Harm	Clear Power Differential Between Victims and Perpetrators	Behavior Must Be Repetitive
Incivility	"Low-intensity deviant behavior with ambiguous intent to harm the target, in violation of workplace norms for mutual respect. Uncivil behaviors are characteristically rude and discourteous, displaying a lack of regard for others" (Andersson & Pearson, 1999, p. 457).	Ambiguous	No, perpetrators can be supervisors, coworkers, customers	No
Bullying	Bullying is a form of repeated aggressive behavior, in which there is an imbalance of power making it difficult for the target to defend himself or herself (see Cowie, Naylor, Rivers, Smith, & Pereira, 2002). This form of aggression is typically targeted to punish a particular person (Zapf & Gross, 2001).	Yes	Yes	Yes
Mobbing	"Mobbing at work means harassing, offending, socially excluding someone or negatively affecting someone's work tasks .... it has to occur repeatedly (e.g., weekly) and regularly (e.g., about six months) ... Mobbing is an escalating process in the course of which the person confronted ends up in an inferior position and becomes the target of systematic negative social acts" (Einarsen, Hoel, Zapf, & Cooper, 2003, p. 15).	No, but victim perceives there is intent	Yes	Yes

(continued)

TABLE 8.1

Distinguishing Between Forms of Interpersonal Mistreatment

Construct	Definitions Cited in the Literature	Harmdoer's Intention to Cause Harm	Clear Power Differential Between Victims and Perpetrators	Behavior Must Be Repetitive
Social undermining	"Behavior intended to hinder, over time, the ability to establish and maintain positive interpersonal relationships, work-related success, and favorable reputation" (Duffy, Ganster, & Pagon, 2002, p. 332).	Yes	No, perpetrators can be supervisors, coworkers, customers	Yes
Emotional abuse	"Repeated hostile verbal and nonverbal, often nonphysical behaviors directed at a person(s) such that the targets' sense of him/herself as a competent worker and person is negatively affected." (Keashly, 2001, p. 234).	Yes	No, perpetrators can be supervisors, coworkers, customers	Yes
Interpersonal deviance	Deviance is "voluntary behavior that violates significant organizational norms and in so doing threatens the well-being of the organization or its members, or both" (Robinson & Bennett, 1995, p. 556). Interpersonal deviance is directed at a member of the organization.	Yes	No	No

interpretation. Furthermore, because workplace incivility overlaps considerably with other forms of interpersonal mistreatment researcher's run the risk of developing measures of incivility that fail to capture its unique qualities. Thus, true variance in measurement promises to be low.

CHALLENGES IN MEASURING INCIVILITY FROM VICTIMS' PERSPECTIVES

Assuming for the moment that researchers could agree on a common conceptual definition of workplace incivility, a formidable challenge would still exist when trying to measure it: Should it be measured from the victim's or the perpetrator's perspective? Most researchers have opted to measure incivility from the victim's perspective, although the perpetrator's perspective also is important. Furthermore, assessing incivility from each of these perspectives presents some unique measurement issues. In this section we examine problems associated with the victim's perspective; in the following section we examine the perpetrator's perspective. Specifically, we focus here on the dissimilarity of norms, impression management, and different forms of self-report bias.

When measuring workplace incivility from the victim's perspective, a fundamental assumption is that all people embrace the same norms for respect and civil behavior. However, challenges can arise when attempting to quantify levels of incivility in situations in which norms are not shared. This might be the case, for example, if a sample consisted of respondents from several different cultural backgrounds. In such a case, researchers may have a collective understanding of what constitutes civil or uncivil behavior, yet survey respondents may hold different views depending on their cultural backgrounds. This divergence in perspectives from researcher to respondent may pose problems for measurement insofar as they may lead to interpretative differences that threaten validity. To ensure the validity and utility of incivility research, efforts should focus on continually updating and refining a catalog of universally accepted uncivil behaviors.

Additionally, some uncivil behaviors may be unique to certain work environments but not present in others. The unique qualities of an individual's profession or work environment can cause challenges for researchers using a general scale across multiple jobs or organizations. For example, some behaviors that may be considered rude in a typical office setting, such as snooping through a coworker's desk, may not be considered rude in other work environments lacking clearly defined work spaces (e.g., nursing stations at hospitals and service areas in restaurants). Conversely, acts of incivility in a restaurant, such as taking food intended for another server's table to your guest's table, is unique to that environment and would not be applicable to incivility in other jobs. Thus, measures of incivility that are not specific to a given work context may fail to capture some germane forms of incivility in specific settings. Likewise, measures that are tailored to a specific work context will not be applicable to multiple settings.

Aside from problems with the subjectivity of defining incivility and difference in the context in which it occurs, many problems stem from the methods that are used to measure it. Given the nature of workplace incivility, it is not surprising that researchers have used self-report surveys or structured interviews to measure it. Although these methods are relatively easy to use and are conducive to measuring incivility, they also may be influenced by errors and biases (see Spector & Rodopman, Chapter 9, present volume). These biases can affect the particular uncivil events recalled (e.g., recall bias, recency effect) or how they are evaluated (e.g., impression management, cognitive dissonance). Additionally, social culture (e.g., regional or national) also can affect perceptions and appraisals of incivility. We now discuss each of these sources of error.

Recall Bias

Recall bias is defined as selective recall of information or events congruent with one's current mood (for more information see Bower, 1981). For example, if a survey respondent were asked how often he or she had experienced uncivil behaviors from coworkers in the past 3 months, recollection of these uncivil behaviors could be impacted by the respondent's mood state at the time the survey was completed. Given that incivility is likely to cause people to feel unhappy or dissatisfied, individuals in a negative mood may recall more uncivil behavior than individuals would in a positive mood. Negative mood may also distort how we perceive interactions with the people we work with. For example, recollection of a coworker not holding the elevator may be viewed as rather innocuous when a respondent is in a positive mood, but may be recalled as uncivil behavior if the respondent were in a negative mood.

This type of bias can affect the measurement of incivility because researchers may not be gathering an accurate report of incivility due to either overinflated or underinflated responses. The biasing effects of mood may be more pronounced when a respondent is asked to recall behavior over a longer period of time (i.e., incivility experienced in the last year). Current incivility instruments vary in terms of the time frame they ask respondents to adopt, with some specifying no time frame at all. Unfortunately there is typically no way to assess the extent to which mood may bias recall in such measures because researchers never can know the "true" level of incivility as experienced.

Recency Effects

Rundus (1971) coined the term *recency effect* when he observed that participants in his experiment were better able to recall words positioned at either the beginning (primacy) or end (recency) of a list. Similarly, victim's accounts of incivility also may be biased by recent uncivil events. Uncivil behavior that closely precedes the measurement of incivility will be better recalled than instances of incivility that happened further in the past (Dillman, Smyth, & Christian, 2009). Since most self-report incivility measures are retrospective in nature, recency effects are very difficult to control for. One potential way would simply be to point out to respondents that recency effects may occur and encourage them to consider their experiences at work over whatever time frame is specified in the instructions.

Another way to combat recency effects would be to ask that respondents report whether they have experienced uncivil behavior each and every day for a relatively short (e.g., 2-week) time period (e.g., "Diary" methodology). The obvious advantage of this approach is that all events are "recent," thereby making their accounts unbiased. Unfortunately diary studies require a much higher level of cooperation from respondents than retrospective studies do, and it has been suggested that the process of keeping a diary may itself bias reporting of certain behaviors (Bolger, Davis, & Rafaeli, 2003).

Impression Management

Impression management is defined as any effort on the part of individuals to control the impressions others have of them (Rosenfeld, Giacalone, & Riordan, 1995). Typically, impression management efforts are aimed at making one appear in a favorable light. Impression management is central to people's efforts to preserve their self-images and to portraying themselves as they desire to be.

It is possible the survey respondents are disinclined to admit that they are the victims of incivility for fear of being viewed as weak or as someone who is disliked by his or her coworkers. Thus, when presented with a list of uncivil behaviors and asked to report which they have experienced, even if a person has experienced them a great deal he or she may report never experiencing them or experiencing them very infrequently. Conversely, impression management efforts potentially could inflate the reporting of uncivil behaviors. It is possible, for example, for survey respondents to portray themselves as victims to prompt sympathy from others (Roth, Synder, & Pace, 1986). This may be the case, for example, if an employee has performed poorly and is unwilling to accept responsibility for his or her poor performance. In this case, the frequency of uncivil behavior the person reports experiencing may be much higher than what actually occurs on the job. From the researchers perspective both forms of impression management are problematic because they misrepresent the true level of incivility respondents experience on the job—a value that, of course, is unknown to the researcher.

Another factor, related closely to impression management that may alter respondents' reports of incivility, is social desirability. Past research has isolated two dimensions of social desirability: self-deception and impression management, which was discussed above (Paulhus, 1991). Consistent with past research on self-deception, respondents may alter their reports of incivility in an attempt to protect their self-esteem or emotional well-being (Sinha & Krueger, 1998; Upshaw & Yates, 1968). This is somewhat different than impression management because it does not involve presentation to others, but rather individuals' views of themselves. Reporting lower or less severe experiences of incivility may also allow the respondent to engage in self-deception and feel that the behaviors are not problematic. Further, reporting incivility may have implications for self-esteem as the respondent may feel he or she is responsible for the incident.

Cognitive Dissonance

Cognitive dissonance has been described as an unpleasant state in which individuals notice a discrepancy between an attitude they hold and their behavior in relation to that attitude. Cognitive dissonance theory (Festinger, 1957) claims that individuals who experience dissonance are motivated to bring their cognitions into closer alignment with their behavior. This dynamic can impact the reporting of incivility insofar as it leads victims to rationalize (i.e., to alter attitudes toward) uncivil behaviors they have experienced. For example, individuals who work in the helping professions, such as nursing or social work, probably have experienced rude or uncivil behavior from patients or clients (Fitzwater & Gates, 2004). However, because they may accept such behavior as normative, such individuals are unlikely to perceive such behaviors as uncivil in an effort to reduce the feelings of dissonance they create. For example, a nurse who consistently cares for abusive patients may be motivated to understand uncivil behavior from the patient's perspective or to explain it away in an effort to reduce any dissonance associated with helping someone who is rude to them.

Cognitive dissonance also could impact respondents' retrospective reports of incivility from coworkers for additional reasons. For example, if an employee had been working in an organization for a long period of time, reporting a high degree of incivility or other forms of mistreatment would make little sense, perhaps, triggering dissonance. After all, why would a person remain in such a hostile environment? Salancik and Pfeffer (1978) pointed out that retrospective reports of job conditions (which would include instances of incivility) are essentially "social constructions" which are often altered in a manner that helps respondents avoid dissonant cognitions. This phenomenon has in fact been shown empirically in the job design literature (e.g., O'Reilly & Caldwell, 1979; Vance & Biddle, 1985).

It also is possible that incivility is dissonant with an individual's perception of himself or herself as a likable, socially accepted coworker. Conversely, a person who views himself or herself negatively may see low levels of incivility on the job as dissonant. Thus, persons who see themselves in a positive or negative light may either underreport or overreport incivility on the job. Although little research has examined this proposition, it has been shown that negative affectivity (NA) is positively related to reports of workplace incivility (Burnfield et al., 2004), and other forms of workplace harassment (Bowling & Beehr, 2006)—findings which are consistent with this proposition. We would hasten to add that this relation is open to other interpretations. Specifically, a person who is high on NA may in fact be perceived negatively by his or her coworkers, and because of this, actually experience higher levels of incivility than those who are low on NA. This, in fact, was found in a recent study by Milam, Spitzmueller, and Penney (2009). Thus, NA may impact both the recollection of incivility as well as its actual occurrence. More research on dissonance effects, and factors that impact such effects, is obviously needed.

Cultural and Subcultural Differences

Cultural or subcultural differences may exist with respect to the perception and reporting of uncivil behavior, although little research has explored this (see Brassell, 2009, for a recent exception). Culture can be defined on a number of different levels (Hofstede, 1980). People from one country may not perceive the same behavior as uncivil as people from another country. For example, in the Japanese culture students do not make eye contact with professors when speaking with them. To an American professor, in contrast, averting one's gaze is likely to be taken as a sign of inattentiveness or outright disrespect (Scholmerich, Leyendecker, & Keller, 1995).

There also may be subcultural differences with respect to what constitutes uncivil behavior. In the United States, for example, it has been shown that people from traditional Southern states (e.g., Arkansas, Louisiana, South Carolina, and Texas) have a higher norm for respect than people who are not from the South (Cohen & Nisbett, 1994). In addition, Southerners react more strongly than non-Southerners when norms of respect are violated and consequently they may report more uncivil behavior (Cohen, 1996; Cohen & Nisbett, 1994, 1997; Cohen, Nisbett, Bowdle, & Schwarz, 1996; Cohen, Vandello, Puente, & Rantilla, 1999).

CHALLENGES IN MEASURING INCIVILITY FROM PERPETRATORS' PERSPECTIVES

Because the aim of most incivility research is to examine the affective reactions of victims of incivility most researchers focus on victims' perspectives (Bowling & Beehr, 2006; Cortina et al., 2001; Pearson, Andersson, & Porath, 2000; Tepper, 2007; Zauderer, 2002). It also is important, however, to measure incivility from the perspective of the perpetrator. Doing this promises to provide a more thorough understanding of the motivational causes of uncivil behavior. Ultimately, this will help organizations to design interventions that will reduce incivility or prevent it from occurring in the first place. We now discuss the challenges associated with measuring incivility from perpetrators' perspectives. Before doing this, however, we briefly review evidence on what causes people to engage in uncivil behavior in the workplace.

Causes of Uncivil Behavior

Although a wealth of research exists on the ramifications of incivility, comparatively little research has investigated its causes. A complete look at the causes of incivility warrants an examination of individual, group, and organizational antecedents.

Individual Causes

A wide range of individual factors account for uncivil behavior. For example, younger employees admit to committing more uncivil acts in the workplace compared to older employees (Bennett & Robinson, 2000; Zellers, Tepper, & Duffy, 2002). It has also been shown that men are more likely than women to instigate incivility, especially when the victim is someone of lower status. Women, on the other hand, are more likely than men to act uncivilly against their superiors (Pearson et al., 2000). Thus, age and gender appear to be demographic predictors of uncivil behavior, although the reasons for this are unclear. It may be, for example, that men and younger people tend to hold somewhat different norms with regard to civility compared to women and older people.

Another individual cause of uncivil behavior in the workplace is past history of being victimized. It has been found, for example, that being a victim of incivility or aggression increases one's likelihood of being a perpetrator (Olweus, 1984). The most logical explanation for this is that social learning processes are at work, that is, people learn uncivil behaviors when they are victims (Robinson & O'Leary-Kelly, 1998). It has also been shown that a history of teasing others may increase the probability that an individual may ultimately engage in workplace incivility. Researchers have defined teasing as "a personal communication directed by an agent toward a target that includes three components: aggression, humor and ambiguity" (Shapiro, Baumeister, & Kessler, 1991, p. 460). Given this definition, teasing is obviously very similar to incivility. Teasing, however, may be done in a completely harmless manner and is often done in organizations to increase morale or even to complement the target. For example, an employee who is highly valued but very messy may be the target of good natured teasing about this from the members of his or her work group.

Shapiro at al. (1991) point out that while teasing can be harmless or even positive, it can also be antisocial; it is the antisocial form of teasing that is similar to incivility. Antisocial teasing is defined as malicious and intended to hurt and humiliate the target. Teasing an employee who is highly overweight would be an example of this—the intent would obviously be to humiliate and belittle the target. According to Eisenberg (1986), teasing that occurs among men tends to be of this variety, most often directed at one's physical appearance. In some cases, however, it is more difficult for targets to determine their tormentors' intent. When the members of a work group repeatedly tease a fellow employee because of her taste in clothes, the intent of this teasing is less clear. Eisenberg found that the teasing that occurs among women tends to be more ambiguous in its intent like this.

A final individual cause of incivility is personality. Although not a great deal of research has examined the direct link between specific personality traits and workplace incivility, a handful of personality variables have been shown to relate to incivility or behaviors similar to incivility. As might be expected, individuals lower in the agreeableness and conscientiousness dimensions of the Big Five personality model (Digman, 1990) are more likely to engage in deviant or counterproductive behaviors (Ones & Viswesvaran, 2001). It has also been shown that individuals with a propensity toward anger and aggression, both verbal and physical, are also likely to commit incivility. Perpetrators also are higher on measures of hyperactivity (Kumpulainen, Rasanen, & Henttonen, 1998) and impulsivity (Slee & Rigby, 1993). Higher levels of negative emotions, or negative affectivity, have been found to relate to increased deviant behavior (Penney & Spector, 2005). It is possible that individuals with greater negative affect engage in more uncivil behavior as well.

Group-Level Causes

While individual-level factors certainly can help facilitate understanding of incivility, it is also true that much employee behavior occurs in a group context. Furthermore, there is ample evidence that the social context of groups may have a strong influence on many individual behaviors including decision making, level of effort to put forth, and risk taking (Forsyth, 1999). It is not surprising then that group context may have an impact on incivility (Glomb & Liao, 2003; Robinson & O'Leary-Kelly, 1998).

While many aspects of group context could potentially impact the prevalence of incivility, the most powerful of these is most likely to be group norms regarding incivility. According to Hackman (1992), norms represent shared standards within groups for what is and what is not acceptable behavior. Thus, it is very likely that norms exist within groups for what is and is not considered uncivil behavior. An academic department where departmental meetings routinely include shouting, interruptions, and other forms of rudeness would be a group where the norms support uncivil behavior. Although such norms alone will not determine whether group members engage in such behavior, they are certainly given strong consideration because members generally strive to conform to group norms (Asch, 1955).

Normative processes within groups also impact incivility more indirectly by governing behavior that may be associated with workplace incivility. For example, Bachrach, Bamberger, and McKinney (2007) showed that groups differ in their norms with regard to the acceptability of alcohol consumption and that these norms are associated with gender-related harassment. Jex and Thomas (2003) also found evidence of shared perceptions of helping behavior or altruism within military units. Units whose members indicate a low level of such behavior may be environments where incivility is likely to occur.

Organizational-Level Causes: Management

Although individual and group-level factors may certainly contribute to incivility, it is also true that employees' behavior occurs in an *organizational* context as well. Organizational factors that may contribute to incivility include things such as organizational structures, rules and policies, management styles, and communication technologies (Vardi & Weitz, 2004). In addition, actions of the organization may create perceptions of injustice or feelings of diminished control in employees leading to incivility (Analoui & Kakabadse, 1992; Spector & Fox, 2005). Each of these factors is discussed next.

Organizations may be structured in a variety of ways (Burton, Erickson, Hakonsson, & Snow, 2004). For example, some organizations are structured according to functional areas (e.g., marketing, accounting, human resources), others by geographical region, and others by product or service. It is also common for organizational designs to be based on multiple factors; that is, an organization may be designed according to traditional functional areas yet draw from these areas for various projects or work for different clients (Joyce, 1986). This is commonly known as a *matrix* organizational structure, and is widely used in a variety of settings including health care, academia, the consumer products industry, and defense contracting. The primary benefit of this type of organizational structure is that it allows an organization to put resources into its most important projects or services, while also allowing a high level of flexibility and improved efficiency (Davis & Lawrence, 1977; Kuprenas, 2003).

It is also true, however, that matrix structures tend to foster conditions that are conducive to incivility. According to De Laat (1994), matrix structures may cause a great deal of dysfunctional conflict and political gamesmanship among managers. This is because project managers are often in the position of competing with functional managers for resources. For example, in a defense contracting firm the manager of an important government-funded project may need several engineers to complete the project. At the same time, the manager of the engineering department may also need engineers for work being done within that department. It is certainly possible that such competition for resources among managers may ultimately lead to incivility.

It has also been shown that employees who work in matrix organizational structures report higher levels of work overload and conflicting role demands compared to employees working in more traditional organizational structures (Joyce, 1986). Given that both work overload and role conflict are associated with a number of employee strains (e.g., Jackson & Schuler, 1985; Spector & Jex, 1998) it is certainly possible that this may lead to higher levels of incivility among employees working within matrix structures. An employee who is dissatisfied, frustrated, and anxious at work may be more likely to lash out at others and instigate a cycle of uncivil behavior (Andersson & Pearson, 1999).

In addition to a formal structure, organizations often have some rules and policies regarding employee misconduct, and these could impact the frequency of workplace incivility. It is common, for example, for organizations to have formal policies in place to address employee misconduct. In most such policies, the penalty becomes more severe with each transgression. According to Trevino (1992), such "progressive discipline" procedures tend to be the most effective in curbing employee misconduct when they are perceived by employees as uniformly and fairly applied to all employees.

In addition to general disciplinary polices, it also is becoming more common for organizations to adopt policies prohibiting specific behaviors that are closely related to incivility. Sexual harassment, for example, often includes many of the same behaviors that are considered under the general rubric of incivility (e.g., a male employee starting rumors about a female employee's love life; Fitzgerald, Drasgow, Hulin, Gelfand, & Magley, 1997). Many organizations in recent years have adopted policies specifically prohibiting sexual harassment (Fitzgerald, 1993), and there is evidence that the presence of such policies does reduce the prevalence of such behavior (Sigal & Jacobsen, 1999). Some organizations have also adopted more general harassment policies that undoubtedly apply to many behaviors that would be considered to be incivility, although little research has examined the impact of such policies (Stockdale, Bison-Rapp, O'Conner, & Gutek, 2004).

Many organizations also have rules and policies designed to curb behaviors that may precipitate workplace incivility. The most common behavior of this type is substance use. It has been shown that substance use contributes to a variety of dysfunctional employee behaviors, including antagonistic or uncivil behavior toward others (Bachrach et al. 2007). In terms of policies, many organizations expressly prohibit substance use on the job and specify penalties associated with this behavior (Mangione, Howland, & Lee, 1998). Many organizations, however, go further than this and attempt to screen out potential substance users during the selection process through preemployment drug testing (Rawlinson, 1989), assessment of personal history (Lehman, Farabee, Holcom, & Simpson, 1995), or personality testing (Hogan & Hogan, 1989).

While structures and policies represent formal organizational factors that may impact the level of incivility, it is also the case that management styles may impact the level of incivility in organizations. In organizations where managers exert control through constant monitoring and checking on employees, employees may grow to resent and distrust managers, which may ultimately increase incivility within an organization (see work on performance monitoring). In contrast, in organizations where managers trust employees to be accountable for their work, and to exercise independent judgment and discretion, employees are more likely to be satisfied with their work and to develop more positive relationships with management. These positive feelings may also impact incivility, but in this case would reduce it.

Advances in communication technology have resulted in reduced face-to-face contact among employees. This increases the chances of miscommunication and may make employees less inhibited in the way they communicate with one another other (Baruch, 2005)—both of these factors may increase incivility. Another consequence of advanced communication technology is that more informal behaviors have become acceptable in the workplace. Part-time work and telecommuting have increased and the traditional work structure of the past no longer applies. The study of incivility has increased in recent years as numerous "good manner" behaviors in the workplace have become obsolete. Increasingly, managers are becoming hesitant to label previously inappropriate behaviors as unacceptable for fear of limiting individuality, freedom, and creativity (Morris, 1996). Developments in technology such as the Internet and e-mail make it possible for employees to work from home as well as to collaborate with individuals across the globe. These innovations and changes, when combined with an increasingly casual environment, can lead to behaviors being perceived as rude or uncivil (Baron & Neuman, 1996; Chen & Eastman, 1997; Martin, 1996; Morand, 1998). As organizational structures have flattened and become increasingly casual, the likelihood that those unintentional behaviors will be perceived as threatening or rude has increased. Screening calls, canceling meetings on short notice, and leaving unwanted trash for others to clean are more prevalent and accepted than before (Andersson & Pearson, 1999).

Incivility in organizations may also be viewed as a response to perceptions of injustice. For example, if an employee perceived that his or her efforts and accomplishments are not recognized, or that there is inequity in their treatment from a coworker, that employee may respond to these perceived inequities by engaging in uncivil behavior (Dorman & Zapf, 2004; Pearson et al., 2005; Spector & Fox, 2005; Vardi & Weitz, 2004). Thus, incivility may be a mechanism for restoring equity or justice.

Incivility can be seen as a mechanism for employees to regain control of a stressful situation. It has been shown that deviant behaviors, which are similar to incivility, often are spurred by attempts to gain more control of one's work (Analoui & Kakabadse, 1992). However, little research has investigated incivility as it relates to autonomy. The effects of autonomy may be situation-dependent, increasing uncivil behavior in certain situations and decreasing it in others. For example, Frone (2003) found that low levels of supervision contribute to higher levels of on-the-job substance use among teenage employees. Vardi and Wiener (1996), however, found that companies with reasonable control systems and supervision are marked by low levels of deviance. Although this research did not examine incivility directly, it implies that either too much or too little autonomy may instigate incivility. In this connection, researchers also could investigate how individual differences in need for autonomy relate to uncivil behavior. It may be the case, for example, that employees who prefer high degrees of autonomy are more likely to become uncivil in response to efforts to control their behavior compared to employees preferring less autonomy.

Measurement Challenges

One of the first challenges in assessing incivility from the perpetrators' perspectives is that perpetrators often view their uncivil behavior, as well as its consequences, differently than victims. This is problematic from a measurement standpoint because victims and perpetrators may interpret and respond to items differently. These differences would cause the most problems with general items such as "To what extent have you acted in an uncivil manner toward a coworker in the last three months?" because such an item is totally dependent on one's definition of uncivil behavior. Other items could be impacted by such differences as well. An item such as "How often are you rude to your coworkers?" also depends on one's definition of rudeness.

Research evidence has supported clear differences in perpetrator and victim perceptions. Baumeister, Stillwell, and Wotman (1990), for example, asked participants to write autobiographical accounts of incidents in which they expressed anger toward another person and incidents in which someone expressed anger toward them. Content analyses of these narratives indicated that incidents in which anger was expressed toward others were portrayed as justifiable and understandable, and perpetrators thought they had only a short-term effect on the victim. Stated differently, perpetrators believed their expression of anger was justified and that their targets would recover quickly. In contrast, participants perceived incidents in which anger was directed at them were arbitrary, unwarranted, or unexplainable, and they believed its impact to be long term. In this case, respondents felt the provocation was quite unjustified and did not feel as though they would recover from it as quickly.

Based on these findings, Baumeister et al. (1990) concluded that the differences in perceptions may arise because victims perceive the event as being the "last straw" in a series of provocations that caused their response. However, perpetrators perceived the event as isolated from all others and believed that their victim's responses were overreactions. These divergent attributions can make measuring incivility from only one perspective misleading if the researcher's goal is to determine prevalence rates of uncivil behavior. Victims may report a higher rate of uncivil behavior compared to perpetrators making the calculation of prevalence rates more difficult. This can be especially problematic if the researcher is trying to establish whether a culture of incivility exists within an organization, that is, a general belief that incivility is tolerated.

More recent research on victims and perpetrators of incivility has found other, sociodemographic characteristics that differentiate victims from perpetrators. Specifically, women and employees with lower status are inclined to be victims; in contrast, men and people of high status are inclined to be perpetrators (Cortina et al., 2001, 2002; Glomb, 2002; Pearson, Andersson, & Wegner, 2001). It has also been found that the personality traits of low agreeableness and high negative affectivity are associated with higher levels of victimization (Milam et al., 2009). Milam et al. (2009), however, also found that relations between both of these personality traits and incivility were mediated by behaviors that annoy or anger coworkers—termed *provocative target behavior*.

An additional problem is that measures of workplace incivility from a perpetrator's perspective are likely to be affected by social desirability bias. This occurs when respondents answer survey questions in a manner that makes them look favorable to others instead of truthfully (Crowne & Marlowe, 1964; Paulhus, 1991). Although all self-report surveys are potentially affected by social desirability bias because of their sensitive nature, questions about having acted uncivilly toward others are likely to arouse high levels of socially desirable responding.

Although not an easy variable to eliminate, there are some strategies that researchers can employ to curb the effect of social desirability, for example, collecting data from multiple different sources such as supervisors and subordinates, multiple ratings of performance variables, or gathering archival data. Statistical methods can also be used by directly measuring social desirability as a latent construct and partialed out the effect (Podsakoff, MacKenzie, Lee, & Podsakoff, 2003). Although social desirability is likely to be less of a concern when respondents believe their responses will be anonymous (Robinson & Bennett, 1995) researchers must remain aware of its potential effects whenever measuring any deviant behavior.

In addition to differences in what constitutes workplace incivility and social desirability, perpetrators' reports of incivility are also likely to be impacted by many of the same biases affecting victims' reports, albeit for slightly different reasons. Recall bias, for example, is likely to be an even bigger problem when perpetrators are asked about incivility than when victims are asked. Baumeister et al. (1990) suggest that perpetrators do not view their uncivil behavior as having much impact on victims; in fact, they do not view their behavior as being uncivil at all. Based on this, uncivil behaviors are likely to be much more "forgettable" to perpetrators than to victims. Thus, we propose that although victims may have difficulty remembering instances of incivility by coworkers, they are likely to be better than perpetrators at remembering such behavior.

Perpetrators' reports probably also will be impacted by recency effects, impression management, and cultural/subcultural variation in what is considered uncivil behavior. Of these potential biases, impression management is likely to exert a stronger impact than victims' reports on perpetrators' reports. Because people are unlikely to desire conveying an impression of incivility to others, impression management motives are likely to cause people to underreport instances where they have engaged in such behavior at work.

A key difference between measuring incivility from victims' and perpetrators' perspectives is that perpetrators have a much higher threshold for deciding what is and what is not incivility. In other words, many behaviors that may be considered uncivil from a victim's perspective might not be considered uncivil by that individual if he or she acted in the same manner. This difference is most problematic when researchers use general questionnaire items such as, "To what extent have you acted uncivilly to a coworker in the past month?" It also is the case, however, that such differences might affect perpetrators' reports even when items are much more specific such as, "To what extent have you cursed at someone at work?"

This is largely due to differences regarding the meaning of the behavior in question (cursing, in this case).

Given these differences in implicit definitions of incivility, along with biases such as social desirability and impression management, we believe that measuring incivility from perpetrators' perspectives is the most formidable challenge in this research domain—much greater, in fact, than measuring incivility from victims' perspectives. Despite these difficulties, the importance of measuring incivility from perpetrators' perspectives cannot be overstated as a key to understanding the causes of such behavior. By understanding this, organizations will be better positioned to design interventions aimed at reducing or eliminating uncivil behavior. With this in mind, we now turn our attention to suggestions for improving the measurement of workplace incivility from both perspectives.

SUGGESTIONS FOR IMPROVING THE MEASUREMENT OF INCIVILITY

As we have indicated, there are important challenges associated with measuring workplace incivility. Furthermore, there are two general issues underlying these challenges: (1) the subjective nature of the incivility construct, and (2) the potential bias associated with asking people to recall and report uncivil behavior. Our suggestions address these two issues.

Clarification of the Workplace Incivility Construct

Recall that Andersson and Pearson (1999) defined incivility as "low-intensity deviant behavior with ambiguous intent to harm the target, in violation of workplace norms for mutual respect. Uncivil behaviors are characteristically rude and discourteous, displaying a lack of regard for others" (p. 457). Most probably would agree that this definition conveys, at least to some extent, the essential nature of workplace incivility. If nothing else it probably allows people to identify an example of a personal experience that fits the definition. However, the abstract nature of this definition makes it difficult to use as a basis for developing valid measures.

Thus, the most important first step is to derive a more concrete definition of incivility. This can be done in several ways. First, we would recommend that organizational scholars undertake more conceptual analysis of the incivility construct. Andersson and Pearson's (1999) conceptual model of workplace incivility is widely cited, and researchers have accepted their definition although it has not served the field well as a basis for measurement.

Another potential way to clarify the incivility construct is to develop items based on qualitative interviews with employees. This inductive approach has been used by Burnfield, Clark, Devendorf, and Jex (2004) to develop a measure of workplace incivility. These researchers conducted 30 open-ended interviews with employees from a variety of organizations and used these responses as the basis for items comprising a self-report measure of incivility comprised of 12 dimensions (9 for incivility originating from constituents within the organization and 3 for customer-based incivility). Although research on this measure is ongoing, preliminary findings have supported its construct validity. Furthermore, this measure provides a much more complete picture of workplace incivility than many other currently available measures.

In addition to clarifying the precise boundaries of workplace incivility, it also would behoove researchers to distinguish incivility from other closely related constructs (e.g., bullying, mobbing, social undermining). A closely related issue is whether workplace incivility is most appropriately viewed as a measured variable or a latent variable. Viewing it as a measured variable suggests that workplace incivility is distinct from other closely related variables and should be assessed directly. Viewing it as a latent variable suggests that other closely related variables simply are forms of the broader construct of workplace incivility. Stated differently, one might view workplace incivility as the root factor underlying many analogous forms of mistreatment in the workplace. This is similar to the argument made by Watson and Clark (1984) in developing their negative affectivity construct. That is, they proposed negative affectivity as a latent variable underlying many forms of dispositional negative emotionality such as trait anxiety, manifest anxiety, and neuroticism. Our view is that workplace incivility is probably best viewed as a latent construct, although much conceptual and empirical work on this issue is still needed.

Improvement of Self-Reported Recollection

As we have noted, retrospective self-reports have been the method of choice for measuring workplace incivility. This is not surprising given its hegemony in organizational research (Scandura & Williams, 2000) and in the social sciences in general. Unfortunately, as we have noted, the retrospective recall problems plaguing such measures render them less than ideal when it comes to assessing incivility.

Enhancing Accuracy of Self-Reports

According to Fowler (1984), survey researchers should take five steps to obtain more accurate responses when they are seeking estimates of factual information from respondents. First, they should reduce the time period about which respondents are asked to report. Instead of asking respondents whether they have experienced a number of uncivil behaviors over a 6-month period, for example, they might reduce that time period to 3 months. This recommendation is based on the fact that information about events decays over time. As a trade-off, shortening the time period is likely to result in obtaining less information from respondents and, as a result, increases the chances that reports of incivility represent short-term fluctuations. Probably the best way to combat this problem would be to employ a longitudinal design, perhaps collecting data at several 3-month intervals.

Fowler's (1984) second recommendation is to ask more questions about the behavior of interest. In the case of workplace incivility, this might involve asking things such as who engaged in the uncivil behavior, where it took place, and perhaps how the person reacted to the uncivil behavior. Crossley (2004) used this approach in a recent study of social undermining, which is similar in nature to workplace incivility. Interestingly, respondents in this study were able to provide fairly vivid accounts of instances in which they had been undermined by others at work from as long as 15 years prior to the study.

The third recommendation is to provide respondents with the chance to reconsider their answers prior to finishing the survey. This can be done if a survey instrument is administered by a trained interviewer who allows respondents to review their answers and to change them if desired. It is possible to do this in self-administered survey instruments as well. This might be done, for example, by including instructions at the end of the instrument encouraging respondents to review their responses and to change them if doing so would result in more accurate depictions of their actual feelings.

Fowler's (1984) fourth recommendation is to reinterview or resurvey people two or more times. According to Fowler (1984), this helps people to remember events because it puts them into the proper time frame. More specifically, the first interview can serve as an anchoring point for people's recall. Despite the potential advantage of facilitating recall, collecting data across more than one time period runs the risk of not having complete data collected at each administration period. Indeed, loss of a number of cases is a natural consequence of readministration given than attrition occurs and opportunities for missing data are compounded.

The fifth recommendation, which is actually an extension of the fourth, is to ask respondents to keep a diary. According to Fowler (1984), minor events such as small changes in health or daily expenditures are difficult for respondents to recall even over relatively short periods of time. Given that many forms of incivility are fairly common in organizations (e.g., interruptions, rudeness on the phone), they may be forgotten by respondents very quickly. Thus, having respondents keep a diary may greatly facilitate recall of these relatively common behaviors. This approach, however, requires a great deal of commitment from respondents and may also result in a great deal of missing data.

Reducing Social Desirability

Although, the recommendations just mentioned may facilitate recall, this is of limited value if what is reported is colored by efforts to promote social desirability. With this in mind, Fowler (1984) also offered suggestions for minimizing social desirability effects when asking respondents sensitive questions.

His first suggestion is to use language in survey instruments that is nonjudgmental. This would involve, for example, emphasizing to respondents the importance of providing accurate information on the survey but not implying that some answers are more valued than others. In the case of incivility by a perpetrator, researchers may emphasize that incivility is a fairly widespread phenomenon in organizations.

Fowler's (1984) second suggestion is to use self-administered survey instruments as opposed to personal interviews (either in person or by telephone). In so doing, respondents will be more willing to admit engaging in negative behaviors than they would if they had to address another person. Because most organizational research is of this nature, the "impersonal touch" already is built in. We note, however, that response rates tend to be lower when surveys are self-administered, so the advantage of obtaining more accurate reports may be offset by lower response rates.

A final suggestion for dealing with social desirability problems is to assure respondents that the information being gathered is confidential or anonymous. This typically is done by stating in a cover letter preceding the survey that responses will be kept confidential and that no one outside of the research staff will be able to associate individual respondents with their answers. In cases where personal identifiers are necessary, for example, when self-reports are matched with data from other sources (cf. Spector, Dwyer, & Jex, 1988), it is common for institutional review boards to require that personal identifiers be eliminated from data sets once the matching has been completed. Participants should be assured these procedures will be followed.

In cases where highly sensitive or personal information is being asked, which could be the case with some forms of workplace incivility, techniques have been designed to ensure that respondents cannot be linked to their answers. For example, Greenberg, Abdel-Latif, Simmons, and Horvitz (1969) developed random response techniques that may be used for asking sensitive questions on surveys. To use this technique, the respondent selects a question on a probability basis from two or more questions (one of which is the sensitive question) without revealing to the interviewer which of these is selected. Each individual's yes or no reply is of no use to the researcher, but all responses in combination, allow the researcher to estimate the proportion of the sample engaging in the behavior that is asked about in the sensitive question.

In addition to these suggestions, our final suggestion is simply to use data collection methods other than, or in combination with, retrospective self-report surveys. Within the social sciences there are a wide variety of non–self-report methods available to researchers (e.g., Webb, Campbell, Schwartz, & Seachrest, 1966), although most are not used in organizational research. These methods are inherently different from self-report surveys providing researchers with different perspectives for future research or intervention design.

Although a complete review of non–self-report methods falls outside the scope of this chapter, we will describe a few that could be used in workplace incivility research. The simplest one is naturalistic observation (Patton, 1990). This involves observing and recording behavior, perhaps in the context of a meeting or other work setting. An obvious problem with this method is that participants may change their behavior if an observer is in the room. This is known as the problem of reactivity. It also is possible, however, that if an observer sat in on meetings on several occasions, participants may get used to it and act in a relatively natural manner. The advantage of observation compared to self-report surveys is that observers may be more accurate in reporting behavior than participant's self-reports.

Another potential alternative to self-reports is the use of archival data (Webb et al., 1966). Organizations store many types of archival records, some of which may be relevant to workplace incivility. If a researcher were to gain access to written memos or letters, for example, these documents could be content-analyzed for the level of incivility expressed, at least in written form. Organizations also may have records of grievances, harassment cases, or other work-related incidents that may gain insight into the level of incivility within an organizational setting. Archival data that are not part of organzational records may also provide information about the level of incivility individuals are likely to experience on a job. The Occupational Network (O*Net) occupation analysis database, for example, contains measures of the extent to which people in different occupations experience interpersonal conflict.

A third alternative to surveys would be focus groups (Stewart & Shamdasani, 1990). Focus groups, which are used frequently in consumer research, are essentially a form of group interviewing. In a typical focus group, a facilitator proposes a set of questions to the group. During the process of discussing each question, the facilitator records notes on a flip chart reflecting the comments made by participants. The main advantage of a focus group over a traditional one-on-one interview is that focus group participants can discuss questions and build on one anothers' ideas. Although focus groups cannot be used to measure individual acts of incivility, this may be a very effective method in measuring the overall level of incivility within organizations or work units.

A final alternative to the use of self-reports is case studies (Yin, 1994). Although the case study typically is viewed as a method of obtaining research ideas, or perhaps crude pilot data, it also could be very useful providing more in-depth insight into phenomena such as workplace incivility. Surveys allow researchers to derive quantitative estimates of the prevalence of workplace incivility, but do not provide much insight into the specific nature of uncivil behavior or its effects. By contrast, case studies of a person who has been the victim of frequent workplace incivility, or of a person who has engaged in a great deal of uncivil behavior, may provide valuable insight into events precipitating such incidents. The obvious disadvantage of using case studies is that the information may be of limited generalizability. Nevertheless, insofar as it provides information that cannot be obtained via surveys, their use should be considered by researchers studying workplace incivility.

CONCLUSION

We have discussed several challenges associated with measuring workplace incivility. Perhaps the most formidable challenge of all regard the development of a clearer definition of workplace incivility that distinguishes it from other related constructs. Assuming that this conceptual barrier could be overcome, self-reports of workplace incivility may be impacted by many biases associated with retrospective recall regardless of whether it is measured from the victim's perspective or perpetrator's perspective. Measuring perpetrators' reports is especially challenging due to differing definitions of what constitutes uncivil behavior, as well as social desirability and impression management issues. Our suggestions for improving the measurement of incivility should be considered seriously by researchers. Our suggestions have to do with improving survey measures and with using alternatives to self-reports. Ultimately, the most effective and insightful way to measure workplace incivility is by using multiple methods and multiple perspectives. Hopefully, our comments will encourage researchers to undertake this challenge.

REFERENCES

Analoui, F., & Kakabadse, A. (1992). Unconventional practices at work: Insight and analysis through participant observation. *Journal of Managerial Psychology, 18*, 449–469.

Andersson, L. M., & Pearson, C. M. (1999). Tit for tat? The spiraling effect of incivility in the workplace. *Academy of Management Review, 24*, 452–471.

Andreou, E. (2001). Bully/victim problems and their association with coping behaviour in conflictual peer interactions among school-age children. *Educational Psychology, 21*, 59–66.

Asch, S. E. (1955). Opinions and social pressure. *Scientific American, 193*, 31–35.

Bachrach, S. B., Bamberger, P. A., & McKinney, V. M. (2007). Harassing under the influence: The prevalence of male heavy drinking, the embeddedness of permissive workplace drinking norms, and the gender harassment of female coworkers. *Journal of Occupational Health Psychology, 12*, 232–250.

Baron, R. A., & Neuman, J. H. (1996). Workplace violence and workplace aggression: Evidence on their relative frequency and potential causes. *Aggressive Behavior, 22*, 161–173.

Baruch, Y. (2005). Bullying on the net: Adverse behavior on e-mail and its impact. *Information & Management, 42*, 361–371.

Baumeister, R. F., Stillwell, A., & Wotman, S. R. (1990). Victim and perpetrator accounts of interpersonal conflict: Autobiographical narratives about anger. *Journal of Personality and Social Psychology, 59*, 994–1005.

Bennett, R. J., & Robinson, S. L. (2000). Development of a measure of workplace deviance. *Journal of Applied Psychology, 85*, 349–360.

Bolger, N., Davis, A., & Rafaeli, E. (2003). Diary methods: Capturing life as it is lived. *Annual Review of Psychology, 54*(1), 579–616.

Bower, G. H. (1981). Mood and memory. *American Psychologist, 36*, 129–148.

Bowling, N. A., & Beehr, T. A. (2006). Workplace harassment from the victim's perspective: A theoretical model and meta-analysis. *Journal of Applied Psychology, 91*, 998–1012.

Brassell, R. G. (2009). *Qualitative cultural differences: A study of workplace incivility.* Unpublished Master's Thesis, Western Kentucky University, Bowling Green, KY.

Burnfield, J. L., Clark, O, L., Devendorf, S. & Jex, S. M. (2004, April). *Understanding workplace incivility: Scale development and validation.* Paper presented at the 19th Annual Conference of the Society for Industrial and Organizational Psychology, Chicago, IL.

Burton, R. M., Eriksen, B., Håkonsson, D. D., Snow, S. C. (2006). *Organizational Design: The Evolving State-of-the-Art.* New York, NY: Springer.

Chen, C. C., & Eastman, W. (1997). Toward a civic culture for multicultural organizations. *Journal of Applied Behavioral Science, 33*, 454–470.

Cohen. D. (1996). Law, social policy, and violence: The impact of regional cultures. *Journal of Personality and Svcial Psychology, 70*, 961–978.

Cohen. D., & Nisbett, R. E. (1994). Self-protection and the culture of honor: Explaining southern violence. *Personality and Social Psychology Bulletin, 20*, 551–567.

Cohen. D., & Nisbett, R. E. (1997). Field experiments examining the culture of honor: The role of institutions perpetuating norms about violence. *Personality and Social Psychology Bulletin, 23*, 1188–1199.

Cohen, D., Nisbett, R. E., Bowdle, B. F., & Schwarz, N. (1996). Insult, aggression, and the southern culture of honor: An "experimental ethnography." *Journal of Personality and Social Psychology, 70*, 945–960.

Cohen, D., Vandello, J., Puente, S., & Rantilla, A. (1999). "When you call me that, smile!" How norms for politeness, interaction styles, and aggression work together in southern culture. *Social Psychology Quarterly, 62*, 257–275.

Cortina, L. M., Lonsway, K. A., Magley, V. J., Freeman, L. V., Hunter, M., Collinsworth, L. L., & Fitzgerald, L. F. (2002). What's gender got to do with it? Incivility in the federal courts. *Law and Social Inquiry, 27*, 235–270.

Cortina, L. M., Magley, V. J., Williams, J. H., & Langhout, R. D. (2001). Incivility in the workplace: Incidence and impact. *Journal of Occupational Health Psychology, 6*, 64–80.

Cowie, H., Naylor, P., Rivers, I., Smith, P. K., & Pereira, B. (2002). Measuring workplace bullying *Aggression and Violent Behavior, 7*, 33–51.

Crossley, C. D. (2004). *Victim's reactions to social undermining.* Unpublished doctoral dissertation, Bowling Green State University, Bowling Green, OH.

Crowne, D. P., & Marlowe, D. (1964). *The approval motive: Studies in evaluative dependency.* New York, NY: Wiley.

Davis, S. M., & Lawrence, P. R. (1977). *Matrix.* Reading, MA: Addison-Wesley.

De Laat, P. B. (1994). Matrix management of projects and power struggles: A case study of an R & D Laboratory. *Human Relations, 47*, 9, 1089–1119.

Digman, J. M. (1990). Emergence of the five-factor model. *Annual Review of Psychology, 41*, 417–440.

Dillman, D. A., Smyth, J., & Christian, L. M. (2009). *Internet, mail and mixed-mode surveys: The tailored design method* (3rd ed.). Hoboken, NJ: Wiley & Sons.

Dorman, C., & Zapf, D. (2004). Customer related social stressors and burnout. *Journal of Occupational Health Psychology, 9*, 61–82.

Duffy, M. K., Ganster, D., & Pagon, M. (2002). Social undermining in the workplace. *Academy of Management Journal, 45*, 331–351.

Duffy, M. K., O'Leary-Kelly, A. M., & Ganster, D. C. (2003). Anti-social work behavior and individual and organizational health. In D. A. Hofmann & L. E. Tetrick (Eds.), *Health and safety in organizations: A multilevel perspective* (pp. 173–200). San Francisco, CA: Jossey-Bass.

Einarsen, S., Hoel, H., Zapf, D., & Cooper, C. L. (2003). The concept of bullying at work: The European tradition. In S. Einarsen, H. Hoel, D. Zapf, & C. L. Cooper (Eds.), *Bullying and emotional abuse in the workplace. International perspectives in research and practice* (pp. 3–30). London, England: Taylor & Francis.

Eisenberg, A. R. (1986). Teasing: Verbal play in two Mexican homes. In B. B. Schieffelin & E. Ochs (Eds.), *Language socialization across cultures* (pp. 182–198). Cambridge, England: Cambridge University Press.

Festinger, L. (1957). *A theory of cognitive dissonance.* Stanford, CA: Stanford University Press.

Fitzgerald, L. F. (1993). Sexual harassment: Violence against women in the workplace. *American Psychologist, 48*, 1070–1076.

Fitzgerald, L. F., Drasgow, F., Hulin, C. L., Gelfand, M. J., & Magley, V. J. (1997). Antecedents and consequences of sexual harassment in organizations: A test of an integrated model. *Journal of Applied Psychology, 82*, 359–378.

Fitzwater, E., & Gates, D. (2004). Clinical consultation. How do you manage the aggressive behavior of cognitively impaired patients? *Rehabilitation Nursing, 29*, 13.

Forsyth, D. R. (1999). *Group dynamics* (3rd ed.). Belmont, CA: Brooks/Cole.

Fowler, F. J. (1984). *Survey research methods.* Beverley Hills, CA: Sage.

Frone, M. R. (2003). Predictors of overall and on-the-job substance use among young workers. *Journal of Occupational Health Psychology, 8*, 39–54.

Glomb, T. M. (2002). Workplace anger and aggression: Informing conceptual models with data from specific encounters. *Journal of Occupational Health Psychology, 7*, 20–36.

Glomb, T. M., & Liao, H. (2003). Interpersonal aggression in work groups: Social influence, reciprocal and individual effects. *Academy of Management Journal, 46*, 486–496.

Greenberg, B. G., Abdel-Latif, A. A., Simmons, W. R., & Horvitz, D. (1969). The unrelated question randomized response model: Theoretical framework. *Journal of the American Statistical Association, 64*, 520–539.

Hackman, J. R. (1992). Group influences on individuals in organizations. In M. D. Dunnette & L. M. Hough (Eds.), *Handbook of industrial and organizational psychology* (2nd ed., Vol. 2, pp. 199–267). Palo Alto, CA: Consulting Psychologists Press.

Hofstede, G. (1980). *Culture's consequences: International differences in work-related values.* Beverly Hills, CA: Sage.

Hogan, J., & Hogan, R. (1989). How to measure employee reliability. *Journal of Applied Psychology, 74*, 273–279.

Jackson, S. E., & Schuler, R. S. (1985). A meta-analysis and conceptual critique of research on role ambiguity and role conflict in work settings. *Organizational Behavior and Human Decision Processes, 36*, 16–78.

Jex, S. M., & Thomas, J. L. (2003). Relations between stressors and group perceptions: Main and mediating effects. *Work & Stress, 17*, 158–169.

Joyce, W. F. (1986). Matrix organization: A social experiment. *The Academy of Management Journal, 29*(3), 536–561.

Keashly, L. (2001). Interpersonal and systemic aspects of emotional abuse at work: The target's perspective. *Violence and Victims, 16*, 233–268.

Kumpulainen, K., Rasanen, E., & Henttonen, I. (1998). The persistence of teacher-reported behavior problems among children aged 8 to 12. *European Child & Adolescent Psychiatry, 7*, 225–234.

Kuprenas, J. A. (2003). Implementation and performance of a matrix organizational structure. *International Journal of Project Management, 21*, 51–62.

Lehman, W. E., Farabee, D. J., Holcom, M. L., & Simpson, D. D. (1995). Prediction of substance use in the workplace: Unique contributions of personal background and work environment variables. *Journal of Drug Issues, 25*, 253–274.

Mangione, T. W., Howland, J., & Lee, M. (1998). *New perspectives for worksite alcohol strategies: Results from a corporate drinking study.* Boston, MA: JSI Research and Training Institute.

Martin, J. (1996). *Miss Manners rescues civilization.* New York, NY: Crown.

Milam, A. C., Spitzmueller, C., & Penney, L. M. (2009). Investigation of individual differences among targets of workplace incivility. *Journal of Occupational Health Psychology, 14*, 58–69.

Morand, D. A. (1998). Getting serious about going casual on the job. *Business Horizons, 41*, 51–56.

Morris, J. (1996, Autumn). Democracy beguiled. *The Wilson Quarterly, 20*, 24–35.

Nunnally, J. C., & Bernstein, I. H. (1994). *Psychometric theory* (3rd ed.). New York, NY: McGraw-Hill.

Olweus, D. (1984). Aggressors and their victims: Bullying at school. In N. Frude & H. Gault (Eds.), *Disruptive behavior in the schools* (pp. 57–76). New York, NY: Wiley.

Ones, D. S., & Viswesvaran, C. (2001). Integrity tests and other criterion-focused personality scales (COPS) used in personnel selection. *International Journal of Selection and Assessment, 9*, 31–39.

O'Reilly, C. A., & Caldwell, D. (1979). Information influence as a determinant of task characteristics and job satisfaction. *Journal of Applied Psychology, 64*, 157–165.

Patton, M. Q. (1990). *Qualitative evaluation methods.* Beverly Hills, CA: Sage.

Paulhus, D. L. (1991). Measurement and control of response bias. In P. Robinson, P. R. Shaver, & L. S. Wrightsman (Eds.), *Measures of personality and social psychological attitudes* (pp. 17–59). San Diego, CA: Academic.

Pearson, C. M., Andersson, L. M., & Porath, C. L. (2000). Assessing and attacking workplace incivility. *Organizational Dynamics, 29*, 123–137.

Pearson, C. M., Andersson, L. M., & Porath, C. L. (2005). Workplace incivility. In S. Fox & P. E. Spector (Eds.), *Counterproductive work behavior: Investigations of actors and targets* (pp. 177–200). Washington, DC: American Psychological Association.

Pearson, C. M., Andersson, L. M., & Wegner, J. A. (2001). When workers flout convention: A preliminary study of workplace incivility. *Human Relations, 54,* 1387–1420.

Penney, L. M., & Spector, P. E. (2005). Job stress, incivility and counterproductive work behavior (CWB): The moderating role of negative affectivity. *Journal of Organizational Behavior, 26,* 777–796.

Podsakoff, P. M., MacKenzie, S. B., Lee, J. Y., & Podsakoff, N. P. (2003). Common method biases in behavioral research: A critical review of the literature and recommended remedies. *Journal of Applied Psychology, 88,* 879–903.

Rawlinson, H. (1989). Pre-employment testing. *Small Business Reports, 14,* 20–27.

Robinson, S. L., & Bennett, R. J. (1995). A typology of deviant workplace behaviors: A multidimensional scaling study. *Academy of Management Journal, 38,* 555–572.

Robinson, S. L., & O'Leary-Kelly, A. M. (1998). Monkey see, monkey do: The influence of work groups on antisocial behavior of employees. *Academy of Management Journal, 41,* 658–672.

Rosenfeld, P. R., Giacalone, R. A., & Riordan, C.A. (1995). *Impression management in organizations: Theory, measurement, and practice.* New York, NY: Routledge.

Roth, D. L., Snyder, C. R., & Pace, L. M. (1986). Dimensions of favorable self-presentation. *Journal of Personality and Social Psychology, 51,* 867–874.

Rundus, D. (1971). Analysis of rehearsal process in free recall. *Journal of Experimental Psychology, 89,* 63–77.

Salancik, G. R., & Pfeffer, J. (1978). A social information processing approach to job attitudes and task design. *Administrative Science Quarterly, 23,* 224–253.

Salmivalli, C. (2001). Feeling good about oneself, being bad to others? Remarks on self-esteem, hostility, and aggressive behavior. *Aggressive & Violent Behavior, 6,* 375–393.

Scandura, T. A., & Williams, E. A. (2000). Research methodology in management: Current practices, trends, and implications for future research. *Academy of Management Journal, 43,* 1248–1264.

Scholmerich, A., Leyendecker, B., & Keller, H. (1995). The study of early interaction in a contextual perspective: Culture, communication, and eye contact. In J. Valsner (Ed.), *Comparative cultural and constructivist perspectives* (pp. 29–50). Norwood, NJ: Albex.

Shapiro, J. P., Baumeister, R. F., & Kessler, J. W. (1991). A three-component model of children's teasing: Aggression, humor and ambiguity. *Journal of Social and Clinical Psychology, 10,* 459–472.

Sigal, J., & Jacobsen, H. (1999). A cross-cultural explanation of factors affecting reactions to sexual harassment: Attitudes and policies. *Public Policy and Law, 5,* 760–785.

Sinha, R. R., & Krueger, J. (1998). Idiographic self-evaluation and bias. *Journal of Research in Personality, 32,* 131–155.

Slee, P. T., & Rigby, T. (1993). Australian school children's self-appraisal of interpersonal relations: The bullying experience. *Child Psychiatry and Human Development, 23,* 273–282.

Spector, P. E., Dwyer, D. J., & Jex, S. M. (1988). Relations of job stressors to affective, health, and performance outcomes: A comparison of multiple data sources. *Journal of Applied Psychology, 73,* 11–19.

Spector, P. E., Fox, S. (2005). The stressor-emotion model of counterproductive work behavior. In S. Fox & P. E. Spector (Eds.), *Counterproductive work behavior: Investigations of actors and targets.* Washington, DC: American Psychological Association.

Spector, P. E., & Jex, S. M. (1998). Development of four self-report measures of job stressors and strain: Interpersonal Conflict at Work Scale, Organizational Constraints Scale, Quantitative Workload Inventory, and Physical Symptoms Inventory. *Journal of Occupational Health Psychology, 3,* 356–367.

Stewart, D., & Shamdasani, R. N. (1990). *Focus groups: Theory and practice.* Newbury Park, CA: Sage.

Stockdale, M. S., Bison-Rapp, S., O'Conner, M., & Gutek, B. A. (2004). Coming to terms with zero tolerance sexual harassment policies. *Journal of Forensic Psychology Practice, 4,* 65–78.

Tepper, B. (2007). Abusive supervision in work organizations: Review, synthesis, and research agenda. *Journal of Management, 33,* 261–289.

Trevino, L. K. (1992). The social effects of punishment in organizations: A justice perspective. *Academy of Management Review, 17,* 647–676.

Upshaw, H. S., & Yates, L. A. (1968). Self-persuasion, social approval and task success as determinants of self-esteem following impression management. *Journal of Experimental Social Psychology, 4*(2), 143–152.

U.S. Bureau of Labor Statistics. (2005). *Survey of workplace violence prevention.* Washington, DC: Author.

U.S. Department of Health and Human Services. (2006). *Workplace violence prevention strategies and research needs.* Washington, DC: Author.

Vance, R. J., & Biddle, T. F. (1985). Task experience and social cues: Interactive effects on attitudinal reactions. *Organizational Behavior and Human Decision Processes, 35,* 252–265.

Vardi, Y., & Weitz, E. (2004). *Misbehavior in organizations: Theory, research and management.* Mahwah, NJ: Lawrence Erlbaum Associates.

Vardi, Y., & Wiener, Y. (1996). Misbehavior in organizations: A motivational framework. *Organization Science, 7,* 151–165.

Watson, D., & Clark, L. (1984). Negative affectivity: The propensity to experience aversive emotional states. *Psychological Bulletin, 96,* 465–490.

Webb, E. J., Campbell, D. T., Schwartz, R. D., & Seachrest, L. (1966). *Unobtrusive measures: Nonreactive research in the social sciences.* Chicago, IL: Rand McNally.

Yin, R. K. (1994). *Case study research: Design and methods* (2nd ed.). Thousand Oaks, CA: Sage.

Zapf, D., & Gross, C. (2001). Conflict escalation and coping with workplace bullying: A replication and extension. *European Journal of Work & Organizational Psychology, 10,* 497–522.

Zauderer, D. G. (2002). Workplace incivility and the management of human capital. *Public Manager, 31,* 36–43.

Zellers, K. L., Tepper, B. J., & Duffy, M. K. (2002). Abusive supervision and subordinates' organizational citizenship behavior. *Journal of Applied Psychology, 87,* 1068–1076.

9

Methodological Issues in Studying Insidious Workplace Behavior

Paul E. Spector and Ozgun B. Rodopman

Since the mid-1990s there has been increasing interest in the study of detrimental behaviors and experiences in the workplace, as reflected in several edited books on the topic (e.g., Fox & Spector, 2005; Sagie, Stashevsky, & Koslowsky, 2003; Vardi & Weitz, 2004). This has represented a shift away from the traditional focus on good employee attitudes and positive contributions to the job through effective performance. Traditionally, most previous attention paid to the negative side of organizational behavior focused on relatively benign (although significant) issues of attendance and turnover (Hulin, Roznowski, & Hachiya, 1985). More recently, however, researchers have become interested in the tendency of employees to engage in a host of hostile and nasty behaviors toward one another that not only undermines the effectiveness of organizations, but that also adversely affects the health and well-being of individuals (e.g., Boswell & Olson-Buchanan, 2004). Such behaviors have been studied under a variety of rubrics, including workplace aggression (Neuman & Baron, 1997, 2005; O'Leary-Kelly, Griffin, & Glew, 1996; Spector, 1975, 1977), bullying (Rayner & Keashly, 2005), deviance (Bennett, Aquino, Reed, & Thau, 2005; Hollinger, 1986; Robinson & Bennett, 1995), emotional abuse (Keashly & Harvey, 2005), incivility (Pearson, Andersson, & Porath, 2005), mobbing (Zapf & Einarsen, 2005), retaliation (Folger & Skarlicki, 2005; Skarlicki & Folger, 1997), and revenge (Bies & Tripp, 2005; Bies, Tripp, & Kramer, 1997). Whereas the relatively rare cases of extreme violence have captured media attention, it is the day-to-day insidious workplace behavior (IWB) that affects large numbers of employees and that just about everyone is likely to encounter or perform themselves at some time or another.

One of the impediments to studying IWB is that there can be reasons for individuals to keep it hidden from view, whether they are themselves perpetrators or targets. Such acts can be sensitive to perpetrators because they might violate social or organizational norms (e.g., civility) or because they might be sanctioned by organizations (e.g., abusive behavior). In some cases they also might lead to legal action, particularly if they occur across genders or races, and can be part of a sexual harassment or racial harassment case (e.g., insulting someone's gender or race). For a target, to complain might be considered a form of disloyalty or tattling and to be known as a victim is to be seen as weak. Thus, researchers confront the challenge of uncovering something that many will be motivated to keep secret.

The goal of this chapter is to discuss issues and strategies in studying the sensitive topic of IWB. We will include treatment of ethical issues, dealing with institutional review boards, gaining access to appropriate samples, research designs, and various approaches to studying these behaviors in addition to using self-report surveys. Our treatment of measurement issues will be limited, as that is the focus of the chapter by Jex, Geimer, Clark, Guidroz, and Yugo (Chapter 8, present volume).

ETHICAL ISSUES IN STUDYING INSIDIOUS WORKPLACE BEHAVIOR

Because of the inherently sensitive nature of IWB, ethical issues are likely to arise in the course of studying it and researchers are bound by professional standards to consider such matters carefully (Lowman, 2006). For example, depending on the behaviors under study, individuals who are identified may be at risk for harm. And at the very least, there is potential for violation of privacy. Furthermore, with research conducted in field settings there also is the possibility of coercion when company management has an interest in having employees participate so it can determine the extent to which IWB is occurring and to identify the particular employees who are engaging in it. These concerns must be salient to researchers whether the participants being studied have engaged in these behaviors themselves, are targets of these behaviors, or have played some other role (e.g., supervisors of victims and perpetrators).

In designing studies of IWB, researchers first need to consider the nature of the behaviors in question. Such behaviors can vary considerably in severity, ranging from milder forms of impoliteness and incivility to severe acts of abuse and harassment. They can be acts that violate organizational policies or even the law. The specific choice of behaviors to study can have implications for the best ways to protect participants. Certainly, harm would be minimal in studies of milder forms of IWB, but they can be considerable in the more severe cases. This would be the case, for example, if individuals are identified who have engaged in acts that are part of a pattern of sexual harassment (Lim & Cortina, 2005).

Working in organizational field settings can present challenges and ethical dilemmas in balancing responsibilities to individual employee participants versus organizations. For example, if a researcher uncovers harmful behaviors, does he or she have a greater responsibility to protect the well-being of an individual employee who is engaging in harmful acts or to the organization that is being harmed? In a real sense, the organization also is a participant in the study deserving of protection, especially when officials have granted permission for the organization to be studied. Thus, researchers need to anticipate possible ethical issues in the design and conduct of a study to balance the rights and welfare of employees and organizations. Much of this can be done by negotiating the conditions and terms under which the study will be conducted and how the data will be handled. This includes clarifying who owns the data, what will be revealed to management, and what will be done if the researcher discovers that an employee has engaged in a specific undesirable behavior (for more on these themes, see Lowman, 2006).

Professional organizations, such as the American Psychological Association (2002), have developed ethical principles (e.g., respect for people's rights and dignity) that may help researchers guide their choices and behaviors with respect to these ethical issues. In practice, Mirvis and Seashore (1979) emphasize the need for a good understanding of different roles (e.g., employee, manager, member of the organization and society) and the complex relationships individuals have in organizations. Researchers should be concerned about clarifying roles, expectations, and responsibilities of the parties involved. That way, they can more easily obtain and maintain top management support as well as participants' trust. At the same time, potential conflicts of interests and unexpected demands by the organization or employees can be avoided. A written agreement or contract is helpful to clarify the terms of the relationship between the researcher and the organization and to set ground rules for dealing with issues such as privacy, identity protection, voluntary participation, claims for data, and proper conduct.

Identity Protection

Because researchers cannot reveal the identities of individuals they do not know, anonymity is the most effective means of identity protection. Most studies of IWB have used anonymous questionnaires that reduce identity concerns by allowing inclusion of severe acts without raising issues of confidentiality. In cases in which researchers wish to combine multiple sources of data, such as matching employee questionnaires to those of coworkers or supervisors, procedures have been developed to allow matching without revealing identities. One such method is to ask individuals to create a secret code and to put it on questionnaires to be completed by the individual and by the coworker or the supervisor. Participants then give the questionnaires to their coworkers or supervisors to complete and return separately to the researcher. Another way of ensuring anonymity is to ask three questions that are sufficiently general to prevent identification but particular enough so that the combination of the answers is distinct for each individual. Examples are first names of grandparents, street number for the earliest remembered address, or name of first-grade teacher. This can be particularly useful in longitudinal studies in which each participant completes two or more questionnaires over time.

Two unconventional methods sometimes used to get responses on sensitive topics, such as theft base rate (Wimbush & Dalton, 1997), are the randomized-response technique and the unmatched-count technique. In the randomized response technique, participants are asked whether they engaged in a particular sensitive behavior. They then flip a coin and respond by saying yes if they either got heads on the coin or if the answer to the sensitive question is yes. No one knows which case is true for a particular individual. However, the difference between the proportion of total yes responses and the expected value of getting heads (0.50) reflects the proportion of people who answer the sensitive question affirmatively.

The unmatched-count technique has two groups of people respond to a series of random questions, of which some are true and some are false for any individual (e.g., I have a brother). The first group is asked to indicate the total number of yes responses to a set of questions. No one knows which questions are affirmed by a particular individual. The second group reports the total number of yes responses to the same set of questions with an additional sensitive question. The difference between the two groups in the total number of yes responses is attributed to the additional sensitive question and reflects the proportion of individuals who agreed to it. Because both techniques focus on aggregate outcomes rather than individual responses, they provide anonymity.

Often, studies are conducted in which participants are, in fact, identified. This is necessary to match questionnaire responses to other sources of data that can be linked only by participants' names. However, when studies are conducted in which individuals identify themselves, care must be taken to inform participants prior to their participation about who will have access to their responses and under what conditions their identities will be revealed to management (e.g., if they indicate engaging in illegal activity). The researcher also must take care in determining what questions to ask. If, for example, some questions concern ongoing behavior that is harmful to the organization or to other people, researchers are obligated ethically to inform management or potential targets for their own safety and well-being. Instructions should make it clear to participants what sorts of responses will be shared with management so there is clear informed consent prior to participation in the study.

Coercion

Another ethical issue in conducting field studies on IWB is the possibility that management will coerce employees into participating. Again, researchers should discuss such issues with management before the research begins to clarify conditions under which data will be collected. Researchers should do their best to convince management to allow completely voluntary participation. They also should avoid participating in studies in which any management coercion is used. If a researcher is uncomfortable with the procedures that will be used, withdrawal from the study may be appropriate, depending upon precisely how coercive management is and what the potential risk might be to employees. Withdrawal might have little cost when the researcher does not work for the organization under study as a consultant or employee. However, if there is a contractual or employment relationship, withdrawal might not be an easy option as it might violate legal and professional commitments made to the organization. In such cases, failure to fulfill professional obligations might itself be an ethical breach. Furthermore, it could have severe financial costs due to loss of a contract or a job. In cases in which withdrawal from a study is not possible, researchers should do their best to inform employees of the purpose of the study and how data will be used, and protect their identities.

SPECIAL CONSIDERATIONS OF INSTITUTIONAL REVIEW BOARDS

Perhaps nothing has had a more chilling effect on the study of sensitive issues like IWB than government regulation, such as institutional review boards (IRBs; Lee, 1993). Countries vary with respect to the extent to which research is regulated, with some having little or no regulation (e.g., China) whereas others have highly advanced systems of research review (e.g., Australia, Canada, and the United States). In the United States IRBs are mandated for institutions that receive federal research funding, which today means all or almost all colleges and universities where research is conducted. By law, these IRBs have jurisdiction over all research conducted at their institutions, even though for most, only a small minority might be federally funded. Thus, all researchers must submit for review all research projects.

A problem with IRBs is that each operates independently and there is no consistency regarding how efficiently they operate, how knowledgeable their members are about research methods and regulations, or how they interpret research regulations. Some IRBs will deny approval to projects simply because they address sensitive issues, such as IWB (Seiler & Murtha, 1980). This is perhaps due, in part, to the lack of familiarity that IRB members have with this sort of organizational research and, in part, to the rigidity with which they attempt to enforce their interpretation of the rules. One of us (Spector) corresponded at length with a graduate student at a university who could not gain IRB approval to conduct a master's thesis study including an anonymous survey of IWB that was similar to work routinely approved by IRBs in North America. The IRB's concern was that the questions were just too sensitive to be asked of participants. By contrast, fortunately, the IRB at our university routinely grants approval to such projects.

In the United States there is a distinction between projects that must be reviewed and those that are exempted from review. If a project carries with it some degree of risk to participants, it will have to be reviewed by the IRB. If risk is minimal, then a project might be deemed exempt from review, although the researcher cannot determine his or her own exemption. Rather, the IRB must be petitioned for an exemption. The advantages to an exempt project are that (a) the process is typically much quicker since it does not have to go to the entire board, (b) the exemption is granted for a longer period of time (5 years) than a project that is reviewed (1 year), and (c) an informed consent form completed by participants is not typically required. Projects are exempted from review in which individuals are not identified, such as with anonymous questionnaires. Studies of publicly observable phenomena also can be exempted if the researcher is merely recording instances of behavior in a public place without identifying individuals. Informed consent should not be required with anonymous surveys because it would identify the individuals who participated in the study, thereby potentially putting them at risk (Lee, 1993). Without signed forms, no one will know for certain who participated. This is an issue that might have to be argued with a particular IRB that insists on having signed informed consent forms for an anonymous survey or other type of study in which participants are not identified.

If individuals can be identified and there is possible risk, which could be the case if individuals admit to engaging in IWB, then review is needed. In most cases, each participant would be asked to sign an informed consent form stating that he or she understands the purpose and risks of the research and agrees to participate. Such a form will indicate the conditions under which data are collected and the purposes to which the data will be put. It also will identify who will have access to the data (e.g., only the researchers or management). It is imperative that researchers doing work in organizations clarify with management all of the issues that are covered by informed consent so there is agreement about precisely what will be done. Although IRBs have power over researchers in their own institutions, they have no power to enforce their policies with outside organizations. This may cause problems for researchers who find themselves caught between requirements of their IRBs and those of the organizations at which they are conducting research.

IRBs can create difficulties for researchers who wish to study IWB. If members of the IRB at a particular institution are unfamiliar with this sort of research, then extra care might have to be taken to explain its purpose, the methodology, and potential risks to participants. Projects in which individuals are not identified should be the easiest to get approved, since risks are minimal. Identification carries the theoretical risk that an individual's supervisor will learn that he or she has engaged in IWB, so it is possible that an IRB will have concerns about such a project unless protections are built-in carefully and described thoroughly.

ACCESSING SAMPLES OF PARTICIPANTS

IWB researchers who need to access appropriate samples of participants are likely to face particular challenges. Whether the focus is on actors or targets, there can be difficulties in locating individuals who have engaged in or who have experienced the behaviors of interest, and then getting them to share their experiences, even anonymously.

Another issue is that for some phenomena, incidence rates can be rather low, with a small proportion of the general working population fitting the specification needed for the study. In that case, either very large samples will have to be taken or subpopulations with higher incidence rates will have to be identified and sampled. With these considerations in mind, we now consider various methods of accessing samples to be used in research on various forms of IWB.

Typical Organizational Survey Techniques

Most studies of IWB are anonymous surveys that use methods commonly applied in organizational survey research (Scandura & Williams, 2000). These methods can be differentiated between surveys conducted internally and those conducted externally to the employing organization, each of which has its own advantages and limitations. Internal surveys are conducted by contacting the management of an organization and getting approval to study their employees. The study is presented to employees as being conducted within their organization with the approval of management. Sometimes it is noted that management is interested in the results and that a report will be provided that reveals the findings. An external survey is conducted outside the employing organization, with participants contacted at home or through nonemploying organizations. This might be done by drawing a sample of individuals in a particular geographic region, such as a city (e.g., Bennett & Robinson, 2000). More commonly, members of a professional society or other vocational group are surveyed. Finally, an approach to sampling readily available to many university-based researchers would be to solicit volunteers among students on campus who are employed part time or full time (e.g., Penney & Spector, 2005).

Internal Surveys

The internal survey enables the study of a single organization or small number of known organizations, thus controlling for a variety of potential confounding variables. It also can result in high response rates, particularly if management supports the study and allows employees to complete the survey on company time. The highest rates often are achieved by conducting the survey in a staff meeting, where all or almost all employees are likely to participate. If the organization management is committed to the study, it might cover the costs of the survey, including copying and postage. There also is a possibility that the survey data could be tied to other data in the organization, some of which might be more objective than survey data, such as employee attendance, health care utilization, and productivity. Of course, linking to such data might compromise anonymity. One disadvantage for the internal survey of a sensitive topic is that employees might not feel comfortable revealing their experiences with IWB, leading to lower response rates, missing data, or dishonest responding. It also can be difficult to find an organization willing to participate in an IWB study given that there might be concerns that conducting such a study might stir up trouble among employees who are disgruntled. There may be a feeling that some things are best left alone.

External Surveys

The external survey typically results in a sample that cuts across many different organizations since it is unlikely that many individuals contacted outside of an organization will have the same employer. Thus, it usually will be more heterogeneous than the typical internal survey in terms of the organizational environment. This can introduce additional variance into the study, which may or may not be desirable depending upon the study's purpose.

However, the external survey often is easier to accomplish since there is no need to get organizational approval to conduct it. Many times, a professional association directory can be acquired from the association or one of its members (e.g., the American Psychological Society and the Society for Industrial and Organizational Psychology provide directories to members). For example, O'Driscoll and his colleagues (2003) recruited managers from the membership list of the New Zealand Institute of Management. Although labor-intensive, survey samples can be drawn from such directories.

One particular population easier to sample on some campuses is employed college students. Often, urban universities enroll large proportions of nontraditional students, who also are employed. Night classes, in particular, can be good sources of full-time employees who might be taking one or more college classes. Many campuses have courses that are popular for those in professions needing to take continuing education courses, such as public school teachers. Volunteers can be solicited both inside (with instructor approval) and outside of class.

An advantage to using external samples is that participants tend to be less anxious about revealing information since the study is not connected to their employers. This is particularly true when studies are conducted on university campuses, where individuals are far removed from work and where they expect that research might be conducted for scientific (i.e., nonorganizationally related) purposes. A potential disadvantage of using student samples is that it is uncertain if the population of employed individuals on campus generalizes to the broader working population. Of course, with most internal surveys, one never can be certain if results generalize beyond the particular organization under study, making it doubtful that threats to external validity are any greater for external surveys than for internal surveys. In fact, research has shown that few differences in IWB were found between research participants from a university sample and a heterogeneous sample of nonuniversity employees from several organizations (Fox, Spector, & Miles, 2001).

Alternative Approaches to Accessing Samples

Lee (1993) has identified seven alternative approaches to accessing samples for studies of sensitive topics that may be adapted to the study of IWB. They involve either finding creative ways to identify and access potential individuals who have had experience with IWB or ways of getting individuals to more readily participate in a study. Specifically, these are (a) list sampling, (b) piggyback surveying, (c) screening, (d) networking, (e) outcropping, (f) advertising, and (g) servicing.

List Sampling

This method requires that a list of individuals be compiled whose members share a particular characteristic of interest. For example, to study the effects of emotions and cognitions on work deviance behavior, Lee and Allen (2002) contacted 1,000 individuals from a list of registered nurses in Ontario, Canada. For their research on work–family conflict, Casper, Martin, Buffardi, and Erdwin (2002) obtained participants from a mailing list of a child-care referral organization. In the case of IWB, participants would be individuals who either have engaged in such acts or who have been targets of them. For their research on racial/ethnic bullying, Fox and Stallworth (2005) recruited participants from membership lists of associations, which specifically target various racial and ethnic groups, such as the Hispanic MBA Association. Most likely, it would have to be a quite specific behavior because it is unlikely that a variety of behaviors classified as IWB would result in individuals appearing on the same list. It also seems more likely that a list would incorporate individuals experiencing more serious rather than less serious behaviors (e.g., a list of those arrested for assault of coworkers is more likely to exist than a list of those who merely are rude). Furthermore, the researcher somehow would have to gain knowledge that an appropriate list exists and then gain access to it. Terpstra and Cook (1985), for example, analyzed data from all sexual harassment cases filed in a 2-year period with the Illinois Department of Human Rights.

Some forms of IWB might be sufficiently serious that organizations create incident reports to keep track of them. If researchers were able to access such reports, it would be possible for them to conduct a study using the reports as data or to identify a population of individuals who could be asked to participate voluntarily in a study. On the actor side, some behaviors might result in organizational sanctions that could be placed in employees' human resource files. Complaints of abusive behavior or sexual harassment, for example, are likely to be reported in an employee's file. On the target side, individuals who seek help with a problem coworker or supervisor might have records that document the incident, which might exist within the employee's file, or some other organizational record.

Of course, a key concern about using such lists within organizations is possible violations of privacy. Because some incidents might appear in records that are not made public, using such reports stands to violate the rights of the employees involved. This would require using special procedures to protect identities. For example, to provide materials that can be analyzed, human resources personnel with access to records might be asked to provide incident reports with identifying information removed. Likewise, personnel with access to names could send anonymous questionnaires to everyone on a particular list asking for voluntary participation in a study. This would keep researchers from being able to identify individuals who met inclusion criteria for the study.

Piggyback Surveying

Sometimes a survey designed for a specific purpose can be added on to an existing survey used for another, broader purpose. This can be particularly useful if the new purpose can be satisfied by using a small number of questions that easily can be added so as neither (a) to add to the burden on participants nor (b) to threaten the validity of the original set of questions. For example, a few additional questions could supplement an organization's periodic climate or job satisfaction survey. Another possibility is to ask a few preliminary screening questions that identify the individual as falling into a subpopulation of interest. This is particularly useful if the characteristic being identified has a frequency of occurrence in the larger population. The identified individuals then could be resurveyed with a larger number of questions. Of course, this would require that the individuals be identified so the researcher would know who to resurvey. In this case, anonymity of responses to the main survey could be maintained by including a special card containing the unique questions that gets returned to the researcher separately. Another option would be to include a few preliminary screening questions with a statement asking respondents who answer a certain way (e.g., all yes) to go to a Web site at which additional questions can be completed.

Screening

When individuals who meet some relatively rare specification are needed (e.g., individuals who have filed a sexual harassment complaint), it may be particularly useful to prescreen a larger population to identify a subgroup to survey. This is likely to be helpful if the data to be collected are fairly extensive, especially if an interview is to be used. In their study of social processes in workplace bullying, for example, Lewis and Orford (2005) contacted participants for an in-depth interview through a national, UK voluntary telephone helpline for victims of workplace bullying. The coordinator of the helpline provided a list of individuals who met the screening criteria by the researchers (e.g., women having severe problems as targets of bullying in the workplace). The prescreening could be conducted using a very brief questionnaire that includes only enough questions to identify potential participants (e.g., through telephone or through in-person canvassing). This can be done inside an organization by using interoffice mail, e-mail, telephone, or by walking between workstations. Of course, the feasibility of each approach depends on employees' access to these various forms of office communication.

This approach is useful only when the study requires a population of individuals who match a particular specification instead of directly comparing those who fit and those who do not fit. In many cases, however, because researchers are interested in comparing individuals who are engaging in IWB (or who are being targeted by acts of IWB) with those who are not, this approach may have only limited value.

Snowball Sampling

With the snowball sampling technique, a researcher uses a set of contacts to enlist others to participate in a study. It can be used to access a general sample (e.g., anyone who works) or a sample of people meeting particular specifications (e.g., managers). For example, in their study of mobbing, Zapf, Knorz, and Kulla (1996) recruited participants for the control group by asking people who contacted one of the authors to give the surveys to others. Illustrating the advantages of this approach, Browne (2005) reported on how snowball sampling allows access to individuals of a special population (i.e., nonheterosexual women), who otherwise are difficult to identify and convince to participate in research. The initial contacts also might be participants in the study, but they don't have to be. For example, students in a class can be asked to distribute questionnaires to people fitting a particular requirement, such as those who are employed full time. In their investigation of dynamics of emotional labor, for example, Brotheridge and Lee (2002) asked undergraduate marketing students to give surveys to family members and other acquaintances who interact with customers as part of their jobs. Each participant can be asked, not only to participate, but also to ask others to do so. This can be accomplished easily via e-mail, in which respondents are asked to complete a survey as well as to forward the request to other qualified individuals.

A potential limitation of the snowball sampling technique is possible bias due to a lack of independence between participants (Lee, 1993). If individuals who participate in the study recruit others who, in turn, recruit still others, there are likely to be personal relationships and shared characteristics among participants. Potentially, this is a problem because participants might influence one another's responses, or because participants might recruit people who share certain perspectives, thereby leading to a restriction of range in key variables. This problem is likely to be minimized, however, if individuals are prohibited from recruiting more than some minimal number of others.

Outcropping

Sometimes, individuals segregate themselves according to a particular characteristic or join a group devoted to people sharing a common experience. Outcropping refers to a researcher enlisting research participants from such groups that contain individuals who meet specified characteristics. For individuals who have been targets of IWB, this might mean locating support groups, either locally or virtually. For example, for their study of mobbing, Zapf et al. (1996) recruited participants from mobbing self-help groups. In similar fashion, Orth, Montada, and Maercker (2006) contacted individuals through a German victim assistance association to survey about their experiences as victims of violent crimes. It also is possible to contact potential participants via contacts made at Web sites. For example, there are a number of Web sites dedicated to workplace bullying, such as bullyonline.org that is a Web-based discussion group hosted by Yahoo.com in which people share their experiences and solutions to workplace bullying. As of February 2010, there were more than 1,200 members, making this a potentially useful place from which to recruit potential volunteers for a study. (For more on bullying, see Neuman and Keashly, Chapter 2, this volume.) There also are likely to be other groups that deal with bullying and other forms of IWB, although these are more likely to take the perspectives of targets than actors.

Several limitations of using outcropping to solicit research participants should be noted. First, of course, one must be able to locate appropriate groups. It seems unlikely that these will exist for all forms of IWB. Furthermore, although Web-based groups might be fairly large, it is unlikely that local groups would be of comparable size. Given that Web-based surveys typically have low response rates (Yang, Levine, Xu, & Lopez Rivas, 2005), sample size is a concern.

Second, concerns may be raised about the generalizability of samples using this approach. After all, members of such groups are likely to differ in key ways from people in general, and study volunteers may be even more unusual. For example, members of Web-based discussion groups are likely to be more computer literate than people who might choose to join live support groups.

Finally, as noted earlier, studying individuals who share common experiences precludes researchers' opportunities to compare such individuals to others who have not had these experiences. Thus, for example, a study of bullying support group members would disallow comparisons between victims of bullying and nonvictims, and such comparisons would be required to draw conclusions about the causes or effects of bullying.

Advertising

A particularly passive approach to sampling involves soliciting participants in advertisements. This can be done by placing ads in the usual media that is used to sell goods and services, such as newspapers or radio. For example, Zapf et al. (1996) recruited mobbing victims by means of newspaper articles on mobbing and local broadcasting. University researchers sometimes use school newspapers to recruit students as participants in research. For example, in their effort to develop a structured interview to measure organizational citizenship behavior, Allen, Facteau, and Facteau (2004) advertised their study in the student newspaper, flyers on campus bulletin boards, and invitations sent to student organizations via e-mail and postal mail. They compensated the participants and offered entry to an additional raffle of $100. The advertisement can give a brief overview of the study (e.g., a survey about work experiences), requirements for participation (e.g., having a rude coworker or boss), remuneration, and instructions on how to sign up. Typically, a modest payment is offered for participation as an inducement. This means that grant support is necessary as the cost of this sort of study (including the advertising itself) can be considerable. This approach frequently is used in medical studies, such as in clinical trials for a new drug or treatment. In these cases, advertisements are used to locate individuals with particular disorders, (e.g., eating disorder or sleep disturbance). This approach is used less often in organizational research.

As with outcropping, the samples drawn using advertisements can be fairly specialized, making generalizability a concern. In addition, given the passive nature of the sampling, there is no way of knowing information about the underlying population that was sampled other than in the most general terms. For example, one might know that an advertisement ran in a newspaper that had a certain number of subscribers, but not how many of those subscribers read the newspaper on a given day, and of those how many read or even saw the advertisement. This makes it difficult, if not impossible, to determine response rates.

Servicing

Sometimes researchers can recruit participants by tying participation in a research study to an offer of service. For example, a program for dealing with workplace stress could be used to solicit volunteers for a research study. The service (e.g., stress management training) might be provided free in exchange for participation in the study. For example, in their study on work attitudes and behaviors, Melamed, Ben-Avi, Luz, and Green (1995) offered individuals a screening examination for cardiovascular disease free of charge. Alternately, the service could be offered for a fee with clients asked to volunteer, perhaps for a remuneration that would be a credit toward partial cost of the service. The feasibility of this approach is based on being able to offer a service that would be in sufficient demand by the sorts of individuals of interest to the researcher (Lee, 1993). This approach is limited to situations in which the researcher has the resources to offer such a service, as such a study could be quite expensive. Likely, this would require a grant that might have as its main purpose the evaluation of an intervention program. The IWB study then could be piggybacked onto it. For example, a program to reduce musculoskeletal disorders could serve as the foundation study from which to add a study of IWB and how it might contribute to workplace injury.

Depending upon how the servicing study is conducted, there can be limitations to generalizability. At one extreme, the servicing approach can be tied to the advertising approach to recruit participants. Researchers can advertise for volunteers to receive an experimental service. At the other extreme, an organization might agree to be a partner in an intervention study in which it makes the service available to employees. In such a study, the researcher will know response rates and be able to compare the characteristics of those sampled to employees in general. Furthermore, an experimental or quasi-experimental design could be used to randomly assign chosen individuals to receive the intervention or to serve as controls.

RESEARCH DESIGNS AND APPROACHES

Various research designs and approaches to conducting research on IWB have been used to varying degrees, each of which has various unique strengths and limitations. These include (a) cross-sectional, single-source surveys, (b) diaries, (c) interviews, (d) focus groups, (e) stress-incident record, (f) observational methods, (g) multisource designs, (h) longitudinal designs, and (i) predictive designs.

Cross-Sectional, Single-Source Surveys

As in the case of most research in the field of organizational behavior (Scandura & Williams, 2000), research on IWB has been dominated by the cross-sectional, single-source survey design (e.g., Fox et al., 2001). Typically, employees are asked to complete an anonymous questionnaire concerning their own acts of IWB or incidents of IWB they have experienced. Anonymity is not required, but often is preferred for reasons previously noted.

Popularity

Cross-sectional, single-source surveys are popular with researchers for at least four fundamental reasons.

1. *Efficiency.* The cross-sectional, single-source design is extremely efficient insofar as it provides data on many variables from large samples at relatively low cost (both in terms of labor and money).

The main cost of this sort of study involves the copying and mailing of questionnaires. If internal surveys are conducted, organizations often will cover these costs. Often, the cost of postage can be avoided by conducting the survey in a group (e.g., a classroom or staff meeting), or by having respondents return them to a drop box, or by interorganization mail. Copy costs also might be eliminated by conducting the survey electronically, either via e-mail or by posting it on a Web site (although there can be costs associated with these procedures, particularly if specialized software or Web-based survey services are used).

2. *Privacy.* Anonymous questionnaires protect participants' privacy. As we noted earlier, researchers cannot reveal an identity that is unknown. This approach enhances the comfort level of participants who may feel that they can respond honestly because their responses cannot be revealed to others—enhancing the validity of responses as a result. Of course, no amount of assurance of anonymity totally will remove all concerns from all participants.

3. *Convenience.* Instruments with established psychometric properties have been developed that are available for use in survey studies. Thus, questionnaires may be assembled readily by using already-published instruments tapping the constructs of interest. Of course, the appropriateness of such research instruments to the situation and population must be determined with great care. Importantly, such instruments can be used with a wide variety of research techniques beyond simply the cross-sectional, single-source design.

4. *Established.* Cross-sectional, single-source designs are well-established among researchers and are likely to be chosen because they have been used traditionally. Such designs have a history of providing publishable results and can be found in all the top journals. Despite complaints from critics about the limitations of this design (e.g., Spector, 1994), and criticisms by reviewers for the top tier journals, it continues to be the dominant approach for many areas of organizational research, including IWB.

Limitations

Despite these considerable benefits, the limitations of cross-sectional, single-source designs are well known and have been discussed at length in the literature (e.g., Spector, 1994). The most serious problem is that this design is not very helpful in testing causal propositions. The first step in determining causation is to establish a relationship among variables (Shadish, Cook, & Campbell, 2002), which this design is able to do. However, the cross-sectional, single-source design cannot provide additional evidence for causality because all data are collected on a single occasion. There is no mechanism by which direction of causal flow can be determined confidently.

A second limitation concerns biases associated with collecting all data from a single source. This design does not provide for the control of common biases among two or more variables, such as social desirability (Crowne & Marlowe, 1964). Thus, it is possible that some factor associated with two variables has biased their measurement and distorted the observed relationship relative to the true relationship between the underlying constructs. For example, perhaps individuals who dislike their supervisors overreport negative things about their supervisors and underreport positive things. If this tendency is strong enough, it might well produce observed correlations among measured variables that are not connected at the construct level. It should be kept in mind that biasing factors can vary considerably among different measured variables (Moorman & Podsakoff, 1992, for example, summarize relationships between social desirability and several organizational variables). Of particular concern with the reporting of sensitive issues is that individuals may try to cultivate favorable impressions by giving socially acceptable answers to sensitive questions rather than accurate responses that potentially may be unflattering.

Diaries

Diaries provide in-depth information about people's real-life experiences over time. They are subjective in the sense that they report perceptions of the outside world. Typically, individuals report various aspects of their experience in the form of a diary entry. In research on stress, for example, Hahn (2000) asked participants to complete diaries for 14 days, during which they reported interpersonal encounters, mood states, coping behaviors, and stress reactions. Detailed information from diaries helped to clarify the relationships between the variables of interest (i.e., locus of control, emotions, and stress) and contributed to the field beyond survey methods.

Diaries also may provide useful insights into IWB because they are not restrictive in their content and because they include regular records of experiences over time. For a diary entry, an individual can be asked to record different aspects of IWB, such as what happened, how and when it happened, who was involved, the context, the feelings experienced, and the outcomes of the event. By providing such "on-line" information about events over time, the diary method is useful for keeping track of IWB and overcomes at least two concerns in studying sensitive topics. First, people may become aware of the effects of some IWB only gradually, which can be seen to unfold over time in their diary entries. Second, because people may forget or incorrectly recall IWB as time passes, immediately recording incidents in a diary provides more accurate and detailed information.

The diary method also can be used to identify patterns of behavior over time and to discover contextual and dispositional factors that influence IWB. However, the use of open-ended narratives as a rich source of information also makes comparisons between multiple diaries difficult. The accuracy of diary entries cannot be verified easily, and participants may find it time consuming and burdensome to keep diaries. So too may researchers find it challenging and time consuming to analyze information contained in diaries. One technological advance that can help with diary studies is the use of Palm Pilots for participants to record their responses (e.g., Yip, 2005). The Palm Pilot can prompt participants to respond at predetermined intervals, and it can be used to enter both ratings with closed-ended scales and open-ended responses. Of course, the recording of detailed narratives would be cumbersome using the devices that require entering characters with a stylus.

Interviews

An interview is a face-to-face dialogue conducted with the aim of gathering rich information about individuals and their experiences. According to Cowie, Naylor, Rivers, Smith, and Pereira (2002), a typical interview evolves through stages of ice-breaking (greeting participants and putting them at ease), building trust (talking with participants until they become comfortable), forming an idea (e.g., personality may influence IWB), and revising the idea (e.g., the situation may overcome the impact of personality). Therefore, interviewers should have the competence, experience, and necessary communication skills for each stage to conduct a successful interview that provides accurate and useful information.

Although the degree of structure in interviews may vary, most involve flexible and responsive formats. For example, Liefooghe and Olafsson (1999) studied bullying in a situational interview format by asking participants to portray hypothetical individuals who are both like and unlike bullies.

Due to their interactive nature, the course of interviews can be shaped and redirected as different topics emerge. Interviewers can elaborate and clarify certain points to get a better picture of IWB. For example, interviews and workshops with more than 700 employees allowed Pearson, Andersson, and Porath (2000) to gain valuable insights into workplace incivility and to define the concept. Typically, to generalize and draw conclusions about a topic, researchers have to conduct a series of interviews, thereby making this method both time consuming and expensive. From participants' perspectives, interviews are appealing and have face validity. However, interviewees may be resistant and unwilling to talk about their experiences regarding sensitive topics. Therefore, interviewers should be trained to deal with the challenges posed by discussing sensitive topics and be skilled in building trust and getting the necessary information without offending the participants. This requires building rapport with interviewees by spending time at the beginning of the interview to get acquainted, starting with some nonthreatening "warm up" questions, and being sensitive to interviewees' reactions to questions. Interviewers must coax rather than force responses and be willing to retreat from a line of questioning when respondents are resistant. It also must be made clear at the beginning of an interview how the data will be used and who will have access to it. In so doing, it also is necessary to clearly specify all procedures that will be used to maintain confidentiality.

Focus Groups

A focus group is a group interview of several people (generally 8 to 12) regarding a particular topic. It proceeds in the form of a roundtable discussion for typically 2 to 3 hours (Cowie et al., 2002). Focus groups are used frequently in marketing research to explore customers' perceptions, feelings, preferences, and motives (Cowie et al., 2002). They are less expensive than individual interviews since several people's responses can be collected simultaneously.

Similarly, the use of focus groups in IWB research may allow researchers to gather in-depth, qualitative information about attitudes and experiences related to IWB. For example, Liefooghe and Olafsson (1999) used focus groups to investigate various perspectives on bullying at work, enabling them to understand the individual and organizational factors influencing this form of IWB. Depending on the purpose of research, a focus group may be composed of individuals who know one another or of individuals who never met before. If the aim of the research is related to the social context of a particular event or situation, then friends and acquaintances should participate in the group discussion to provide different perspectives on the same event. For example, the study of an aggressive climate in a department might best involve the main actors to provide converging information about the nature, antecedents, and context of the events in question. However, if the aim of research is to gather general information, then it would be preferable to get independent input from people who have no prior association and therefore no shared biases or perspectives. For example, a study of antecedents of incivility might be informed best by a variety of perspectives and experiences to enrich the breadth and generalizability of the information obtained.

Another concern about group composition occurs when individuals are asked to disclose information about sensitive topics. Under such conditions some people may feel more comfortable discussing topics with people they know, whereas others may feel more comfortable doing so around strangers. The former case is more likely when asking about public behavior that was not directed toward others in the group (e.g., talking about the behavior of others who are not present). The latter case would be more likely when behavior is not known widely among group members, and when there is a potential risk of conflict or embarrassment. However, some individuals might be unwilling to discuss particularly sensitive topics in groups, making the individual interview or even less public methods necessary.

Typically several focus groups are conducted in a study to gather information from multiple groups. Researchers can compare data from different groups and attempt to identify similarities, differences, and trends in the perceptions and opinions across groups. Sometimes focus groups provide pilot data to inform a main study, which then might use closed-ended questionnaires. Alternately, focus groups can provide data that are analyzed and interpreted in their own right. This can be time consuming since it requires having coders conduct content analyses of recordings or transcripts of the focus group interactions.

One final caution is that focus groups provide high-quality information if individuals can voice their opinions freely and if a few participants do not dominate the discussion. Thus, a skilled facilitator is required to get the most out of this technique. The facilitator must maintain a civil climate throughout the discussion by intervening if group members get into conflicts or direct unkind remarks to one another. He or she also must moderate the discussion and encourage those who are quiet to share experiences and give their reactions. One approach that can be used is to go around the table and ask each person to respond to a specific question.

Stress Incident Record

The Stress Incident Record (SIR; Keenan & Newton, 1985) is an open-ended written survey approach in which participants are asked to relate a prior stressful incident and then to answer questions about it. The open-ended responses are content analyzed by trained judges who place them into mutually exclusive categories along one or more dimensions (e.g., the target of behavior or the type of behavior), forming categorical variables with each case falling into one category of each dimension. With IWB incidents, the variable might have target categories of coworker, subordinate, or supervisor. Judges categorize the incidents along one dimension at a time, with multiple judges being used to establish interjudge agreement. Inferential statistics then are used to test relationships between the categorical variable that is formed by content analysis and other variables. For example, Narayanan, Menon, and Spector (1999) related categories of stressors to gender and job type.

Interested in studying workplace stress, Keenan and Newton (1985) included instructions asking participants to "recall an incident that made you feel anxious, annoyed, upset, or frustrated, or aroused your feelings in some other way" (p. 152). Several additional studies using the SIR have found that participants often mentioned IWB as a stressful event (e.g., Narayanan et al., 1999). Of note, this method need not be limited to the study of stress; it can be adapted to the study of IWB by asking participants to relate incidents in which they either engaged in IWB or were targets of such behavior.

The SIR approach allows participants to generate experiences that are salient to themselves instead of having the researcher assume a priori what is important. This can be particularly useful at early stages of research in which the boundary conditions of a phenomenon are unknown. For example, the SIR approach has been useful in exploring emerging topics such as e-mail bullying (Burroughs & Gruys, 2004). It also allows researchers to revise and update existing lists of IWB.

There are several disadvantages to this approach. First, it requires participants to have a sufficient level of written language skill to relate incidents accurately. Second, participants' motivation can be an issue given that many individuals might not like writing. Third, studies using the SIR find that many participants will indicate they cannot think of an incident about which to report. Fourth, content analysis can be labor intensive, particularly when there are a large number of incidents to categorize. Fifth, moving beyond these practical limitations, there also is a concern about possible biases that may affect the sorts of incidents that people choose to relate. For example, in keeping with a well-established attributional bias (Jones & Harris, 1967), individuals asked to report incidents of negative behavior are likely to blame others for it rather than taking personal responsibility.

Observational Methods

Observational methods provide access to events and behaviors as they occur in naturalistic settings as opposed to laboratory settings. Besides direct observation, audio recordings, video recordings, and surveillance records may be used to provide data on IWB. This is particularly useful for studying overt physical behavior that can be noted via systematic observations. For example, Palmstierna and Wistedt (1987) designed the Staff Observation Aggression Scale (SOAS) to monitor and assess the frequency, nature, and severity of aggression on psychiatric wards. The greatest advantage of this method is that it allows researchers to watch events as they occur instead of relying on the biased and imperfect recall of events by participants. Using this technique, researchers also have direct information about what happened before and after certain events, making antecedents and consequences readily discernible.

Observational techniques may be particularly useful for studying aggressive responses directed toward employees who work with clients (e.g., psychiatric ward nurses) or customers (e.g., convenience store clerks). However, observations may be time consuming and may capture only a subset of all events in the workplace. Furthermore, in keeping with the established phenomenon of demand characteristics (Orne, 1962), individuals who know that they are being observed are likely to act differently than they normally would do. They also may act differently than they would do in locations that are not monitored. Furthermore, ethical issues (e.g., privacy violation) and practical considerations (e.g., increases in stress) may arise when using such methods.

Multisource Designs

The multisource design builds upon the single-source design by adding data on one or more variables from one or more additional sources. Typically, the core of the study is the employee survey, but at least some variables are assessed independently. Alternative sources can consist of others in positions to complete questionnaires about an employee. These may include clients/customers, coworkers, observers, spouses/significant others, or supervisors.

For example, Skarlicki and Folger (1997) linked employees' perceptions of justice to coworkers' reports of the employees' retaliation (including IWB). Fox, Spector, Goh, and Bruursema (2007) collected data on counterproductive work behavior (including IWB) and stressors from both employees and coworkers. In these studies, it is assumed that the alternative sources (coworkers or supervisors) have sufficient knowledge of the target participants' IWB.

Studies that have compared coworkers with target participants' own reports have found a moderate level of convergence between them. For example, Penney and Spector (2005) found a correlation of .29 between the two sources for a measure of incivility and .30 for a measure of counterproductive work behavior directed against other people. Bruk-Lee and Spector (2006) reported even higher levels of convergence for interpersonal conflict, with a correlation of .37 for conflict with coworkers and .42 for conflict with supervisors.

Alternative sources don't have to be limited to questionnaires completed by others. Data from incident reports and records also can be used. Perlow and Latham (1993), for example, linked employees' scores on a personality scale to records of dismissal for abusing clients. In another study Dietz, Robinson, Folger, Baron, and Schulz (2003) related official violent crime rates from FBI reports in various communities to workplace aggression in plants in those same communities. The workplace aggression incidents were obtained from official company reports, which were recorded over 14 months by security personnel from statements by involved parties.

The main advantage of using additional sources of data is the control of potential shared biases across variables. If data collection for two variables is independent, then the chances of confounding by biasing factors are reduced. To use our earlier example, employees' dislike for a supervisor might have little impact on a measure taken independently of those employees.

Of course, it is not always possible to totally separate the sources in such a way that the common source of bias is eliminated completely. A coworker or supervisor providing an alternative source of data might be quite aware of employees' feelings toward that supervisor, and that might well bias judgments in the same way that it does for the employees themselves. To control this sort of bias, there should be minimal contact between focal employees and alternate sources, which is not always feasible. Spector and Jex (1991), for example, did this in their study of job characteristics. They had job analysts rate characteristics of employees' jobs based on written materials and not by direct observation of employees.

Longitudinal Designs

The longitudinal design introduces the element of time that can be helpful for drawing causal conclusions. Data are collected at two or more times by assessing the same variables on repeated occasions. Importantly, the longitudinal design is not a panacea, or what Meehl (1971) might have referred to as an "automatic inference-machine" (p. 147). Collecting data more than once does not allow for causal inferences to be drawn automatically, and it might not be much of an advantage over cross-sectional designs in many cases. To be able to draw a causal conclusion, observations must be taken over the course of the causal event, that is, one must make observations both before and after an event occurs to show that the event had not yet happened at Time 1, but that it had occurred at Time 2.

For example, if we wish to show that IWB is caused by a workplace event, we would have to demonstrate that IWB had not occurred prior to the event occurring but rather that IWB occurred after the event. Most of the phenomena we study are not discrete events but rather chronic conditions that might require exposure over time before having any impact on employees. Thus, to be conducted appropriately, longitudinal studies must include assessments of employees both before and after they are affected by the conditions. To do this, the length of time required before observed effects can be seen must fall within the period of study.

This is not to suggest that longitudinal designs are of limited value. Quite the contrary. However, the longitudinal strategy is complex and can involve considerable work to determine appropriate time frames that should be used. In many cases, what might make most sense is to take initial measurements of employees quite early in their organizational tenure, before they have had much exposure to conditions of interest. A series of measurements taken over time can help map how exposure might affect the variables of interest, and this can help provide data that would lend confidence to the conclusion that the relationships of interest are causal in nature.

It is useful to design a longitudinal study that incorporates a specific condition or event that changes over the course of the study for some but not all people. One approach is to use a quasi-experimental design to compare employees in different organizations that underwent different conditions. For example, Greenberg (2006) compared employees at two hospitals where pay was reduced among employees at one but not the other. Measures of insomnia were taken for all participants at several times before and after the change had occurred.

Another approach that does not compare employees from different organizations or units is illustrated by a study by Manning, Osland, and Osland (1989) that investigated the consequences of smoking cessation on job attitudes, job tension, and mood. A sample of employees was surveyed twice, 12 to 16 months apart. A question was included asking about smoking on both occasions, allowing for the classification of participants according to whether they quit smoking between Times 1 and 2. Results showed that job satisfaction and mood were the same for ex-smokers as for those in the other groups at Time 1 but were worse at Time 2. This design provides stronger evidence than a cross-sectional design of a causal link between smoking cessation and the outcomes studied since it was able to show no differences at Time 1 but a change at Time 2. Of course, results are not conclusive since smoking cessation might have been confounded with other variables that were the real cause of the outcomes.

Such a design might be applied to the study of IWB by looking at the impact of a specific change on IWB or perhaps the impact of exposure to a particular IWB on hypothesized variables. For example, the impact of conditions on IWB could be examined in a study in which some stressful event (e.g., forced overtime) is assessed in relation to IWB. The impact of IWB on people might be studied by looking at the impact of gaining or losing a hostile coworker or supervisor who made an individual endure IWB. In both cases the change could be assessed by comparing participants' reports between Times 1 and 2 to see if there was a change. An alternative, although somewhat weaker approach, is to compare participants who switch jobs in cases in which the conditions in question are present and those in which these conditions are absent. The limitation to this approach, however, is that the change in the condition in question is confounded with the overall change in jobs.

Predictive Designs

A predictive design is one in which a variable measured at one point in time is used to predict another variable assessed at a later date. The predictive design is distinguished from the longitudinal design in that in the predictive design the same variables are not measured repeatedly. This design is popular in employee selection research in which measures of personal characteristics (e.g., ability) are used to predict subsequent job performance (e.g., Anderson, Lievens, Van Dam, & Ryan, 2004).

This design also has been used to investigate the role of personality in IWB. For example, Roberts, Hams, Bogg, Goldberg, Shiner, and Caspi (2005) found that personality characteristics (e.g., constraint and negative emotionality) at age 16 predicted counterproductive behavior at age 26. Likewise, Perlow and Latham (1993) showed that locus of control predicted subsequent aggressive behavior at work. And Gottfredson and Holland (1990) found that expected satisfaction was linked significantly to a measure of counterproductive work behavior collected 4 months later.

CONCLUSION: RESEARCH STRATEGIES

Research on IWB has become mainstream and no longer can be considered a new and understudied area. Approaches taken in the early stages of the development of this area no longer will suffice if we are to make progress in understanding its complex causes and consequences. This means that researchers should use a variety of methods, such as those discussed here, rather than relying simply on those that are most convenient or familiar.

Specifically, it is time to move beyond cross-sectional, single-source survey designs and to utilize a variety of complementary methods to study IWB more thoroughly. This is not to say that the cross-sectional, single-source design should be abandoned, as it can be very useful as a first step in testing a hypothesis about relationships among variables. However, the first step shouldn't be the last step, and there are too few studies using other methods to help rule out competing explanations for observed results.

The use of new methods should not be limited to only those that easily generate quantitative data. Such methods tend to assess chronic and ongoing conditions of work and the frequency of particular behaviors. Needed are studies that look at particular instances of behavior in response to episodic experiences at work. In this regard, some qualitative methods can be quite useful, and material collected from diaries, focus groups, interviews, and other open-ended approaches can be content-analyzed to allow quantitative analysis. Such methods should be used in combination with the more typically used closed-ended methods to incorporate the use of converging operations in IWB research to assess the extent to which different methods yield identical conclusions.

At least part of the reason for the avoidance of some methods undoubtedly has to do with the publication preferences—both perceived and real—of our top journals. At least one reason for the popularity of certain methods is that they can generate large amounts of quantitative data efficiently, thus enabling the use of structural equation modeling and other complex analytical techniques toward which reviewers of top-tier journals seem predisposed. Studies using other methods, particularly those that are more qualitative in nature, are likely to be at least perceived to encounter greater resistance in the editorial process. However, based on our observations, this is not well founded. In fact, we believe that there is a bias among the editors of top journals toward publishing research that is especially novel in nature, even though it may be somewhat less rigorous. Researchers attacking new questions are likely to prefer efficient methods, such as the cross-sectional, single-source survey for early research. Subsequent follow-up studies using more rigorous and difficult methods might not be attempted because of concerns that such studies will be mere replications with little of the novelty that editors of top journals seem to prefer. We encourage our colleagues to reconsider these beliefs and to take the bold step of using less well-established research techniques when it comes to studying IWB.

IWB is a vibrant and growing area of research that has attracted a great deal of attention in our field. Research has established relationships between IWB and quite a few other variables that are potential causes and consequences, although there is insufficient research using methods that can lead us confidently to causal conclusions. We know that individuals with particular personality characteristics and those who perceive their jobs in certain ways are likely to report engaging in various forms of IWB (e.g., Fox et al., 2001; Neuman & Baron, 2005). Furthermore, reports of IWB relate to a number of attitudinal and well-being variables (e.g., Spector & Fox, 2005). Now, however, the stage is set for additional work to be conducted that ties all these variables together in a way that helps us understand and control IWB. We hope that our discussion of the methodological issues associated with studying IWB will facilitate this process.

REFERENCES

Allen, T. D., Facteau, J. D., & Facteau, C. L. (2004). Structured interviewing for OCB: Construct validity, faking, and the effects of question type. *Human Performance, 17*, 1–24.

American Psychological Association. (2002). *Ethical principles of psychologists and code of conduct.* Washington, DC: Author.

Anderson, N., Lievens, F., Van Dam, K., & Ryan, A. M. (2004). Future perspectives on employee selection: Key directions for future research and practice. *Applied Psychology: An International Review, 53*, 487–501.

Bennett, R. J., Aquino, K., Reed, A., II, & Thau, S. (2005). The normative nature of employee deviance and the impact of moral identity. In S. Fox & P. E. Spector (Eds.), *Counterproductive work behavior: Investigations of actors and targets* (pp. 107–125). Washington, DC: American Psychological Association.

Bennett, R. J., & Robinson, S. L. (2000). Development of a measure of workplace deviance. *Journal of Applied Psychology, 85*, 349–360.

Bies, R. J., & Tripp, T. M. (2005). The study of revenge in the workplace: Conceptual, ideological, and empirical issues. In S. Fox & P. E. Spector (Eds.), *Counterproductive work behavior: Investigations of actors and targets* (pp. 65–81). Washington, DC: American Psychological Association.

Bies, R. J., Tripp, T. M., & Kramer, R. M. (1997). At the breaking point: Cognitive and social dynamics of revenge in organizations. In R. A. Giacalone & J. Greenberg (Eds.), *Antisocial behavior in organizations* (pp. 18–36). Thousand Oaks, CA: Sage.

Boswell, W. R., & Olson-Buchanan, J. B. (2004). Experiencing mistreatment at work: The role of grievance filing, mistreatment, and employee withdrawal. *Academy of Management Journal, 47*, 129–139.

Brotheridge, C. M., & Lee, R. T. (2002). Testing a conservation of resources model of the dynamics of emotional labor. *Journal of Occupational Health Psychology, 7,* 57–67.

Browne, K. (2005). Snowball sampling: Using social networks to research non-heterosexual women. *International Journal of Social Research Methodology: Theory & Practice, 8,* 47–60.

Bruk-Lee, V., & Spector, P. E. (2006). The social stressors-counterproductive work behaviors link: Are conflicts with supervisors and coworkers the same? *Journal of Occupational Health Psychology, 11,* 145–156.

Burroughs, S. M., & Gruys, M. L. (2004, April). *Establishing law and order in cyberspace: Understanding and controlling e-mail bullying.* Paper presented at the meeting of the Society for Industrial and Organizational Psychology, Chicago, IL.

Casper, W. J., Martin, J. A., Buffardi, L. C., & Erdwin, C. J. (2002). Work-family conflict, perceived organizational support, and organizational commitment among employed mothers. *Journal of Occupational Health Psychology, 7,* 99–108.

Cowie, H., Naylor, P., Rivers, I., Smith, P. K., & Pereira, B. (2002). Measuring workplace bullying. *Aggression and Violent Behavior, 7,* 33–51.

Crowne, D. P., & Marlowe, D. (1964). *The approval motive.* New York, NY: John Wiley.

Dietz, J., Robinson, S. L., Folger, R., Baron, R. A., & Schulz, M. (2003). The impact of community violence and an organization's procedural justice climate on workplace aggression. *Academy of Management Journal, 46,* 317–326.

Folger, R., & Skarlicki, D. P. (2005). Beyond counterproductive work behavior: Moral emotions and deontic retaliation versus reconciliation. In S. Fox & P. E. Spector (Eds.), *Counterproductive work behavior: Investigations of actors and targets* (pp. 83–105). Washington, DC: American Psychological Association.

Fox, S., & Spector, P. E. (Eds.). (2005). *Counterproductive work behavior: Investigations of actors and targets.* Washington, DC: American Psychological Association.

Fox, S., Spector, P. E., Goh, A., & Bruursema, K. (2007). Does your coworker know what you're doing? Convergence of self- and peer-reports of counterproductive work behavior. *International Journal of Stress Management, 14,* 41–60.

Fox, S., Spector, P. E., & Miles, D. (2001). Counterproductive work behavior (CWB) in response to job stressors and organizational justice: Some mediator and moderator tests for autonomy and emotions. *Journal of Vocational Behavior, 59,* 291–309.

Fox, S., & Stallworth, L. E. (2005). Racial/ethnic bullying: Exploring links between bullying and racism in the US workplace. *Journal of Vocational Behavior, 66,* 438–456.

Gottfredson, G. D., & Holland, J. L. (1990). The longitudinal test of the influence of congruence: Job satisfaction, competency utilization, and counterproductive behavior. *Journal of Counseling Psychology, 37,* 389–398.

Greenberg, J. (2006). Losing sleep over organizational injustice: Attenuating insomniac reactions to underpayment inequity with supervisory training in interactional justice. *Journal of Applied Psychology, 91,* 57–68.

Hahn, S. E. (2000). The effects of locus of control on daily exposure, coping and reactivity to work interpersonal stressors: A diary study. *Personality and Individual Differences, 29,* 729–748.

Hollinger, R. C. (1986). Acts against the workplace: Social bonding and employee deviance. *Deviant Behavior, 7,* 53–75.

Hulin, C. L., Roznowski, M., & Hachiya, D. (1985). Alternative opportunities and withdrawal decisions: Empirical and theoretical discrepancies and an integration. *Psychological Bulletin, 97,* 233–250.

Jones, E. E., & Harris, V. A. (1967). The attribution of attitudes. *Journal of Experimental Social Psychology 3*, 1-24.

Keashly, L., & Harvey, S. (2005). Emotional abuse in the workplace. In S. Fox & P. E. Spector (Eds.), *Counterproductive work behavior: Investigations of actors and targets* (pp. 201–235). Washington, DC: American Psychological Association.

Keenan, A., & Newton, T. J. (1985). Stressful events, stressors and psychological strains in young professional engineers. *Journal of Occupational Behavior, 6*, 151–156.

Lee, K., & Allen, N. J. (2002). Organizational citizenship behavior and workplace deviance: The role of affect and cognitions. *Journal of Applied Psychology, 87*, 131–142.

Lee, R. M. (1993). *Doing research on sensitive topics*. Thousand Oaks, CA: Sage.

Lewis, S. E., & Orford, J. (2005). Women's experiences of workplace bullying: Changes in social relationships. *Journal of Community and Applied Social Psychology, 15*, 29–47.

Liefooghe, A., & Olafsson, R. (1999). "Scientists" and "amateurs": Mapping the bullying domain. *International Journal of Manpower, 20*, 39–49.

Lim, S., & Cortina, L. M. (2005). Interpersonal mistreatment in the workplace: The interface and impact of general incivility and sexual harassment. *Journal of Applied Psychology, 90*, 483–496.

Lowman, R. L. (2006). *The ethical practice of psychology in organizations* (2nd ed.). Washington, DC: American Psychological Association.

Manning, M. R., Osland, J. S., & Osland, A. (1989). Work-related consequences of smoking cessation. *Academy of Management Journal, 32*, 606–621.

Meehl, P. E. (1971). High school yearbooks: A reply to Schwarz. *Journal of Abnormal Psychology, 77*, 143–148.

Melamed, S., Ben-Avi, Irit, Luz, J., & Green, M. S. (1995). Objective and subjective work monotony: Effects on job satisfaction, psychological distress, and absenteeism in blue-collar workers. *Journal of Applied Psychology, 80*, 29–42.

Mirvis, P. H., & Seashore, S. E. (1979). Being ethical in organizational research. *American Psychologist, 34*, 766–780.

Moorman, R. H., & Podsakoff, P. M. (1992). A meta-analytic review and empirical test of the potential confounding effects of social desirability response sets in organizational behavior research. *Journal of Occupational and Organizational Psychology, 65*, 131–149.

Narayanan, L., Menon, S., & Spector, P. E. (1999). Stress in the workplace: A comparison of gender and occupations. *Journal of Organizational Behavior, 20*, 63–73.

Neuman, J. H., & Baron, R. (1997). Aggression in the workplace. In R. A. Giacalone & J. Greenberg (Eds.), *Antisocial behavior in organizations* (pp. 37–67). Thousand Oaks, CA: Sage.

Neuman, J. H., & Baron, R. A. (2005). Aggression in the workplace: A social-psychological perspective. In S. Fox & P. E. Spector (Eds.), *Counterproductive work behavior: Investigations of actors and targets* (pp. 13–40). Washington, DC: American Psychological Association.

O'Driscoll, M. P., Poelmans, S., Spector, P. E., Kalliath, T., Allen, T. D., Cooper, C. L., & Sanchez, J. I. (2003). Family-responsive interventions, perceived organizational and supervisor support, work–family conflict, and psychological strain. *International Journal of Stress Management, 10*, 326–344.

O'Leary-Kelly, A. M., Griffin, R. W., & Glew, D. J. (1996). Organization-motivated aggression: A research framework. *Academy of Management Review, 21*, 225–253.

Orne, M. T. (1962). On the social psychology of the psychological experiment: With particular reference to demand characteristics and their implications. *American Psychologist, 17,* 776–783.

Orth, U., Montada, L., & Maercker, A. (2006). Feelings of revenge, retaliation motive, and post-traumatic stress reactions in crime victims. *Journal of Interpersonal Violence, 21,* 229–243.

Palmstierna, T., & Wistedt, B. (1987). Staff observation aggression scale: Presentation and evaluation. *Acta Psychiatrica Scandinavia, 76,* 657–663.

Pearson, C. M., Andersson, L. M., & Porath, C. L. (2000). Assessing and attacking workplace incivility. *Organizational Dynamics, 29,* 123–137.

Pearson, C. M., Andersson, L. M., & Porath, C. L. (2005). Workplace incivility. In S. Fox & P. E. Spector (Eds.), *Counterproductive work behavior: Investigations of actors and targets* (pp. 177–200). Washington, DC: American Psychological Association.

Penney, L. M., & Spector, P. E. (2005). Job stress, incivility, and counterproductive work behavior (CWB): The moderating role of negative affectivity. *Journal of Organizational Behavior, 26,* 777–796.

Perlow, R., & Latham, L. L. (1993). Relationship of client abuse with locus of control and gender: A longitudinal study. *Journal of Applied Psychology, 78,* 831–834.

Rayner, C., & Keashly, L. (2005). Bullying at work: A perspective from Britain and North America. In S. Fox & P. E. Spector (Eds.), *Counterproductive work behavior: Investigations of actors and targets* (pp. 271–296). Washington, DC: American Psychological Association.

Roberts, B. W., Hams, P., Bogg, T., Goldberg, L., Shiner, R., & Caspi, A. (2005, April). *Personality influences on work outcomes: Three longitudinal studies across decades.* Paper presented at the meeting of the Society for Industrial and Organizational Psychology, Los Angeles, CA.

Robinson, S. L., & Bennett, R. J. (1995). A typology of deviant workplace behaviors: A multidimensional scaling study. *Academy of Management Journal, 38,* 555–572.

Sagie, A., Stashevsky, S., & Koslowsky, M. (Eds.). (2003). *Misbehaviour and dysfunctional attitudes in organizations.* Hampshire, United Kingdom: Palgrave MacMillan.

Scandura, T. A., & Williams, E. A. (2000). Research methodology in management: Current practices, trends, and implications for future research. *Academy of Management Journal, 43,* 1248–1264.

Seiler, L. H., & Murtha, J. M. (1980). Federal regulation of social research using "human subjects": A critical assessment. *American Sociologist, 15,* 146–156.

Shadish, W. R., Cook, T. D., & Campbell, D. T. (2002). *Experimental and quasi-experimental designs for generalized causal inference.* Boston, MA: Houghton Mifflin.

Skarlicki, D. P., & Folger, R. (1997). Retaliation in the workplace: The roles of distributive, procedural, and interactional justice. *Journal of Applied Psychology, 82,* 434–443.

Spector, P. E. (1975). Relationships of organizational frustration with reported behavioral reactions of employees. *Journal of Applied Psychology, 60,* 635–637.

Spector, P. E. (1977). What to do with significant multivariate effects in multivariate analyses of variance. *Journal of Applied Psychology, 62,* 158–163.

Spector, P. E. (1994). Using self-report questionnaires in OB research: A comment on the use of a controversial method. *Journal of Organizational Behavior, 15,* 385–392.

Spector, P. E., & Fox, S. (2005). A model of counterproductive work behavior. In S. Fox & P. E. Spector (Eds.), *Counterproductive workplace behavior: Investigations of actors and targets* (pp. 151–174). Washington, DC: American Psychological Association.

Spector, P. E., & Jex, S. M. (1991). Relations of job characteristics from multiple data sources with employee affect, absence, turnover intentions and health. *Journal of Applied Psychology, 76,* 46–53.

Terpstra, D. E., & Cook, S. E. (1985). Complainant characteristics and reported behaviors and consequences associated with formal sexual harassment charges. *Personnel Psychology, 38,* 559–574.

Vardi, Y., & Weitz, E. (2004). *Misbehavior in organizations: Theory, research, and management.* Mahwah, NJ: Lawrence Erlbaum Associates.

Wimbush, J. C., & Dalton, D. R. (1997). Base rate for employee theft: Convergence of multiple methods. *Journal of Applied Psychology, 82,* 756–763.

Yang, L. Q., Levine, E. L., Xu, X., & Lopez Rivas, G. E. (2005, May). *Affect, job satisfaction and counterproductive work behavior.* Unpublished paper, University of South Florida, Tampa.

Yip, T. (2005). Sources of situational variation in ethnic identity and psychological well-being: A Palm Pilot study of Chinese American students. *Personality and Social Psychology Bulletin, 31,* 1603–1616.

Zapf, D., & Einarsen, S. (2005). Mobbing at work: Escalated conflicts in organizations. In S. Fox & P. E. Spector (Eds.), *Counterproductive work behavior: Investigations of actors and targets* (pp. 237–270). Washington, DC: American Psychological Association.

Zapf, D., Knorz, C., & Kulla, M. (1996). On the relationship between mobbing factors, and job content, social work environment, and health outcomes. *European Journal of Work and Organizational Psychology, 5,* 215–237.

Section 4

Integration

10

Issues and Challenges in Studying Insidious Workplace Behavior

Marissa S. Edwards and Jerald Greenberg

In Chapter 1 of this volume we defined insidious workplace behavior (IWB) as a form of intentionally harmful workplace behavior that is legal, subtle and low level (rather than severe), repeated over time, and directed at individuals or organizations. In other words, IWB is not a unique type of behavior itself but a set of characteristics that describe various types of deviant behavior. Exemplifying this point, this book addresses several types of deviant behavior, including aggression, sabotage, revenge, incivility, sexist humor and harassment, and lying, as well as the challenges of measuring and researching IWB. Throughout their discussions, the authors emphasize that although IWB may appear innocuous, it can have genuine and significant negative implications for employees and organizations alike. It is our hope that this volume will inspire not only further theoretical work but ultimately efforts to reduce IWB in the workplace.

In this chapter, we integrate the perspectives offered in the current volume with existing literature to offer a snapshot of the study of IWB as it stands today. In so doing, we draw on theoretical and empirical work into constructs such as workplace deviance (Robinson & Bennett, 1995) and counterproductive work behavior (Fox & Spector, 2005), as well as studies of interpersonal mistreatment (e.g., bullying, Rayner, 1997; incivility, Pearson & Porath, 2005). We do this by addressing several fundamental issues. In question form, these are (a) Who is most likely to engage in IWB? (b) What motivates IWB in work settings? (c) Who are the most likely targets of IWB? (d) What forms do IWB take? (e) How do targets, observers, and organizations respond to IWB when it occurs? and (f) What are the long-term consequences of IWB for individuals and organizations? Finally, we conclude this chapter by discussing some of the challenges facing future researchers in this field. These include (a) promoting definitional clarity,

(b) conducting research designed to develop valid scales for measuring IWB, (c) establishing sound theories that inspire research and explain underlying processes, and ultimately (d) establishing clear guidance for organizational practitioners.

ACTORS: WHO ENGAGES IN IWB?

Compared to more extreme and visible acts of deviance, IWB, by nature, is difficult to detect. Usually, unless targets come forward to identify perpetrators, acts of IWB go undetected and unreported (Cortina & Magley, 2009). This poses challenges for researchers attempting to study such behavior (Fox & Spector, 1999). Among these is the fact that relatively little is known about the characteristics of those who engage in IWB (i.e., actors). Despite this, two particular characteristics of actors have emerged in the literature as individual-level determinants of IWB, which we now examine: (a) gender and (b) personality characteristics. Given the limited research on IWB, this requires us to draw on research that examines only some forms of IWB and to extrapolate from related forms of deviant behavior that may not be as insidious in nature.

Gender Differences

Overall, research has revealed that males engage in more aggressive and antisocial behavior than females (Eagly & Steffen, 1986; Junger-Tas, Terlouw, & Klein, 1994; Zapf & Einarsen, 2003; Zeichner, Parrott, & Frey, 2003). In several studies, more people indicated that they were subjected to workplace bullying, sexual harassment, and physical aggression from men than from women. For example, in Rayner's (1997) study of bullying in the United Kingdom, 67% of bullies were male, although this finding may be attributed to the high number of men in supervisory roles. Concerning sexual harassment, a survey of undergraduate college students in the United States revealed that, compared to women, men were twice as likely to engage in sexual harassment and three times as likely to engage in sexually coercive behavior (Ménard, Hall, Phung, Ghebrial, & Martin, 2003). We note, however, that because men and women tend to engage in different types of IWB, researchers' failures to distinguish between different types of IWB in their research results in an incomplete picture of this phenomenon. For example, research suggests that female bullies use covert tactics (e.g., isolating employees, reducing autonomy, and spreading rumors), whereas men use more overt tactics (e.g., engaging in public criticism, yelling, and physical violence). For this reason, women are less inclined than men to be noticed, making their apparent incidence rate lower (Zapf, Einarsen, Hoel, & Vartia, 2003), although in reality, men and women engage in workplace bullying with equal frequency.

Neurological Evidence

In an interesting experiment, Singer et al. (2006) found significant gender differences in experimental participants' responses to a particular form of IWB—cheating someone out of earned outcomes. Participants in this study played a financial investment game with several others, including confederates who either deliberately cheated them out of their fair share of money earned in the game (i.e., "unfair" players) or who paid them what they deserved (i.e., "fair" players). Following the game, participants underwent functional magnetic resonance imaging (fMRI) scans while observing both fair and unfair confederates receiving painful electric shocks. Both male and female participants who witnessed fair players receive shocks showed activity in areas of the brain associated with empathy (namely, the fronto-insular and anterior cingulate cortices). However, men and women differed in their responses to unfair players who were shocked. Women displayed a similar degree of activity in empathy-related pain regions while viewing unfair players receiving shocks, but men viewing such individuals showed no such activation. Instead, men experienced a surge of activity in areas of the brain associated with pleasure and rewards (i.e., nucleus accumbens).

Although, as Singer et al. (2006) note, further research is required to establish whether gender differences are specific to revenge involving forms of retaliation beyond physical pain, findings are enlightening insofar as they suggest that reactions to socially inappropriate behavior have a biological basis. As such, they represent a useful adjunct to evidence suggesting that biological differences may be responsible for the differential tendencies of men and women to engage in IWB (Knight, Guthrie, Page, & Fabes, 2002).

This newly developing explanation takes its place along already established explanations, such as those based on differences in social learning and the development of gender roles, to which we now turn.

Social Learning Theory

Initially proposed by Bandura (1977), social learning theory (SLT) suggests that individual behavior is influenced by observational learning and, in turn, modeling the behaviors and reactions of others. In a series of classic experiments Bandura reported that individuals are inclined to imitate a model's behavior when that model (a) is a powerful figure, (b) is rewarded for engaging in the behavior, and (c) shares key characteristics with the observer.

Applied to IWB, SLT provides a useful explanation for why individuals engage in deviant behavior in the workplace. Specifically, SLT suggests that male employees who have learned by observing other males (who are similar to them) that behaving in a particular way in which they are inclined to act (e.g., using threats, intimidation, physical violence, revenge, etc.) results in positive consequences (e.g., compliance with a request, increased work performance) will be likely to engage in such behavior themselves. By contrast, women are historically less powerful (although that has been changing rapidly) and are not rewarded for engaging in an aggressive manner, thereby making them less inclined to engage in IWB (Moffitt, Caspi, Rutter, & Silva, 2001).

Gender Role Theory

Researchers also have called upon gender role theory (Eagly, 1987) to explain sex differences in deviant behavior. According to gender role theory, men and women face societal pressures to behave in ways that are consistent with their gender roles and this leads them to internalize cultural expectations about gender-appropriate behaviors (Kidder, 2002). Specifically, gender roles are "shared expectations about appropriate conduct that apply to individuals on the basis of their socially identified sex" (Eagly & Wood, 1991, p. 309). Much of the research exploring how gender role expectations explain sex differences in deviant behavior has focused on specific acts of deviance, namely, violence and aggression. This research reveals that men are more likely than women to be perpetrators of these acts (for a recent review, see Archer, 2004). According to gender role theory this is because men are socially reinforced and rewarded for engaging in behaviors consistent with stereotypical beliefs about masculinity, such as aggressiveness (for a review, see Crooks, Goodall, Baker, & Hughes, 2006).

In their review of the results of several meta-analyses of the sex-difference research, Eagly and Wood (1991) observed that empirical evidence strongly supports gender role theory, and recent studies support this conclusion. Kidder's (2002) study of nurses and engineers, for example, revealed significant gender differences in the performance of organizational citizenship behaviors (i.e., altruism and civic virtue), consistent with hypotheses based on gender role theory. As several authors have noted, social stereotypes also reflect these expectations about male and female behavior (Eagly, Wood, & Diekman, 2000). As Grossman and Wood (1993) note, women typically are expected to be friendly, emotionally expressive, and to display concern for others, whereas men are expected to be aggressive, independent, assertive, and stoic. The fact that males and females generally fulfill different social roles, particularly in domestic and occupational settings, further reinforces these gender stereotypes (Eagly et al., 2000).

Personality Differences

In research examining individual-level predictors of IWB, among the most widely studied personality variables are narcissism, Machiavellianism, and negative affectivity. We now examine these as potential antecedents of IWB.

Narcissism

The construct of subclinical narcissism, developed by Raskin and Hall (1979), was based on a definition of narcissistic personality disorder (NPD) found in the *Diagnostic and Statistical Manual of Mental Disorders (DSM)*. In contrast to the psychiatric disorder, Lee and Ashton (2005) identify narcissism as a "normal" personality variable typically exhibited in behaviors including "dominance, exhibitionism, and exploitation as well as feelings of superiority and entitlement" (p. 1572). We focus on this normal conceptualization here and review some of the studies that link it to IWB.

First, we note that researchers have identified a positive association between narcissism and aggressive behavior (Penney & Spector, 2002). As Penney and Spector (2002) observe, one of the most prevalent conceptualizations used to explain this relationship is the theory of threatened egotism proposed by Baumeister, Smart, and Boden (1996). Specifically, this theory suggests that violent or aggressive behavior may occur under conditions of "threatened egotism"—that is, when a person's favorable self-appraisal is challenged externally. Baumeister et al. (1996) argued further that individuals high in narcissism, who generally have inflated and unrealistically high levels of self-esteem, are likely to be particularly sensitive to such threats. Research has shown that narcissists are, in fact, predisposed to engage in aggressive behavior (Bushman & Baumeister, 1998).

Following from research suggesting that ego-threatening events occur frequently in organizational settings, Penney and Spector (2002) sought to determine the extent to which relationships existed between narcissism, trait anger, counterproductive work behavior (CWB), and various job constraints (e.g., faulty equipment, inadequate training). Specifically, they proposed that situational constraints (i.e., circumstances or contexts that keep employees from using their skills and talents to achieve satisfactory job performance) may be perceived as ego threatening to the extent that they prevent individuals from performing to the best of their ability, not allowing them to learn about the effectiveness of their performance. The theory of threatened egotism suggests that due to their extreme need to feel superior to others, individuals high in narcissism will perceive more events or situations as ego threatening, leading them to respond with anger and frustration, thereby triggering aggressive behavior (in keeping with the classic frustration-aggression hypothesis; Berkowitz, 1989). Penney and Spector's (2002) results were in keeping with this idea: Highly narcissistic individuals reported feeling angry more often and engaged in more CWB than those who were low in narcissism.

More recently, Judge, LePine, and Rich (2006) shed additional light on this relationship. These researchers measured narcissism in a sample of workers along with their self-evaluations of deviant behavior and their supervisors' ratings of these workers' deviant behavior. They found that narcissism was linked positively to self-evaluations of workplace deviance and to their supervisor's evaluations of their workplace deviance, although narcissism was a stronger predictor of the self-reported deviance. As Judge et al. put it, "narcissism appears to reflect a grandiose self-view" (p. 771), suggesting that it may be risky to employ highly narcissistic people in jobs in which accurate perceptions of self are necessary or when 360-degree ratings are used.

To summarize, although there have only been a few studies on narcissism in organizations, their findings suggest that narcissism may play a key role in IWB, especially when it comes to recognizing one's own behavior in this regard. Because the existing research is only preliminary and has not focused specifically on IWB per se, it's clear that additional research examining this association is in order.

Machiavellianism

Another trait that is linked to certain types of IWB is Machiavellianism (Christie & Geis, 1970), defined as "a strategy of social conduct that involves manipulating others for personal gain, often against the other's self-interest" (Wilson, Near, & Miller, 1996, p. 285). Machiavellianism is associated with lying, superficial charm, low levels of morality, and the tendency to manipulate others for personal gain (McHoskey, Worzel, & Szyarto, 1998). People with high levels of Machiavellianism display jealousy and envy in the workplace (Vecchio, 2000), low levels of ethical conflict (Mudrack, 1993), and high levels of boredom (Marušic, Bratko, & Zarevski, 1995).

The possibility of a connection between Machiavellianism and IWB is suggested by Bennett and Robinson (2000), who found that Machiavellianism scores were correlated positively with measures of interpersonal and organizational deviance. Further research supports this connection as well. For example, in a study assessing people's ability to justify participating in different types of organizational sabotage, Giacalone and Knouse (1990) reported that individuals who scored high on Machiavellianism more readily justified engaging in sabotage (and in the related acts of manipulating and controlling information) than those who scored low on this dimension of personality.

Research also has found that highly Machiavellian people are inclined to engage in deceptive behavior (Bond & Rao, 2004; Vrij, 2000). This is reported in literature reviewed by Kashy and DePaulo (1996), which reveals that the manipulative use of lying represents the core behavioral attribute of highly Machiavellian individuals. As these authors note, such individuals lie, cheat, and exploit others so long as they believe that they will not be detected. In their study of the frequency of lying in everyday social interactions, Kashy and DePaulo found that individuals scoring high in Machiavellianism and social adroitness (an additional measure of manipulativeness) told more lies than their low-scoring counterparts. This was especially so for lies designed to protect participants from embarrassment and loss of face and for lies designed to advance or protect their own interests. Although people engage in deception for many different reasons, as Grover (Chapter 7, present volume) correctly points out, these findings suggest that the particular types of lies that people tell are likely to be based in part on the degree of Machiavellianism they possess.

We are unaware of any studies linking Machiavellianism to workplace bullying but extrapolating from research on schoolyard bullying suggests a possible relationship. For example, noting that bullies engage in socially manipulative behavior (e.g., spreading rumors), Sutton and Keogh (2000) hypothesized that high levels of Machiavellianism are positively related to bullying. To test this, they categorized subsamples of 198 school children as either bullies, victims, both bullies and victims, or neither (controls) based on their responses to self-reported measures of Machiavellianism, attitudes toward bullying victims, and actual bullying behavior. As expected, bullies scored significantly higher than controls on Machiavellianism. Furthermore, highly Machiavellian children reported lower levels of sympathy for victims. In a subsequent study Andreou (2004) found that school children who bullied others and who experienced bullying themselves (i.e., bully-victims) had high levels of Machiavellianism and reported having little faith in human nature. To the extent that these findings may be generalized to organizations, they suggest that considerable insight may be gleaned from including Machiavellianism as a variable in future studies of IWB.

Negative Affectivity

Negative affectivity (NA) is a stable personality trait characterized by a propensity to experience negative cognitions, negative emotions (e.g., guilt and anger), and to interpret neutral events in a negative manner (Watson & Clark, 1984). Not surprisingly, NA has been linked to adverse psychological outcomes, such as depression, anxiety, eating disorders, and illicit substance use (Kashdan, Vetter, & Collins, 2005; Myers, Aarons, Tomlinson, & Stein, 2003; Norton, Sexton, Walker, & Norton, 2005; Pryor & Wiederman, 1996). Germane to IWB, we note that a positive relationship between deviant behavior and NA has been reported. For example, Aquino, Lewis, and Bradfield (1999) found a direct relationship between NA and deviance, such that when experiencing an aversive emotional state, employees were more likely to engage in deviance that was interpersonal (e.g., hurtful verbal remarks) as opposed to organizational in nature (e.g., sabotaging equipment). This may be based on the way high NAs interpret the world. Specifically, Penney and Spector (2005) suggest when confronted with ambiguous and potentially aversive behavior (e.g., incivility), high NAs may be inclined to perceive that an actor intended to harm them, thereby leading to the heightened negative cognitions and emotions associated with retaliation and revenge.

In a study exploring individual differences in vengefulness (i.e., the disposition to seek revenge following interpersonal harm), McCullough, Bellah, Kilpatrick, and Johnson (2001) surveyed undergraduate students who recently had been offended by someone in their lives. Participants completed baseline measures of key variables and were contacted for follow-up 8 weeks later. Analyses revealed that individuals with higher vengefulness scores spent more time ruminating about the original offenses, were less forgiving of offenders, less satisfied with life, and had higher degrees of NA. They also found that vengeful individuals remained motivated to seek revenge over time to a greater degree than were less vengeful individuals. As McCullough et al. (2001) observed, this suggests that a vengeful disposition may lead individuals to retaliate in response to personal grievances. Additional research suggests that vengeful individuals are inclined to experience negative cognitions and emotions, and to interpret situations accordingly, which contributes to their desires for revenge (McCullough et al., 2001).

In a study seeking to replicate previous findings in CWB research, Penney and Spector (2005) examined the relationships between CWB, NA, and job stressors, workplace incivility, and interpersonal conflict. They found that NA was positively related to CWB, and that it moderated the relationship between experienced job stressors and CWB. Specifically, although participants reported engaging in low levels of CWB when perceived job stressors were low, high NAs reported significantly greater levels of CWB than low NAs when job stressors were perceived to be at high levels. According to Penney and Spector (2005), high NAs engaging in CWB may reflect their (maladaptive) attempt to cope with highly stressful situations.

Cultural Differences

Considering the profound ways in which national culture influences social behavior in organizations (Moodian, 2008), it appears potentially valuable to consider its influence on IWB. As Luthar and Luthar (2002) observed in their review of sexual harassment research, ethnicity and cultural values strongly influence the acceptability and perceptions of sexual behavior in different countries. Specifically, using Hofstede's (2001) cultural dimensions, the authors suggest that men are likely to sexually harass women in countries that rank lower in individualism (e.g., Mexico), higher in power distance (e.g., Brazil), higher in masculinity (e.g., Japan), and higher uncertainty avoidance (e.g., Guatemala). Based on a review of the available evidence, Luthar and Luthar argue convincingly that cultural values and norms influence sexual harassment.

In addition to sexual harassment, Hofstede's (2001) cultural dimensions have been used to predict individuals' likelihoods of engaging in self-deceptive enhancement (i.e., the tendency to give genuinely believed but exaggerated self-assessments of one's personal performance) and impression management (i.e., presenting oneself in a positive light as a means of maintaining a favorable image; Paulhus, 1998). In this connection, Lalwani, Shavitt, and Johnson (2006) hypothesized that participants from individualist cultures would be more likely than those from collectivist cultures to engage in deception and less likely to engage in impression management. Confirming this, the authors found that participants from the United States scored higher on measures of self-deceptive enhancement and lower on impression management than those from Singapore.

Tinsley and Weldon (2003) also used the collectivism–individualism dimension to explore managers' responses to workplace conflict. These researchers found that although American managers were no more likely than Chinese managers to express a desire for revenge, they were significantly more likely to communicate directly when being revengeful. Furthermore, in accordance with the notion that shame is used frequently as a form of social control and to shape individual behavior in collectivistic cultures (see Parkinson, Fischer, & Manstead, 2005), Chinese managers expressed a stronger desire than American managers to shame employees and to teach them moral lessons.

In summary, to the extent that certain behaviors fulfill cultural goals and are deemed more acceptable in some cultures than others, it is not surprising that cultural norms and values influence individuals' likelihoods of engaging in some forms of IWB. In keeping with current interactionist thinking (e.g., Joyce, Slocum, & Von Glinow, 2007), however, we should note that the propensity to engage in IWB is likely to be a complex interaction of individual, situational, and cultural forces.

TRIGGERS: WHAT MOTIVATES IWB?

Employees may engage in IWB for a variety of reasons. As suggested by Neuman and Keashly (Chapter 2, present volume), several reasons are suggested directly by the literature on workplace aggression, such as the desire to retaliate against harmdoers, and the experiencing of emotions such as fear, anger, and shame. This is not to say, however, that aggressive behavior cannot also occur in the absence of readily discernible triggers. In the case of workplace bullying, for example, Salin (2003) identified several precipitating factors—notably, changes in the composition of work groups, organizational changes, and crises associated with restructuring. Specifically, Salin (2003) suggests that such conditions promote perceptions of competition among employees along with raised levels of stress and feelings of powerlessness and uncertainty. This, in turn, triggers bullying among employees—both because they are displacing anger toward employers who left them feeling frustrated and because that frustration motivates them to regain lost feelings of control and certainty in the workplace. In keeping with this theorizing, the means, motive, and opportunity (MM&O) framework proposed by Neuman and Keashly (Chapter 2, present volume) provides a useful heuristic for understanding IWB insofar as it highlights the contribution of each element and the interactions between them in the production, management, and prevention of the most aggressive forms of IWB.

In their review of studies examining revenge in the workplace, Bies and Tripp (2005) suggest that revenge is a provoked behavior that arises as a result of (a) feelings of disappointment and frustration following goal obstruction; (b) violations of organizational rules, norms, or promises (e.g., a betrayal of confidence); or (c) attacks on one's personal status or power, such as personal insults and unjustified criticism. These authors note that unfair or harsh treatment from superiors, in particular, can lead employees to retaliate. In this respect, McCullough et al. (2001) note that three subsidiary goals can underlie revenge: (a) a desire to get even and restore a sense of moral equilibrium, (b) a desire to demonstrate to offenders that their behavior will not be tolerated, and (c) a desire by victims to save face by indicating that they are worthy of being treated with respect.

In the present volume, Jones (Chapter 4) explicitly addresses employees' desires for revenge following IWB and proposes that violations of core needs and arousal of justice motives ultimately motivate people to engage in revenge. It is particularly interesting that participants in Jones's study experienced IWB for 12 months prior to engaging in revenge, prompting the question of why employees went so long without retaliating. Jones suggests that employees initially may have refrained from reacting due to (a) fear of negative consequences, (b) the need to maintain a working relationship with perpetrators, or (c) a lack of perceived opportunities to retaliate. Jones also highlights the crucial role of attributions in the revenge process, suggesting that the desire for revenge is triggered once targets believe that actors could have and should have refrained from engaging in the unwelcome behavior.

Potential motives for another form of IWB, sabotage, are the focus of Seabright, Ambrose, and Schminke's chapter (Chapter 3, present volume). These authors identify five reasons why workers engage in sabotage identified in the literature: (a) to retaliate against whose who have treated them unfairly, (b) to display their capacity to assert power, (c) to express their feelings of frustration, (d) to facilitate their work, and (e) to alleviate boredom and have fun. They argue further that the employees' affect (positive/negative) and goal state (instrumental/expressive) motivate them to engage in sabotage. Seabright et al. also predict that the various causes of sabotage lead to differential goals and affective states and that these subsequently influence whether sabotage is insidious or overt in nature. Testing this idea, these researchers found that acts of insidious sabotage were precipitated by feelings of powerlessness and triggered by instrumental goals and positive affect. By contrast, extreme acts of sabotage were precipitated by perceptions of injustice and were motivated by negative affect and expressive goals. This work represents an important contribution to the sabotage literature because it integrates previous findings regarding the causal role of cognition and emotion in IWB and because it examines the differential effects of instrumental versus expressive goals on behavior.

The importance of instrumental motives for IWB also is stressed by Boxer and Ford (Chapter 6, present volume), who argue that sexist humor can serve a functional purpose in organizations. Specifically, these authors suggest that men use humor for several reasons, such as to enhance their self-images, to build or maintain their organizational status, and to delineate the boundaries of their social groups. This approach is consistent with O'Leary-Kelly, Paetzold, and Griffin (2000), who conceive of sexual harassment as aggressive behavior that may be driven by instrumental motives (e.g., asserting power). Likewise, Berdahl (2007) suggested that harassment is motivated by the desire to protect or enhance social status when it is threatened. Such instrumental purposes of IWB enrich our understanding of the motives underlying decisions to engage in IWB.

Grover's (Chapter 7, present volume) analysis of the reasons why employees tell lies in the workplace also suggests that instrumental motives play a role. For example, Grover explains that managers may lie in the face of corporate failure as a means of maintaining a positive self-image or to achieve favorable outcomes when negotiating with others. Grover notes further that individuals are motivated to lie to different organizational audiences for different reasons. Namely, whereas superiors may lie to subordinates to maintain confidentiality expected of them in keeping with their positions, subordinates may lie to superiors to avoid punishment following wrongdoing.

In summary, IWB appears to be driven by a variety of instrumental motives: to harm others, to release frustration and anger following interpersonal mistreatment, or to reject the status quo. Bullies can achieve power and status in an organization if their mistreatment of other employees translates into valued outcomes, sexist humor can be used to generate amusement and enhance self-esteem, and lying can be used as an effective negotiation tactic.

TARGETS: WHO IS VICTIMIZED BY IWB?

In addition to examining potential perpetrators of IWB, researchers also are interested in identifying its potential targets (i.e., victims). Ultimately, just about anyone can be a target of IWB. For example, Grover (Chapter 7, present volume) notes that people may lie to coworkers, superiors, subordinates, or customers. Adding to this, Seabright et al. (Chapter 3, present volume) note that IWB in the form of sabotage is more likely to be targeted at organizations than individuals. With this in mind, we now consider various individual characteristics of targets that research suggests are most predictive of being targets of IWB. However, because the choice of targets goes beyond individual differences, we also examine organizational conditions as well.

Individual Characteristics of Targets

Based on current research, the individual characteristics that are most predictive of being targeted for IWB are gender, social competence, and negative affectivity.

Gender

Research examining the extent to which gender influences the likelihood of becoming a victim of IWB has produced mixed results. Although females are at significantly greater risk than males of experiencing sexual harassment (Berdahl & Moore, 2006; Foote & Goodman-Delahunty, 2005), most studies of workplace bullying suggest that males and females are equally likely to be targeted (e.g., Rayner, 1997). One exception, however, is Quine's (2002) survey of junior doctors in the United Kingdom, in which a slightly greater percentage of females (43%) than males (32%) reported being the targets of bullying. The results of a recent study in Denmark (Ortega, Høgh, Pejtersen, Feveile, & Olsen, 2009) examined the prevalence of bullying in male-dominated occupations (e.g., manual labor) and female-dominated occupations (e.g., health care). Although the results did not reveal gender differences within the groups, the risk of experiencing bullying was greater for both occupations. As the authors observed, "the gender ratio and/or its interaction with type of work might be an influential risk factor for bullying" (p. 424).

With respect to the gender of perpetrators and targets, a survey of over 5,000 Irish employees from a range of professions found that 55% of females reported being bullied by other females, 41% reported being bullied by males, and 4% were bullied by both males and females. By contrast, the majority (82%) of males reported being bullied only by other males (Health and Safety Authority, 2001). Rayner (1997) also found that although women reported being bullied to similar degrees by both men and women, men were most likely to report being bullied by other men.

She attributes the much lower proportion of female-to-male bullying to the fact that males hold a greater proportion of managerial positions than females and that people may be reluctant to bully individuals who hold higher level organizational positions. (As we note later, however, upward deviance does, in fact, occur.)

In a study that sought to determine whether being part of a gender minority at work increased the risk of victimization, Eriksen and Einarsen (2004) surveyed over 6,000 assistant nurses. They found that the proportion of nurses who reported being bullied during the previous 6 months was over twice as high for males (10.2%) as it was for females (4.3%). The authors explain this by noting that males may be considered a threat to the traditionally female-dominated culture of the nursing profession and their minority status makes them highly visible targets. Additional research supports the notion that gender interacts with organizational level to increase the risk of victimization. For example, in their national survey of British workers, Hoel, Cooper, and Faragher (2001) found that men at all levels reported being bullied to a greater extent than women, but women in senior management positions experienced the highest rates of bullying in the entire sample.

Sexual harassment is a form of behavior that sometimes manifests itself as IWB. With respect to this form of behavior, research indicates that women are far more likely than men to be victims (Berdahl & Moore, 2006). For example, 22% of female employees in Australia reported experiencing sexual harassment during the course of their working lives compared to only 7% for males (Human Rights and Equal Opportunity Commission, 2008). In keeping with this, it is not surprising that women report harassment 2 to 7 times more than men (Foote & Goodman-Delahunty, 2005). In a study of different forms of harassment experienced by female students in an academic setting, Cortina, Swan, Fitzgerald, and Waldo (1998) found that 49% of undergraduate students and 53% of graduate students had experienced some form of harassment "at least once or twice" during their time at the university.

Furthermore, research suggests that certain characteristics increase a woman's risk of being sexually harassed. One such factor is the possession of nontraditional, egalitarian views about the role of women in society. This was observed in a lab experiment involving 120 male students who were encouraged by a male confederate to send pornographic material to a female they believed to be their female interaction partner

(Dall'Ara & Maass, 1999). The confederate described the woman in question as being either egalitarian or traditional in role orientation. Researchers reported that men were more likely to harass (i.e., to send the pornographic material to) a woman with egalitarian views regarding gender roles than one with traditional views. Additionally, the confederate required fewer prompts to get participants to send the material to a woman who held egalitarian views than one who held traditional views. Interestingly, men who harassed the egalitarian woman held particular characteristics: They scored highly on the Likelihood to Harass (LHS) scale, they held sexist views, they strongly identified with being male, and they engaged in low levels of self-monitoring. Based on these findings, the researchers emphasize, egalitarian women may be at increased risk of harassment from men meeting a particular profile, possibly because such men feel threatened by women who hold competitive, nontraditional views about gender equity.

Despite its importance, gender is only one of several individual characteristics that may contribute to victimization (for a comprehensive review of these factors, see Zapf). We now examine two others, social competence and negative affectivity (Zapf & Einarsen, 2003).

Social Competence

Research suggests that people with limited social skills are more likely to be victims than those with highly developed social skills. This may be because perpetrators target individuals who are considered particularly vulnerable because they are unlikely to retaliate or even to speak up about the undesirable behavior (Zapf & Einarsen, 2003; Zapf & Gross, 2001). In addition to making them attractive targets for bullies, these characteristics also influence how victims cope with the bullying once targeted. Zapf (1999), for example, conducted a comprehensive study of employees' beliefs about the causes of mobbing (bullying perpetrated by a group of people) in the workplace. To assess the extent to which organizational, social, and individual factors contributed to bullying, participants completed multiple questionnaire measures, including ones designed to assess psychological dysfunctions, conflict behavior, and stigmatization, from which an unassertiveness/avoidance scale was generated. Findings revealed that victimized employees who scored high in unassertiveness/avoidance exhibited the poorest conflict management skills (e.g., scoring low in compromising and integrating), and also reported a significantly greater level of depression and anxiety than other participants in the sample. As Zapf (1999) observed, these individuals tried to steer clear of conflict as much as possible. They also tended to concede to bullies and were unable to sustain viable social support networks or to integrate with their work groups. In other words, they had generally weaker social skills than their fellow employees.

Further insight into this issue may be derived from research on schoolyard bullying. For example, Fox and Boulton (2005) conducted a study designed to determine the extent to which victims and nonvictims of bullying differed with respect to a range of social competencies. Participants were 330 children between 9 and 11 years of age who completed a social skills questionnaire containing items based from the social competency and victimization literature. Specifically, the children were asked to rate how similar they believed they were to each of the 20 descriptors on the social skills questionnaire (e.g., "Fights back when picked on"), and also to rate bullying victims and nonvictims in their classes on each item. For categorization purposes, children also provided the names of classmates who frequently were bullied. In addition, the children's teachers also rated certain victims and nonvictims in their classes. Analyses of ratings by self, peers, and teachers converged to reveal five social skills characteristics linked to victimization: (a) displaying behavioral vulnerability (e.g., looking frightened), (b) encouraging bullying behavior by being unassertive (e.g., giving in to the bully with little or no protest), (c) rewarding and thereby reinforcing the bullying behavior (e.g., crying), (d) displaying provocative behavior (e.g., annoying other children), and (e) being reserved and quiet (e.g., speaking very quietly).

It is important to note that the studies of social competence we have reviewed here focus only on one form of IWB, bullying, and on behavior occurring outside the workplace. For these reasons, their generalization to other forms of IWB, particularly in organizations, cannot be assumed. Still, this research provides insight into a potentially important determinant of victimization, one that begs to be tested with respect to various forms of IWB.

Negative Affectivity

Just as higher levels of the trait of NA are associated with increased propensity to engage in IWB, as we noted earlier, it is also the case that the state of negative affectivity is linked to victimization. That is, targets frequently experience the negative moods and emotions associated with high levels of negative affect. Furthermore, victims of bullying in particular report low self-esteem, somatic complaints, high levels of anxiety, and depressive symptomatology (Quine, 2001; Zapf & Einarsew, 2003). As we will discuss, however, it is unclear whether individuals who are generally unhappy, anxious, and feel negatively about themselves are specifically targeted by perpetrators in the first place or if these characteristics emerge following extended periods of victimization.

In one of the first studies to examine the relationship between bullying and various individual and organizational factors, Vartia (1996) found significant positive correlations between bullying, neuroticism, and self-esteem among 949 municipal employees. Although victims were more neurotic and had lower levels of self-esteem than nonvictims, these relationships became statistically nonsignificant after controlling for various aspects of the work environment (e.g., autonomy and monotony of the work) and organizational climate (e.g., communication climate and social climate). Although these findings reveal that the role of individual personality is eclipsed by organizational variables when it comes to bullying, Vartia (1996) suggests that personality factors may play important roles before the effects of environmental factors take hold, such as when perpetrators initially select their victims. In the absence of data to test this effect, however, this possibility should be considered speculative.

Partly in response to Vartia's (1996) appeal for well-designed studies on the role of victims' personalities in bullying, Coyne, Seigne, and Randall (2000) conducted an organizational case study. This investigation involved samples from two major organizations in which the researchers attempted to match victim and control participants on key variables (e.g., age, gender, job status, and marital status). All 120 participants completed an inventory measuring traits that closely corresponded to the Big Five personality factors. The researchers found statistically significant differences between victims and nonvictims of bullying, particularly with respect to stability (neuroticism), extroversion, and independence. Specifically, victims were highly fearful, suspicious, passive, and introverted, and reported difficulty coping with situations. Importantly, a weighted grouping of personality traits strongly predicted victimization, suggesting that employees at greater risk of being bullied could potentially be identified before they become targets (Coyne et al., 2000).

A subsequent study by the same authors found similar results. Specifically, compared to nonvictims of bullying, victims scored significantly lower than control participants with respect to emotional stability, appearing stressed, being fearful and suspicious of others, and also perceiving work environments more negatively (Coyne, Smith-Lee Chong, Seigne, & Randall, 2003). Taken together, these studies strongly suggest that negative affectivity is a risk factor for victimization by workplace bullies. At present, we are unaware of any studies that have explored this characteristic of targets with respect to other forms of IWB.

It is important to note that researchers studying the characteristics of victims of IWB, particularly those involving psychiatric symptoms (e.g., Coggan, Bennett, Hooper, & Dickinson, 2003; Matthiesen & Einarsen, 2001), find it difficult to determine the direction of causality. Were symptoms present before a harmful episode occurred, contributing to mistreatment (or perceptions thereof), or did symptoms emerge in response to victimization? Furthermore, there may be a potential artifact at work, with personality characteristics influencing how workplace behaviors are perceived. For example, Wislar, Richman, Fendrich, and Flaherty (2002) reported that employees with high degrees of neuroticism and narcissism were significantly more likely to report experiencing sexual harassment or abusive work practices than were other employees. It may be that individuals with greater propensities to feel anxious, suspicious, and tense also will interpret workplace behavior more negatively, sensitizing them to be aware of abuse and harassment. In the case of bullying, employees who have low self-esteem may be more likely to interpret their colleagues' ambiguous behavior as negative and directed at them, and to feel bullied as a result.

The direction of causality also is of concern in studies of workplace aggression. For example, we know that victims of workplace aggression tend to experience low levels of self-esteem (Harvey & Keashly, 2003). However, existing research does not reveal the extent to which individuals may have had low levels of self-esteem prior to being victimized (Lindemeier, 1996). Do individuals with low levels of self-esteem put themselves in situations in which victimization by aggressors occurs, does victimization lower people's levels of self-esteem, or do both occur? Until rigorous prepost studies are conducted to establish the direction of causality, this question will remain unanswered, pointing to an important gap in the IWB literature.

The Role of Power Differentials

Beyond various individual characteristics, the positions individuals hold in their hierarchical organizations relative to others also are likely to affect their risk of victimization. In particular, employees in lower-level positions generally have less power, visibility, and voice in their organizations than those in supervisory or management roles. This makes them prime targets of interpersonal mistreatment—particularly at the hands of those with greater organizational status and power, such as managers. As Neuman and Keashly (Chapter 2, present volume) remind us, subordinates are inclined to have only limited opportunities to respond to abuses from superiors. Moreover, they are likely to be disinclined to take action that may threaten their livelihoods. Accordingly, it is not surprising that Neuman and Keashly report that 65% of employees victimized by their superiors express interest in leaving their organizations because of the high degree of distress they suffered from mistreatment. And, given that the most widely occurring targets of aggressive behavior were subordinates victimized by their own superiors, this is a potentially serious problem.

This is not to say, however, that supervisors cannot also become targets of IWB. Indeed, data from Jones's (Chapter 4, present volume) study suggests that people in power frequently are targets of retaliatory behavior. Specifically, 70% of participants blamed their immediate supervisors for the initial mistreatments that triggered their desires for revenge. As Jones observes, individuals may be motivated to engage in acts of revenge to restore a sense of control and power, especially if the perpetrator is in a more powerful position. This may be one reason why supervisors are targeted. Indeed, research indicates that cases of "contrapower harassment" (i.e., when a target has greater formal organizational power than a perpetrator; Benson, 1984) are not as rare as first considered. In a recent study conducted at a large American university, Lampman, Phelps, Bancroft, and Beneke (2009) sought to determine the rate of contrapower harassment, which they defined as acts of bullying, incivility, and sexual attention by students directed at staff members. Consistent with research suggesting that this is a common occurrence (e.g., De Souza & Fansler, 2003; McKinney, 1990), Lampman et al. (2009) revealed that almost all female (96%) and male (99%) faculty members had experienced at least one incident of bullying or incivility from a student. Additionally, 26% of female and 37% of male faculty members experienced some form of sexual behavior from students. Similarly, emerging research on the phenomenon of upward bullying (Branch, Ramsay, & Barker, 2007) supports the notion that managers are often bullied by lower level employees. Now that we know that the phenomenon of contrapower harassment exists, the time has come to explore in future research its antecedents, consequences, and the processes underlying its occurrence. We consider this to be a key item to be placed on the agenda of future IWB researchers.

ACTION: WHAT FORMS DOES IWB TAKE?

"You know it when you see it," is something that is said about many forms of behavior. In the case of IWB, however, this phrase is not applicable both because people often do not see the behavior in question and because scientists cannot always agree on what it is in the first place. For these reasons it is particularly important to be able to identify the various forms that IWB takes. We introduced this issue in Chapter 1 of this volume, including a summary of how IWB relates to other forms of deviant behavior. Here, we expand on this by discussing how some of the contributors to this volume have addressed this question.

One of the challenges associated with identifying the various forms of IWB is that some of the same behaviors that widely are considered counterproductive or deviant also may be categorized as insidious. At issue is the extent to which the behavior in question meets our defining characteristics of IWB (identified in this book's opening chapter)—namely, that the behaviors are (a) intentionally harmful, (b) legal, (c) low level, (d) repetitive, and (e) targeted either at individuals or organizations.

Indeed, there is considerable overlap between the different concepts addressed by the contributors to this book. For example, Neuman and Keashly (Chapter 2, present volume) refer to "aggressive workplace behavior," which can take several interrelated forms. As noted by Cowie, Naylor, Rivers, Smith, and Pereira (2002), bullying is widely regarded to be a subset of aggressive behavior, harassment constitutes bullying of a sexual nature, and harassment and incivility are closely interrelated (Lim & Cortina, 2005). In their chapter, Neuman and Keashly provide a comprehensive account of the wide variety of behaviors that constitute workplace aggression, such as being treated in a rude or disrespectful manner, being lied to, being subjected to sexist remarks, and being threatened with physical harm. Incivility (Pearson, Chapter 5, present volume) also appears to share some similarities involving rude, insensitive, or disrespectful behavior, although it does not tend to extend to more extreme acts, such as threats of violence (see also Pearson, Andersson, & Wegner, 2001). We note as well that several of the contributors to this book have addressed some of the behaviors described here as forms of IWB in their own right, such as lies (Grover, Chapter 7) and sexist remarks (Boxer & Ford, Chapter 6).

The stealthy and frequently ambiguous nature of IWB means that it is generally difficult to detect, allowing individuals to engage in IWB for long periods of time before they are caught. Indeed, it may not be until IWB persists over protracted periods of time that anything inappropriate appears to have occurred on a cumulative basis. Indeed, serious consequences may not arise until targets have suffered for weeks, months, or even years. Two reasons for this may be identified. First, it takes time for someone to eventually recognize a pattern in which the cumulative impact of the insidious acts appears. Second, over time the odds are increased that the perpetrator will cross the line into the realm of blatantly unacceptable behavior. Consider, for example, physical aggression. In some forms (e.g., light hits), this may be considered IWB, but when accumulated, these seemingly innocuous behaviors may result in adverse psychological outcomes of a serious nature, resulting in posttraumatic stress disorder, anxiety, depression, and even suicide (Matthiesen & Einarsen, 2004; Vartia, 2001).

Neuman and Baron (2005) utilized Buss's (1961) typology of aggression to classify eight types of workplace aggression, including many of the behaviors addressed in the present volume. For example, these authors classified sexual harassment as active, verbal, and direct aggression, and sabotage as active, physical, and indirect aggression. However, sexual harassment can take many forms, including inappropriate touching and staring. This typology demonstrates the numerous forms that incivility can take and classifies them along several dimensions, such as, giving the target the silent treatment (verbal, passive, and direct), showing up late for meetings held by the target (physical, passive, and indirect), and making rude or disrespectful comments (verbal, active, and direct). Given that Neuman and Baron's (2005) framework focuses on aggressive behavior, however, it does not include lying and revenge. We believe that developing a comprehensive typology of IWB that incorporates these behaviors along with others is an important task for scholars to complete in the future.

With respect to motives underlying IWB, Seabright et al. (Chapter 3, present volume) make the point that employees who engage in sabotage do not always seek to harm their intended targets. Namely, their definition incorporates behaviors ranging from destroying or vandalizing equipment and property in an effort to retaliate against an organization to subverting organizational policies and procedures. Sometimes, subverting policies and procedures actually improves organizational effectiveness in the long run. For example, if an employee believes that an organization's workplace health and safety procedures are not protecting workers effectively, he or she may choose to ignore the current standards and adopt a different set of practices. Although these may begin as idiosyncratic, they ultimately may become institutionalized as their effectiveness is demonstrated over time. Disregarding policies is likely to lower productivity in the short term, but an organization stands to benefit in the long term if circumventing the current safety procedures leads to better, safer procedures in the future. It is important to note that in such positive cases, and when acts of vandalism are major and immediately detectable, the behavior in question would not be considered IWB.

Sabotage, like other varieties of deviant workplace behavior, may be considered IWB only when it takes the specific forms in keeping with our definition. Put differently, sabotage and revenge are not observable behaviors per se but rather motives underlying certain behaviors that may manifest themselves as IWB. After all, one cannot see sabotage or revenge but acts assumed to be motivated by the desire to achieve these ends. In contrast, hitting someone lightly or telling a sexist joke are observable forms of behavior that may be insidious. Furthermore, bullying is not a particular act but a set or class of behaviors that may be undertaken with the intention of harming another; although as we indicated, its motives may be complex.

Picking up on this complexity, Grover (Chapter 7, present volume) argues that individuals tell different types of lies in the workplace to achieve differential outcomes and that not all forms of lying should be considered inherently negative. For example, managers may be required to conceal certain aspects of situations to protect the privacy of individuals or the security of their organizations as a whole. Similarly, employees may tell "white lies" to coworkers as a means of improving their peers' self-esteem and sense of competence. Thus, saying "you look nice today" or "you did a good job," even if untrue, may not be negative in nature if these utterances are meant to be (and actually are) taken in a positive manner.

As we emphasized in Chapter 1, our definition of IWB specifies that the behavior must be performed with the intention of causing harm, thereby excluding acts of negligence and mistakes from the domain of IWB. With this in mind, we caution once more that it is important to take into consideration actors' intentions for engaging in a particular behavior when attempting to identify it as insidious in nature. As we indicated in the opening chapter of this volume, actors' intentions frequently are ambiguous and the degree of ambiguity often depends on the forms of IWB in which they engage. For example, actively insulting a colleague and belittling her in front of others ostensibly may appear to be more harmful than, say, failing to inform her of a new rule or ignoring her during team meetings, although depending on the specifics this might not be the case. We acknowledge that such ambiguity contributes to the challenge of studying IWB, but we are note alone in imposing a potentially (and inherently) ambiguous criterion. Indeed, as Pearson notes (Chapter 5, this volume) despite inherent ambiguity in distinguishing incivility from other forms of aggressive behavior, the concept of incivility has been studied successfully as have systematic efforts to minimize it in the workplace. Following this lead, we claim that the ambiguity surrounding IWB is not a fatal flaw in its conceptualization so much as it is an inherent quality of the concept itself.

SHORT-TERM RESPONSES: HOW DO VICTIMS AND ORGANIZATIONS REACT TO IWB?

After IWB has occurred it is up to individual victims to decide how they will respond, if at all. Then, once organizational officials come to know about a perpetrator's IWB, they must decide how to respond.

Responses of Individual Victims

After IWB has occurred, victims and witnesses (e.g., coworkers) may respond in various ways. For example, they may withhold their concerns from management (i.e., engage in employee silence; Greenberg & Edwards, 2009), they may report the behavior to those capable of initiating effective change (i.e., engage in whistle-blowing; Miceli & Near, 2005; Near & Miceli, 1985), they may address the situation themselves (e.g., by confronting or retaliating against perpetrators), or finally, they may leave their organizations altogether.

These behaviors are in keeping with Hirschman's (1970) typology for explaining reactions to declines in organizational performance. Specifically, he suggested that loyal employees will voice their concerns (e.g., actively expressing their displeasure), whereas less loyal employees will be inclined to exit (e.g., physically leave), thereby ending their relationships with their organizations. Extending Hirschman's typology, Farrell (1983) proposed that unhappy employees might engage in "neglect," which involves negligent or slack behavior (e.g., being frequently late or absent from work). These three themes—voice (speaking up about mistreatment), neglect (doing nothing about mistreatment), and exit (leaving the organization)—characterize responses to various forms of IWB reported in the literature.

Research indicates that employees frequently refrain from expressing their concerns about interpersonal mistreatment in a formal manner. For example, Cortina and Magley (2009) recently found that only 1% to 6% of survey participants filed formal complaints about acts of incivility suffered in the workplace. This is not surprising in view of the fact that many victims are unwilling to jeopardize their positions or to prolong their psychological distress by taking formal action. However, victims of incivility may respond informally, but the particular way in which they do so differs according to their gender. As shown by Pearson and Porath (2005), men are likely to retaliate and attempt to get even with those who were uncivil toward them, whereas women are disinclined from confronting perpetrators. Instead, in Pearson and Porath's study, women disengaged from the situation by confiding in their friends and family.

Studies of workplace bullying and harassment also suggest that victims respond in a variety of ways (Rayner, Hoel, & Cooper, 2002). For example, Lutgen-Sandvik's (2006) qualitative study of observers of bullying (many of whom were targets as well) revealed five major ways in which employees responded to the mistreatment: (a) exodus (e.g., quitting, threatening to quit, requesting a transfer), (b) collective voice (e.g., mutually supporting colleagues), (c) reverse discourse (e.g., making contact with powerful allies or filing a formal grievance), (d) subversive disobedience (e.g., retaliation), and (e) confrontation (e.g., challenging the bully directly in a face-to-face interaction). Lutgen-Sandvik (2006) furthermore emphasized that employees' responses formed a "motivated trajectory," with people using different strategies over time: "Workers use one tactic, assess its effect, use another tactic, assess its effect, use another tactic, assess, and so on; they also use different strategies in combination … [people] do not give up; they continue trying to end abuse until exiting the organization" (p. 427).

In summary, it's apparent that victims respond to IWB in a variety of ways although the extent to which these responses differ as a function of the specific form of IWB involved is not yet clear. There appear to be some general similarities (e.g., filing formal complaints) although we don't yet know if people's specific responses to IWB vary according to the particular form of IWB involved (i.e., act dependent) or if people show consistent styles in their responses to various forms of IWB (i.e., victim dependent). Of course, it's also possible that these two factors interact such that certain people respond to certain forms of IWB in one way, whereas other combinations result in different responses. We believe that categorizing responses to various forms of IWB and identifying moderators of these reactions is a fundamental task that must be completed by researchers studying IWB in the future.

Responses of Organizational Officials

After a victim reports IWB to an organizational official or after officials discover acts of IWB themselves, they must decide how to respond. Will they be passive and do nothing, or will they take some form of remedial action? The general answer is: Just as individual victims sometimes fail to respond to IWB, so too do organizational officials.

Near and Miceli (1995) suggested that organizations sometimes fail to punish perpetrators because they are highly dependent on these individuals and cannot afford to risk losing their services. Similarly, officials may tacitly approve of a perpetrator's ostensibly negative behavior because they believe it is instrumental in bringing about some desired short-term end (e.g., a manager's incivilities may be keeping subordinates from slacking). For these reasons, officials may turn a blind eye to the mistreatment. This assumes, of course, that the behavior in question with some credibility can be labeled "innocuous" and "under the radar," as IWB is by definition. Officials' passivity also seems to assume that there is an implicit cost–benefit analysis going on, with the perceived benefits of maintaining the behavior (e.g., productivity resulting from the harmdoer's actions) outweighing the costs (e.g., the harm done to the individuals involved).

In considering why organizations often fail to address employees' complaints of sexual harassment, Pierce, Smolinski, and Rosen (1998) refer to a "deaf ear syndrome" in which various factors promote nonresponsiveness. Gathering data from several sources (e.g., literature, media case examples, and interviews with litigators of sexual harassment cases), these researchers identified major themes associated with organizational inaction: (a) inadequate policies and procedures to deal with sexual harassment (e.g., vague definitions of unacceptable behavior and poorly written policies), (b) managerial reactions and rationalizations (e.g., blaming the target, minimizing the severity of the harassment), and (c) organizational qualities that inhibit taking action (e.g., family-owned businesses or those with poor human resource systems and policies). Importantly, Pierce et al.'s (1998) analysis suggests that many of these failings can be remedied with appropriate interventions and training. Also, because sensitivity to sexual harassment may have grown among human resources professionals in the years since Pierce et al.'s (1998) study (Armstrong, 2006), it's possible that some of the themes—particularly, inadequate policies and procedures—are less viable today.

Neuman and Keashly (Chapter 2, present volume) propose that there may be an additional dynamic involved that leads organizations to be proactive about not punishing IWB. Specifically, policies and practices in some contemporary organizations explicitly reward employees who pursue organizational goals at the expense of others, even if it requires engaging in ruthless and antagonistic behavior. For example, in her review of some of the potential antecedents of bullying, Salin (2003) observes that an employee who is rewarded on the basis of team performance may be motivated to punish and expel poorly performing team members. Similarly, in organizations in which there is significant internal competition to achieve profits and employees are rewarded on the basis of individual achievement, employees may sabotage the performance of others to improve their own ranking. In addition to the serious psychological consequences this can have on employees as we indicated earlier, such practices are dangerous because they tacitly reinforce such harmful behavior in the future by sending the message that there's nothing wrong with such behavior, or even that it is condoned. In turn, this may desensitize employees to the inappropriateness of such behaviors, encouraging their occurrence in the future—both directly among perpetrators (through instrumental conditioning) and indirectly among observers (through observational conditioning).

This theme is repeated in several places in this book. For example, Boxer and Ford (Chapter 6, present volume) offer such an argument in their analysis of sexist humor, suggesting that a "normative climate of tolerance" can create hostile climates within organizations, thereby permitting (if not tacitly endorsing) a range of negative, discriminatory behaviors toward women to become institutionalized (i.e., accepted and integrated as part of everyday behavior). Seabright et al. (Chapter 3, present volume) likewise suggest that apparent organizational tolerance for seemingly unacceptable behavior effectively lowers the normative threshold for many forms of workplace deviance. And in this same vein, Grover (Chapter 7, present volume) suggests that if management fails to address individual instances of deception, lying may become a habituated workplace behavior. And this, in turn, threatens to erode public confidence and trust in organizations as lying to employees and customers becomes widespread.

In summary, research reveals that individuals are inclined to use a variety of coping strategies in response to IWB but that very few file formal complaints. Moreover, once such behaviors come to the attention of management, perpetrators are unlikely to be disciplined. As a result, perpetrators tend to behave with impunity, making it business as usual among offenders. However, as we will emphasize later in this chapter, there are good reasons to attempt to turn this around by promoting appropriate action.

CONSEQUENCES: WHAT IS THE LONG-TERM IMPACT OF IWB?

Thus far, we have identified the types of responses in which individuals and organizations may engage immediately following IWB (e.g., making formal complaints, being silent, etc.). In so doing, we implied that there are negative long-term effects of being victimized by IWB but until now, we only hinted at them. Here, we will be explicit about these effects. In addition to describing the potentially harmful long-term, cumulative impact of IWB on individuals and organizations that most would expect, we will point to some positive byproducts as well.

Negative Impact

Although there are likely to be long-term negative consequences of all types of IWB, evidence sheds light primarily on three forms—bullying, incivility, and sexist humor. In the case of workplace bullying, the emotional effects of victimization have been well documented. These include depression (Liefooghe & Olafsson, 1999) and posttraumatic stress disorder (Leymann & Gustafsson, 1996; Matthiesen & Einarsen, 2004), which is associated with a number of adverse symptoms, including intrusive memories of the traumatic event, difficulty sleeping, difficulty concentrating, and high levels of emotional distress.

Pearson (Chapter 5, present volume) explicitly considered the emotional and behavioral consequences of incivility, noting that targets commonly experience anger, fear, and sadness following victimization (Pearson & Porath, 2005), emotions that may lead to decreased work effort, poorer work quality, reduced interactions with coworkers—and ultimately, leaving the company. In similar fashion, Cortina, Magley, Williams, and Langhout (2001) found that the more personal encounters employees had with incivility on their jobs, the more they experienced psychological distress (e.g., depression and anxiety), the lower were their levels of work satisfaction, and the greater were their intentions to leave their organizations.

The negative psychological and behavioral consequences of sexual harassment also have been documented extensively (Avina & O'Donohue, 2002; Fitzgerald, 1993; Van Roosmalen & McDaniel, 1998). In their review of sexist humor in the workplace, Boxer and Ford (Chapter 6, present volume) argue that sexually oriented jokes, teasing, and innuendos represent a subtle form of harassment that can cause psychological distress in females when experienced over long periods of time. The authors also note that the long-term organizational consequences of sexist humor include low employee morale, low organizational loyalty, increased competition, and low work group cohesiveness in groups involving both men and women.

Clearly, IWB can have a variety of adverse consequences for targets. In line with our definition of IWB and the work of previous researchers, we suggest that one of the challenges for researchers is to establish how variations in the severity, frequency, and duration of deviant behavior affects employees.

When IWB involves the direct victimization of individuals (e.g., being a target of bullying), the resulting consequences depend in great part on employees' responses. For example, when victims retaliate against perpetrators directly, perpetrators may become targets of deviant behavior themselves. However, given that many victims have direct reporting relationships with perpetrators, they may be reluctant to retaliate. Consequently, they may express their negative reactions indirectly, such as by striking back at the organization itself (e.g., by engaging in sabotage or by bad-mouthing the organization to others), which can have negative implications for productivity, costs, and reputation (DiBattista, 1996; Rindova, Williamson, Petkova, & Sever, 2005). Rayner and Keashly (2005) identified three additional organizational costs stemming from bullying: recruiting new employees to replace those who resign, opportunity costs arising from displaced employee effort (e.g., lower productivity), and the investigative and litigation costs associated with addressing official complaints.

Despite these unfavorable outcomes, there is reason to believe that organizations may face even more sinister consequences if employees refrain from taking action or if management fails to respond, thereby allowing IWB to continue unchecked. Specifically, in the case of incivility, Pearson (Chapter 5, present volume) points to evidence showing that incivility can escalate between actors and targets to the point of aggression and physical violence. She suggests, therefore, that minor episodes of incivility should not be ignored because they may mark the initial phases of a serious spiral of deviance that begins with IWB but that may escalate to violence worthy of newspaper headlines.

Seabright et al. (Chapter 3, present volume) make an analogous point with respect to workplace sabotage. Specifically, they describe the contagious nature of IWB: Employees who witness IWB learn vicariously to model such behavior (whether aimed at one or more targets) to the extent that they are able to associate its occurrence with desirable outcomes (e.g., power). This implies that managers should intervene swiftly to stop IWB as soon as they become aware of it. Failing to do so threatens to launch a spiral of contagion resulting in the escalation of the behavior. Paul and Townsend (1996) observe more generally that failing to respond to wrongdoing appropriately or retaliating against those employees who speak up can lead to reduced morale among employees, litigation fees, reduced profits, and costs to organizational reputation. Clearly, IWB is bad enough but systematically ignoring it may make matters worse.

Positive Byproducts

Despite the costly and problematic nature of IWB, we should note that responding to IWB also might have positive consequences. For the most part, such benefits all fall into the category of "learning from a bad experience," or as the saying goes, "what doesn't kill you makes you stronger."

We see this, for example, in Jones's (Chapter 4, present volume) report that some employees reported feeling empowered after engaging in revenge. In similar fashion, Pearson (Chapter 5, present volume) also found that some targets of incivility eventually came to view their experience as a source of strength and learning. Namely, some individuals reported that they sought to understand and cope with their experience, which they did by learning about issues such as conflict management, by seeking counseling to help them reframe their interpretations of the situation, or by consulting attorneys to learn about their legal rights as employees. We also suggest that IWB can help to promote relationships between coworkers and increase team cohesiveness to the extent that victims confide in their colleagues and receive a supportive and empathic response. These positive individual results stand to have long-term organizational consequences, particularly with respect to promoting organizational attachment (Lee & Mitchell, 1994).

The same kind of benefits would apply to organizations' reactions to IWB as well. For example, from a policy perspective, organizations that have learned from critical incidents with respect to IWB stand to benefit. Specifically, experience with addressing IWB can stimulate efforts to lead to a range of improvements to human resources systems (e.g., the implementation of systems of punishment). Likewise, they also may encourage the development of whistle-blowing policies in organizations and the improvement of legislation designed to protect whistle-blowers (or its implementation in nations in which laws provide no such protection; Lewis, 2002).

In closing this section, we caution that the benefits described here are incidental byproducts of efforts to address IWB and *not* benefits that should be sought by engaging in IWB. To do so would be akin to exposing oneself to toxic material because people who become ill receive extra attention from loved ones and because of the first-hand lessons to be learned about the experience of illness. Indeed, there are more adaptive ways to achieve such results. Just as medical doctors research and attempt to cure human illness, management researchers should study IWB so that efforts can be undertaken to reduce or eliminate it. Its consequences dramatically outweigh any incidental benefits that may accrue.

THE FUTURE: CHALLENGES AHEAD

Now that we have addressed several of the key issues raised in this book and have positioned them relative to the broader literature on workplace deviance, the stage is set for us to identify the key challenges we face as scholars attempting to further our understanding of IWB and as practitioners attempting to manage IWB in organizations. Specifically, we focus on three preliminary challenges—promoting definitional clarity, overcoming measurement and research obstacles, and establishing sound theoretical bases. Then, once these challenges have been met (i.e., once we have clean conceptualizations, valid measures, and insightful theories to guide research) the stage is set for researchers to design and test interventions designed to stem the tide of IWB and, ultimately, for managers to implement them. We describe these challenges next and enumerate them in summary form in Table 10.1

Promoting Definitional Clarity

As IWB emerges as a field of study, scientists face the challenge of defining it in a manner that distinguishes it from related constructs (see our Chapter 1, present volume) and that differentiates its various forms. However, the various types of IWB described in this book incorporate more subjectivity than desired to make this possible.

TABLE 10.1

Ordered Challenges in Studying and Managing IWB

Preliminary Challenges
1. Clarify conceptualizations of IWB using qualitative analyses
2. Conduct research that allows valid measures of IWB to be developed
3. Develop preliminary theories of IWB based on descriptive research

Ongoing Challenges
4. Create IWB interventions following from theories
5. Test interventions following from theories
6. Revise preliminary theories based on intervention results
7. Create and test new interventions based on revised theories
8. Repeat Steps 6 and 7 as necessary until stable theories and effective interventions result

For example, Neuman and Keashly (Chapter 2, present volume) offer a dictionary definition of the term *insidious*—namely, stealthy actions that inflict subtle harm on one or more targets in a gradual manner. Likewise, we earlier defined IWB as *a form of intentionally harmful workplace behavior that is legal, subtle and low level (rather than severe), repeated over time, and directed at individuals or organizations.* Importantly, the terms *low level* and *subtle* leave considerable room for interpretation and illustrate that many forms of IWB depend largely on the perceptions of the target. Not that this justifies this state of affairs, but subjectivity characterizes the definitions of basic psychological concepts (e.g., learning usually is defined as *"a relatively permanent change in performance resulting from experience,"* in which *relatively* is inherently subjective).

As noted by Jex, Geimer, Clark, Guidroz, and Yugo (Chapter 8, present volume) in their discussion of measurement issues surrounding workplace incivility, subjectivity is problematic in that it allows people to differ greatly in their interpretations of situations. For example, what may concern one employee as incivility or sexist teasing another may perceive as entirely harmless while still another may consider serious affronts. In other words, there may be individual differences in thresholds for recognizing or responding to IWB. This problem is exacerbated by the fact that various forms of IWB involve some behaviors that are very similar in appearance. For example, several of the aggressive behaviors cited by Neuman and Keashly (Chapter 2, present volume) also may be classified as incivility (e.g., being treated in a rude or disrespectful manner, being given the silent treatment), bullying (e.g., being put down in front of others, being the target of rumors or gossip), or sexual harassment (e.g., being subjected to sexist remarks, being subjected to suggestive or offensive stories).

In this regard, Jex et al. propose empirical procedures for establishing definitional clarity. Specifically, they suggest that this may be accomplished by conducting conceptual analyses and by conducting qualitative interviews. Keltner, Capps, Kring, Young, and Heerey (2001) provide an example of this procedure in their conceptual analysis of teasing. Specifically, after noting problems inherent in current definitions of teasing they offered their own definition that helped clarify existing conceptual ambiguities and that incorporated a variety of behaviors that may be considered teasing. The authors subsequently reviewed empirical studies on teasing and used this as a basis for explicating the conditions under which people tease others, developmental changes in the nature and content of teasing, and variations in teasing across social contexts (e.g., considering the relationship between teasers and targets). We believe that it would be fruitful for researchers to conduct similar analyses of various forms of IWB to enable them to be understood more completely and differentiated with greater clarity.

Qualitative interviews also promise to provide valuable information about employees' perceptions of and experiences with IWB, providing a potentially useful first step toward establishing definitional clarity. An excellent example of this procedure may be seen in Pearson et al.'s (2001) multimethod study of incivility, which sought to determine how incivility was related to other types of workplace mistreatment and to explore its consequences for both individuals and organizations. After conducting focus groups and semistructured interviews, and administering questionnaires to over 600 employees, the researchers questioned subject-matter experts in an attempt to compare the various findings. This approach allowed the authors to establish that, although incivility involves a myriad of behaviors, it differs in intensity from aggression. Furthermore, incivility was found to differ from petty tyranny (Ashforth, 1994) in that individuals engaging in incivility may or may not differ from their targets with respect to status, whereas for similar acts to be considered petty tyranny, actors must have formal power over their targets (Pearson et al., 2001). Qualitative studies of this type promise to yield useful findings when attempting to define all forms of IWB and to differentiate them from one another. Once this is accomplished it will be possible to revisit our conceptualization of IWB in an informed manner.

Overcoming Measurement and Research Obstacles

Commenting on definitional clarity in the field of organizational behavior, Locke (2003) observed that good definitions of constructs are essential to scientific advancement because they guide researchers in their efforts to establish valid measures. After all, it's difficult to measure what is ill-defined and equally difficult to study what cannot be measured. In this book, Jex et al. (Chapter 8) and Spector and Rodopman (Chapter 9) describe several ways in which this problem is particularly vexing in the case of measuring IWB.

Reliance on Self-Reports

A key problem in measuring IWB is that self-reports—the organizational scientist's tool of choice—cannot be trusted when measuring IWB because targets, perpetrators, and organizations may be motivated to conceal such behavior from others, and for different reasons. Perpetrators might fear being punished, victims might be concerned about being seen as disloyal, and organizations might wish to avoid negative publicity.

Jex et al. (Chapter 8, present volume) offer recommendations for improving the measurement of incivility using self-report methods that also may be applicable to other forms of IWB. Based on Fowler's (1984) suggestions for increasing the accuracy of survey data, these involve (a) reducing the time periods about which employees are asked to think when referencing past events; (b) asking more questions about the phenomenon under investigation; (c) allowing study participants time to consider their responses before finishing a survey measure; (d) reinterviewing participants multiple times or using a diary method of data method to facilitate recall; (e) utilizing approaches to reduce social desirability, such as making participants aware of the anonymity or confidentiality of their responses; and (f) utilizing additional data collection methods, such as naturalistic observation, focus groups, or case studies.

Ethical Considerations

When studying IWB researchers need to be aware of the possibility of coming across acts that contravene organizational policies (e.g., sexual harassment). In such cases, researchers must decide where their loyalties lie—to the individual who has disclosed engaging in IWB or to the organization. To avoid such ethical dilemmas, researchers should establish clear a priori guidelines as to how such incidents will be handled and precisely what will be revealed to management. We agree with Spector and Rodopman's (Chapter 9, present volume) emphasis on the importance of assuring participants of anonymity as an effective way of avoiding this problem while simultaneously allowing valid data to be collected.

Institutional Review Board Compliance

The sensitive nature of IWB will likely require researchers to provide higher degrees of detail than usual about their proposed research protocol to institutional review boards (IRBs). This high level of detail also may be useful in reassuring host organizations about precisely what the researcher intends to do. And because IRBs cannot enforce external organizations to comply with their standards, researchers providing such detail help ensure that management is aware of the requirements (e.g., obtaining informed consent from participants) and of their intent to comply with them. Typically, this means that researchers have to withhold the identities of employees who have behaved inappropriately. Although officials may request this information, it is incumbent upon researchers not to stray from their preagreed arrangements with participants and the host organization (which, of course, must meet IRB guidelines).

Gaining Access to Research Participants

It is probably not difficult to envision the challenges faced by researchers desiring to gain access to actors and targets of IWB who will be studied. Indeed, prospective participants are likely to be reluctant to share their experiences even if anonymity is assured. A manifestation of this challenge noted by Spector and Rodopman (Chapter 9, present volume) is that it usually is difficult to obtain appropriate sample sizes for phenomena whose base rates are low. Consequently, researchers may be required to sample large numbers of employees or to identify relevant subpopulations with higher incidence rates to obtain sufficiently large samples to allow for conducting powerful statistical analyses. To help open doors, we recommend following Liamputtong's (2007) guidelines for researching sensitive topics. Among other things, this involves making participants partners in the research by explaining to them the important roles they play in addressing a serious problem in the workplace—and one to which they clearly can relate.

We believe that questioning participants in detail about their experiences and specifically exploring the contexts in which the behavior occurred is extremely important in IWB research, particularly at this early stage of development. As we already mentioned, gaining a comprehensive understanding of who engages in the behavior, the circumstances in which it occurs, the specific actions involved, and the reactions of the victim and witnesses can help differentiate the various types of IWB and thus promote definitional clarity. Additionally, given the sensitive nature of IWB research, we argue that adopting measures to reduce social desirability in responding is particularly important and should increase the validity of the obtained data. In this regard as well, Liamputtong's (2007) recommendations promise to be useful.

Establishing Sound Theories

Our colleagues and we have emphasized throughout this book that IWB is an emerging field of research. This may be seen in the highly descriptive nature of the investigations reported. The many observational and survey studies described on these pages do not test theories but rather provide insight that ultimately may be drawn upon as the basis for developing theories. Although some authors (e.g., Neuman & Keashly, Chapter 2, present volume) have found it useful to organize their descriptive efforts in terms of conceptual frameworks, it's clear that formal theories of IWB have not yet been developed. Although these descriptive approaches are important, particularly during the early stages of conceptual development (Greenberg & Tomlinson, 2004), we argue that now may be the time to begin developing theory as a means of explicating the psychological processes underlying IWB.

Higgins (2004) suggests several characteristics of a "good" or useful theory that are relevant here:

1. It must be testable that it will generate research to support or disconfirm it.
2. It must be consistent, noncontradictory, and coherent, so that clear and specific predictions can be generated.
3. It must be economical, such that it should have few parameters compared to competing theories.
4. It should be generalizable, in that its applicability should not be restricted to its original sample or data set.
5. It should explain current findings in the literature.

Higgins (2004) emphasizes that all of these attributes contribute to what he considers the primary purpose of a theory—that is, to generate research. As he notes, "The acid test for a theory is whether its logic compels a process of reasoning that concludes with an implication, often surprising, that suggests new research that might not otherwise have been done—research that ends in a discovery" (p. 142). Though what constitutes a "good" theory will always be a contentious issue, we suggest that these attributes provide a useful initial checklist for researchers to use when developing theory in the field of IWB.

Establishing Practical Guidelines

Considering the costs of IWB, we believe that researchers should make it an ongoing priority to develop effective techniques for minimizing or eliminating it. We outline the general steps in doing this in Table 10.1 (Steps 4 through 8). These require developing theories that withstand tests of actual behavior measured in the field. For example, if a theory suggests that IWB will be reduced under certain conditions, then interventions that create such conditions should be introduced and their efficacy should be tested. Where interventions fail, the theory should be revised and new interventions should be developed from it. Ultimately, this process of revising theories based on the results of interventions should be repeated until our theories result in a set of highly effective interventions. For more on the process of developing theory-based applications, including detailed examples, we refer readers to Greenberg and Lind (2000).

Contributors to this book have expressed ideas that are germane to the process of developing and testing theory-based applications. Most notable in this regard is Neuman and Keashly (Chapter 2, present volume), who emphasize the importance of using organizational policies to establish precisely what constitutes acceptable and unacceptable behavior and how unacceptable behavior will be addressed. Specifically, they note that although organizational codes of conduct and zero-tolerance policies may be useful for mitigating extreme forms of IWB, such as by keeping bullying and sexist jokes from escalating into overt sexual harassment, they are unlikely to be of use in addressing minor forms of IWB, such as incivility. In part, this is because it is easy for perpetrators to deny engaging in minor acts and to dismiss them as innocuous if they do admit to them.

We agree with Neuman and Keashly that it may be more effective in such cases to take a proactive approach to managing IWB by encouraging leaders to serve as models of the prosocial, collaborative and nonthreatening behaviors that are incompatible with IWB. In other words, we believe that fostering a supportive organizational climate may be particularly useful in discouraging people from engaging in IWB (Egan, 1994). Now, we believe, the time has come to develop interventions aimed at fostering supportive organizational climates and testing their effectiveness in reducing IWB. Where effective, the theories used to derive the interventions should remain intact but where the interventions fail, theories should be revised, and new interventions based on them should be tested. It is with this in mind that we present Steps 4 through 8 in Table 10.1 as an ongoing and iterative process.

CONCLUSION

It is an intriguing observation about human behavior that some of its most interesting and potent forms are not always the most obvious but seemingly, the most subtle. We see this, for example, in literature examining such prosaic phenomena as where people sit relative to one another (e.g., Greenberg, 1976), the amount of time people spend waiting for one another (e.g., Greenberg, 1989), and what they fail to say to one another (e.g., Greenberg & Edwards, 2009). Such seemingly minor and usually difficult-to-notice behaviors often have particularly important effects in the workplace, where ongoing relationships between parties of differing power levels play a major role in determining how people treat one another in the course of daily interaction.

This general observation is most certainly applicable to IWB, the class of behaviors chronicled throughout this book and on which we have focused in this chapter. Despite its potential value as a topic of research and as a matter worthy of consideration by organizational practitioners, systematic efforts to study IWB and to manage it effectively are in their infancy. This is understandable considering that studies of various forms of IWB have been largely unconnected to one another and lacking a unified conceptual framework. Hopefully, our analyses in this chapter will inspire our colleagues to advance this burgeoning field by developing such integrated models. To the extent that we may have paved the way for this to occur, we will have satisfied our major objective in preparing this chapter.

REFERENCES

Andreou, E. (2004). Bully/victim problems and their association with Machiavellianism and self-efficacy in Greek primary school children. *British Journal of Educational Psychology, 74,* 297–309.

Aquino, K., Lewis, M. U., Bradfield, M. (1999). Justice constructs, negative affectivity, and employee deviance: A proposed model and empirical test. *Journal of Organizational Behavior, 20,* 1073–1091.

Archer, J. (2004). Sex differences in aggression in real-world settings: A meta-analytic review. *Review of General Psychology. 8*, 291–322.

Armstrong, M. (2006). *A handbook of human resource management practice* (10th ed.). Philadelphia, PA: Kogan Page.

Ashforth, B. (1994). Petty tyranny in organizations. *Human Relations, 47*, 755–778.

Avina, C., & O'Donohue, W. (2002). Sexual harassment and PTSD: Is sexual harassment diagnosable trauma? *Journal of Traumatic Stress, 15*, 69–75.

Bandura, A. (1977). *Social learning theory*. Englewood Cliffs, NJ: Prentice Hall.

Baumeister, R. F., Smart, L., & Boden, J. M. (1996). Relation of threatened egotism to violence and aggression: The dark side of high self-esteem. *Psychological Review, 103*, 5–33.

Bennett, R. J. & Robinson, S. L. (2000). Development of a measure of workplace deviance. *Journal of Applied Psychology, 85*(3), 349–360.

Benson, K. (1984). Comments on Crocker's "An analysis of university definitions of sexual harassment." *Signs, 9*, 516–519.

Berdahl, J. L. (2007). Harassment based on sex: Protecting social status in the context of gender hierarchy. *Academy of Management Review, 32*, 641–658.

Berdahl, J. L., & Moore, C. (2006). Workplace harassment: Double jeopardy for minority women. *Journal of Applied Psychology, 91*, 426–436.

Berkowitz, L. (1989). The frustration-aggression hypothesis: Examination and reformulation. *Psychological Bulletin, 106*, 59–73.

Bies, R. J., & Tripp, T. M. (2005). The study of revenge in the workplace: Conceptual, ideological, and empirical issues. In S. Fox & P. E. Spector (Eds.), *Counterproductive work behavior: Investigations of actors and targets* (pp. 65–81). Washington, DC: American Psychological Association.

Bond, C. F., Jr., & Rao, S. R. (2004). Lies travel: Mendacity in a mobile world. In P. A. Granhag & L. A. Strömwall (Eds.), *The detection of deception in forensic contexts* (pp. 127–147). New York, NY: Cambridge University Press.

Branch, S., Ramsay, S., & Barker, M. (2007). Managers in the firing line: The contributing factors of workplace bullying by staff: An interview study. *Journal of Management and Organization, 13*, 264–281.

Bushman, B. J., & Baumeister, R. F. (1998). Threatened egotism, narcissism, self-esteem, and direct and displaced aggression: Does self-love or self-hate lead to violence? *Journal of Personality and Social Psychology, 75*, 219–229.

Buss, A. H. (1961). *The psychology of aggression*. New York, NY: Wiley.

Christie, R., & Geis, F. L. (1970). *Studies in Machiavellianism*. New York: Academic Press.

Coggan, C., Bennett, S., Hooper, R., & Dickinson, P. (2003). Association between bullying and mental health status among a sample of 3,265 New Zealand adolescents. *International Journal of Mental Health Promotion, 5*, 16–22.

Cortina, L. M., & Magley, V. J. (2009). Patterns and profiles of response to incivility in organizations. *Journal of Occupational Health Psychology, 14*, 272–288.

Cortina, L. M., Magley, V. J., Williams, J. H., & Langhout, R. D. (2001). Incivility in the workplace: Incidence and impact. *Journal of Occupational Health Psychology, 6*, 64–80.

Cortina, L. M., Swan, S., Fitzgerald, L. F., & Waldo, C. (1998). Sexual harassment and assault: Chilling the climate for women in academia. *Psychology of Women Quarterly, 22*, 419–441.

Cowie, H., Naylor, P., Rivers, I., Smith, P. K., & Pereira, B. (2002). Measuring workplace bullying. *Aggression and Violent Behavior, 7*, 33–51.

Coyne, I., Seigne, E., & Randall, P. (2000). Predicting workplace victim status from personality. *European Journal of Work and Organizational Psychology, 9*, 335–349.

Coyne, I., Smith-Lee Chong, P., Seigne, E., & Randall, P. (2003). Self and peer nominations of bullying: An analysis of incident rates, individual differences and perceptions of the work environment. *European Journal of Work and Organizational Psychology, 12*, 209–228.

Crooks, C. V., Goodall, G. R., Baker, L. B., & Hughes, R. (2006). Preventing violence against women: Engaging the fathers of today and tomorrow. *Cognitive and Behavioral Practice, 13*, 82–93.

Dall'Ara, E., & Maass, A. (1999). Studying sexual harassment in the laboratory: Are egalitarian women at higher risk? *Sex Roles, 41*, 681–704.

De Souza, E., & Fansler, A. G. (2003). Contrapower sexual harassment: A survey of students and faculty members. *Sex Roles, 48*, 529–542.

DiBattista, R. A. (1996). Forecasting sabotage events in the workplace. *Public Personnel Management, 25*, 41–52.

Eagly, A. H. (1987). *Sex differences in social behavior: A social-role interpretation*. Hillsdale, NJ: Lawrence Erlbaum Associates.

Eagly A. H., & Steffen, V. J. (1986). Gender and aggressive behavior: A meta-analytic review of the social psychological literature. *Psychological Bulletin 119*, 410–421.

Eagly, A. H., & Wood, W. (1991). Explaining sex differences in social behavior: A meta-analytic perspective. *Personality and Social Psychology Bulletin, 17*, 306–315.

Eagly, A. H., Wood, W., & Diekman, A. B. (2000). Social role theory of sex differences and similarities: A current appraisal. In T. Eckes & H. M. Trautner (Eds.), *The developmental social psychology of gender* (pp. 123–174). Mahwah, NJ: Lawrence Erlbaum Associates.

Egan, G. (1994). *Working the shadow side: A guide to positive behind-the-scenes management*. San Francisco, CA: Jossey-Bass.

Eriksen, W., & Einarsen, S. (2004). Gender minority as a risk factor of exposure to bullying at work: The case of male assistant nurses. *European Journal of Work and Organizational Psychology, 13*, 473–492.

Farrell, D. (1983). Exit, voice, loyalty, and neglect as responses to job dissatisfaction: A multidimensional scaling study. *Academy of Management Journal, 26*, 596–607.

Fitzgerald, L. F. (1993). Sexual harassment: Violence against women in the workplace. *American Psychologist, 48*, 1070–1076.

Foote, W. E., & Goodman-Delahunty, J. (2005). *Evaluating sexual harassment: Psychological, social, and legal considerations in forensic examinations*. Washington, DC: American Psychological Association.

Fowler, F. J. (1984). *Survey research methods*. Beverley Hills, CA: Sage.

Fox, C. L., & Boulton, M. J. (2005). The social skills problems of victims of bullying: Self, peer and teacher perceptions. *British Journal of Educational Psychology, 75*(2), 313–328.

Fox, S., & Spector, P. E. (1999). A model of work frustration-aggression. *Journal of Organizational Behavior, 20*, 915–931.

Fox, S., & Spector, P. E. (2005). *Counterproductive work behavior: Investigations of actors and targets*. Washington, DC: American Psychological Association.

Giacalone, R. A., & Knouse, S. B. (1990). Justifying wrongful employee behavior: The role of personality in organizational sabotage. *Journal of Business Ethics, 9*, 55–61.

Greenberg, J. (1976). The role of seating position in group interaction: A review, with applications for group trainers. *Group and Organization Studies, 1*, 310–327.

Greenberg, J. (1989). The organizational waiting game: Delay as a status-asserting and status-neutralizing tactic. *Basic and Applied Social Psychology, 10,* 13–26.

Greenberg, J., & Lind, E. A. (2000). The pursuit of organizational justice: From conceptualization to implication to application. In C. L. Cooper & E. A. Locke (Eds.), *I/O Psychology: What we know about theory and practice* (pp. 72–108). Oxford, England: Blackwell.

Greenberg, J., & Edwards, M. S. (2009). *Voice and silence in organizations.* Bingley, England: Emerald.

Greenberg, J., & Tomlinson, E. C. (2004). Situated experiments in organizations: Transplanting the lab to the field. *Journal of Management, 30,* 703–724.

Grossman, M., & Wood, W. (1993). Sex differences in intensity of emotional experience: A social role interpretation. *Journal of Personality and Social Psychology, 65,* 1010–1022.

Harvey, S., & Keashly, L. (2003). Predicting the risk for aggression in the workplace: Risk factors, self-esteem, and time at work. *Social Behavior and Personality, 31,* 807–814.

Health and Safety Authority. (2001). *Report of the task force on the prevention of workplace bullying.* Dublin, Ireland: The Stationary Office.

Higgins, E. T. (2004). Making a theory useful: Lessons handed down. *Personality & Social Psychology Review, 8,* 138–145.

Hirschman, A. O. (1970). *Exit, voice and loyalty: Responses to declines in firms, organizations and states.* Cambridge, MA: Harvard University Press.

Hoel, H., Cooper, C. L., & Faragher, B. (2001). The experience of bullying in Great Britain: The impact of organizational status. *European Journal of Work and Organizational Psychology, 10,* 443–465.

Hofstede, G. (2001). *Culture's consequences* (2nd ed.). Thousand Oaks, CA: Sage.

Human Rights and Equal Opportunity Commission. (2008). *Sexual harassment: Serious business.* Sydney, Australia: Author.

Joyce, W., Slocum, J. W., & Von Glinow, M. A. (2007). Person-situation interaction: Competing models of fit. *Journal of Organizational Behavior, 3,* 265–280.

Judge, T. A., LePine, J. A., & Rich, B. L. (2006). Loving yourself abundantly: Relationship of the narcissistic personality to self and other perceptions of workplace deviance, leadership, and task and contextual performance. *Journal of Applied Psychology, 91,* 762–776.

Junger-Tas, J., Terlouw, G. J., & Klein, M. W. (Eds.). (1994). *Delinquent behavior among young people in the western world.* Amsterdam, Netherlands: Kugler.

Kashdan, T. B., Vetter, C., & Collins, R. L. (2005). Substance use in young adults: Associations with personality and gender. *Addictive Behaviors, 30,* 259–269.

Kashy, D. A., & DePaulo, B. M. (1996). Who lies? *Journal of Personality and Social Psychology, 70,* 1037–1051.

Keltner, D., Capps, L., Kring, A. M., Young, R. C., & Heerey, E. A. (2001). Just teasing: A conceptual analysis of teasing and empirical review. *Psychological Bulletin, 127,* 229–248.

Kidder, D. L. (2002). The influence of gender on the performance of organizational citizenship behaviors. *Journal of Management, 28,* 629–648.

Knight, G. P., Guthrie, I. K., Page, M. C., & Fabes, R. A. (2002). Emotional arousal and gender differences in aggression: A meta-analysis. *Aggressive Behavior, 28,* 266–393.

Lalwani, A. K., Shavitt, S., & Johnson, T. (2006). What is the relation between cultural orientation and socially desirable responding? *Journal of Personality & Social Psychology, 90,* 165–178.

Lampman, C., Phelps, A., Bancroft, S., & Beneke, M. (2009). Contrapower harassment in academia: A survey of faculty experience with student incivility, bullying, and sexual attention. *Sex Roles, 60,* 331–346.

Lee, K., & Ashton, M. C. (2005). Psychopathy, Machiavellianism, and narcissism in the Five-Factor Model and the HEXACO model of personality structure. *Personality and Individual Differences, 38*, 1571–1582.

Lee, T., & Mitchell, R. (1994). Organizational attachment: Attitudes and actions. In J. Greenberg (Ed.), *Organizational behavior: State of the science* (pp. 122–156). Mahwah, NJ: Lawrence Erlbaum Associates.

Lewis, D. (2002). Whistleblowing procedures at work: What are the implications for human resource practitioners? *Business Ethics, 11*, 202–209.

Leymann, H., & Gustafsson, A. (1996). Mobbing at work and the development of post-traumatic stress disorders. *European Journal of Work and Organizational Psychology, 5*, 251–275.

Liamputtong, P. (2007). *Researching the vulnerable: A guide to sensitive research methods.* Thousand Oaks, CA: Sage.

Liefooghe, A., & Olafsson, R. (1999). "Scientists" and "amateurs": Mapping the bullying domain. *International Journal of Manpower, 20*, 39–49.

Lim, S., & Cortina, L. M. (2005). Interpersonal mistreatment in the workplace: The interface and impact of general incivility and sexual harassment. *Journal of Applied Psychology, 90*, 483–496.

Lindemeier, B. (1996, June). Mobbing. Krankheitsbild und Intervention desBetriebsarztes [Bullying: Symptoms and intervention of the company physician]. *Die Berufsgenossenschaft*, 428–431.

Locke, E. A. (2003). Good definitions: The epistemological foundation of scientific progress. In J. Greenberg (Ed.) *Organizational behavior: The state of the science* (2nd ed., pp. 415–444). Mahwah, NJ: Lawrence Erlbaum Associates.

Lutgen-Sandvik, P. (2006). Take this job and …: Quitting and other forms of resistance to workplace bullying. *Communication Monographs, 73*, 406–433.

Luthar, V. K., & Luthar H. K. (2002). Using Hofstede's cultural dimensions to explain sexually harassing behaviors in an international context. *International Journal of Human Resource Management, 13*, 268–284.

Marušic, I., Bratko, D., & Zarevski, P. (1995). Self-reliance and some personality traits: Sex differences. *Personality and Individual Differences, 19*, 941–943.

Matthiesen, S. B., & Einarsen, S. (2001). MMPI-2 configurations among victims of bullying at work. *European Journal of Work and Organizational Psychology, 10*, 467–484.

Matthiesen, S. B., & Einarsen, S. (2004). Psychiatric distress and symptoms of PTSD among victims of bullying at work. *British Journal of Guidance and Counseling, 32*, 335–356.

McCullough, M. E., Bellah, C. G., Kilpatrick, S. D., & Johnson, J. L. (2001). Vengefulness: Relationships with forgiveness, rumination, well-being, and the Big Five. *Personality and Social Psychology Bulletin, 27*, 601–610.

McHoskey, J. W., Worzel, W., & Szyarto, C. (1998). Machiavellianism and psychopathy. *Journal of Personality and Social Psychology, 74*, 192–210.

McKinney, K. (1990). Sexual harassment of university faculty by colleagues and students. *Sex Roles, 23*, 421–438.

Ménard, K. M., Hall, G. C. N., Phung, A. H., Ghebrial, M. F. E., & Martin, L. (2003). Gender differences in sexual harassment and coercion in college students. *Journal of Interpersonal Violence, 18*, 1222–1239.

Miceli, M. P., & Near, J. P. (2005). Standing up or standing by: What predicts blowing the whistle on organizational wrongdoing? In J. Martocchio (Ed.), *Research in personnel and human resources management* (Vol. 24, pp. 95–136). Greenwich, CT: JAI.

Moffitt, T. E., Caspi, A., Rutter, M., & Silva, P. A. (2001). *Sex differences in antisocial behaviour.* New York, NY: Cambridge University Press.

Moodian, M. A. (2008). *Contemporary leadership and intercultural competence: Exploring the cross-cultural dynamics within organizations.* Thousand Oaks, CA: Sage.

Mudrack, P. E. (1993). An investigation into the acceptability of workplace behaviors of a dubious ethical nature. *Journal of Business Ethics, 12,* 517–524.

Myers, M. G., Aarons, G. A., Tomlinson, K., & Stein, M. B. (2003). Social anxiety, negative affectivity and substance use among high school students. *Psychology of Addictive Behaviors, 17,* 277–283.

Near, J. P., & Miceli, M. P. (1985). Organizational dissidence: The case of whistle-blowing. *Journal of Business Ethics, 4,* 1–16.

Near, J. P., & Miceli, M. P. (1995). Effective whistle-blowing. *Academy of Management Review, 20,* 679–708.

Neuman, J. H., & Baron, R. A. (2005). Aggression in the workplace: A social psychological perspective. In S. Fox, & P. E. Spector (Eds.), *Counterproductive workplace behavior: Investigations of actors and targets* (pp. 13–40). Washington, DC: American Psychological Association.

Norton, P. J., Sexton, K. A., Walker, J. R., & Norton, G. R. (2005). Hierarchical model of vulnerabilities for anxiety: Replication and extension with a clinical sample. *Cognitive Behaviour Therapy, 34,* 49–63.

O'Leary-Kelly, A. M., Paetzold, R. L., & Griffin, R. W. (2000). Sexual harassment as aggressive behavior: An actor-based perspective. *Academy of Management Review, 25,* 372–388.

Ortega, A., Høgh, A., Pejtersen, J. H., Feveile, H., & Olsen, O. (2009). Prevalence of workplace bullying and risk groups: A representative population study. *International Archives of Occupational and Environmental Health, 82,* 417–426.

Parkinson, B., Fischer, A. H., & Manstead, A. S. R. (2005). *Emotion in social relations: Cultural, group and interpersonal processes.* New York, NY: Psychology Press.

Paul, R. J., & Townsend, J. B. (1996). Don't kill the messenger! Whistle-blowing in America: A review with recommendations. *Employee Responsibilities and Rights Journal, 9,* 149–161.

Paulhus, D. L. (1998). Intrapersonal and intrapsychic adaptiveness of trait self-enhancement: A mixed blessing? *Journal of Personality and Social Psychology, 75,* 1197–1208.

Pearson, C., Andersson, L., & Wegner, J. (2001). When workers flout convention: A preliminary study of workplace incivility. *Human Relations, 54,* 1387–1419.

Pearson, C. M., & Porath, C. L. (2005). On the nature, consequences and remedies of workplace incivility: No time for "nice"? Think again. *Academy of Management Executive, 19,* 1–12.

Penney, L. M., & Spector, P. (2002). Narcissism and counterproductive behavior: Do bigger egos mean bigger problems? *International Journal of Selection and Assessment, 10,* 126–134.

Penney, L. M., & Spector, P. E. (2005). Job stress, incivility, and counterproductive work behavior (CWB): The moderating role of negative affectivity. *Journal of Organizational Behavior, 26,* 777–796.

Pierce, E., Smolinski, C. A., & Rosen, B. (1998). Why sexual harassment complaints fall on deaf ears. *Academy of Management Executive, 12,* 41–54.

Pryor, T., & Wiederman, M. W. (1996). Substance use and impulsive behaviors among adolescents with eating disorders. *Addictive Behaviors, 21,* 269–272.

Quine, L. (2001). Workplace bullying in nurses. *Journal of Health Psychology, 6,* 73–84.

Quine, L. (2002). Workplace bullying in junior doctors: Questionnaire survey. *British Medical Journal, 324,* 878–879.

Raskin, R. N., & Hall, C. S. (1979). A narcissistic personality inventory. *Psychological Reports, 45,* 590.

Rayner, C. (1997). The incidence of workplace bullying. *Journal of Community and Applied Social Psychology, 7,* 199–208.

Rayner, C., Hoel, H., & Cooper, C. L. (2002). *Workplace bullying: What we know, who is to blame, and what can we do?* London: Taylor & Francis.

Rayner, C., & Keashly, L. (2005). Bullying at work: A perspective from Britain and North America. In S. Fox & P. E. Spector (Eds.), *Counterproductive work behavior: Investigations of actors and targets* (pp. 271–296). Washington, DC: American Psychological Association.

Rindova, V., Williamson, I. O., Petkova, A. P., & Sever, J. M. (2005). Being good or being known: An empirical examination of the dimensions, antecedents, and consequences of organizational reputation. *Academy of Management Journal, 48,* 1033–1050.

Robinson, S. L., & Bennett, R. J. (1995). A typology of deviant workplace behaviors: A multidimensional scaling study. *Academy of Management Journal, 38,* 555–572.

Salin, D. (2003). Ways of explaining workplace bullying: A review of enabling, motivating and precipitating structures and processes in the work environment. *Human Relations, 56,* 1213–1232.

Singer, T., Seymour, B., O'Doherty, J. P., Stephan, K. E., Dolan, R. J., & Frith, C. D. (2006). Empathic neural responses are modulated by the perceived fairness of others. *Nature, 439,* 466–469.

Sutton, J., & Keogh, E. (2000). Social competition in school: Relationships with bullying, Machiavellianism and personality. *British Journal of Educational Psychology, 70,* 443–456.

Tinsley, C., & Weldon, E. (2003). Responses to a normative conflict among American and Chinese managers. *International Journal of Cross-Cultural Management, 3,* 181–192.

Van Roosmalen, E., & McDaniel, S. A. (1998). Sexual harassment in academia: A hazard to women's health. *Women and Health, 28,* 33–54.

Vartia, M. A. (1996). The sources of bullying: psychological, work environment and organisational climate. *European Journal of Work and Organisational Psychology, 5,* 203–214.

Vartia, M. (2001). Consequences of workplace bullying with respect to the well-being of its targets and the observers of bullying. *Scandinavian Journal of Work Environment and Health, 27,* 63–69.

Vecchio, R. P. (2000). Negative emotion in the workplace: Employee jealousy and envy. *International Journal of Stress Management, 7,* 161–179.

Vrij, A. (2000). *Detecting lies and deceit: The psychology of lying and the implications for professional practice.* New York, NY: Wiley.

Watson, D., & Clark, L. A. (1984). Negative affectivity: The disposition to experience aversive emotional states. *Psychological Bulletin, 96,* 465-490.

Wilson, D. S., Near, D., & Miller, R. R. (1996). Machiavellianism: A synthesis of evolutionary and psychological literatures. *Psychological Bulletin, 19,* 285–299.

Wislar, J. S., Richman, J. A., Fendrich, M., & Flaherty, J. A. (2002). Sexual harassment, generalized workplace abuse and drinking outcomes: The role of personality vulnerabilities. *Journal of Drug Issues, 32,* 1071–1089.

Zapf, D. (1999). Organizational, work group related and personal causes of mobbing/bullying at work. *International Journal of Manpower, 20,* 70–85.

Zapf, D., & Einarsen, S. (2003). Individual antecedents of bullying: Victims and per-petrators. In S. E. Einarsen, H. Hoel, D. Zapf, & C. L. Cooper (Eds.), *Bullying and emotional abuse in the workplace. International perspectives in research and practice* (pp. 165–184). London, England: Taylor & Francis.

Zapf, D., Einarsen, S. E., Hoel, H., & Vartia, M. (2003). Empirical findings on bullying in the workplace. In S. E. Einarsen, H. Hoel, D. Zapf, & C. L. Cooper (Eds.), *Bullying and emotional abuse in the workplace: International perspectives in research and practice* (pp. 103–126). New York, NY: Taylor & Francis.

Zapf, D., & Gross, C. (2001). Conflict escalation and coping with workplace bullying: A replication and extension. *European Journal of Work and Organizational Psychology, 10*, 497–522.

Zeichner, A., Parrott, D. J., & Frey, F. C. (2003). Gender differences in laboratory aggression under response choice conditions. *Aggressive Behavior, 29*, 95–106.

Author Index

Subject Index